THE SEVEN★POWER SUMMIT

Documents from
the Summits of
Industrialized Countries
1975–1989

The Summit of the Arch, Paris, July 14-16, 1989. Heads of delegations (left to right): Jacques Delors, European Communities; Ciriaco de Mita, Italy; Margaret Thatcher, United Kingdom; George Bush, United States; François Mitterand, France; Helmut Kohl, Federal Republic of Germany; Brian Mulroney, Canada; and Sousuke Uno, Japan.

THE SEVEN★POWER SUMMIT

Documents from the Summits of Industrialized Countries 1975–1989

Compiled and Edited by
PETER I. HAJNAL

Introduction by
JOHN J. KIRTON

KRAUS INTERNATIONAL PUBLICATIONS
A Division of The Kraus Organization Limited
Millwood, New York

First printing 1989

Printed in the United States of America

The paper used in this publication meets the minimum
requirements of American National Standard for
Information Science--Permanence of Papers for Printed
Library Materials, ANSI Z39.48-1984.

Library of Congress Cataloging-in-Publication Data

The Seven-power summit.
Bibliography: p.
Includes Index.
1. International economic relations—Congresses.
2. Economic policy—Congresses. I. Hajnal, Peter I.,
1936-
HF1352.S48 1989   337   89-2692
ISBN 0-527-37319-2

TABLE OF CONTENTS

San Juan *continued*

LONDON (UNITED KINGDOM), 7–8 MAY 1977

BONN, 16–17 JULY 1978

TOKYO, 28–29 JUNE 1979

TOKYO *continued*

VENICE, 22–23 JUNE 1980

OTTAWA, 20–21 JULY 1981

OTTAWA *continued*

VERSAILLES, 4–6 JUNE 1982

LONDON *continued*

BONN, 2–4 MAY 1985

TOKYO, 4–6 MAY 1986

VENICE, 8–10 JUNE 1987

TORONTO, 19–21 JUNE 1988

TORONTO *continued*

PARIS, 14–16 JULY 1989

PARIS *continued*

ABBREVIATIONS AND ACRONYMS

AID	Association internationale de développement
AIDS	Acquired immune deficiency syndrome
ANC	African National Congress
ASEAN	Association of South East Asian Nations
CDE	Conference on Disarmament in Europe
CIEC	Conference on International Economic Co-operation
CMEA	Council for Mutual Economic Co-operation
COMECON	Council for Mutual Economic Co-operation
CSCE	Conference on Security and Co-operation in Europe
EC	European Community (-ies)
EEC	European Economic Community
EFTA	European Free Trade Association
EMS	European Monetary System
ESA	European Space Agency

FAO	Food and Agriculture Organization of the United Nations
FMI	Fonds monétaire international
G-7	Group of Seven Finance Ministers
GATT	General Agreement on Tariffs and Trade
GDP	Gross domestic product
GNP	Gross national product
HFSP	Human Frontier Science Program
IAEA	International Atomic Energy Agency
IBRD	International Bank for Reconstruction and Development
ICAO	International Civil Aviation Organization
ICSU	International Council of Scientific Unions
IDA	International Development Association
IEA	International Energy Agency
IFAD	International Fund for Agricultural Development
IMF	International Monetary Fund
IMO	International Maritime Organization
INF	Intermediate-Range Nuclear Forces
ISO	International Organization for Standardization
MBD	Million barrels a day
MBFR	Mutual and Balanced Force Reductions

MIGA	Multilateral Investment Guarantee Agency
MTNs	Multilateral Trade Negotiations
NATO	North Atlantic Treaty Organization
NIEs	Newly Industrializing Economies
OCDE	Organisation de coopération et de développement économique
ODA	Official Development Assistance
OECD	Organisation for Economic Co-operation and Development
OIT	Organisation internationale du travail
OPEC	Organization of the Petroleum Exporting Countries
PNB	Produit national brut
SADCC	Southern African Development Coordination Conference
SDRs	Special Drawing Rights
START	Strategic Arms Reduction Talks
UDF	United Democratic Front (South Africa)
UN	United Nations
UNCTAD	United Nations Conference on Trade and Development
UNEP	United Nations Environment Programme
UNFDAC	United Nations Fund for Drug Abuse Control
URSS	Union des républiques socialistes soviétiques

USSR	Union of Soviet Socialist Republics
WHO	World Health Organization
WMO	World Meteorological Organization
World Bank	International Bank for Reconstruction and Development [also used as joint name for International Bank for Reconstruction and Development and IDA]
World Bank Group	International Bank for Reconstruction and Development, International Development Association, and International Finance Corporation

FOREWORD

This work presents in one volume the full texts of documents of the first fifteen summit meetings of the heads of state or government of the seven major industrialized countries and representatives of the European Communities. It also provides lists of national and European Community delegations to these meetings—called variously economic summits, summits of industrialized countries, and, increasingly, seven-power summits—and a selective bibliography of monographs, journal articles and parts of works dealing with the summits.

Different categories of summit documents exist. The best-known type, referred to as the final communiqué or declaration, is issued at the conclusion of each summit and usually published in newspapers of record and in press releases of the governments of the participating countries; in recent years, however, newspapers have not always printed complete texts of these major final documents.

Declarations or statements on political and other special topics, harder to obtain than the final communiqués, have become a frequent product of the summits. An even more elusive type of document is the chairman's summary, in which the head of the host country's delegation gives his or her evaluation and impressions at the end of the summit. Such summaries—along with statements given by other principal members of the host delegation—have been collected in this volume, as have documents of a less formal type: transcripts of press conferences or press releases. End-of-summit summaries and press conferences of heads of delegations other than those of the host country are not included here. The Introduction discusses in detail the nature and significance of the various types of summit documents.

In case of variant texts of particular summit documents, the most complete version has been chosen for inclusion. Texts from each host country were selected whenever possible, augmented when warranted on the basis of documents found in other sources. Occasionally, texts were edited slightly to ensure standard spelling and punctuation.

It is hoped that this book will be a useful source of reference for those concerned with international economics and finance and with the process and substance of negotiations at the summit level.

I gratefully acknowledge the assistance of the following organizations: the Department of External Affairs, Ottawa, Canada; the Ottawa embassies of France, the Federal Republic of Germany, Italy, Japan, and the United States; the British High Commission in Ottawa; the Department of State, Washington, D.C.; the Istituto Affari Internazionali, Rome; the Royal Institute of International Affairs, London; and the Presse-und Informationsamt der Bundesregierung, Bonn. All were generous in supplying documents and information.

I thank the Social Sciences and Humanities Research Council of Canada, and the University of Toronto, for a grant-in-aid and other assistance in the completion of this work. I owe a debt of gratitude to the University of Toronto's Centre for International Studies, and especially to the Centre's Research Director, Professor John J. Kirton and his staff, for their valuable suggestions and other help. Last but not least, I thank my wife, Edna, for her editorial assistance. All have contributed to whatever merit this work may have; I am, of course, solely responsible for any errors or omissions.

Peter I. Hajnal
Toronto, Canada
August 1989

INTRODUCTION:

THE SIGNIFICANCE OF THE SEVEN-POWER SUMMIT

John J. Kirton*

Since its inception in 1975, the annual summit of the leaders of the world's major industrial democracies and the European Community has come to occupy center stage in the continuing struggle to create order out of anarchy in the world's economic and political life. From its fragile beginnings as an ad hoc response to the international chaos of the early 1970s, this regular gathering of heads of state and government, foreign ministers, and finance ministers has rapidly grown to become one of the more developed and effective institutions in world affairs. Indeed, with its unrivaled combination of predominant power and common purpose, the summit and its allied institutions are slowly supplementing, and in some respects replacing, the much more venerable, more familiar, and better documented multilateral organizations of the United Nations

*Professor John J. Kirton is Co-Director of Research, Centre for International Studies, University of Toronto, Toronto, Canada.

(UN) and Atlantic Alliance systems as the leading force in contemporary international governance. For students of international relations, and of the domestic polities and economies of the many countries of the North, South and even East where the summit's impact extends, the development of a richer understanding of the summit's deliberations and decisions is a vital intellectual task.[1]

THE SUMMIT AS AN INTERNATIONAL INSTITUTION

The importance of the seven-power summit is apparent from its remarkable development as an international institution in so short a period of time. In sharp contrast to such milestones in the historic process of organizing internationally as the birth of the League of Nations and UN, the summit did not arise through a single grand act of political architecture and construction producing an edifice intended to last for all time. Rather, much like the Concert of Europe that preserved peace and prosperity in the central global system throughout the early nineteenth century, the modern summit emerged

---

[1]The existing scholarly literature on the summit, while expanding, remains rather sparse, particularly in comparison to the mountains of material on the institutions of the United Nations system and the Atlantic Alliance. The major full-length works on the summit are: Robert D. Putnam and Nicholas Bayne, *Hanging Together: Cooperation and Conflict in the Seven-Power Summits,* rev. ed. (Cambridge, Mass.: Harvard University Press, 1987); Georges de Menil and Anthony M. Solomon, *Economic Summitry* (New York: Council on Foreign Relations, 1983); Cesare Merlini, ed., *Economic Summits and Western Decision-Making* (London: Croom Helm; New York: St. Martin's Press in association with the European Institute of Public Administration, 1984); David Watt, *Next Steps for Summitry: Report of the Twentieth Century Fund International Conference on Economic Summitry; Background Paper* (New York: Priority Press, 1984); Georges de Menil, *Les Sommets économiques: les politiques nationales à l'heure de l'interdépendance* (Paris: Economica, 1983); Michael J. Artis and Sylvia Ostry, *International Economic Policy Coordination* (London: Routledge & Kegan Paul, 1986); and Leonard Waverman and Thomas Wilson, eds., "Macroeconomic Coordination and the Summit," *Canadian Public Policy* 15 (February 1989), Special Issue.

through a continuing and cumulative, if uneven, investment of political will by the powers that counted, in response to crises with which the old order and international organizations were unable to cope.[2]

The summit began as a meeting, called as a one-time event by French President Valéry Giscard d'Estaing in Rambouillet, France, in the autumn of 1975. However, the very success of this gathering, a new set of international challenges, pressure from the Japanese, domestic electoral calculations in the United States, and the particular global vision of United States Secretary of State Henry Kissinger inspired President Gerald Ford to repeat the experiment at San Juan, Puerto Rico the following year. After that, the summit quickly became a permanent, predictable fixture of the international political cycle. At each summit, the leaders themselves set and announce the host of next year's late spring or summer rendez-vous before they depart.[3]

Equally predictable has been the membership, and the ever-increasing list of frustrated claimants for inclusion. Invitations to the first summit went to only six select States: France the host, the United States, the United Kingdom, Germany, Japan, and Italy. These six added Canada in 1976

---

[2]Richard Elrod, "The Concert of Europe: A Fresh Look at an International System," *World Politics* 28 (January 1976): 159–74, and William Wallace, "Political Issues at the Summits: A New Concert of Powers?" in *Economic Summits and Western Decision-Making,* ed. Cesare Merlini, 137–52. See also Robert Jervis, "From Balance to Concert: A Study of International Security Co-operation," in *Co-operation under Anarchy,* ed. Kenneth A. Oye (Princeton: Princeton University Press, 1985), 58–79.

[3]The decision on the rotation for hosting the annual summit is now rigidly defined, according to the sequence of hosting for the first round from 1975 to 1981. The sequence—France, the United States, the United Kingdom, the Federal Republic of Germany, Japan, Italy, Canada—reflects in very general terms the relative influence wielded by each country at the summit as a result of its material capability and historic role in creating the summit institution. The major remaining ambiguity about this precise order of precedence is the rather remote possibility of the European Community being introduced into the hosting rotation (presumably after Canada) at some point in the future.

and the European Community in 1977. But they then closed the doors to this most exclusive club, leaving middle-power aspirants such as Australia and Spain languishing on the outside.

Those admitted to the cozy atmosphere inside have, not surprisingly, grown comfortable lingering ever longer in the confines of this powerful and prestigious club. The day-and-a-half encounters at Rambouillet and Puerto Rico have expanded steadily, despite the pressing domestic demands on busy leaders, to reach the three-day session of the Paris Summit of 1989. For those leaders who arrive early or stay late to conduct bilateral meetings, the summit experience has proven to be worth an even longer investment of time. No other international event—from the annual autumn opening of the UN General Assembly, through the occasional North Atlantic Treaty Organization (NATO) Heads of Government meetings, to the Commonwealth or francophone summits held every two years, and the now annual summits the United States holds with its superpower counterpart—comes close to commanding such a large and automatic part of presidents' and prime ministers' time.[4]

As the length of the meeting has expanded, so has the process of preparation. In the early days the host leader simply

---

[4]The one possible exception is the twice-yearly European Community summit which emerged at the same time as the seven-power summit in response to very similar forces. However, with its much more limited major-power membership and impact on global affairs, the European Summit is more comparable to such other regular regional summits as the annual Canada–United States summit that began in 1985 or the annual summit of eight Latin American countries that commenced in 1988. Evidence for the centrality of the seven-power summit, in the admittedly easy case of Canada, can be found in John J. Kirton, "Managing Global Conflict: Canada and International Summitry," in *Canada Among Nations 1987: A World of Conflict,* ed. Maureen A. Molot and Brian W. Tomlin (Toronto: James Lorimer, 1988), 22–40. The only overriding claim to seven-power summit attendance on a leader's time appears to be an imminent national election, as evidenced by British Prime Minister Margaret Thatcher's early departure from the Venice summit of 1987.

dispatched a few officials to meet with other governments several months in advance of the event. In 1977, when Jimmy Carter became U.S. President, he appointed a trusted advisor, with cabinet rank, to work on summit preparations on a full-time, year-round basis. Since that time all countries have employed specially designated personal representatives or "sherpas," who normally serve on a continuing basis for several years.[5] These sherpas meet formally on at least four occasions throughout the year preceding the summit, as well as at the opening of, and throughout the summit itself. They are supported by an elaborately layered network of "sous-sherpas" (usually one from the foreign ministry and one from the finance ministry), "sous-sous-sherpas," and political directors. Their quest for consensus, which is a key feature of the summit process, is advanced through the annual or semi-annual ministerial deliberations of the major international economic institutions, notably the International Monetary Fund (IMF), the World Bank, and the Organisation for Economic Co-operation and Development (OECD). The effort generally culminates in a grand tour by the host head of government to the capitals of his or her colleagues for bilateral meetings in advance of the summit. There has even been, on occasion, a triumvirate of leaders meeting together to discuss the forthcoming event, and structured consultations on the part

---

[5]The term "sherpa" comes from the native porters or bearers who assist mountain climbers in the Himalayas. The term preserves the fiction that these individuals serve only the most modest functions, and the fact that the summit is a forum where individual leaders have a unique ability to transcend entrenched bureaucracies and professional advisers and make decisions for themselves. The phrase, and the formal designation of *personal* representative, shows the strong bias and key feature of the summit as an antibureaucratic, transcendently political institution devoid of a separate organization or secretariat and dependent on the individual leaders involved. For the views of sherpas on the summit, see John Hunt and Henry Owen, "Taking Stock of the Seven-Power Summits: Two Views," *International Affairs* 60, no. 4 (Autumn 1984): 657–61; Robert Armstrong, *Economic Summits: A British Perspective* (Toronto: Centre for International Studies, University of Toronto, 1988); Pascal Lamy, *The Economic Summit and the European Community* (Toronto: Centre for

of the summit host with countries and groups of countries left outside.[6]

Such meticulous preparation has set the stage for a considerably more ambitious, intense and consequential gathering than the founders, with their penchant for fireside chats in the library, anticipated. The length of the communiqués in this collection demonstrates that the agenda of the summiteers has steadily expanded, despite the recurrent efforts of the leaders to shorten the document they must approve—and the host must read—at the meeting's end. As the political declarations, accompanying statements, and chairmen's summaries indicate most clearly, the agenda of the summits has also widened: the explicit economic focus of the first meeting soon expanded to embrace political, security, social, environmental and a host of other subjects. At the same time the role of the summit has grown: the early emphasis on familiarization, education and deliberation has given way, however unevenly, to firm decision-making, backed by ongoing consultation, effective implementation, and the creation of a new family of summit-related institutions to reinforce the work.[7]

International Studies, University of Toronto, 1988); Allan Gotlieb, *Canada and the Economic Summits: Power and Responsibility* (Toronto: Centre for International Studies, University of Toronto, 1987); and Sylvia Ostry, *Summitry: The Medium and the Message* (Toronto: Centre for International Studies, University of Toronto, 1988).

[6]For example, prior to the Toronto summit of 1988, Canadian foreign minister Joe Clark met with the ministers from the newly formed Group of Eight major Latin American Countries to discuss their concerns about the forthcoming Toronto summit, especially with regard to debt relief. The Canadians also gave some consideration to sending Prime Minister Mulroney to the Soviet Union, in his role as summit host, prior to the event. The most advanced step in this process of global linkage has come from French President Mitterand, who invited the leaders of fifteen developing countries from around the world to meet with him, and the other heads of the summit seven in Paris in the days preceding the opening of the 1989 summit, and who received a letter to the Seven from Mr. Gorbachev during the summit itself.

[7]The allied institutions of the seven-power summit are the Group of Five Finance Ministers expanded into the Group of Seven Finance Ministers at the Tokyo summit of 1986, the Trade Ministers Quadrilateral, "summit seven" foreign ministers' meetings

A clear consequence of the increasing international importance of the summits has been their increasing visibility, and controversy, in domestic political life.[8] Despite continuing criticism from journalists who proclaim the gatherings to be a waste of time, the few hundred media representatives who waited under the gray skies at Rambouillet in 1975 had swelled to the army of 4,000 who attended the leaders in the splendor of Venice in 1987 and the modernity of Toronto in 1988, and the 6,000 at Paris in 1989 during the Bicentennial of the French Revolution. Propelled by such attention from the shapers of attitudes of domestic audiences, the summits have entered into the planning and process of national elections, as leaders employ the world's most high-profile international stage to secure maximum political advantage back home. Indeed, the summit, notably in the case of the United States, the United Kingdom and Canada, has sometimes appeared as if its primary purpose was to serve as the international committee to re-elect whichever of its "old boy" members, or protégés, was up for re-election that year. Not surprisingly, such dynamics have inspired criticism from opposition leaders and domestic organizations claiming that their government's summit performance, or the summit itself, has let the country down.

---

on the margins of the UN General Assembly, and the one-time gathering called by President Reagan (minus France) to deal with arms control and East–West relations vis-à-vis the Soviet Union. Below the ministerial level there exist: the Group of Seven Finance deputies; and seven-power groups at lower levels to operate summit-created regimes on airline hijacking, the spread of ballistic missile technologies, and other subjects. In early 1988 West German Foreign Minister Hans-Dietrich Genscher also called for a special meeting of the foreign ministers of the summit countries. On the role of the Group of Seven Finance Ministers, see Yoichi Funabashi, *Managing the Dollar: From the Plaza to the Louvre* (Washington, D.C.: Institute for International Economics, 1988).

[8]On the domestic dimensions of the summit, see Kurt Becker, "Between Image and Substance: The Role of the Media," in *Economic Summits and Western Decision-Making*, ed. Merlini, 153–66, and Robert D. Putnam, "Diplomacy and Domestic Politics: The Logic of Two-Level Games," *International Organization* 42, no. 3 (Summer 1988): 427–60.

THE SUMMIT SYSTEM AND INTERNATIONAL ORDER

Such overwhelming attention is a natural product of the pageantry, power, and potential that arises when seven of the world's most powerful countries meet at the highest political level to deal with the most difficult issues of the day; it is also commensurate with the larger significance of the summit in the process of building international order. For, taken as a whole, the summit system represents the third, and in some respects the most effective, great wave of international institution-building in the post-war era.[9]

The first such wave began in the dying days and immediate aftermath of the Second World War when the victorious powers, organized as the United Nations against the axis powers, erected in the UN system an integrated network of increasingly universal institutions—the Security Council, General Assembly, and functional agencies—to create and manage a new international order. Despite its many achievements, however, the UN system suffered from a fundamental flaw in design that left it increasingly unable to cope with a rapidly evolving world. In organizing its Security Council, it assigned the task of preserving international political order, not to a coherent group of countries with common values and similar political systems, but to a pentarchy of permanent veto powers whose divided attachments to capitalism and communism, democracy and totalitarianism, proved to be a recipe for paralysis and ineffectiveness. Moreover, in the Security Council privilege was poorly correlated with power, as membership in the victorious wartime coalition gave the United Kingdom, France and China rights and responsibilities well beyond their capacity to

---

[9]For a more detailed discussion of this process, cast in terms of the "old" and "new" internationalism, see John W. Holmes and John J. Kirton, eds., *Canada and the New Internationalism* (Toronto: Canadian Institute of International Affairs, and Centre for International Studies, University of Toronto, 1988).

contribute to the collective task. And in the reigning institutions of the UN economic system—the IMF and the World Bank—the United States received unique privileges that its wealth at the time justified, but that its declining power has rendered increasingly inappropriate with each passing decade.

The second wave of postwar international institution-building was designed to cope with the crisis of the cold war that crippled the core of the UN system so soon after its creation. It consisted of the array of more restricted, Atlantic-centered, multilateral institutions that began with NATO and the General Agreement on Tariffs and Trade (GATT), and continued with the Organisation for European Economic Co-operation and its successor, the OECD, and the International Energy Agency (IEA). As a successor or supplement to the UN system, this Atlantic network sacrificed breadth of membership and accumulation of maximum capability, in order to secure commonality of purpose against the security threat on a single, vital, regional front. With six of the seven summit country participants members of NATO and the IEA, and with all seven country summiteers members of the GATT and OECD, Atlanticism remains a considerable force in world affairs. Yet the addition of large numbers of small and middle powers has contributed far more political diversity and disagreement than needed capability, and has inhibited the ease and speed of making and enforcing required decisions. Moreover the absence of Japan from NATO and France from the IEA have been increasingly costly omissions, as the threats to western security have expanded well beyond Europe, have grown to embrace more than military and associated political challenges, and increasingly have required the rapidly rising power of Japan in response.[10]

---

[10]For a more optimistic view, see *No Other Way: Canada and International Security Institutions,* ed. John W. Holmes (Toronto: Centre for International Studies, University of Toronto, 1987).

The third wave of international institution-building, centered in the summit system, was called into being by the inability of the established UN and Atlantic networks to cope with the cascading crises of the early 1970s. The failure of the IMF to deal with the collapse of the Bretton Woods international monetary regime in 1971, the failure of the Atlantic institutions to respond effectively to the Mid-East oil and political shocks of 1973, and the failure of the UN system to prevent the Indian nuclear explosion and respond to the demands for a New International Economic Order in 1974 dramatically demonstrated the need for a new forum for organizing the increasingly beleaguered industrial democracies of the North and replacing the old order they had created with a fundamentally reformed successor.

The seven-power summit represented a unique effort to combine the new powers that counted to provide political leadership at the highest level to an international political and economic system that seemed to be out of control. Taken together, the countries of the summit command well over half of the world's gross national product and control a lesser but still decisive share of the world's modern military might. With the presence of the European Community, they represent an overwhelming majority of the population of the world's industrialized North. The summit also provides a central, comprehensive forum to consider and cope with the major challenges of the global system as a whole because of the rich array of special relationships and institutional affiliations that its member countries have with the countries of the East and South. And with membership limited to the same major industrial democracies, of whatever internal political complexion and ideology, this forum combines commonality of purpose with diversity of political debate. Moreover, the combination of limited membership, common political and economic systems, and vigorous disagreement about what to do leads to a rare ease and effectiveness in decision-making and provides some protection for minority opinion in a consensus-oriented forum. Nowhere else in the current international institutional firmament is there such an accessible concentration of commonality, coherence and decisive capability.

PRODUCING THE SUMMIT DOCUMENTS

The documents in this collection, which record the results of these efforts, come in four classes, each with its own distinctive significance and contribution in the complex summit constellation. Heading the hierarchy is the formal communiqué, often referred to as a "declaration," read by the host with regal ceremony at the conclusion of each summit, as his or her colleagues sit assembled on stage. These texts are the scriptures of the summit, the central achievement whose creation consumes much of the summit preparatory activity during the preceding year.

The production of this communiqué characteristically begins the previous autumn, when the sherpas first meet to share insights about the political priorities and constraints their leaders face. Once the range of the politically possible is defined, the sherpas at their second meeting in early winter usually discuss the general structure and likely agenda of the summit that year. The third sherpa meeting, held about two months later, addresses the specifics of what the leaders will discuss and what the communiqué might say. The fourth sherpa meeting, which takes place within the month prior to the summit, tends to focus on the more precise language of the "thematic paper" which is, in effect, a draft communiqué that increasingly guides and is shaped by the sherpas' deliberations throughout the first half of the summit year.

From the night prior to the summit to the morning of the last day, the sherpas are constantly working at the side of their leaders or among themselves to advise the heads of their delegations, carry out the heads' instructions, and ensure that the final version of the communiqué will reflect the consensus that the leaders themselves create during their three days together. During the second night of the summit the sherpas may meet to prepare an almost final draft. Sometimes the finance sous-sherpas assist by drafting specific references on matters such as exchange rates, for review by finance ministers, before the sherpas take them up. Although these passages usually prevail, some sherpas, ever jealous of their prerogatives, insist they have no status and treat them with cavalier disregard.

The grand finale for the sherpas comes the night before the final day of the summit when, perhaps aided by their political directors, they labor through the night to produce the document which the leaders will approve in the morning and the host will read in the afternoon. Because this is genuinely a document of the heads themselves, the sherpas end their sometimes sleepless night by referring all remaining disagreements, carefully ensconced in square brackets in the draft text, to the leaders, for resolution at their final meetings. It is hardly surprising that in this process the English language sometimes gets mangled, or that precise commitments about national responsibilities or particular programs get relegated to an appendix.

Ranking second in the hierarchy of summit scripture is the political declaration, which sometimes appears in plural form. This now standard feature of a summit's paper product is still a contribution that is somewhat in dispute. Led by the French prior to the 1989 Paris Summit, there are some who claim that the summit is, or should be, an economic forum, where the "high" political issues of global peace and security have no place. This doctrine rides roughshod over several realities— that some summits have made their greatest contribution in the realm of high politics, that the most important political issues of the moment naturally demand the attention of the most powerful leaders of the most powerful States, and that most elected heads of government, along with their citizens, are much more comfortable talking about politics than about the dismal technical details of exchange rate reference zones, schemes for macroeconomic policy performance surveillance and the like. Thus, the leaders have talked about high politics since the first summit. And, to avoid damaging speculation about what they have talked about and to signal their agreement to allies and adversaries on the outside, they have since 1978 issued at least one statement about the political subjects they have discussed.

In order to preserve the economic nature of the communiqué, these political statements have been issued as separate documents. They have covered a variety of topics, have been issued as one or several statements, and have appeared under a variety of titles. But they generally remain faithful to the core consensus that the summit's political communiqué ought to deal principally with the great issues of East–West relations (including the legacy of the Second World War and the front-line powder keg of the Middle East) and threats to the states system and its great-power protectors themselves.

To produce these political statements, the sherpas share their table with the political directors—a group composed of the most senior foreign ministry official responsible for global political affairs in each member government. Because it must often reflect the fast-moving political situation of the moment, the preparation of the political statement begins much later in the annual summit cycle than that of the communiqué itself. Typically the political directors join the sherpas at their fourth meeting, and bring with them a draft political declaration they have prepared among themselves. Given traditional French ambivalence about the role of political items in the summit, and the desire of sherpas to retain control of the summit preparation process in the face of foreign ministry officials, there is a recent tradition of the sherpas discarding the political directors' proposed document and starting the drafting process anew. The political directors, however, tend to gain the upper hand at the summit itself, when it is they, rather than the communiqué-preoccupied sherpas, who in practice have the most to contribute to the jointly drafted final text.

To cope with other political issues, such as regional security, and other matters where the great-power plutocrats have more particular interests and a greater propensity to disagree, there has evolved, over the years of the summit, a third class of documents: the chairman's summary, delivered by the host head at the end of the summit as an additional indication of what was discussed or agreed. Chairmen's summaries come in several forms. They may be oral statements (transcribed by those in attendance) or previously prepared written documents. Moreover, they may be merely the unilateral impressions of the host, or may be a collective statement agreed upon by all the heads prior to their release.

Professional diplomats struggling to save face for their leaders or to secure collective legitimization for their prized issues tend to see substantial significance in the particular form the summary takes, or whether an item gets into only the summary rather than the political declaration or the communiqué itself. But to the media army waiting impatiently outside for any scrap of news to feed to their expensive satellites hovering hungrily above, the particular title on the piece of paper matters much less. Their interpretation is, from a practical political standpoint, a reasonable one, because such summaries are prepared and issued by the host head (with the assistance of his or her sherpa). It is the host head who has a *primus inter pares* status, reflecting the fact that it is ultimately his or her summit and that it is his or her responsibility to see that all goes well. At the Toronto Summit, in 1988, the traditional chairman's summary was dispensed with in favor of an agreed statement from the foreign ministers that was approved by the heads. This process resulted in a document that appeared almost as weighty as the political declaration itself.

These prerogatives of the host head of government have given rise to a fourth class of documents: the press releases or press briefings that the host head may provide throughout the summit itself. The three-day event is, of course, a frenzy of competitive briefings, as the sherpas, ministers, officials and press spokespersons of each delegation struggle to get out the version of what went on that is most favorable to them. But in this process the words of the host leader have a special status. Given the ultimate responsibility of the host to ensure that none of his or her colleagues lose face at a summit, a well-timed press statement on an issue that the leaders refused collectively to endorse can help a friend whose help will in turn be needed in future years. The host leader can also begin, in however fragile a manner, the process where issues become legitimized and perhaps, eventually, decisively dealt with by the summit itself in future years.

The overall importance and different classes of these documents reflect in part the status of the various participants in the summit. Because each summit involves not only the country's head of state or government, but its foreign minister and finance minister as well, it assembles a uniquely powerful combination of politicians and portfolios from the great ministries of state, unmatched by any other international institution or regular summit forum. Beyond this general formula for participation, however, the actual composition of national delegations is a striking testament to the diversity of political conditions and governmental structures in the member countries, and the resilience of the summit forum in adapting to their needs. Thus the European Community sends as a "head" every year the President of the Commission headquartered in Brussels. But it also sends the President of its Council in those years when the Community presidency is held by a member whose head is not already at the summit as the leader of a member country. The French have also participated in a formula for a two-headed delegation. For in the years of domestic political "co-habitation" between socialist President François Mitterrand and center-right Prime Minister Jacques Chirac, both leaders would represent France at the summit, with the latter taking the seat otherwise occupied by the French Minister of Finance. The fraternity of ministers has, however, had some compensation. For not only were the summit's founders recreating as heads a forum they had enjoyed so much when they were finance ministers themselves, but in 1980, when an untimely death deprived the Japanese delegation of their Prime Minister, their Foreign Minister substituted at the summit as the Japanese head.

The claims of the European Community and the French to occasional double representation at the top has helped Germany use the formula to good effect at the ministerial level, where the Germans have enjoyed an extra seat every year. Because Germany routinely has a coalition government in which the Free Democratic Party (FDP) is the constant element, that country sends to the summit not only its Finance Minister, who comes from the larger coalition partner, but also its Minister of Economics, who represents the FDP in this domain. Nor is it conceivable that this extra economic minister would lead the summiteers to ask, under the principle of equality and substitution, that the other German minister stay at home. For he, in the person of Hans-Dietrich Genscher, is a summit legend, and a personal repository of its institutional memory, having been at every summit in the fifteen-year history of the event. The Japanese have also followed the German precedent, by sending their Minister of International Trade and Industry to the finance ministers' summit conclaves. But even with these modifications, the summit remains one of the world's most exclusive clubs.

INTERPRETING THE SUMMIT DOCUMENTS

Unlike the UN and Atlantic institutions, with their gargantuan bureaucracies generating mountains of documentation on a daily basis, the record of the summit's deliberations and decisions is extraordinarily sparse. This sparseness is not an unintended defect of the summit system. Rather, it is a deliberate and central feature of its design. For, much like a cabinet at the domestic level in a parliamentary system, the summiteers have known from the beginning that in order to be effective in their deliberative and decision-making tasks, the norms of confidentiality, and occasionally even secrecy, must prevail. Indeed, the President of one of the summit's founding countries once expressed the view that the ideal summit would be one in which the leaders met in total secrecy, released an announcement only several weeks after the conclusion of the meeting, and revealed in it not what had been discussed or decided, but only that the meeting had taken place. While such a philosophy has not prevailed in practice—if only because the attendance of several thousand journalists provides the elected politicians present with too great a temptation to talk—summits such as Puerto Rico were able to discuss in secrecy sensitive issues, some of which may have remained beyond public knowledge to this day.

This pronounced penchant for privacy means, paradoxically, that the documents that are released publicly by the summiteers are of great importance. Because these documents are so scarce and short, each word, phrase, and sentence commands a significance far beyond its apparent simplicity. Behind each passage lies a particular act of political creativity—generating the ringing declarations that signal a historic new consensus, or the hard-fought and narrowly won language that exhaustion and the need to rush to the final communiqué-reading creates. In fact, even the most incomprehensible and ungrammatical passages—and they occur in these summit documents—signal a rich story of political struggle overwhelmed by a need for resolution beyond all else. And even the most anodyne, technical passages that appear to be (and probably were) drafted by civil servants, and seem likely to put the average citizen to sleep, speak volumes about the considerable degree of order that the summit process has engendered and imposed on an anarchic world.

The documents in this collection thus reflect the drama of the debate, the struggle for dominance, and the quest for leadership among seven of the most powerful countries of the world. Because the summit takes place at the highest political level possible, among individuals who have no domestic equals, these documents provide an intensely personal story, and one of great importance for those who sit below. Summit declarations are compelling because they are so final, for citizens inside and outside the summit countries alike. There is no higher collective authority to whom a decision at a summit can be appealed—until the summit itself convenes again in another year's time.

This compilation of the summit's documentary record through the fifteen years of its existence thus performs three vital functions. In the first place, it provides a detailed record of the ever-expanding and changing agenda of world politics over the past decade and a half. The collection of the topics that the summit addresses each year is a uniquely comprehensive, precise and meaningful synthesis of the preoccupations, priorities and emerging problems in the global system. In contrast to institutions that deliberately avoid taking up particular issues, or spend their energies consumed by only a few such issues, there are few consequential items or developments of the world's politics, economy, and even society that the leaders do not address, even if all are not always revealed in the formal summit documents themselves.

As valuable as this portrait is, the summit's subjects are more than just a static snapshot of the global agenda. Rather, they are a dynamic saga of the politics of agenda formation and legitimation in world affairs. They thus reveal the proliferating demands that peoples place on government, the increasing interdependence of a more closely connected world, the migration of topics from the sovereignty-encrusted realm of domestic politics to the plane of international deliberation, the slow acceptance of shared new challenges in the modern world, and even the recognition by the privileged and their plutocrats of the concerns of those on the outside. In shaping the summit agenda, each member tries to guide the focus of world attention, share its foreign policy preoccupations with others, solicit support and understanding, or get others to help carry a burden they no longer can bear themselves.

In this process, the summit highlights not only the global agenda but the foreign policies of its major actors. The second contribution of these documents, then, is to reveal the real, as opposed to declaratory, foreign policies of the participants, by recording, however indirectly, their positions on the pressing issues of the day.[11] Occasionally, when national responsibili-

---

[11]For a systematic identification of the positions of the individual members, and their success in translating these into the final text of summit documents, see: Timothy Heeney, *Canadian Foreign Policy and the Seven Power Summits* (Toronto: Centre for

ties and commitments are articulated on a national basis (and drafted in practice by the country concerned), the identification of national policy preferences is easy. Far more often, however, the challenge of uncovering each country's true positions is a more creative task. In accordance with the core norms of a concert system, the summit documents are consensus decisions that do not criticize anyone and in the aggregate compliment all. Still, after the many rounds of collective drafting and approval, these documents reveal, in inserted paragraphs, specific sentences, subordinate clauses, and even adjectives, the distinct national imprint, and at times the vital interests, of the particular country that produced them.

Third, these documents provide a comprehensive record not only of the issues and the positions, but also of the decisions that count in contemporary world affairs. Despite a recurrent desire for deliberative rather than decision-making summits, and a persistent cynicism about the willingness or ability of the leaders to keep their summit commitments once the gathering is over, the summits generally do arrive at a consensus and make decisions that stick. The assembled documents thus present the most detailed available record of the values, principles, norms and decisions that are reshaping international order in world politics and economics today. Their power lies not in their status as the articulation of the

---

International Studies, University of Toronto, 1988); Michael Pons, *West German Foreign Policy and the Seven Power Summits* (Toronto: Centre for International Studies, University of Toronto, 1988); François Roberge, *French Foreign Policy and the Seven Power Summits* (Toronto: Centre for International Studies, University of Toronto, 1988); Daizo Sakurada, *Managing the International Political Economy: Japan's Seven Power Summit Diplomacy* (Toronto: Centre for International Studies and University of Toronto/York University Joint Centre on Asia-Pacific Studies, University of Toronto, 1989); Blair Dimock, *The Benefits of Teamplay: Italy and the Seven Power Summits* (Toronto: Centre for International Studies, University of Toronto, 1989); and Robert Hornung, *Sharing Economic Responsibility: The United States and the Seven Power Summits* (Toronto: Centre for International Studies, University of Toronto, 1989).

preferences of fading imperial powers or the desiderata of disembodied "regimes", but in their role as the contemporary conclusions and creations of the great powers acting in concert to impose order on an otherwise messy and dangerous world.

This collection thus provides a comprehensive, systematic compilation of one of the most important sets of documents of our time. Although the texts of the summit documents are made available to the attending journalists at each summit, and the major documents are printed in full in such elite newspapers as *The New York Times,* they are not readily available to the public whose lives they will affect. Moreover, the summit governments themselves, despite the wealth of documentation they prepare for the media at each summit, usually offer no collection of the entire past record—and thus no easy way to see if the so-called new ideas and first-time breakthroughs are really new, or if the summiteers have even lived up to their commitments of the previous years. The one existing collection of summit documents includes only the final communiqués and political declarations of each gathering, while omitting the chairman's summaries and briefings that provide context and significance to the event.[12] The latter is material with high public importance but often lost to commentators who subsequently try to assess the importance of the summit. This collection is therefore a necessary preliminary to the systematic work required to answer the most critical questions about the summit and its achievements.

For students of both international and domestic politics, then, these are documents that matter. Long after the leaders have flown home, their diplomats in dialogue with difficult foreigners, officials engaged in bureaucratic battles with recalcitrant colleagues in other departments, and leaders tempted to backslide in the parochial heat of the political

---

[12]Istituto Affari Internazionali, *Economic Summits, 1975–1986: Declarations* (Isola San Giorgio, Italy: Fondazione Cini, 1987).

moment, wave these summit documents at their adversaries, have them waved back at them in turn, and see the provisions of those documents having real, continuing political force. Cheat they can and do, but in the cozy world of summitry, they are inhibited from becoming repeat offenders by the knowledge that they are likely to have their transgressions noticed, and by the certainty that they will have to confront, face to face, their powerful peers in less than one year's time. And should peer pressure alone be insufficient, there is the recognition that those sitting around the table have the ability to do great damage to one's interests if they so choose. If government at home is ultimately defined as a monopoly of the legitimate means of coercion, the international governance of the summit ultimately depends on its oligopoly of the effective powers of persuasion and punishment.

Summit decisions are thus able to bite deeply, and effectively, into the intractable reaches of domestic politics and international institution-building, some of which have long remained immune to the ordinary diplomatic processes of the post-Westphalian world. They can and do impose discipline on the domestic economies of those powerful countries beyond the effective reach of the old international institutions formally charged with this purpose. And they define the parameters, priorities, principles and work programs for the international institutions of the previous two generations. In short, these texts are not just pious expressions of passing politeness from preoccupied politicians but documents that matter in the real world of politics and economics at the national, international and global level alike.

The Summits

Rambouillet

15–17 November 1975

RAMBOUILLET (FRANCE), 15–17 NOVEMBER 1975

DELEGATIONS

France

Valéry Giscard d'Estaing, *President*
Jean Sauvagnargues, *Minister of External Affairs*
Jean-Pierre Fourcade, *Minister of the Economy and Finance*
Raymond Barre, *Personal Representative (Sherpa)*

Germany (Federal Republic)

Helmut Schmidt, *Federal Chancellor*
Hans-Dietrich Genscher, *Federal Foreign Minister*
Hans Apel, *Federal Minister of Finance*
Manfred Lahnstein, *Personal Representative (Sherpa)*

Italy

Aldo Moro, *President of the Council of Ministers*
Mariano Rumor, *Minister for Foreign Affairs*

Italy *continued*

Emilio Colombo, *Minister of the Treasury*
Rinaldo Ossola *Personal Representative (Sherpa)*

Japan

Takeo Miki, *Prime Minister*
Kiichi Miyazawa, *Minister for Foreign Affairs*
Masayoshi Ohira, *Minister of Finance*
Nobuhiko Ushiba, *Personal Representative (Sherpa)*

United Kingdom

Harold Wilson, *Prime Minister*
James Callaghan, *Secretary of State for Foreign and Commonwealth Affairs*
Denis Healey, *Chancellor of the Exchequer*
John Hunt, *Personal Representative (Sherpa)*

United States

Gerald Ford, *President*
Henry Kissinger, *Secretary of State*
William E. Simon, *Secretary of the Treasury*
George P. Shultz, *Personal Representative (Sherpa)*

DECLARATION OF RAMBOUILLET

November 17, 1975

The Heads of State and Government of France, the Federal Republic of Germany, Italy, Japan, the United Kingdom of Great Britain and Northern Ireland, and the United States of America met in the Château de Rambouillet from 15th to 17th November 1975, and agreed to declare as follows:

1. In these three days we held a searching and productive exchange of views on the world economic situation, on economic problems common to our countries, on their human, social and political implications, and on plans for resolving them.

2. We came together because of shared beliefs and shared responsibilities. We are each responsible for the government of an open, democratic society, dedicated to individual liberty and social advancement. Our success will strengthen, indeed is essential to, democratic societies everywhere. We are each responsible for assuring the prosperity of a major industrial economy. The growth and stability of our economies will help the entire industrial world and developing countries to prosper.

3. To assure in a world of growing interdependence the success of the objectives set out in this declaration, we intend to play our own full part and strengthen our efforts for closer international cooperation and constructive dialogue among all countries, transcending differences in stages of economic development, degrees of resource endowment and political and social systems.

4. The industrial democracies are determined to overcome high unemployment, continuing inflation and serious energy problems. The purpose of our meeting was to review our progress, identify more clearly the problems that we must overcome in the future, and to set a course that we will follow in the period ahead.

5. The most urgent task is to assure the recovery of our economies and to reduce the waste of human resources involved in unemployment. In consolidating the recovery, it is essential to avoid unleashing additional inflationary forces which would threaten its success. The objective must be growth that is steady and lasting. In this way, consumer and business confidence will be restored.

6. We are confident that our present policies are compatible and complementary and that recovery is under way. Nevertheless, we recognize the need for vigilance and adaptability in our policies. We will not allow the recovery to falter. We will not accept another outburst of inflation.

7. We also concentrated on the need for new efforts in the areas of world trade, monetary matters and raw materials, including energy.

8. As domestic recovery and economic expansion proceed, we must seek to restore growth in the volume of world trade. Growth and price stability will be fostered by maintenance of an open trading system. In a period where pressures are developing for a return to protectionism, it is essential for the main trading nations to confirm their commitment to the principles of the OECD [Organisation for Economic Co-operation and Development] pledge and to avoid resorting to measures by which they could try to solve their problems at the expense of others, with damaging consequences in

the economic, social and political fields. There is a responsibility on all countries, especially those with strong balance-of-payments positions and on those with current deficits, to pursue policies which will permit the expansion of world trade to their mutual advantage.

9. We believe that the multilateral trade negotiations should be accelerated. In accordance with the principles agreed to in the Tokyo Declaration, they should aim at achieving substantial tariff cuts, even eliminating tariffs in some areas, at significantly expanding agricultural trade and at reducing non-tariff measures. They should seek to achieve the maximum possible level of trade liberalization therefrom. We propose as our goal completion of the negotiations in 1977.

10. We look to an orderly and fruitful increase in our economic relations with socialist countries as an important element in progress in détente, and in world economic growth. We will also intensify our efforts to achieve a prompt conclusion of the negotiations concerning export credits.

11. With regard to monetary problems, we affirm our intention to work for greater stability. This involves efforts to restore greater stability in underlying economic and financial conditions in the world economy. At the same time, our monetary authorities will act to counter disorderly market conditions, or erratic fluctuations, in exchange rates. We welcome the rapprochement, reached at the request of many other countries, between the views of the U.S. and France on the need for stability that the reform of the international monetary system must promote. This rapprochement will facilitate agreement through the IMF [International Monetary Fund] at the next session of

the Interim Committee in Jamaica on the outstanding issues of international monetary reform.

12. A cooperative relationship and improved understanding between the developing nations and the industrial world is fundamental to the prosperity of each. Sustained growth in our economies is necessary to growth in developing countries; and their growth contributes significantly to health in our own economies. The present large deficits in the current accounts of the developing countries represent a critical problem for them and also for the rest of the world. This must be dealt with in a number of complementary ways. Recent proposals in several international meetings have already improved the atmosphere of the discussion between developed and developing countries. But early practical action is needed to assist the developing countries. Accordingly, we will play our part, through the IMF and other appropriate international fora, in making urgent improvements in international arrangements for the stabilization of the export earnings of developing countries and in measures to assist them in financing their deficits. In this context, priority should be given to the poorest developing countries.

13. World economic growth is clearly linked to the increasing availability of energy sources. We are determined to secure for our economies the energy sources needed for their growth. Our common interests require that we continue to cooperate in order to reduce our dependence on imported energy through conservation and the development of alternative sources. Through these measures as well as international cooperation between producer and consumer countries, responding to the long-term interests of both, we shall spare no effort in order to ensure more balanced conditions and a harmonious and steady development in the world energy market.

14. We welcome the convening of the Conference on International Economic Co-operation scheduled for December 16. We will conduct this dialogue in a positive spirit to assure that the interests of all concerned are protected and advanced. We believe that industrialized and developing countries alike have a critical stake in the future success of the world economy and in the cooperative political relationships on which it must be based.

15. We intend to intensify our cooperation on all these problems in the framework of existing institutions as well as in all the relevant international organizations.

SOURCE: France, Ministère des affaires étrangères, *La politique étrangères de la France: textes et documents, 2e semestre 1975* (Paris: La Documentation française, 1976), pp. 173–75; U.S., Department of State, *Bulletin,* No. 1902 (December 8, 1975): 805–807; Great Britain, Foreign and Commonwealth Office, *Declarations of Annual Economic Summits, 1975–1986* (London, 198—): A1, Rambouillet, 1–3 [unpublished]; *Economic Summits, 1975–1986: Declarations* (Rome: Istituto Affari Internazionali, 1987): 13–16.

San Juan

27–28 June 1976

SAN JUAN (PUERTO RICO), 27–28 JUNE 1976

DELEGATIONS

Canada

Pierre Elliot Trudeau, *Prime Minister*
Allan J. MacEachen, *Secretary of State for External Affairs*
Donald MacDonald, *Minister of Finance*
Ivan Head, *Personal Representative (Sherpa)*

France

Valéry Giscard d'Estaing, *President*
Jean Sauvagnargues, *Minister of External Affairs*
Jean-Pierre Fourcade, *Minister of the Economy and Finance*
Raymond Barre, *Personal Representative (Sherpa)*

Germany (Federal Republic)

Helmut Schmidt, *Federal Chancellor*
Hans-Dietrich Genscher, *Federal Foreign Minister*
Hans Apel, *Federal Minister of Finance*
Manfred Lahnstein, *Personal Representative (Sherpa)*

13

Italy

Aldo Moro, *President of the Council of Ministers*
Mariano Rumor, *Minister for Foreign Affairs*
Emilio Colombo, *Minister of the Treasury*
Mario Mondello, *Personal Representative (Sherpa)*

Japan

Takeo Miki, *Prime Minister*
Kiichi Miyazawa, *Minister for Foreign Affairs*
Masayoshi Ohira, *Minister of Finance*
Bunroku Yoshino, *Personal Representative (Sherpa)*

United Kingdom

James Callaghan, *Prime Minister*
Anthony Crosland, *Secretary of State for Foreign and Commonwealth Affairs*
Denis Healey, *Chancellor of the Exchequer*
John Hunt, *Personal Representative (Sherpa)*

United States

Gerald Ford, *President*
Henry Kissinger, *Secretary of State*
William E. Simon, *Secretary of the Treasury*
George P. Shultz, *Personal Representative (Sherpa)*

JOINT DECLARATION OF
THE INTERNATIONAL CONFERENCE

June 28, 1976

The Heads of State and Government of Canada, France, the Federal Republic of Germany, Italy, Japan, the United Kingdom of Great Britain and Northern Ireland and the United States of America met at Dorado Beach, Puerto Rico, on the 27th and 28th of June, 1976, and agreed to the following declaration:

The interdependence of our destinies makes it necessary for us to approach common economic problems with a sense of common purpose and to work toward mutually consistent economic strategies through better cooperation.

We consider it essential to take into account the interests of other nations. And this is most particularly true with respect to the developing countries of the world.

It was for these purposes that we held a broad and productive exchange of views on a wide range of issues. This meeting provided a welcome opportunity to improve our mutual understanding and to intensify our cooperation in a number of areas. Those among us whose countries are members of the European Economic Community intend to make their efforts within its framework.

At Rambouillet, economic recovery was established as a primary goal and it was agreed that the desired stability depends upon the underlying economic and financial conditions in each of our countries.

Significant progress has been achieved since Rambouillet. During the recession there was widespread concern regarding the longer-run vitality of our economies. These concerns have proved to be unwarranted. Renewed confidence in the future has replaced doubts about the economic and financial outlook. Economic recovery is well under way and in many of our countries there has been substantial progress in combatting inflation and reducing unemployment. This has improved the

15

situation in those countries where economic recovery is still relatively weak.

Our determination in recent months to avoid excessive stimulation of our economies and new impediments to trade and capital movements has contributed to the soundness and breadth of this recovery. As a result, restoration of balanced growth is within our grasp. We do not intend to lose this opportunity.

Our objective now is to manage effectively a transition to expansion which will be sustainable, which will reduce the high level of unemployment which persists in many countries and will not jeopardize our common aim of avoiding a new wave of inflation. That will call for an increase in productive investment and for partnership among all groups within our societies. This will involve acceptance, in accordance with our individual needs and circumstances, of a restoration of better balance in public finance, as well as of disciplined measures in the fiscal area and in the field of monetary policy and in some cases supplementary policies, including incomes policy. The formulation of such policies, in the context of growing interdependence, is not possible without taking into account the course of economic activity in other countries. With the right combination of policies we believe that we can achieve our objectives of orderly and sustained expansion, reducing unemployment and renewed progress toward our common goal of eliminating the problem of inflation. Sustained economic expansion and the resultant increase in individual well-being cannot be achieved in the context of high rates of inflation.

At the meeting last November, we resolved differences on structural reform of the international monetary system and agreed to promote a stable system of exchange rates which emphasized the prerequisite of developing stable underlying economic and financial conditions.

With those objectives in mind, we reached specific under-standings, which made a substantial contribution to the IMF meeting in Jamaica. Early legislative ratification of these agreements by all concerned is desirable. We agreed to improve cooperation in order to further our ability to counter disorderly market conditions and increase our understanding of economic problems and the corrective policies that are needed. We will continue to build on this structure of consultations.

Since November, the relationship between the dollar and most of the main currencies has been remarkably stable. However, some currencies have suffered substantial fluctuations.

The needed stability in underlying economic and financial conditions clearly has not yet been restored. Our commitment to deliberate, orderly and sustained expansion, and to the indispensable companion goal of defeating inflation, provides the basis for increased stability.

Our objective of monetary stability must not be undermined by the strains of financing international payments imbalances. We thus recognize the importance of each nation managing its economy and its international monetary affairs so as to correct or avoid persistent or structural international payments imbalances. Accordingly, each of us affirms his intention to work toward a more stable and durable payments structure through the application of appropriate internal and external policies.

Imbalances in world payments may continue in the period ahead. We recognize that problems may arise for a few developed countries which have special needs, which have not yet restored domestic economic stability, and which face major payments deficits. We agree to continue to cooperate with others in the appropriate bodies on further analysis of these problems with a view to their resolution. If assistance in financing transitory balance-of-payments deficits is necessary to avoid general disruptions in economic growth, then it can best be provided by multilateral means coupled with a firm program for restoring underlying equilibrium.

In the trade area, despite the recent recession, we have been generally successful in maintaining an open trading system. At the OECD [Organisation for Economic Co-operation and Development] we reaffirmed our pledge to avoid the imposition of new trade barriers.

Countries yielding to the temptation to resort to commercial protectionism would leave themselves open to a subsequent deterioration in their competitive standing; the vigor of their economies would be affected while at the same time chain reactions would be set in motion and the volume of world trade would shrink, hurting all countries. Wherever departures from the policy set forth in the recently renewed OECD trade pledge occur, elimination of the restrictions involved is essential and urgent. Also, it is important to avoid deliberate exchange rate policies which would create severe distortions in trade and lead to a resurgence of protectionism.

We have all set ourselves the objective of completing the Multilateral Trade Negotiations by the end of 1977. We hereby reaffirm that objective and commit ourselves to make every effort through the appropriate bodies to achieve it in accordance with the Tokyo Declaration.

Beyond the conclusion of the trade negotiations we recognize the desirability of intensifying and strengthening relationships among the major trading areas with a view to the long-term goal of a maximum expansion of trade.

We discussed East–West economic relations. We welcomed in this context the steady growth of East–West trade, and expressed the hope that economic relations between East and West would develop their full potential on a sound financial and reciprocal commercial basis. We agreed that this process warrants our careful examination, as well as efforts on our part to ensure that these economic ties enhance overall East–West relationships.

We welcome the adoption, by the participating countries, of converging guidelines with regard to export credits. We hope that these guidelines will be adopted as soon as possible by as many countries as possible.

In the pursuit of our goal of sustained expansion, the flow of capital facilitates the efficient allocation of resources and thereby enhances our economic well-being. We, therefore, agree on the importance of a liberal climate for international investment flows. In this regard, we view as a constructive development the declaration which was announced last week when the OECD Council met at the Ministerial level.

In the field of energy, we intend to make efforts to develop, conserve and use rationally the various energy resources and to assist the energy development objectives of developing countries.

We support the aspirations of the developing nations to improve the lives of their peoples. The role of the industrialized democracies is crucial to the success of their efforts. Cooperation between the two groups must be based on mutual respect, take into consideration the interests of all parties and reject unproductive confrontation in favor of sustained and concerted efforts to find constructive solutions to the problems of development.

The industrialized democracies can be most successful in helping the developing countries meet their aspirations by agreeing on, and cooperating to implement, sound solutions to their problems which enhance the efficient operation of the international economy. Close collaboration and better coordination are necessary among the industrialized democracies. Our efforts must be mutually supportive, not competitive. Our efforts for international economic cooperation must be considered as complementary to the policies of the developing countries themselves to achieve sustainable growth and rising standards of living.

At Rambouillet, the importance of a cooperative relationship between the developed and developing nations was affirmed; particular attention was directed to following up the results of the Seventh Special Session of the UN [United Nations] General Assembly, and especially to addressing the balance-of-payments problems of some developing countries. Since then, substantial progress has been made. We welcome the constructive spirit which prevails in the work carried out in the framework of the Conference on International Economic Co-operation, and also the positive results achieved in some areas at UNCTAD IV [the fourth session of the United Nations Conference on Trade and Development] in Nairobi. New measures taken in the IMF have made a substantial contribution to stabilizing the export earnings of the developing countries and to helping them finance their deficits.

We attach the greatest importance to the dialogue between developed and developing nations in the expectation that it will achieve concrete results in areas of mutual interest. And we reaffirm our countries' determination to participate in this process in the competent bodies, with a political will to succeed, looking toward negotiations in appropriate cases. Our common goal is to find practical solutions which contribute to an equitable and productive relationship among all peoples.

SOURCE: U.S., Department of State, *Bulletin,* No. 1935 (July 26, 1976): 121–23; Great Britain, Foreign and Commonwealth Office, *Declarations of Annual Economic Summits, 1975–1986* (London, 198—): A2, Puerto Rico, 1–4 [unpublished]; *Economic Summits, 1975–1986: Declarations* (Rome: Istituto Affari Internazionali, 1987): 19–24.

PRESIDENT FORD'S REMARKS
AT THE CONCLUSION OF THE CONFERENCE

June 28, 1976

We have just concluded two days of very productive discussions on a number of issues of great importance to us all. Our talks were characterized by a seriousness of purpose, a firm desire to improve our understanding of one another's views, and a common commitment to strengthen constructive cooperation among all nations.

During the course of our discussions, we reached agreement in several significant areas. These are set out in the declaration that we have just adopted.

First, we are confident about the future economic and financial outlook for our countries. All of us are committed to achieving sustainable growth which will reduce unemployment without jeopardizing our common aim of avoiding a new wave of inflation. We recognize that the sustained economic expansion we seek and the resultant increase in individual well-being cannot be achieved in the context of high inflation rates.

We agreed that our objective of monetary stability must not be undermined by the strains of financing payments imbalances. Each nation should manage its economy and its international monetary affairs so as to correct or avoid persistent or structural international payments imbalances.

We have recognized that problems may arise for a few developed countries which have special needs, which have not yet restored domestic economic stability, and which face major payments deficits. We agreed that if assistance in financing transitory balance-of-payments deficits is necessary to avoid general disruptions in economic growth, it can best be provided by multilateral means, in conjunction with a firm program for restoring underlying equilibrium.

The industrialized democracies can be most successful in helping developing nations by agreeing on and working together to implement sound solutions to their own problems, solutions which enhance the efficient operation of the international economy. Our efforts must be mutually supportive rather than competitive. We remain determined to continue the dialogue with the developing countries to achieve concrete results.

We agreed on the importance of maintaining a liberal climate for the flow of international investment. We agreed to examine carefully the various aspects of East–West economic contacts so that they enhance overall East–West relations.

Together, the results of our discussions represent a significant step forward in cooperation among the industrial democracies. They establish positive directions which will benefit not only our peoples but the international economy as a whole.

In conclusion, let me add a personal note. I was greatly impressed with the candid and friendly atmosphere here. Our countries have come through a difficult period. Our cooperation during this period has not only contributed to the resolution of problems but has in fact significantly strengthened relations among our countries and among the industrialized democracies as a whole.

We can be proud of this record and of our nations' abilities to meet the severe challenges we have faced. In my view, the spirit of Rambouillet, which was carried forward to these meetings in Puerto Rico, has strengthened prospects for progress by the industrialized democracies in a number of key areas. If we nurture the sense of common purpose and vision which has characterized these discussions, we have an opportunity to shape events and better meet the needs of our citizens and all the world.

SOURCE: U.S., Department of State, *Bulletin,* No. 1935 (July 26, 1976): 118–19.

NEWS CONFERENCE BY SECRETARY KISSINGER AND TREASURY SECRETARY SIMON

June 28, 1976

Secretary Kissinger: Let me say that basically the purpose of this conference was to enable the leaders of the industrial democracies, a group of nations that between them have 60 percent of the world's GNP [gross national product], to discuss a number of economic issues and to discuss a number of issues where economic and political considerations merge, such as East–West and North–South issues. They discussed them in a very free and relaxed atmosphere.

It was not a question of reading prepared statements at each other; but as Prime Minister Callaghan said, there was usually one of the leaders who introduced one of the issues, and then there was a free and easy discussion.

We believe that on the major issues confronting these countries a large degree of understanding was reached that should help encourage the economic processes, and it should also enable the countries represented here to work together on international issues such as those that were mentioned in the communiqué. But what no communiqué can reflect is the many conversations that took place at the side, the attitude of the participants that reflected the conviction that they represented parallel values and the realization that their destinies were linked together.

With this, let us answer your specific questions.

Q. Can any of you quantify the type of assistance that is in mind for Italy?

Secretary Kissinger: There was no specific discussion of any particular amount nor indeed of the framework within which assistance can take place. There is a general statement in this document that we would apply to all circumstances in which there are persistent or temporary disequilibria and perhaps Bill can explain its significance better.

23

Secretary Simon: Well, there is an existing agreement in the International Monetary Fund that loans can be made on a supplementary basis when resources are needed to forestall or to cope with a temporary problem in the international monetary system that is impairing its proper functioning, and we discussed the possibility of, if something like this were needed— as I believe the communiqué says verbatim—what type [of] mechanism should be brought into place for transitory financing for balance-of-payments purposes under very stringent economic conditions.

Q. May I ask the first Secretary [laughter]—given the fact that you said we should not expect any dramatic developments out of this, can you give us an idea of any changes that might come about as a result of this meeting, or any new directions that U.S. policy might take?

Secretary Kissinger: Well, first of all, one cannot expect that the foreign policy of major countries can be redesigned every six months, and if that were to happen, that would be a reason for alarm rather than for congratulations.

On the economic side, all of the countries face the situation now that the recession which seemed to be the dominant problem at Rambouillet has turned to a greater or lesser degree in the various countries into a recovery problem, and the problem that had to be discussed was how to sustain this recovery without inflation.

On the East–West trade, this was not discussed at Rambouillet at all, and we agreed to study the various implications of the relationship between state economies and market economies so that commerce can develop to the mutual benefit and cannot be used for political purposes.

With respect to North–South, there was a very full and detailed discussion in the light of the experience which we have all had at UNCTAD in Nairobi and at the meeting of the Conference on International Economic Co-operation in Paris as to how the industrialized countries, the industrialized democracies, that between them contribute almost the entire development effort—the Socialist countries contribute nothing—how those countries can cooperate for the mutual benefit of both developed and developing countries and for the benefit of the world economy. That, too, was not an entirely new direction, but a new emphasis on which very fruitful discussions took place.

Q. Can you tell us anything, Mr. Secretary, about the President's talks with Giscard, Moro, Callaghan, Miki?

Secretary Kissinger: Of course, one of the great benefits of these meetings is the ability to exchange ideas not only in a meeting room but on a bilateral basis. And with the various leaders there was an exchange because, obviously, with the Italian Prime Minister, there was a discussion of the implications of what political developments might occur in Italy that could be most conducive to reform, and we got the assessment of the Italian leaders.

We will see the Japanese Prime Minister again on Wednesday in Washington, so this was more in the nature of a preliminary talk.

The talk with President Giscard d'Estaing concerned the review of the entire world situation, including some topics that were not discussed in the general session, such as the Middle East and Africa. And you will remember I said it is only to point out why there were no bilaterals with certain other people, that the President has seen Prime Minister Trudeau two weeks ago and will see Chancellor Schmidt two weeks from now. So, this is the essence of his conversations.

Q. Did you get any further in the North–South deal, on getting a common approach?

Secretary Kissinger: I don't think it is possible—nor did we attempt—to get all the details of a common approach in a meeting of a day and a half, but there was a general understanding that there should be a common approach or at least a parallel approach.

There was also a general understanding, as the communiqué reflects, that the developed countries can make their best contribution by putting forward sound positions rather than wait for proposals to be put to them and let themselves be driven by the negotiating tactics of a particular conference, and it was agreed that we would work closely together in preparation for other meetings.

Q. Mr. Secretary, in view of the fact that much of the developing payment deficit results from oil, was that discussed, any stand to be taken on that question?

Secretary Kissinger: Well, there was a general discussion of the energy problem but more from the point of view of what the industrial democracies can do to reduce their dependence on it, and there were general discussions of the economic aspects of balance-of-payments deficits which I will let Secretary Simon answer.

Secretary Simon: There was one important point, if I understand your question and statement correctly, that the balance-of-payments problem stems entirely from oil—that is not correct. Obviously the quadrupling of the oil price had a significant part to play, but there are those countries who have not sufficiently adjusted their economic policies to compensate for the increased cost of oil, and these adjustments, while difficult politically and socially, must indeed be made. And it was in that framework—of the responsibilities of nations in surplus as well as in deficit—that we discussed the balance-of-payments problems, that President Ford explained to the participants this year the United States is going to have a dramatic swing of $15–$16 billion in our current account balance, from a $12 billion surplus last year to approximately $3 billion deficit this year. We view this with equanimity and indeed—as other countries in surplus positions should, too.

Q. Mr. Secretary Simon, should we interpret the communiqué to indicate that Prime Minister Miki is receptive to the idea of revaluating the yen?

Secretary Simon: When we talk about revaluation of a currency, the Japanese yen is a floating currency that is subjected to the market evaluation, if you will, and that is what occurs. Now there are occasions which—I don't say the Japanese have been guilty of—where one can artificially attempt for a time to peg a rate, but I have not seen this occur, no. Floating rates, the market sets the rate.

Q. Mr. Secretary, was there any discussion at all of southern Africa and Rhodesia?

Secretary Kissinger: Not in the meetings as such, but at the fringes of the meetings.

Q. Was there anything decided about it?

Secretary Kissinger: There was no attempt made to decide anything. As I pointed out after my meetings with [South African] Prime Minister [John] Vorster, he has now to consider several problems with his colleagues, and we are consulting various black African States and various of our allies before we can formulate the precise next move, but we also insist that the process which was set in motion is still underway and in our view has a chance of continuing.

We also have called attention in Britain, and I want to do it here, about the central role that Britain can play with respect to Rhodesia, and it is a responsibility which we have the impression—indeed the British Government has said it is willing to exercise.

Q. Aside from having the agreement that there should be a common approach to it, do you know already or do you have a hint in which direction the North–South—

Secretary Kissinger: There was a rather full discussion of various of the topics that have been on the international agenda, and experts and others will work on that in the spirit of this meeting in the weeks ahead.

Q. I would like to ask Secretary Simon what the prospects are for the British pound and how this was discussed at the meeting.

Secretary Simon: Number one, we don't discuss other currencies of other countries. That is for obvious reasons. Going back to the Jamaica agreement, one of the basic tenets of that agreement was that exchange rate stability would only be achieved when we achieved underlying economic stability; and as countries adjust to the durable inflation problems and other problems today their currencies indeed will stabilize, and actually most currencies in recent months, since the Jamaica agreement, have been remarkably stable. There have been a few notable exceptions, due to the fundamental economic problems which are being corrected.

Q. How much of the $5 billion have the British drawn down?

Secretary Simon: I don't have that figure, and if I did I am not sure that that figure should not be announced, if indeed it should be at all, by the U.K. officials, not by an American finance official.

Q. Mr. Secretary, was there any discussion with Giscard on the possible French force to Lebanon?

Secretary Kissinger: That issue is not at this particular moment acute. The French Government knows our attitude, and it is parallel to their own, which is to say that, if under conditions of cease-fire, if all of the parties should invite a French force, and if the French Government were prepared to send one, it could play a potentially useful role, but it is not now being discussed, and our impression is that the Arab League force will be the principal international instrument that is being used.

SOURCE: U.S., Department of State, *Bulletin,* No. 1935 (July 26, 1976): 119–21.

London

7–8 May 1977

LONDON (UNITED KINGDOM), 7–8 MAY 1977

DELEGATIONS

Canada

Pierre Elliot Trudeau, *Prime Minister*
Donald Jamieson, *Secretary of State for External Affairs*
Donald MacDonald, *Minister of Finance*
Ivan Head, *Personal Representative (Sherpa)*

France

Valéry Giscard d'Estaing, *President*
Raymond Barre, *Prime Minister and Minister of Economy and Finance*
Louis de Guiringaud, *Minister of External Affairs*
Bernard Clappier, *Personal Representative (Sherpa)*

Germany (Federal Republic)

Helmut Schmidt, *Federal Chancellor*
Hans-Dietrich Genscher, *Federal Foreign Minister*
Hans Apel, *Federal Minister of Finance*
Manfred Lahnstein, *Personal Representative (Sherpa)*

Italy

Giulio Andreotti, *President of the Council of Ministers*
Arnaldo Forlani, *Minister for Foreign Affairs*
Gaetano Stammati, *Minister of the Treasury*
Umberto La Rocca, *Personal Representative (Sherpa)*

Japan

Takeo Fukuda, *Prime Minister*
Iichiro Hatoyama, *Minister for Foreign Affairs*
Hideo Bō, *Minister of Finance*
Bunroku Yoshino, *Personal Representative (Sherpa)*

United Kingdom

James Callaghan, *Prime Minister*
David Owen, *Secretary of State for Foreign and Commonwealth Affairs*
Denis Healey, *Chancellor of the Exchequer*
John Hunt, *Personal Representative (Sherpa)*

United States

Jimmy Carter, *President*
Cyrus Vance, *Secretary of State*
W. Michael Blumenthal, *Secretary of the Treasury*
Henry Owen, *Personal Representative (Sherpa)*

European Communities

Roy Jenkins, *President of the Commission*
Crispin Tickell, *Personal Representative (Sherpa)*

DECLARATION:
DOWNING STREET SUMMIT CONFERENCE

May 8, 1977

In two days of intensive discussion at Downing Street we have agreed on how we can best help to promote the well-being both of our own countries and of others.

The world economy has to be seen as a whole; it involves not only cooperation among national governments but also strengthening appropriate international organizations. We were reinforced in our awareness of the interrelationship of all the issues before us, as well as our own interdependence. We are determined to respond collectively to the challenges of the future.

Our most urgent task is to create more jobs while continuing to reduce inflation. Inflation does not reduce unemployment. On the contrary, it is one of its major causes. We are particularly concerned about the problem of unemployment among young people. We have agreed that there will be an exchange of experience and ideas on providing the young with job opportunities.

We commit our governments to stated economic growth targets or to stabilization policies which, taken as a whole, should provide a basis for sustained non-inflationary growth, in our own countries and worldwide and for reduction of imbalances in international payments.

Improved financing facilities are needed. The International Monetary Fund must play a prominent role. We commit ourselves to seek additional resources for the IMF and support the linkage of its lending practices to the adoption of appropriate stabilization policies.

We will provide strong political leadership to extend opportunities for trade to strengthen the open international trading system, which will increase job opportunities. We reject protectionism: it would foster unemployment, increase inflation and undermine the welfare of our peoples. We will give a new impetus to the Tokyo Round of Multilateral Trade Negotiations. Our objective is to make substantive progress in key areas in

1977. In this field structural changes in the world economy must be taken into consideration.

We will further conserve energy and increase and diversify energy production, so that we reduce our dependence on oil. We agree on the need to increase nuclear energy to help meet the world's energy requirements. We commit ourselves to do this while reducing the risks of nuclear proliferation. We are launching an urgent study to determine how best to fulfill these purposes.

The world economy can only grow on a sustained and equitable basis if developing countries share in that growth. We are agreed to do all in our power to achieve a successful conclusion of the CIEC [Conference on International Economic Co-operation] and we commit ourselves to a continued constructive dialogue with developing countries. We aim to increase the flow of aid and other real resources to those countries. We invite the COMECON [Council for Mutual Economic Co-operation] countries to do the same. We support multilateral institutions such as the World Bank, whose general resources should be increased sufficiently to permit its lending to rise in real terms. We stress the importance of secure private investments to foster world economic progress.

To carry out these tasks we need the assistance and cooperation of others. We will seek that cooperation in appropriate international institutions, such as the United Nations, the World Bank, the IMF, the GATT [General Agreement on Tariffs and Trade], and OECD. Those among us whose countries are members of the European Economic Community intend to make their efforts within its framework.

In our discussions we have reached substantial agreement. Our firm purpose is now to put that agreement into action. We shall review progress on all the measures we have discussed here at Downing Street in order to maintain the momentum of recovery.

The message of the Downing Street Summit is thus one of confidence:

—in the continuing strength of our societies and the proven democratic principles that give them vitality;

—that we are undertaking the measures needed to over-come problems and achieve a more prosperous future.

APPENDIX TO DOWNING STREET SUMMIT DECLARATION

WORLD ECONOMIC PROSPECTS

Since 1975 the world economic situation has been improving gradually. Serious problems, however, still persist in all of our countries. Our most urgent task is to create jobs while continuing to reduce inflation. Inflation is not a remedy to unemployment but one of its major causes. Progress in the fight against inflation has been uneven. The needs for adjustment between surplus and deficit countries remain large. The world has not yet fully adjusted to the depressive effects of the 1974 oil price rise.

We commit our governments to targets for growth and stabilization which vary from country to country but which, taken as a whole, should provide a basis for sustained non-inflationary growth worldwide.

Some of our countries have adopted reasonably expansionist growth targets for 1977. The governments of these countries will keep their policies under review, and commit themselves to adopt further policies, if needed to achieve their stated target rates and to contribute to the adjustment of payments imbalances. Others are pursuing stabilization policies designed to provide a basis for sustained growth without increasing inflationary expectations. The governments of these countries will continue to pursue those goals.

These two sets of policies are interrelated. Those of the first group of countries should help to create an environment conducive to expansion in the others without adding to inflation. Only if growth rates can be maintained in the first group and increased in the second, and inflation tackled successfully in both, can unemployment be reduced.

We are particularly concerned about the problem of unemployment among young people. Therefore we shall promote the training of young people in order to build a skilled and flexible labor force so that they can be ready to take advantage of the upturn in economic activity as it develops. All of our governments, individually or collectively, are taking appropriate measures to this end. We must learn as much as possible from each other and agree to exchange experiences and ideas.

Success in managing our domestic economies will not only strengthen world economic growth but also contribute to success in four other main economic fields to which we now turn—balance-of-payments financing, trade, energy, and North–South relations. Progress in these fields will in turn contribute to world economic recovery.

BALANCE-OF-PAYMENTS FINANCING

For some years to come oil-importing nations, as a group, will be facing substantial payments deficits and importing capital from OPEC [Organization of the Petroleum Exporting Countries] nations to finance them. The deficit for the current year could run as high as $45 billion. Only through a reduction in our dependence on imported oil and a rise in capacity of oil-producing nations to import can that deficit be reduced.

This deficit needs to be distributed among the oil-consuming nations in a pattern compatible with their ability to attract capital on a continuing basis. The need for adjustment to this pattern remains large, and it will take much international cooperation and determined action by surplus as well as deficit countries, if continuing progress is to be made. Strategies of adjustment in the deficit countries must include emphasis on elimination of domestic sources of inflation and improvement in international cost-price relationships. It is important that industrial countries in relatively strong payments positions should ensure continued adequate expansion of domestic demand, within prudent limits. Moreover these countries, as well as other countries in strong payments positions, should promote increased flows of long-term capital exports.

The International Monetary Fund must play a prominent role in balance-of-payments financing and adjustment. We therefore strongly endorse the recent agreement of the Interim Committee of the IMF to seek additional resources for that organization and to link IMF lending to the adoption of appropriate stabilization policies. These added resources will strengthen the ability of the IMF to encourage and assist member countries in adopting policies which will limit payments deficits and warrant their financing through the private markets. These resources should be used with the conditionality and flexibility required to encourage an appropriate pace of adjustment.

This IMF proposal should facilitate the maintenance of reasonable levels of economic activity and reduce the danger of resort to trade and payments restrictions. It demonstrates cooperation between oil-exporting nations, industrial nations in stronger financial positions, and the IMF. It will contribute materially to the health and progress of the world economy. In pursuit of this objective, we also reaffirm our intention to strive to increase monetary stability.

We agreed that the international monetary and financial system, in its new and agreed legal framework, should be strengthened by the early implementation of the increase in quotas. We will work towards an early agreement within the IMF on another increase in the quotas of that organization.

TRADE

We are committed to providing strong political leadership for the global effort to expand opportunities for trade and to strengthen the open international trading system. Achievement of these goals is central to world economic prosperity and the effective resolution of economic problems faced by both developed and developing countries throughout the world.

Policies of protectionism foster unemployment, increase inflation and undermine the welfare of our peoples. We are therefore agreed on the need to maintain our political commitment to an open and non-discriminatory world trading system. We will seek both nationally and through the appropriate international institutions to promote solutions that create new jobs and consumer benefits through expanded trade and to avoid approaches which restrict trade.

The Tokyo Round of multilateral trade negotiations must be pursued vigorously. The continuing economic difficulties make it even more essential to achieve the objectives of the Tokyo Declaration and to negotiate a comprehensive set of agreements to the maximum benefit of all. Toward this end, we will seek this year to achieve substantive progress in such key areas as:

(i)   A tariff reduction plan of broadest possible application designed to achieve a substantial cut and harmonization and in certain cases the elimination of tariffs;

(ii) Codes, agreements and other measures that will facilitate a significant reduction of non-tariff barriers to trade and the avoidance of new barriers in the future and that will take into account the structural changes which have taken place in the world economy;

(iii) A mutually acceptable approach to agriculture that will achieve increased expansion and stabilization of trade, and greater assurance of world food supplies.

Such progress should not remove the right of individual countries under existing international agreements to avoid significant market disruption.

While seeking to conclude comprehensive and balanced agreements on the basis of reciprocity among all industrial countries we are determined, in accordance with the aims of the Tokyo Declaration, to ensure that the agreements provide special benefits to developing countries.

We welcome the action taken by governments to reduce counter-productive competition in officially supported export credits and propose that substantial further efforts be made this year to improve and extend the present consensus in this area.

We consider that irregular practices and improper conduct should be eliminated from international trade, banking and commerce, and we welcome the work being done toward international agreements prohibiting illicit payments.

ENERGY

We welcome the measures taken by a number of governments to increase energy conservation, and most recently the program announced by the President of the United States. The increase in demand for energy and oil imports continues at a rate which places excessive pressure on the world's depleting hydrocarbon resources. We agree therefore on the need to do everything possible to strengthen our efforts still further.

We are committed to national and joint efforts to limit energy demand and to increase and diversify supplies. There will need to be greater exchanges of technology and joint research and development aimed at more efficient energy use, improved recovery and use of coal and other conventional resources, and the development of new energy sources.

Increasing reliance will have to be placed on nuclear energy to satisfy growing energy requirements and to help diversify sources of energy. This should be done with the utmost precaution with respect to the generation and dissemination of material that can be used for nuclear weapons. Our objective is to meet the world's energy needs and to make peaceful use of nuclear energy widely available, while avoiding the danger of the spread of nuclear weapons. We are also agreed that, in order to be effective, non-proliferation policies should as far as possible be acceptable to both industrialized and developing countries alike. To this end, we are undertaking a preliminary analysis to be completed within two months of the best means of advancing these objectives, including the study of terms of reference for international fuel cycle evaluation.

The oil-importing developing countries have special problems both in securing and in paying for the energy supplies needed to sustain their economic development programs. They require additional help in expanding their domestic energy production and to this end we hope the World Bank, as its resources grow, will give special emphasis to projects that serve this purpose.

We intend to do our utmost to ensure, during this transitional period, that the energy market functions harmoniously, in particular through strict conservation measures and the development of all our energy resources. We hope very much that the oil-producing countries will take these efforts into account and will make their contribution as well.

We believe that these activities are essential to enable all countries to have continuing energy supplies now and for the future at reasonable prices consistent with sustained non-inflationary economic growth; and we intend through all useful channels to concert our policies in continued consultation and cooperation with each other and with other countries.

NORTH–SOUTH RELATIONS

The world economy can only grow on a sustained and equitable basis if developing countries share in that growth. Progress has been made. The industrial countries have maintained an open market system despite a deep recession. They have increased aid flows, especially to poorer nations. Some $8 billion will be available from the IDA [International Development Association] for these nations over the next three years, as we join others in fulfilling pledges to its fifth replenishment. The IMF has made available to developing countries, under its compensatory financing facility, nearly an additional $2 billion last year. An

International Fund for Agricultural Development has been created, based on common efforts by the developed OPEC and other developing nations.

The progress and the spirit of cooperation that have emerged can serve as an excellent base for further steps. The next step will be the successful conclusion of the Conference on International Economic Co-operation and we agreed to do all in our power to achieve this. We shall work:

(i) To increase the flow of aid and other real resources from the industrial to developing countries, particularly to the 800 million people who now live in absolute poverty; and to improve the effectiveness of aid;

(ii) To facilitate developing countries' access to sources of international finance;

(iii) To support such multilateral lending institutions as the World Bank, whose lending capacity, we believe, will have to be increased in the years ahead to permit its lending to increase in real terms and widen in scope;

(iv) To promote the secure investment needed to foster world economic development;

(v) To secure productive results from negotiations about the stabilization of commodity prices and the creation of a Common Fund for individual buffer stock agreements and to consider problems of the stabilization of export earnings of developing countries; and

(vi) To continue to improve access in a non-disruptive way to the markets of industrial countries for the products of developing nations.

It is desirable that these actions by developed and developing countries be assessed and concerted in relation to each other and to the larger goals that our countries share. We hope that the World Bank, together with the IMF, will consult with other developed and developing countries in exploring how this could best be done.

The well-being of the developed and developing nations are bound up together. The developing countries' growing prosperity benefits industrial countries, as the latter's growth benefits developing nations. Both developed and developing nations have a mutual interest in maintaining a climate conducive to stable growth worldwide.

SOURCE: Great Britain, Foreign and Commonwealth Office, *Declarations of Annual Economic Summits, 1975–1986* (London, 198—): A3, London, 1–8 [unpublished]; U.S., Department of State, *Bulletin,* No. 1980 (June 6, 1977): 583–86; *Economic Summits, 1975–1986: Declarations* (Rome: Istituto Affari Internazionali, 1987): 27–36.

Bonn

16–17 July 1978

BONN, 16–17 JULY 1978

DELEGATIONS

Canada

Pierre Elliot Trudeau, *Prime Minister*
Donald Jamieson, *Secretary of State for External Affairs*
Jean Chrétien, *Minister of Finance*
Robert Johnstone, *Personal Representative (Sherpa)*

France

Valéry Giscard d'Estaing, *President*
Louis de Guiringaud, *Minister of External Affairs*
René Monory, *Minister of the Economy and Finance*
Bernard Clappier, *Personal Representative (Sherpa)*

Germany (Federal Republic)

Helmut Schmidt, *Federal Chancellor*
Hans-Dietrich Genscher, *Federal Foreign Minister*
Hans Matthöfer, *Federal Minister of Finance*
Otto Lambsdorff, *Federal Minister of Economics*
Manfred Lahnstein, *Personal Representative (Sherpa)*

Italy

Giulio Andreotti, *President of the Council of Ministers*
Arnaldo Forlani, *Minister for Foreign Affairs*
Filippo Maria Pandolfi, *Minister of the Treasury*
Umberto La Rocca, *Personal Representative (Sherpa)*

Japan

Takeo Fukuda, *Prime Minister*
Sunao Sonoda, *Minister for Foreign Affairs*
Tatsuo Murayama, *Minister of Finance*
Hiromichi Miyazaki, *Personal Representative (Sherpa)*

United Kingdom

James Callaghan, *Prime Minister*
David Owen, *Secretary of State for Foreign and
    Commonwealth Affairs*
Denis Healey, *Chancellor of the Exchequer*
John Hunt, *Personal Representative (Sherpa)*

United States

Jimmy Carter, *President*
Cyrus Vance, *Secretary of State*
W. Michael Blumenthal, *Secretary of the Treasury*
Henry Owen, *Personal Representative (Sherpa)*

European Communities

Roy Jenkins, *President of the Commission*
Crispin Tickell, *Personal Representative (Sherpa)*

DECLARATION

July 17, 1978

The Heads of State and Government of Canada, the Federal Republic of Germany, France, Italy, Japan, the United Kingdom of Great Britain and Northern Ireland and the United States of America met in Bonn on 16th and 17th July 1978. The European Community was represented by the President of the European Council and by the President of the European Commission for discussion of matters within the Community's competence.

1. We agreed on a comprehensive strategy covering growth, employment and inflation, international monetary policy, energy, trade and other issues of particular interest to developing countries. We must create more jobs and fight inflation, strengthen international trading, reduce payments imbalances, and achieve greater stability in exchange markets. We are dealing with long-term problems, which will only yield to sustained efforts. This strategy is a coherent whole, whose parts are interdependent. To this strategy, each of our countries can contribute; from it, each can benefit.

GROWTH, EMPLOYMENT AND INFLATION

2. We are concerned, above all, about worldwide unemployment, because it has been at too high a level for many years, because it hits hardest at the most vulnerable sections of the population, because its economic cost is high and its human cost higher still. We will act, through measures to assure growth and develop needed skills, to increase employment. In doing this, we will build on the progress that has already been made in the fight against inflation and will seek new successes in that fight. But we need an improvement in growth where that can be achieved without rekindling inflation in order to reduce extremes of balance-of-payments surpluses and deficits. This will reduce

47

destabilizing exchange-rate movements. Improved growth will help to reduce protectionist pressures. We need it also to encourage the flow of private investment, on which economic progress depends. We will seek to reduce impediments to private investment, both domestically and internationally. Better growth is needed to ensure that the free world is able to develop to meet the expectations of its citizens and the aspirations of the developing countries.

3. A program of different actions by countries that face different conditions is needed to assure steady non-inflationary growth. In countries whose balance-of-payments situation and inflation rate do not impose special restrictions, this requires a faster rise in domestic demand. In countries where rising prices and costs are creating strong pressures, this means taking new measures against inflation.

—Canada reaffirmed its intention, within the limits permitted by the need to contain and reduce inflation, to achieve higher growth of employment and an increase in output of up to five percent.

—As a contribution to avert the worldwide disturbances of economic equilibrium, the German delegation has indicated that by the end of August it will propose to the legislative bodies additional and quantitatively substantial measures up to one percent of GNP [Gross National Product], designed to achieve a significant strengthening of demand and a higher rate of growth. The order of magnitude will take account of the absorptive capacity of the capital market and the need to avoid inflationary pressures.

—The President of the French Republic has indicated that, while pursuing its policy of reduction of the rate of inflation, the French Government agrees, as a contribution to the common effort, to increase by an amount of about 0.5 percent of GNP the deficit of the budget of the State for the year 1978.

—The Italian Prime Minister has indicated that the Government undertakes to raise the rate of economic growth in 1979 by 1.5 percentage points with respect to 1978. It plans to achieve this goal by cutting public current expenditure while stimulating investment with the aim of increasing employment in a non-inflationary context.

—The Prime Minister of Japan has referred to the fact that his Government is striving for the attainment of the real growth target for fiscal year 1978, which is about 1.5 percentage points higher than the performance of the previous year, mainly through the expansion of domestic demand. He has further expressed his determination to achieve the said target by taking appropriate measures as necessary. In August or September he will determine whether additional measures are needed.

—The United Kingdom, having achieved a major reduction in the rate of inflation and improvement in the balance of payments, has recently given a fiscal stimulus equivalent to rather over one percent of GNP. The Government intends to continue the fight against inflation so as to improve still further the prospects for growth and employment.

—The President of the United States stated that reducing inflation is essential to maintaining a healthy U.S. economy and has therefore become the top priority of U.S. economic policy. He identified the major actions that have been taken and are being taken to counter inflation in the United States: tax cuts originally proposed for fiscal year 1979 have now been reduced by $10 billion; government expenditure projections for 1978 and 1979 have been reduced; a very tight budget is being prepared for 1980; steps are being taken to reduce the direct contribution by government regulations or restrictions to rising costs and prices, and a voluntary program has been undertaken to achieve deceleration of wages and prices.

—The meeting took note with satisfaction that the common approach of the European Community already agreed at Bremen would reinforce the effectiveness of this program.

ENERGY

4. In spite of some improvement, the present energy situation remains unsatisfactory. Much more needs to be done.

5. We are committed to reduce our dependence on imported oil.

6. We note that the European Community has already agreed at Bremen the following objectives for 1985: to reduce the Community's dependence on imported energy to fifty percent, to limit net oil imports, and to reduce to 0.8 the ratio between the rate of increase in energy consumption and the rate of increase in gross domestic product.

7. Recognizing its particular responsibility in the energy field, the United States will reduce its dependence on imported oil. The U.S. will have in place by the end of the year a comprehensive policy framework within which this effort can be urgently carried forward. By year-end, measures will be in effect that will result in oil import savings of approximately 2.5 million barrels per day by 1985. In order to achieve these goals, the U.S. will establish a strategic oil reserve of 1 billion barrels; it will increase coal production by two-thirds; it will maintain the ratio between growth in gross national product and growth in energy demand at or below 0.8; and its oil consumption will grow more slowly than energy consumption. The volume of oil imported in 1978 and 1979 should be less than that imported in 1977. In order to discourage excessive consumption of oil and to

encourage the movement toward coal, the U.S. remains determined that the prices paid for oil in the U.S. shall be raised to the world level by the end of 1980.

8. We hope that the oil-exporting countries will continue to contribute to a stable world energy situation.

9. Looking to the longer term, our countries will review their national energy programs with a view to speeding them up. General energy targets can serve as useful measures of the progress achieved.

10. Private and public investment to produce energy and to use it more efficiently within the industrial world should be increased. This can contribute significantly to economic growth.

11. The further development of nuclear energy is indispensable, and the slippage in the execution of nuclear power programs must be reversed. To promote the peaceful use of nuclear energy and reduce the risk of nuclear proliferation, the nuclear fuel cycle studies initiated at the London Summit should be pursued. The President of the United States and the Prime Minister of Canada have expressed their firm intention to continue as reliable suppliers of nuclear fuel within the framework of effective safeguards. The President intends to use the full powers of his office to prevent any interruption of enriched uranium supply and to ensure that existing agreements will be respected. The Prime Minister intends that there shall be no interruption of Canadian uranium supply on the basis of effective safeguards.

12. Coal should play an increasingly important role in the long term.

13. Joint or coordinated energy research and development should be carried out to hasten the development of new, including renewable, energy sources and the more efficient use of existing sources.

14. In energy development, the environment and human safety of the population must be safeguarded with greatest care.

15. To help developing countries, we will intensify our national development assistance programs in the energy field and we will develop a coordinated effort to bring into use renewable energy technologies and to elaborate the details within one year. We suggest that the OECD will provide the medium for cooperation with other countries.

16. We stress the need for improvement and coordination of assistance for developing countries in the energy field. We suggest that the World Bank explore ways in which its activities in this field can be made increasingly responsive to the needs of the developing countries, and to examine whether new approaches, particularly to financing hydrocarbon exploration, would be useful.

TRADE

17. We reaffirm our determination to expand international trade, one of the driving forces for more sustained and balanced economic growth. Through our joint efforts we will maintain and strengthen the open international trading system. We appreciate and support the progress as set forth in the Framework of Understanding on the Tokyo Round of Multilateral Trade Negotiations made public in Geneva on July 13, 1978, even though within this Framework of Understanding some difficult and important issues remain unresolved.

The successful conclusion of these negotiations, the biggest yet held, would mean not just a major trade-liberalization program extending over the 1980s, but the most important progress yet made in the GATT in relation to non-tariff measures. Thus the GATT rules would be brought more closely into line with the requirements of the next decade—particularly in relation to safeguards—in ways which would avoid any weakening of the world trading system and be of benefit to all trading countries, developed and developing alike. A substantially higher degree of equity and discipline in the international trading system would be achieved by the creation of new mechanisms in many fields for consultation and dispute settlement. Uniform application of the GATT rules is vital and we shall move in that direction as soon as possible.

In all areas of the negotiations, the Summit countries look forward to working even more closely with the developing countries. We seek to ensure for all participants a sound and balanced result, which adequately takes into account the needs of developing countries, for example, through special and differential treatment, and which brings about their greater participation in the benefits and obligations of the world trading system.

At last year's Downing Street Summit we rejected a protectionist course for world trade. We agreed to give a new impetus to the Tokyo Round. Our negotiators have fulfilled that commitment. Today we charge them, in cooperation with the other participants, to resolve the outstanding issues and to conclude successfully the detailed negotiations by December 15, 1978.

18. We note with satisfaction the renewal of the pledge to maintain an open-market oriented economic system made by the OECD Council of Ministers last month. Today's world economic problems cannot be solved by relapsing into open or concealed protectionism.

19. We welcome the statement on positive adjustment policy made by the OECD Ministers. There must be a readiness over time to accept and facilitate structural change. Measures to prevent such change perpetuate economic inefficiency, place the burden of structural change on trading partners and inhibit the integration of developing countries into the world economy. We are determined in our industrial, social, structural and regional policy initiatives to help sectors in difficulties, without interfering with international competition and trade flows.

20. We note the need for countries with large current accounts deficits to increase exports and for countries with large current accounts surpluses to facilitate increases in imports. In this

context, the United States is firmly committed to improve its export performance and is examining measures to this end. The Prime Minister of Japan has stated that he wishes to work for the increase of imports through the expansion of domestic demand and various efforts to facilitate imports. Furthermore, he has stated that in order to cope with the immediate situation of unusual surplus, the Government of Japan is taking a temporary and extraordinary step of calling for moderation in exports with the aim of keeping the total volume of Japan's exports for the fiscal year of 1978 at or below the level of fiscal year 1977.

21. We underline our willingness to increase our cooperation in the field of foreign private investment flows among industrialized countries and between them and developing countries. We will intensify work for further agreements in the OECD and elsewhere.

22. In the context of expanding world economic activity, we recognize the requirement for better access to our countries' markets for the products of the developing countries. At the same time we look to increasing readiness on the part of the more advanced developing countries to open their markets to imports.

RELATIONS WITH DEVELOPING COUNTRIES

23. Success in our efforts to strengthen our countries' economies will benefit the developing countries, and their economic progress will benefit us. This calls for joint action on the basis of shared responsibility.

24. In the years ahead the developing countries, particularly those most in need, can count on us for an increased flow of financial assistance and other resources for their development. The Prime Minister of Japan has stated that he will strive to double Japan's official development assistance in three years.

We deeply regret the failure of the COMECON countries to take their due share in the financial assistance to developing countries and invite them once more to do so.

25. The poorer developing countries require increased concessional aid. We support the soft loan funds of the World Bank and the three regional development banks. We pledge our governments to support replenishment of the International Development Association on a scale that would permit its lending to rise annually in real terms.

26. As regards the more advanced developing countries, we renew our pledge to support replenishment of the multilateral development banks' resources, on the scale needed to meet the growing needs for loans on commercial terms. We will encourage governmental and private co-financing of development projects with these banks.

The cooperation of the developing countries in creating a good investment climate and adequate protection for foreign investment is required if foreign private investment is to play its effective role in generating economic growth and in stimulating the transfer of technology.

We also refer to our efforts with respect to developing countries in the field of energy as outlined in paragraphs 15 and 16.

27. We agreed to pursue actively the negotiations on a Common Fund to a successful conclusion and to continue our efforts to conclude individual commodity agreements and to complete studies of various ways of stabilizing export earnings.

INTERNATIONAL MONETARY POLICY

28. The erratic fluctuations of the exchange markets in recent months have had a damaging effect on confidence, investment and growth throughout the world. Essentially, exchange rate stability can only be achieved by attacking the fundamental problems which have contributed to the present large balance-of-

payments deficits and surpluses. Implementation of the policies described above in the framework of a concerted program will help to bring about a better pattern of world payments balances and lead to greater stability in international exchange markets. This stability will in turn improve confidence and the environment for sustained economic growth.

29. Although exchange rates need to respond to changes in underlying economic and financial conditions among nations, our monetary authorities will continue to intervene to the extent necessary to counter disorderly conditions in the exchange markets. They will maintain extensive consultation to enhance these efforts' effectiveness. We will support surveillance by the International Monetary Fund to promote effective functioning of the international monetary system.

30. The representatives of the European Community informed the meeting of the decision of the European Council at Bremen on 6-7 July to consider a scheme for a closer monetary cooperation. The meeting welcomed the report and noted that the Community would keep the other participants informed.

CONCLUSION

31. It has been our combined purpose to attack the fundamental economic problems that our countries confront.

The measures on which we have agreed are mutually reinforcing. Their total effect should thus be more than the sum of their parts. We will now seek parliamentary and public support for these measures.

We cannot hope to achieve our purposes alone. We shall work closely together with other countries and within the appropriate international institutions; those among us whose countries are members of the European Community intend to make their efforts within this framework.

We have instructed our representatives to convene by the end of 1978 in order to review this Declaration. We also intend to have a similar meeting among ourselves at an appropriate time next year.

SOURCE: U.S., Department of State, *Bulletin,* No. 2018 (September 1978): 2–4; Great Britain, Foreign and Commonwealth Office, *Declarations of Annual Economic Summits, 1975–1986* (London, 198—): A4, Bonn, 1–8 [unpublished]; *Economic Summits, 1975–1986: Declarations* (Rome: Istituto Affari Internazionali, 1987): 39–48.

STATEMENT ON AIR-HIJACKING

July 17, 1978

The Heads of State and Government, concerned about terrorism and the taking of hostages, declare that their governments will intensify their joint efforts to combat international terrorism. To this end, in cases where a country refuses extradition or prosecution of those who have hijacked an aircraft and/or do not return such aircraft, the Heads of State and Government are jointly resolved that their governments shall take immediate action to cease all flights to that country. At the same time, their governments will initiate action to halt all incoming flights from that country or from any country by the airlines of the country concerned.

They urge other governments to join them in this commitment.

SOURCE: Great Britain, Foreign and Commonwealth Office, *Political Declarations and Statements of Annual Economic Summits, 1978–1986* (London, 198—) [unpublished]; *Economic Summits, 1975–1986: Declarations* (Rome: Istituto Affari Internazionali, 1987): 48.

Tokyo

28–29 June 1979

TOKYO, 28–29 JUNE 1979

DELEGATIONS

Canada

Joe Clark, *Prime Minister*
Flora MacDonald, *Secretary of State for External Affairs*
John Crosbie, *Minister of Finance*
Robert Johnstone, *Personal Representative (Sherpa)*

France

Valéry Giscard d'Estaing, *President*
Jean-François Poncet, *Minister of External Affairs*
René Monory, *Minister of the Economy and Finance*
Bernard Clappier, *Personal Representative (Sherpa)*

Germany (Federal Republic)

Helmut Schmidt, *Federal Chancellor*
Hans-Dietrich Genscher, *Federal Minister for Foreign Affairs*
Hans Matthöfer, *Federal Minister of Finance*

Germany (Federal Republic) *continued*

Otto Lambsdorff, *Federal Minister of Economics*
Manfred Lahnstein, *Personal Representative (Sherpa)*

Italy

Giulio Andreotti, *President of the Council of Ministers*
Arnaldo Forlani, *Minister for Foreign Affairs*
Filippo Maria Pandolfi, *Minister of Finance*
Umberto La Rocca, *Personal Representative (Sherpa)*

Japan

Masayoshi Ohira, *Prime Minister*
Sunao Sonoda, *Minister for Foreign Affairs*
Ippeo Kaneko, *Minister of Finance*
Hiromichi Miyazaki, *Personal Representative (Sherpa)*

United Kingdom

Margaret Thatcher, *Prime Minister*
Peter Carrington, *Secretary of State for Foreign and
    Commonwealth Affairs*
Geoffrey Howe, *Chancellor of the Exchequer*
Robert Armstrong, *Personal Representative (Sherpa)*

United States

Jimmy Carter, *President*
Cyrus Vance, *Secretary of State*
W. Michael Blumenthal, *Secretary of the Treasury*
Henry Owen, *Personal Representative (Sherpa)*

European Communities

Roy Jenkins, *President of the Commission*
Crispin Tickell, *Personal Representative (Sherpa)*

DECLARATION

June 29, 1979

The Heads of State and Government of Canada, the Federal Republic of Germany, France, Italy, Japan, the United Kingdom of Great Britain and Northern Ireland, and the United States of America met in Tokyo on the 28th and 29th of June, 1979. The European Community was represented by the President of the European Council and by the President of the European Commission for discussion of matters within the Community's competence.

1. The agreements reached at the Bonn Summit helped to improve the world economy. There was higher growth in some countries, a reduction of payments imbalances, and greater currency stability.

2. But new challenges have arisen. Inflation, which was subsiding in most countries, is now regaining its momentum. Higher oil prices and oil shortage have reduced the room for manoeuver in economic policy in all our countries. They will make inflation worse and curtail growth, in both the industrial and developing countries. The non-oil developing countries are among the biggest sufferers.

We are agreed on a common strategy to attack these problems. The most urgent tasks are to reduce oil consumption and to hasten the development of other energy sources.

Our countries have already taken significant actions to reduce oil consumption. We will intensify these efforts.

The European Community has decided to restrict 1979 oil consumption to 500 million tons (10 million barrels a day) and to maintain Community oil imports between 1980 and 1985 at an annual level not higher than in 1978. The Community is monitoring this commitment and France, Germany, Italy and the United Kingdom have agreed to recommend to their Community partners that each member country's contribution to these annual levels be specified. Canada, Japan, and the U.S. will each achieve the adjusted import levels to which they are pledged in the IEA [International Energy Agency] for 1979, will maintain their imports in 1980 at a level not higher than these 1979 levels, and will be monitoring this.

The seven countries express their will to take as goals for a ceiling on oil imports in 1985, the following figures:

—For France, Germany, Italy,[*] and the United Kingdom: the 1978 figure.

—Canada, whose oil production will be declining dramatically over the period between now and 1985, will reduce its annual average rate of growth of oil consumption to 1%, with the consequent reduction of oil imports by 50,000 barrels per day by 1985. Canada's targets for imports will therefore be 0.6 million barrels per day.

—Japan adopts as a 1985 target a level not to exceed the range between 6.3 and 6.9 million barrels a day. Japan will review this target periodically and make it more precise in the light of current developments and growth projections, and do their utmost to reduce oil imports through conservation, rationalization of use and intensive development of alternative energy sources in order to move toward lower figures.

—The United States adopts as a goal for 1985 import levels not to exceed the levels either of 1977 or the adjusted target for 1979, i.e., 8.5 million barrels per day.

These 1985 goals will serve as reference to monitor both energy conservation and the development of alternative energy sources.

---

[*]Italy's commitment with reference to the 1978 level is accepted in the context of the overall commitment of the European Community.

A high-level group of representatives of our countries and of the EEC [European Economic Community] Commission, within the OECD [Organisation for Economic Co-operation and Development], will review periodically the results achieved. Slight adjustments will be allowed to take account of special needs generated by growth. In fulfilling these commitments, our guiding principle will be to obtain fair supplies of oil products for all countries, taking into account the differing patterns of supply, the efforts made to limit oil imports, the economic situation of each country, the quantities of oil available, and the potential of each country for energy conservation.

We urge other industrialized countries to set similar objectives for themselves.

We agree to take steps to bring into the open the working of oil markets by setting up a register of international oil transactions. We will urge oil companies and oil-exporting countries to moderate spot market transactions. We will consider the feasibility of requiring that at the time of unloading crude oil cargoes, documents be presented indicating the purchase price as certified by the producer country. We will likewise seek to achieve better information on the profit situation of oil companies and on the use of the funds available to these companies.

We agree on the importance of keeping domestic oil prices at world market prices or raising them to this level as soon as possible. We will seek to minimize and finally eliminate administrative action that might put upward pressure on oil prices that result from domestic underpricing of oil and to avoid new subsidies which would have the same effect.

Our countries will not buy oil for governmental stockpiles when this would place undue pressure on prices; we will consult about the decisions that we make to this end.

3. We pledge our countries to increase as far as possible coal use, production, and trade, without damage to the environment. We will endeavor to substitute coal for oil in the industrial and electrical sectors, encourage the improvement of coal transport,

maintain positive attitudes toward investment for coal projects, pledge not to interrupt coal trade under long-term contracts unless required to do so by a national emergency, and maintain, by measures which do not obstruct coal imports, those levels of domestic coal production which are desirable for reasons of energy, regional and social policy.

We need to expand alternative sources of energy, especially those which will help to prevent further pollution, particularly increases of carbon dioxide and sulphur oxides in the atmosphere.

Without the expansion of nuclear power generating capacity in the coming decades, economic growth and higher employment will be hard to achieve. This must be done under conditions guaranteeing our peoples' safety. We will cooperate to this end. The International Atomic Energy Agency can play a key role in this regard.

We reaffirm the understanding reached at the Bonn Summit with respect to the reliable supply of nuclear fuel and minimizing the risk of nuclear proliferation.

New technologies in the field of energy are the key to the world's longer-term freedom from fuel crises. Large public and private resources will be required for the development and commercial application of those technologies. We will ensure that these resources are made available. An International Energy Technology Group linked to the OECD, IEA and other appropriate international organizations will be created to review the actions being taken or planned domestically by each of our countries, and to report on the need and potential for international collaboration, including financing.

We deplore the decisions taken by the recent OPEC [Organization of the Petroleum Exporting Countries] Conference. We recognize that relative moderation was displayed by certain of the participants. But the unwarranted rises in oil prices nevertheless agreed are bound to have very serious economic and social consequences. They mean more worldwide inflation and less growth. That will lead to more unemployment, more balance-of-payments difficulty, and will endanger stability in developing and developed countries of the world alike. We remain ready to examine with oil-exporting countries how to define supply and demand prospects on the world oil market.

4. We agree that we should continue with the policies for our economies agreed at Bonn, adjusted to reflect current circumstances. Energy shortages and high oil prices have caused a real transfer of incomes. We will try, by our domestic economic policies, to minimize the damage to our economies. But our options are limited. Attempts to compensate for the damage by matching income increases would simply add to inflation.

5. We agree that we must do more to improve the long-term productive efficiency and flexibility of our economies. The measures needed may include more stimulus for investment and for research and development; steps to make it easier for capital and labor to move from declining to new industries; regulatory policies which avoid unnecessary impediments to investment and productivity; reduced growth in some public sector current expenditures; and removal of impediments to the international flow of trade and capital.

6. The agreements reached in the Tokyo Round are an important achievement. We are committed to their early and faithful implementation. We renew our determination to fight protectionism. We want to strengthen the GATT [General Agreement on Tariffs and Trade], both to monitor the agreements reached in the MTNs [multilateral trade negotiations] and as an instrument for future policy in maintaining the open world trading system. We will welcome the full participation of as many countries as possible in these agreements and in the system as a whole.

7. We will intensify our efforts to pursue the economic policies appropriate in each of our countries to achieve durable external equilibrium. Stability in the foreign exchange market is essential for the sound development of world trade and the global economy. This has been furthered since the Bonn Summit

by two important developments—the November 1st, 1978 program of the United States in conjunction with other monetary authorities, and the successful emergence of the European Monetary System. We will continue close cooperation in exchange market policies and in support of the effective discharge by the IMF of its responsibilities, particularly its surveillance role and its role in strengthening further the international monetary system.

8. Constructive North–South relations are essential to the health of the world economy. We for our part have consistently worked to bring developing countries more fully into the open world trading system and to adjust our economies to changing international circumstances. The problems we face are global. They can only be resolved through shared responsibility and partnership. But this partnership cannot depend solely on the efforts of the industrialized countries. The OPEC countries have just as important a role to play. The latest decision substantially to increase oil prices will also severely increase the problems facing developing countries without oil resources, as well as the difficulties for developed countries in helping them. The decision could even have a crippling effect on some of the developing countries. In this situation we recognize, in particular, the need for the flow of financial resources to the developing countries to increase, including private and public, bilateral and multilateral resources. A good investment climate in developing countries will help the flow of foreign investment.

We are deeply concerned about the millions of people still living in conditions of absolute poverty. We will take particular account of the poorest countries in our aid programs.

Once more we urge COMECON [Council for Mutual Economic Co-operation] countries to play their part.

We will place more emphasis on cooperation with developing countries in overcoming hunger and malnutrition. We will urge multilateral organizations to help these countries to develop effective food sector strategies and to build up the storage capacity needed for strong national food reserves. Increased bilateral and multilateral aid for agricultural research will be particularly important. In these and other ways we will step up our efforts to help these countries develop their human resources, through technical cooperation adapted to local conditions.

We will also place special emphasis on helping developing countries to exploit their energy potential. We strongly support the World Bank's program for hydrocarbon exploitation and urge its expansion. We will do more to help developing countries increase the use of renewable energy; we welcome the World Bank's coordination of these efforts.

SOURCE: U.S., Department of State, *Bulletin,* No. 2029 (August 1979): 8–9; Great Britain, Foreign and Commonwealth Office, *Declarations of Annual Economic Summits, 1975–1986* (London, 198—): A5, Tokyo, 1–5 [unpublished]; *Economic Summits, 1975–1986: Declarations* (Rome: Istituto Affari Internazionali, 1987): 51–56.

SPECIAL STATEMENT OF THE SUMMIT ON INDOCHINESE REFUGEES

June 28, 1979

The plight of refugees from Vietnam, Laos and Cambodia poses a humanitarian problem of historic proportions and constitutes a threat to the peace and stability of Southeast Asia. Given the tragedy and suffering which are taking place, the problem calls for an immediate and major response.

The Heads of State and Government call on Vietnam and other countries of Indochina to take urgent and effective measures so that the present human hardship and suffering are eliminated. They confirm the great importance they attach to the immediate cessation of the disorderly outflow of refugees without prejudice to the principles of free emigration and family reunification.

The Governments represented will, as part of an international effort, significantly increase their contributions to Indochinese refugee relief and resettlement—by making more funds available and by admitting more people, while taking into account the existing social and economic circumstances in each of their countries.

The Heads of State and Government request the Secretary-General of the United Nations to convene a conference as soon as possible with a view to attaining concrete and positive results. They extend full support to this objective and are ready to participate constructively in such a conference.

The Heads of State and Government call on all nations to join in addressing this pressing problem.

SOURCE: Japan, Ministry of Foreign Affairs, *Special Statement of the Summit on Indochinese Refugees, June 28, 1979* [Tokyo; supplied by the Embassy of Japan, Ottawa, Canada]; Great Britain, Foreign and Commonwealth Office, *Political Declarations and Statements of Annual Economic Summits, 1978–1986* (London, 198—) [unpublished]; U.S., Department of State, *Bulletin,* No. 2029 (August 1979): 5; *Economic Summits, 1975–1986: Declarations* (Rome: Istituto Affari Internazionali, 1987): 57.

PRIME MINISTER OHIRA'S CONCLUDING STATEMENT AT THE JOINT NEWS CONFERENCE

June 29, 1979

To this Summit there have gathered a great number of members of the press from Japan and from outside Japan, and for showing your interest in what goes on in the Summit, I would like to express our appreciation. Because of security considerations, we may have caused you many inconveniences, but I hope you understand this.

Our conference during the past two days has been extremely useful, but in order for the fruit of our discussions to be appreciated in various parts of the world, much depends on you, members of the press. I would be grateful for your cooperation.

I am going to shortly ask various Heads of State and Government to speak, but as the host, I would first like to give my overall evaluation.

In this Summit we have welcomed three new members of whom one is the first woman Prime Minister to the Summit, and the other is the youngest Prime Minister. The two new Prime Ministers have contributed much to the success of the conference with their charm and wisdom. The third new member is somewhat older, me, and I would refrain from making any comment.

Although nearly half of the members in this Summit are new, I believe our Summit has been able to create an extremely close human relation on the basis of the spirit of mutual support of the Summit, which I believe is an important product of our endeavor.

This Summit has been held ... at the time when the attention of the world is focused on the oil problem. In order to respond to the situation, it has been said that our Summit will be a failure unless bold and concrete measures are agreed upon.

Shortly the communiqué will be distributed to you, but from the viewpoint of both immediate measures and medium- and long-term points of view, I believe we have been able to reach concrete consensus that can respond to meet the expectations of the world.

As the Prime Minister of Japan, to give the specific goal of our effort to the year 1985 has taken considerable amount of courage, but recognizing the fact that we all live in a global community faced with the oil anxiety, and recognizing the need for placing our economy on a stable basis well into the future, I felt it was necessary for us to agree to that statement.

In areas other than oil, we have discussed questions such as inflation and employment—showing strong interest in protecting industrial democracies—from long-term and fundamental points of view. Although industrialized economies find ourselves in respective economic difficulties, the Summit leaders have shown strong interest in the relationship with the developing nations. I have found this very encouraging. The old economies of the world are in the same boat. By sharing the new sense of responsibility and new sense of partnership, I would like to see the constructive relationship and cooperation be developed further.

Further, in the present Summit, following up on what was taken up in the last Summit in Bonn, we adopted a statement on air hijacking which I will now read.

This is concerning the statement. At the request of the Heads of State and Government who participated in the Summit, I, in my capacity of chairman of the meeting, am pleased to make the following statement which concerns the Declaration on Air Hijacking issued in Bonn in July, 1978.

PRESS RELEASE ON AIR-HIJACKING

"The Heads of State and Government expressed their pleasure with the broad support expressed by other States for the Declaration on Hijacking made at the Bonn Summit in July 1978. They noted that procedures for the prompt implementation of the Declaration have been agreed upon and that to date enforcement measures under the Declaration have not been necessary.

"They also noted with satisfaction the widespread adherence to the conventions dealing with unlawful interference with international civil aviation. The extensive support for these conventions and the Bonn Declaration on Hijacking reflects the acceptance by the international community as a whole of the principles expressed therein."

This is the statement.

Also, in the present Summit, we have adopted a special statement on the question of refugees from Indochina, which is another major fruit [sic]. Japan itself feels we must make our utmost contribution to the solution of this problem, and I would like to see that the statement be transmitted to other various countries and various international organizations and invite their further participation in international efforts on this question. This has been an unprecedentedly important international event, but this Tokyo Summit has now come to its safe and successful conclusion, and next year we have unanimously agreed to meet again in Italy. We look forward to our reunion in Italy.

And I would like to take this opportunity to express our heartfelt appreciation to all the people, both within and without Japan, who have supported this meeting.

Because we have taken unexpected, unprecedentedly elaborate security measures in connection with the convening of this Summit—and I know we have dealt inconveniences with many people, but because of their cooperation we have been able to successfully carry this conference. I thank all of these people concerned.

SOURCE: Japan, Ministry of Foreign Affairs, *Press Release on Air-Hijacking, June 29, 1979* [Tokyo; supplied by the Embassy of Japan, Ottawa, Canada]; U.S., Department of State, *Bulletin,* No. 2029 (August 1979): 2–3; Great Britain, Foreign and Commonwealth Office, *Political Declarations and Statements of Annual Economic Summits, 1978–1986* (London, 198—) [unpublished]; *Economic Summits, 1975–1986: Declarations* (Rome: Istituto Affari Internazionali, 1987): 57–58.

Venice

22–23 June 1980

VENICE, 22–23 JUNE 1980

DELEGATIONS

Canada

Pierre Elliot Trudeau, *Prime Minister*
Mark MacGuigan, *Secretary of State for External Affairs*
Allan J. MacEachen, *Minister of Finance*
Klaus Goldschlag, *Personal Representative (Sherpa)*

France

Valéry Giscard d'Estaing, *President*
Jean-François Poncet, *Minister of External Affairs*
René Monory, *Minister of the Economy and Finance*
Bernard Clappier, *Personal Representative (Sherpa)*

Germany (Federal Republic)

Helmut Schmidt, *Federal Chancellor*
Hans-Dietrich Genscher, *Federal Minister for Foreign Affairs*
Hans Matthöfer, *Federal Minister of Finance*

Germany (Federal Republic) *continued*

Otto Lambsdorff, *Federal Minister of Economics*
Horst Schulmann, *Personal Representative (Sherpa)*

Italy

Francesco Cossiga, *President of the Council of Ministers*
Emilio Colombo, *Minister for Foreign Affairs*
Filippo Maria Pandolfi, *Minister of the Treasury*
Renato Ruggiero, *Personal Representative (Sherpa)*

Japan

[Prime Minister Masayoshi Ohira died a few days before the
    Venice Summit]
Saburo Okita, *Minister for Foreign Affairs*
Noboru Takeshita, *Minister of Finance*
Kiyoaki Kikuchi, *Personal Representative (Sherpa)*

United Kingdom

Margaret Thatcher, *Prime Minister*
Peter Carrington, *Secretary of State for Foreign and
    Commonwealth Affairs*
Geoffrey Howe, *Chancellor of the Exchequer*
Robert Armstrong, *Personal Representative (Sherpa)*

United States

Jimmy Carter, *President*
Edmund Muskie, *Secretary of State*
William Miller, *Secretary of the Treasury*
Henry Owen, *Personal Representative (Sherpa)*

European Communities

Roy Jenkins, *President of the Commission*
Crispin Tickell, *Personal Representative (Sherpa)*

DECLARATION

June 23, 1980

I. INTRODUCTION

1. In this, our first meeting of the 1980s, the economic issues that have dominated our thoughts are the price and supply of energy and the implications for inflation and the level of economic activity in our own countries and for the world as a whole. Unless we can deal with the problems of energy, we cannot cope with other problems.

2. Successive large increases in the price of oil, bearing no relation to market conditions and culminating in the recent decisions by some members of the Organization of [the] Petroleum Exporting Countries (OPEC) at Algiers, have produced the reality of even higher inflation and the imminent threat of severe recession and unemployment in the industrialized countries. At the same time they have undermined and in some cases virtually destroyed the prospects for growth in the developing countries. We believe that these consequences are increasingly coming to be appreciated by some of the oil-exporting countries. The fact is that the industrialized countries of the free world, the oil-producing countries, and the non-oil developing countries depend upon each other for the realization of their potential for economic development and prosperity. Each can overcome the obstacles to that development, but only if all work together, and with the interests of all in mind.

3. In this spirit we have discussed the main problems that confront us in the coming decade. We are confident in the ability of our democratic societies, based on individual freedom and social solidarity, to meet these challenges. There are no quick or easy solutions; sustained efforts are needed to achieve a better future.

II. INFLATION

4. The reduction of inflation is our immediate top priority and will benefit all nations. Inflation retards growth and harms all sectors of our societies. Determined fiscal and monetary restraint is required to break inflationary expectations. Continuing dialogue among the social partners is also needed for this purpose. We must retain effective international coordination to carry out this policy of restraint, and also to guard against the threat of growing unemployment and worldwide recession.

5. We are also committed to encouraging investment and innovation, so as to increase productivity, to fostering the movement of resources from declining into expanding sectors so as to provide new job opportunities, and to promoting the most effective use of resources within and among countries. This will require shifting resources from government spending to the private sector and from consumption to investment, and avoiding or carefully limiting actions that shelter particular industries or sectors from the rigors of adjustment. Measures of this kind may be economically and politically difficult in the short term, but they are essential to sustained non-inflationary growth and to increasing employment which is our major goal.

6. In shaping economic policy, we need a better understanding of the long-term effects of global population growth, industrial expansion and economic development generally. A study of trends in these areas is in hand, and our representatives will keep these matters under review.

III. ENERGY

7. We must break the existing link between economic growth and consumption of oil, and we mean to do so in this decade. This strategy requires conserving oil and substantially increasing production and use of alternative energy sources. To this end, maximum reliance should be placed on the price mechanism,

and domestic prices for oil should take into account representative world prices. Market forces should be supplemented, where appropriate, by effective fiscal incentives and administrative measures. Energy investment will contribute substantially to economic growth and employment.

8. We welcome the recent decisions of the European Community (EC), the International Energy Agency (IEA) and the Organisation for Economic Co-operation and Development (OECD) regarding the need for long-term structural changes to reduce oil consumption, continuing procedures to monitor progress, the possible use of oil ceilings to deal with tight market conditions, and coordination of stock policies to mitigate the effect of market disruption. We note that the member countries of the IEA have agreed that their energy policies should result in their collective 1985 net oil imports being substantially less than their existing 1985 group objective, and that they will quantify the reduction as part of their continuing monitoring efforts. The potential for reduction has been estimated by the IEA Secretariat, given existing uncertainties, at around 4 million barrels a day (MBD).

9. To conserve oil in our countries:

—We are agreed that no new base-load, oil-fired generating capacity [*sic*] should be constructed, save in exceptional circumstances, and that the conversion of oil-fired capacity [*sic*] to other fuels should be accelerated.

—We will increase efforts, including fiscal incentives where necessary, to accelerate the substitution of oil in industry.

—We will encourage oil saving investments in residential and commercial buildings, where necessary by financial incentives and by establishing insulation standards. We look to the public sector to set an example.

—In transportation, our objective is the introduction of increasingly fuel-efficient vehicles. The demand of consumers and competition among manufacturers are already leading in this direction. We will accelerate this progress, where appropriate, by arrangements or standards for improved automobile fuel efficiency, by gasoline pricing and taxation decisions, by research and development, and by making public transport more attractive.

10. We must rely on fuels other than oil to meet the energy needs of future economic growth. This will require early, resolute, and wide-ranging actions. Our potential to increase the supply and use of energy sources other than oil over the next ten years is estimated at the equivalent of 15–20 MBD of oil. We intend to make a coordinated and vigorous effort to realize this potential. To this end, we will seek a large increase in the use of coal and enhanced use of nuclear power in the medium-term, and a substantial increase in production of synthetic fuels, in solar energy and other sources of renewable energy over the longer term.

11. We shall encourage the exploration and development of our indigenous hydrocarbon resources in order to secure maximum production on a long-term basis.

12. Together we intend to double coal production and use by early 1990. We will encourage long-term commitments by coal producers and consumers. It will be necessary to improve infrastructures in both exporting and importing countries, as far as is economically justified, to ensure the required supply and use of coal. We look forward to the recommendations of the International Coal Industry Advisory Board. They will be considered promptly. We are conscious of the environmental risks associated with increased coal production and combustion. We will do everything in our power to ensure that increased use of fossil fuels, especially coal, does not damage the environment.

13. We underline the vital contribution of nuclear power to a more secure energy supply. The role of nuclear energy has to be increased if world energy needs are to be met. We shall therefore have to expand our nuclear generating capacity. We will continue to give the highest priority to ensuring the health and safety of the public and to perfecting methods for dealing with spent fuels and disposal of nuclear waste. We reaffirm the importance of ensuring the reliable supply of nuclear fuel and minimizing the risk of nuclear proliferation.

14. The studies made by the International Nuclear Fuel Cycle Evaluation Group, launched at the London Summit in 1977, are a significant contribution to the use of nuclear energy. We welcome their findings with respect to: increasing predictable supplies; the most effective utilization of uranium sources, including the development of advanced technologies; and the minimization of proliferation risks, including support of International Atomic Energy Agency (IAEA) safeguards. We urge all countries to take these findings into account when developing policies and programs for the peaceful use of nuclear energy.

15. We will actively support the recommendations of the International Energy Technology Group, proposed at the Tokyo Summit last year, for bringing new energy technologies into commercial use at the earliest feasible time. As far as national programs are concerned, we will by mid-1981 adopt a two-phased approach; first, listing the numbers and types of commercial scale plants to be constructed in each of our countries by the mid-1980s, and, second, indicating quantitative projections for expanding production by 1990, 1995 and 2000, as a basis for future actions. As far as international programs are concerned, we will join others in creating an international team to promote collaboration among interested nations on specific projects.

16. A high-level group of representatives of our countries and of the EEC Commission will review periodically the results achieved in these fields.

17. Our comprehensive energy strategy is designed to meet the requirements of the coming decade. We are convinced that it can reduce the demand for energy, particularly oil, without hampering economic growth. By carrying out this strategy we expect that, over the coming decade, the ratio between increases in collective energy consumption and economic growth of our countries will be reduced to about 0.6, that the share of oil in our total energy demand will be reduced from fifty-three percent now to about forty percent by 1990, and that our collective consumption of oil in 1990 will be significantly below present levels so as to permit a balance between supply and demand at tolerable prices.

18. We continue to believe that international cooperation in energy is essential. All countries have a vital interest in a stable equilibrium between energy supply and demand. We would welcome a constructive dialogue on energy and related issues between energy producers and consumers in order to improve the coherence of their policies.

IV. RELATIONS WITH DEVELOPING COUNTRIES

19. We are deeply concerned about the impact of the oil price increases on the developing countries that have to import oil. The increase in oil prices in the last two years has more than doubled the oil bill of these countries, which now amounts to over $50 billion. This will drive them into ever increasing indebtedness, and put at risk the whole basis of their economic growth and social progress, unless something can be done to help them.

20. We approach in a positive spirit the prospect of global negotiations in the framework of the United Nations and the formulation of a new International Development Strategy. In particular, our object is to cooperate with the developing countries in energy conservation and development, expansion of exports, enhancement of human skills, and the tackling of underlying food and population problems.

21. A major international effort to help these countries increase their energy production is required. We believe that this view is gaining ground among oil-exporting countries. We ask the World Bank to examine the adequacy of the resources and the mechanisms now in place for the exploration, development and production of conventional and renewable energy sources in oil-importing developing countries, to consider means, including the possibility of establishing a new affiliate or facility by which it might improve and increase its lending programs for energy assistance, and to explore its findings with both oil-exporting and industrial countries.

22. We are deeply conscious that extreme poverty and chronic malnutrition afflict hundreds of millions of people of developing countries. The first requirement in these countries is to improve their ability to feed themselves and reduce their dependence on food imports. We are ready to join with them and the international agencies concerned in their comprehensive long-term strategies to increase food production, and to help improve national as well as international research services. We will support and, where appropriate, supplement initiatives of the World Bank and of the Food and Agriculture Organization of the United Nations (FAO) and to improve grain storage and food handling facilities. We underline the importance of wider membership of the new Food Aid Convention so as to secure at least ten million tons of food aid annually and of an equitable replenishment of the International Fund for Agricultural Development.

23. High priority should be given to efforts to cope with population growth and to existing United Nations and other programs for supporting these efforts.

24. We strongly support the general capital increase of the World Bank, increases in the funding of the regional development banks, and the sixth replenishment of the International

Development Association.[1] We would welcome an increase in the rate of lending of these institutions, within the limits of their present replenishments, as needed to fulfill the programs described above. It is essential that all members, especially the major donors, provide their full contributions on the agreed schedule.

25. We welcome the report of the Brandt Commission.[2] We shall carefully consider its recommendations.

26. The democratic industrialized countries cannot alone carry the responsibility of aid and other different contributions to developing countries: it must be equitably shared by the oil-exporting countries and the industrialized Communist countries. The Personal Representatives are instructed to review aid policies and procedures and other contributions to developing countries and to report back their conclusions to the next Summit.

V. MONETARY PROBLEMS

27. The situation created by large oil-generated payments imbalances, in particular those of oil-importing developing countries, requires a combination of determined actions by all countries to promote external adjustment and effective mechanisms for balance-of-payments financing. We look to the international capital market to continue to play the primary role in rechanneling the substantial oil surplus funds on the basis of sound lending standards. We support the work in progress by our monetary authorities and the Bank for Interna-

---

[1]The International Development Association (IDA), the concessional financing arm of the World Bank, obtains its funds chiefly from the contributions of its wealthiest members. Replenishments are arranged every three years through negotiations among the donors of IDA.—Ed.

[2]*North–South: A Programme for Survival; Report of the Independent Commission on International Development Issues.* Cambridge, Mass.: MIT Press, 1980.—Ed.

tional Settlements designed to improve the supervision and security of the international banking system. The private banks could usefully supplement these efforts.

28. Private lending will need to be supplemented by an expanded role for international institutions, especially the International Monetary Fund. We are committed to implementing the agreed increase in the IMF quotas, and to supporting appropriate borrowing by the Fund, if needed to meet financing requirements of its members. We encourage the IMF to seek ways in which it could, within its guidelines on conditionality, make it more attractive for countries with financing problems to use its resources. In particular, we support the IMF's examination of possible ways to reduce charges on credits to low-income developing countries. The IMF and the World Bank should work closely together in responding to these problems. We welcome the Bank's innovative lending scheme for structural adjustment. We urge oil-exporting countries to increase their direct lending to countries with financial problems, thus reducing the strain on other recycling mechanisms.

29. We reaffirm our commitment to stability in the foreign exchange markets. We note that the European Monetary System (EMS) has contributed to this end. We will continue close cooperation in exchange market policies so as to avoid disorderly exchange rate fluctuations. We will also cooperate with the IMF to achieve more effective surveillance. We support continuing examination by the IMF of arrangements to provide for a more balanced evolution of the world reserve system.

VI. TRADE

30. We are resolved further to strengthen the open world trading system. We will resist pressures for protectionist actions, which can only be self-defeating and aggravate inflation.

31. We endorse the positive conclusion of the Multilateral Trade Negotiations, and commit ourselves to early and effective implementation. We welcome the participation of some of our developing partners in the new non-tariff codes and call upon others to participate. We also call for the full participation of as many countries as possible in strengthening the system of the General Agreement on Tariffs and Trade. We urge the more advanced of our developing partners gradually to open their markets over the coming decade.

32. We reaffirm our determination to avoid a harmful export credit race. To this end we shall work with the other participants to strengthen the International Arrangement on Export Credits, with a view to reaching a mutually acceptable solution covering all aspects of the Arrangement by 1 December 1980.[3] In particular, we shall seek to bring its terms closer to current market conditions and reduce distortions in export competition, recognizing the differentiated treatment of developing countries in the Arrangement.

33. As a further step in strengthening the international trading system, we commit our governments to work in the United Nations toward an agreement to prohibit illicit payments to foreign government officials in international business transactions. If that effort falters, we will seek to conclude an agreement among our countries, but open to all, with the same objective.

VII. CONCLUSIONS

34. The economic message from this Venice Summit is clear. The key to success in resolving the major economic challenges which the world faces is to achieve and maintain a balance

---

[3]See Editor's note, page 127.

between energy supply and demand at reasonable levels and at tolerable prices. The stability of the world economy, on which the prosperity of every individual country relies, depends upon all of the countries concerned, recognizing their mutual needs and accepting their mutual responsibilities. Those among us whose countries are members of the European Community intend to make their efforts within this framework. We, who represent seven large industrialized countries of the free world, are ready to tackle our own problems with determination and to work with others to meet the challenges of the coming decade, to our own advantage and to the benefit of the whole world.

SOURCE: U.S., Department of State, *Bulletin,* No. 2041 (August 1980): 8–11; *Economic Summits, 1975–1986: Declarations* (Rome: Istituto Affari Internazionali, 1987): 61–70; Great Britain, Foreign and Commonwealth Office, *Declarations of Annual Economic Summits, 1975–1986* (London, 198—): A6, Venice, 1–8 [unpublished].

STATEMENT ON THE TAKING OF
DIPLOMATIC HOSTAGES

June 22, 1980

Gravely concerned by recent incidents of terrorism involving the taking of hostages and attacks on diplomatic and consular premises and personnel, the Heads of State and Government reaffirm their determination to deter and combat such acts. They note the completion of work on the International Convention Against the Taking of Hostages and call on all States to consider becoming parties to it as well as to the Convention on the Prevention and Punishment of Crimes Against Internationally Protected Persons of 1973.

The Heads of State and Government vigorously condemn the taking of hostages and the seizure of diplomatic and consular premises and personnel in contravention of the basic norms of international law and practice. The Heads of State and Government consider it necessary that all governments should adopt policies which will contribute to the attainment of this goal and to take appropriate measures to deny terrorists any benefits from such criminal acts. They also resolve to provide to one another's diplomatic and consular missions support and assistance in situations involving the seizure of diplomatic and consular establishments or personnel.

The Heads of State and Government recall that every State has the duty under international law to refrain from organizing, instigating, assisting or participating in terrorist acts in another State or acquiescing in organized activities within its territory directed towards the commission of such acts, and deplore in the strongest terms any breach of this duty.

SOURCE: U.S., Department of State, *Bulletin,* No. 2041 (August 1980): 7; *Economic Summits, 1975–1986: Declarations* (Rome: Istituto Affari Internazionali, 1987): 70–71; Great Britain, Foreign and Commonwealth Office, *Political Declarations and Statements of Annual Economic Summits, 1978–1986* (London, 198—) [unpublished].

STATEMENT ON REFUGEES

June 22, 1980

The Heads of State and Government are deeply concerned at the plight of the ever-increasing number of refugees throughout the world. Hundreds of thousands have already left the Indochinese peninsula and Cuba, many of them taking the risk of fleeing across the open seas. Pakistan and Iran have received almost one million refugees from Afghanistan. In Africa refugees number several millions.

The Heads of State and Government note with great regret that the refugee population continues to grow and that, despite major international relief efforts, their suffering continues. They pay tribute to the generosity and forbearance with which countries in the regions affected have received refugees. For their part, the countries represented at this Summit have already responded substantially to appeals for assistance to and resettlement of refugees. They will continue to do so, but their resources are not unlimited. They appeal to others to join with them in helping to relieve this suffering.

But, however great the effort of the international community, it will be difficult to sustain it indefinitely. The problem of refugees has to be attacked at its root.

The Heads of State and Government therefore make a vigorous appeal to the governments responsible for it to remove the causes of this widespread human tragedy and not to pursue policies which drive large numbers of their people from their own countries.

SOURCE: U.S., Department of State, *Bulletin,* No. 2041 (August 1980): 7; *Economic Summits, 1975–1986: Declarations* (Rome: Istituto Affari Internazionali, 1987): 71; Great Britain, Foreign and Commonwealth Office, *Political Declarations and Statements of Annual Economic Summits, 1978–1986* (London, 198—) [unpublished].

POLITICAL TOPICS (AFGHANISTAN)

June 22, 1980

In seeking here in Venice to define a global economic strategy and to show our united determination to make it a reality, we are consciously accepting the responsibility that falls to the three great industrialized areas of the world—North America, Western Europe and Japan—to help create the conditions for harmonious and sustained economic growth. But we cannot do this alone: others, too, have a part to play.

However, present circumstances oblige us to emphasize that our efforts will only bear fruit if we can at the same time preserve a world in which the rule of law is universally obeyed, national independence is respected and world peace is kept. We call on all countries to join us in working for such a world and we welcome the readiness of non-aligned countries and regional groups to accept the responsibilities which this involves.

We therefore reaffirm hereby that the Soviet military occupation of Afghanistan is unacceptable now and that we are determined not to accept it in the future. It is incompatible with the will of the Afghan people for national independence, as demonstrated by their courageous resistance, and with the security of the States of the region. It is also incompatible with the principles of the United Nations Charter and with efforts to maintain genuine détente. It undermines the very foundations of peace, both in the region and in the world at large.

We fully endorse in this respect the views already expressed by the overwhelming majority of the international community, as set out by the United Nations General Assembly in Resolution No. ES-VI/2 of 14th January 1980 and by the Islamic Conference at both its recent sessions.

Afghanistan should be enabled to regain the sovereignty, territorial integrity, political independence and non-aligned character it once enjoyed. We therefore call for the complete withdrawal of Soviet troops and for the Afghan people to be left free again to determine their own future.

We have taken note of today's announcement of the withdrawal of some Soviet troops from Afghanistan. In order to make a useful contribution to the solution of the Afghan crisis, this withdrawal, if confirmed, will have to be permanent and continue until the complete withdrawal of the Soviet troops. Only thus will it be possible to re-establish a situation compatible with peace and the rule of law and thereby with the interests of all nations.

We are resolved to do everything in our power to achieve this objective. We are also ready to support any initiative to this end, such as that of the Islamic Conference. And we shall support every effort designed to contribute to the political independence and to the security of the States of the region.

Those governments represented at this meeting which have taken a position against attendance at the Olympic Games vigorously reaffirm their positions.

SOURCE: U.S., Department of State, *Bulletin,* No. 2041 (August 1980): 7; *Economic Summits, 1975–1986: Declarations* (Rome: Istituto Affari Internazionali, 1987): 72–73; Great Britain, Foreign and Commonwealth Office, *Political Declarations and Statements of Annual Economic Summits, 1978– 1986* (London, 198—) [unpublished].

STATEMENT ON HIJACKING
[DELIVERED BY PRIME MINISTER COSSIGA]

June 22, 1980

At the request of the Heads of State and Government who participated in the Summit, I, in my capacity as chairman of the meeting, am pleased to make the following statement which concerns the Declaration on Air-Hijacking issued in Bonn in July 1978. The Heads of State and Government expressed their satisfaction at the broad support of the international community for the principles set out in the Bonn Declaration of July 1978 as well as in the international conventions dealing with unlawful interference with civil aviation. The increasing adherence to these conventions and the responsible attitude taken by States with respect to air-hijacking reflect the fact that these principles are being accepted by the international community as a whole.

While enforcement measures under the Declaration have not yet been necessary, the Heads of State and Government emphasize that hijacking remains a threat to international civil aviation and that there can be no relaxation of efforts to combat this threat. To this end they look forward to continuing cooperation with all other governments.

SOURCE: U.S., Department of State, *Bulletin,* No. 2041 (August 1980): 7; *Economic Summits, 1975–1986: Declarations* (Rome: Istituto Affari Internazionali, 1987): 73–74; Great Britain, Foreign and Commonwealth Office, *Political Declarations and Statements of Annual Economic Summits, 1978–1986* (London, 198—) [unpublished].

PRIME MINISTER COSSIGA'S
CONCLUDING STATEMENT

June 23, 1980

May I thank, on behalf of all the Heads of Government—I thank all of you not only for being here but also for your collaboration in this Summit through the information that you, the press, have provided. This is the final press conference, the traditional press conference we have after a Summit, and it is up to me as chairman, president of this Summit of the seven industrialized countries of the West.

The message, I think, emerging from this Venice Summit, at the beginning of the 1980s—the beginning of a difficult decade—is a message of unity, solidarity, and cooperation.

You have before you the text of the final communiqué, or if not, it will be distributed to you. And yesterday you received the text on consultation that was taking place on the political themes. The problems that we've had to deal with in these two days, as you already understand, were numerous and by no means easy and nobody, I think, would have maintained that we could give an immediate response or reply or final reply, because, of course, this is never reality, either in history or in politics.

The truth emerging from this Summit is that the seven major industrialized countries are agreed on the strategy which should guide us in facing the challenges that we have before us. We also agree that our unity and solidarity is not enough in a world which is increasingly interdependent. We are all responsible for the fate of this world—industrialized countries and developing countries, oil-producing countries and oil-consuming countries. In the communiqué, I think you will find an appeal to this general sense of a joint responsibility.

As you already know, the central problem that we discussed was that of energy, and we have set out a strategy which involves specific actions to save oil but also an accelerated or speedy effort to produce alternative sources of energy—alternative to oil—including nuclear energy, whose contribution is essential for a better balance between supply and demand in the energy field.

We've decided on the general lines for the decade and how we are to monitor the execution of this program.

We have decided on the need to fight inflation, but we've also agreed that we will help investment to create more jobs, improving the economic structures in our countries. In particular, in the energy field, there will be new investments which can create new jobs, which is very important to solve what is a human, social, political problem; one of the most important, that of youth.

We also discussed in depth the problems of the less rich countries. And it is our intention to confirm our commitment, but at the same time, we wish to make aware of this commitment— what should be a general opinion, a general commitment, a general responsibility—the other industrialized countries, all of them, including the Communist industrialized countries and the oil-producer countries.

The increasing cost of oil doesn't only harm the industrialized countries but creates situations which sometimes are unbearable, especially in developing countries. And the problem cannot be solved merely through the recycling undertaken by private banks. In the final communiqué, you will find what other measures we intend to adopt in this field.

Venice has been the host in the past ten days of two summit meetings, two important meetings at the highest political level. In the first, that of the nine Heads of State, Heads of Government of the European Community, we found, in spite of the fears of many, the confirmation of the real vital unity of the Community. In this second meeting at the highest political level, which is drawing to an end today, we've taken economic and political decisions and indicated lines of action to reinforce international cooperation in the decade which is only now opened.

From Venice, then, we leave with a new spirit. We thank this marvelous city for its hospitality, with a spirit and a sense of openness to the world which has characterized the history of this beautiful city.

SOURCE: U.S., Department of State, *Bulletin,* No. 2041 (August 1980): 1.

Ottawa

20–21 July 1981

OTTAWA, 20–21 JULY 1981

DELEGATIONS

Canada

Pierre Elliot Trudeau, *Prime Minister*
Mark MacGuigan, *Secretary of State for External Affairs*
Allan J. MacEachen, *Minister of Finance*
Allan Gotlieb, *Personal Representative (Sherpa)*

France

François Mitterand, *President*
Claude Cheysson, *Minister of External Relations*
Jacques Delors, *Minister for the Economy, Finance and Budget*
Jean-Marcel Jeanneney, *Personal Representative (Sherpa)*

Germany (Federal Republic)

Helmut Schmidt, *Federal Chancellor*
Hans-Dietrich Genscher, *Federal Minister for Foreign Affairs*

Germany (Federal Republic) *continued*

Hans Matthöfer, *Federal Minister of Finance*
Otto Lambsdorff, *Federal Minister of Economics*
Horst Schulmann, *Personal Representative (Sherpa)*

Italy

Giovanni Spadolini, *President of the Council of Ministers*
Emilio Colombo, *Minister for Foreign Affairs*
Beniamino Andreatta, *Minister of the Treasury*
Sergio Berlinguer, *Personal Representative (Sherpa)*

Japan

Zenko Suzuki, *Prime Minister*
Sunao Sonoda, *Minister for Foreign Affairs*
Michio Watanabe, *Minister of Finance*
Kiyoaki Kikuchi, *Personal Representative (Sherpa)*

United Kingdom

Margaret Thatcher, *Prime Minister*
Peter Carrington, *Secretary of State for Foreign and Commonwealth Affairs*
Geoffrey Howe, *Chancellor of the Exchequer*
Robert Armstrong, *Personal Representative (Sherpa)*

United States

Ronald Reagan, *President*
Alexander Haig, *Secretary of State*
Donald Regan, *Secretary of the Treasury*
Myer Rashish, *Personal Representative (Sherpa)*

European Communities

Gaston Thorn, *President of the Commission*
Fernand Spaak, *Personal Representative (Sherpa)*

DECLARATION OF THE OTTAWA SUMMIT

July 21, 1981

1. We have met at a time of rapid change and great challenge to world economic progress and peace. Our meeting has served to reinforce the strength of our common bonds. We are conscious that economic issues reflect and affect the broader political purposes we share. In a world of interdependence, we reaffirm our common objectives and our recognition of the need to take into account the effects on others of policies we pursue. We are confident in our joint determination and ability to tackle our problems in a spirit of shared responsibility, both among ourselves and with our partners throughout the world.

THE ECONOMY

2. The primary challenge we addressed at this meeting was the need to revitalize the economies of the industrial democracies, to meet the needs of our own people and strengthen world prosperity.

3. Since the Venice Summit the average rate of inflation in our countries has fallen, although in four of them inflation remains in double figures. In many countries unemployment has risen sharply and is still rising. There is a prospect of moderate economic growth in the coming year but at present it promises little early relief from unemployment. The large payments deficits originating in the 1979–80 oil price increase have so far been financed without imposing intolerable adjustment burdens but are likely to persist for some time. Interest rates have reached record levels in many countries and, if long sustained at these levels, would threaten productive investment.

4. The fight to bring down inflation and reduce unemployment must be our highest priority and these linked problems must be tackled at the same time. We must continue to reduce inflation if we are to secure the higher investment and sustainable growth on which the durable recovery of employment depends. The balanced use of a range of policy instruments is required. We must involve our peoples in a greater appreciation of the need for change: change in expectations about growth and earnings, change in management and labor relations and practices, change in the pattern of industry, change in the direction and scale of investment, and change in energy use and supply.

5. We need in most countries urgently to reduce public borrowing; where our circumstances permit or we are able to make changes within the limits of our budgets, we will increase support for productive investment and innovation. We must also accept the role of the market in our economies. We must not let transitional measures that may be needed to ease change become permanent forms of protection or subsidy.

6. We see low and stable monetary growth as essential to reducing inflation. Interest rates have to play their part in achieving this and are likely to remain high where fears of inflation remain strong. But we are fully aware that levels and movements of interest rates in one country can make stabilization policies more difficult in other countries by influencing their exchange rates and their economies. For these reasons, most of us need also to rely on containment of budgetary deficits, by means of restraint in government expenditures as necessary. It is also highly desirable to minimize volatility of interest rates and exchange rates; greater stability in foreign exchange and financial markets is important for the sound development of the world economy.

7. In a world of strong capital flows and large deficits it is in the interests of all that the financial soundness of the international banking system and the international financial institutions be fully maintained. We welcome the recently expanded role of the IMF in financing payments deficits on terms which encourage needed adjustment.

8. In shaping our long-term economic policies, care should be taken to preserve the environment and the resource base of our planet.

RELATIONS WITH DEVELOPING COUNTRIES

9. We support the stability, independence and genuine non-alignment of developing countries and reaffirm our commitment to cooperate with them in a spirit of mutual interest, respect and benefit, recognizing the reality of our interdependence.

10. It is in our interest as well as in theirs that the developing countries should grow and flourish and play a full part in the international economic system commensurate with their capabilities and responsibilities and become more closely integrated in it.

11. We look forward to constructive and substantive discussions with them, and believe the Cancún Summit offers an early opportunity to address our common problems anew.

12. We reaffirm our willingness to explore all avenues of consultation and cooperation with developing countries in whatever forums may be appropriate. We are ready to participate in preparations for a mutually acceptable process of global negotiations in circumstances offering the prospect of meaningful progress.

13. While growth has been strong in most middle-income developing countries, we are deeply conscious of the serious economic problems in many developing countries, and the grim poverty faced especially by the poorer among them. We remain ready to support the developing countries in the efforts they make to promote their economic and social development within the framework of their own social values and traditions. These efforts are vital to their success.

14. We are committed to maintaining substantial and, in many cases, growing levels of Official Development Assistance and will seek to increase public understanding of its importance. We will direct the major portion of our aid to poorer countries, and will participate actively in the United Nations Conference on the Least Developed Countries.

15. We point out that the strengthening of our own economies, increasing access to our markets, and removing impediments to capital flows contribute larger amounts of needed resources and technology and thereby complement official aid. The flow of private capital will be further encouraged in so far as the developing countries themselves provide assurances for the protection and security of investments.

16. The Soviet Union and its partners, whose contributions are meager, should make more development assistance available, and take a greater share of exports of developing countries, while respecting their independence and non-alignment.

17. We will maintain a strong commitment to the international financial institutions and work to ensure that they have, and use effectively, the financial resources for their important responsibilities.

18. We attach high priority to the resolution of the problems created for the non-oil developing countries by the damaging effects on them of the high cost of energy imports following the two oil price shocks. We call on the surplus oil-exporting countries to broaden their valuable efforts to finance development in non-oil developing countries, especially in the field of energy. We stand ready to cooperate with them for this purpose and to explore with them, in a spirit of partnership, possible mechanisms, such as those being examined in the World Bank, which would take due account of the importance of their financial contributions.

19. We recognize the importance of accelerated food production in the developing world and of greater world food security, and the need for developing countries to pursue sound agricultural and food policies; we will examine ways to make increased resources available for these purposes. We note that the Italian Government has in mind to discuss within the European Community proposals to be put forward in close cooperation with the specialized UN institutions located in Rome for special action in this field primarily directed to the poorest countries.

20. We are deeply concerned about the implications of world population growth. Many developing countries are taking action to deal with that problem, in ways sensitive to human values and dignity; and to develop human resources, including technical and managerial capabilities. We recognize the importance of these issues and will place greater emphasis on international efforts in these areas.

TRADE

21. We reaffirm our strong commitment to maintaining liberal trade policies and to the effective operation of an open multilateral trading system as embodied in the GATT [General Agreement on Tariffs and Trade].

22. We will work together to strengthen this system in the interest of all trading countries, recognizing that this will involve structural adaptation to changes in the world economy.

23. We will implement the agreements reached in the Multilateral Trade Negotiations and invite other countries, particularly developing countries, to join in these mutually beneficial trading arrangements.

24. We will continue to resist protectionist pressures, since we recognize that any protectionist measure, whether in the form of overt or hidden trade restrictions or in the form of subsidies to prop up declining industries, not only undermines the dynamism of our economies but also, over time, aggravates inflation and unemployment.

25. We welcome the new initiative represented by the proposal of the Consultative Group of Eighteen that the GATT Contracting Parties convene a meeting at Ministerial level during 1982, as well as that of the OECD [Organisation for Economic Co-operation and Development] countries in their program of study to examine trade issues.

26. We will keep under close review the role played by our countries in the smooth functioning of the multilateral trading system with a view to ensuring maximum openness of our markets in a spirit of reciprocity, while allowing for the safeguard measures provided for in the GATT.

27. We endorse efforts to reach agreement by the end of this year on reducing subsidy elements in official export credit schemes.

ENERGY

28. We are confident that, with perseverance, the energy goals we set at Venice for the decade can be achieved, enabling us to break the link between economic growth and oil consumption through structural change in our energy economies.

29. Recognizing that our countries are still vulnerable and energy supply remains a potential constraint to a revival of economic growth, we will accelerate the development and use of all our energy sources, both conventional and new, and continue to promote energy savings and the replacement of oil by other fuels.

30. To these ends we will continue to rely heavily on market mechanisms, supplemented as necessary by government action.

31. Our capacity to deal with short-term oil market problems should be improved, particularly through the holding of adequate levels of stocks.

32. In most of our countries progress in constructing new nuclear facilities is slow. We intend in each of our countries to encourage greater public acceptance of nuclear energy, and respond to public concerns about safety, health, nuclear waste management and non-proliferation. We will further our efforts in the development of advanced technologies, particularly in spent fuel management.

33. We will take steps to realize the potential for the economic production, trade and use of coal and will do everything in our power to ensure that its increased use does not damage the environment.

34. We also intend to see to it that we develop to the fullest possible extent sources of renewable energy such as solar, geothermal and biomass energy. We will work for practical achievements at the forthcoming United Nations Conference on New and Renewable Sources of Energy.

35. We look forward to improved understanding and cooperation with the oil-exporting countries in the interests of the world economy.

EAST–WEST ECONOMIC RELATIONS

36. We also reviewed the significance of East–West economic relations for our political and security interests. We recognized that there is a complex balance of political and economic interests and risks in these relations. We concluded that consultations and, where appropriate, coordination are necessary to ensure that, in the field of East–West relations, our economic policies continue to be compatible with our political and security objectives.

37. We will undertake to consult to improve the present system of controls on trade in strategic goods and related technology with the USSR.

CONCLUSION

38. We are convinced that our democratic, free societies are equal to the challenges we face. We will move forward together and with all countries ready to work with us in a spirit of cooperation and harmony. We have agreed to meet again next year and have accepted the invitation of the President of the French Republic to hold this meeting in France. We intend to maintain close and continuing consultation and cooperation with each other.

SOURCE: Canada, Department of External Affairs, *Economic Summits, 1975–1987: Declarations* (Ottawa, 198—): Tab 14, 1–11 [unpublished]; U.S., Department of State, *Bulletin,* No. 2053 (August 1981): 8–9; *Economic Summits, 1975–1986: Declarations* (Rome: Istituto Affari Internazionali, 1987): 77–83; Great Britain, Foreign and Commonwealth Office, *Declarations of Annual Economic Summits, 1975-1986* (London, 198—): A7, Ottawa, 1–6 [unpublished].

CHAIRMAN'S SUMMARY OF POLITICAL ISSUES

July 21, 1981

1. Our discussion of international affairs confirmed our unity of view on the main issues that confront us all. We are determined to face them together in a spirit of solidarity, cooperation and responsibility.

2. We all view with concern the continuing threats to international security and stability. Lasting peace can only be built on respect for the freedom and dignity of nations and individuals. We appeal to all governments to exercise restraint and responsibility in international affairs and to refrain from exploiting crises and tensions.

3. In the Middle East, we remain convinced that a solution must be found to the Arab–Israeli dispute. We all deplore the escalation of tension and continuing acts of violence now occurring in the region. We are deeply distressed by the scale of destruction, particularly in Lebanon, and the heavy civilian loss of life on both sides. We call on all States and parties to exercise restraint, in particular to avoid retaliation which only results in escalation; and to forego acts which could lead, in the current tense situation in the area, to further bloodshed and war.

4. We are particularly concerned, in this respect, by the tragic fate of the Lebanese people. We support the efforts now in progress to permit Lebanon to achieve a genuine national reconciliation, internal security and peace with its neighbors.

5. In East–West relations, we are seriously concerned about the continuing build-up of Soviet military power. Our concern is heightened by Soviet actions which are incompatible with the exercise of restraint and responsibility in international affairs. We ourselves, therefore, need a strong defense capability. We will be firm in insisting on a balance of military capabilities and on political restraint. We are prepared for dialogue and cooperation to the extent that the Soviet Union makes this possible. We are convinced of the importance of working towards balanced and verifiable arms control and disarmament agreements in pursuit of undiminished security at lower levels of armament and expenditure.

6. We welcome the fact that, at the Madrid Conference on Security and Co-operation in Europe, Western countries have just taken another major initiative aimed at defining the area to be covered by the measures the proposed European Disarmament Conference would negotiate. Equally important, they have proposed a number of human rights provisions that would give new hope for individuals deprived of their freedom. We believe that Soviet acceptance of these initiatives would enable a balanced conclusion of the Madrid meeting and a substantial reduction of tension in Europe.

7. As regards Afghanistan, about which we publicly stated our firm and unanimous position at last year's Venice Summit, we note that the situation remains unchanged. Therefore, with the overwhelming majority of nations, we continue to condemn the Soviet military occupation of Afghanistan. We support international efforts to achieve the complete withdrawal of Soviet troops and to restore to the Afghan people, who are fighting a war of liberation, their right to determine their own future. We note with approval the constructive proposal of the European Council for an international conference to bring about this result and call upon the Soviet Union to accept it. We are grateful for the report given us by Foreign Secretary Carrington on his recent visit to Moscow, and his discussions there, on behalf of the Ten,[1] on the international conference proposal.

8. Believing as we do that the Kampuchean people are entitled to self-determination, we welcome and support the Declaration of the International Conference on Kampuchea.

---

[1]The ten wealthiest industrialized member States of the International Monetary Fund: Belgium, Canada, Federal Republic of Germany, France, Italy, Japan, The Netherlands, Sweden, the United Kingdom, and the United States.—ED.

9. Together with other States and regional organizations, we are resolved to do what is necessary to enhance regional security and to ensure a peace built on the independence and dignity of sovereign nations. All peoples should be free to chart their own course without fear of outside intervention. To that end, we shall continue to promote peaceful resolution of disputes and to address underlying social and economic problems. We reaffirm our conviction that respect for independence and genuine non-alignment are important for international peace and security.

10. Recalling the statement on refugees adopted at the Venice Summit, we are seriously concerned over the growing plight of refugees throughout the world. We reaffirm our support for international relief efforts and our appeal to all governments to refrain from actions which can lead to massive flows of refugees.

SOURCE: Canada, Department of External Affairs, *Economic Summits, 1975– 1987: Declarations* (Ottawa, 198—): Tab 15, 1–4 [unpublished]; U.S., Department of State, *Bulletin,* No. 2053 (August 1981): 14–15; *Economic Summits, 1975–1986: Declarations* (Rome: Istituto Affari Internazionali, 1987): 83–85; Great Britain, Foreign and Commonwealth Office, *Political Declarations and Statements of Annual Economic Summits, 1978–1986* (London, 198—) [unpublished].

OTTAWA SUMMIT STATEMENT ON TERRORISM

July 21, 1981

1. The Heads of State and Government, seriously concerned about the active support given to international terrorism through the supply of money and arms to terrorist groups, and about the sanctuary and training offered terrorists, as well as the continuation of acts of violence and terrorism such as aircraft hijacking, hostage-taking and attacks against diplomatic and consular personnel and premises, reaffirm their determination vigorously to combat such flagrant violations of international law. Emphasizing that all countries are threatened by acts of terrorism in disregard of fundamental human rights, they resolve to strengthen and broaden action within the international community to prevent and punish such acts.

2. The Heads of State and Government view with particular concern the recent hijacking incidents which threaten the safety of international civil aviation. They recall and reaffirm the principles set forth in the 1978 Bonn Declaration and note that there are several hijackings which have not been resolved by certain States in conformity with their obligations under international law. They call upon the governments concerned to discharge their obligations promptly and thereby contribute to the safety of international civil aviation.

3. The Heads of State and Government are convinced that, in the case of the hijacking of a Pakistan International Airlines aircraft in March, the conduct of the Babrak Karmal government of Afghanistan, both during the incident and subsequently in giving refuge to the hijackers, was and is in flagrant breach of its international obligations under the Hague Convention to which Afghanistan is a party, and constitutes a serious threat to air safety. Consequently the Heads of State and Government propose to suspend all flights to and from Afghanistan in implementation of the Bonn Declaration unless Afghanistan immediately takes steps to comply with its obligations. Furthermore, they call upon all States which share their concern for air safety to take appropriate action to persuade Afghanistan to honor its obligations.

4. Recalling the Venice Statement on the Taking of Diplomatic Hostages, the Heads of State and Government approve continued cooperation in the event of attacks on diplomatic and consular establishments or personnel of any of their governments. They undertake that in the event of such incidents, their governments will immediately consult on an appropriate response. Moreover, they resolve that any State which directly aids and abets the commission of terrorist acts condemned in the Venice Statement, should face a prompt international response. It was agreed to exchange information on terrorist threats and activities, and to explore cooperative measures for dealing with and countering acts of terrorism, for promoting more effective implementation of existing anti-terrorist conventions, and for securing wider adherence to them.

SOURCE: Canada, Department of External Affairs, *Economic Summits, 1975– 1987: Declarations* (Ottawa, 198—): Tab 16, 1–3 [unpublished]; U.S., Department of State, *Bulletin,* No. 2053 (August 1981): 16; *Economic Summits, 1975–1986: Declarations* (Rome: Istituto Affari Internazionali, 1987): 86–87; Great Britain, Foreign and Commonwealth Office, *Political Declarations and Statements of Annual Economic Summits, 1978–1986* (London, 198—) [unpublished].

PRIME MINISTER TRUDEAU'S
CONCLUDING STATEMENT

July 21, 1981

I should wish first on behalf of my colleagues at the table here to express our welcome to the press here and in accordance with the practices, established practices, and as chairman of the Summit meeting this year, I must make a statement summarizing the main points we have dealt with in the course of the last few days, and each of my colleagues will in turn speak to you.

The Ottawa Summit was met [*sic*] at a time of rapid change and great challenge to world economic progress and peace. East–West relations have been affected by the increase in the armed forces of the USSR and its ever increasing presence in the world. The political and economic situation of many countries has made it difficult for them to adapt to the new changes. The members of the Summit meeting have also been victims of these changes, and whatever we have attempted to do in the course of the last years was not necessarily carried out. We have had to reexamine the situation and restructure our activities so that, of course, there has been some pessimism about this Summit.

Of course, it seemed to have been a difficult one but in my dual capacity as a participant and chairman I am able to say, "No, the pessimists were not justified." We have met for many hours, and these contacts have promoted mutual trust and confidence in facing the crises we may have to—which challenge us. We've had very comprehensive discussions and frank discussions during our meetings. We have not tried to hide our divergences. We realize that we are dealing with economies which have different structures and have different reactions to the evolving situation. We have agreed that we could not revitalize our economies by isolating ourselves from one another. We have agreed on the fundamentals and realize we must take into account in our politics the impact it may have on our partners.

The whole burden of that fight cannot be made on monetary policy alone. And third, levels and movements of interest rates in one country can make life more difficult for other countries by influencing the exchange rates. This is something to which we must all remain sensitive and which we must try to minimize. We must also pursue responsible trade policies.

Over the years, as Summit partners, we have warned against succumbing to the temptation of protection. These warnings have served us well. If we had drifted into protectionism, we might have conjured up an economic crisis similar to that of the 1930s. We have reiterated our strong commitment to an open, liberal, and multilateral trading system. We have agreed to deal with trade distortions. But we are determined not to lay the burdens of adjustment at the doorstep of our neighbors. We are looking forward to working with others on a trade agenda for the 1980s. I regard this consensus about trade policy as one of the most important to have emerged from our meeting, not least for a major trading nation like Canada.

One of the uncertainties hovering over this Summit was how it would deal with the North–South relationship. It's no secret to anyone that I attach very great importance to that relationship as an element of fundamental equity, of mutual interests and benefits, and of global security.

The Ottawa Summit was the first of a series of important meetings this year where the North–South relationship will be at the center of the agenda. It seemed important to me, therefore, that the signal emanating from Ottawa should be clear and that it should be positive. For the signal to be persuasive, it had to come from all of us jointly. That was the purpose of much of the travel, that as chairman of this year's meetings, I undertook in the weeks immediately preceding the Summit.

The world looked to the Ottawa Summit for some sign of movement, some basis for hope that progress is possible, that the logjam can be broken. I'm very pleased with what we've been able to achieve. Our discussions showed a common appreciation of the magnitude of the problem and a common readiness to respond to it. There is now a disposition on the part of all Summit countries to pursue any opportunity for meaningful progress, including what are known as "global negotiations." That openness to the process of global negotiations represents a consensus which did not exist before our Summit and seemed very remote not too many months ago.

The message we send from this meeting to the developing countries is the following: First, we respect your independence and support genuine non-alignment as a contribution to international peace and stability and as a basis for cooperation. Second, we look to you to play a full part in the international economic system and to become closely integrated to it. Third, we are ready to participate with you in preparations for a process of global negotiations. Fourth, we appreciate the problems of energy supply which you are encountering and are prepared to join with the surplus oil-exporting countries in examining how best we might jointly help you in developing your indigenous energy reserves. Five, we recognize the importance of more food production in your countries and of greater world [food] security and will try to make increased resources available for these purposes. Six, we will maintain our strong multilateral commitment to the international financial institutions and to the role they have played in alleviating the problems of development. And lastly, we will direct the major portion of our aid to the poorer countries.

On the occasion of this year's Summit meeting, it seemed to us we could not ignore the fact that the strengthening of the armed forces in the Soviet Union has had an impact on the resources of our country and on the orientations which we have had to follow. We are convinced of the need for a strong defense capability, but we're also open to the possibility of dialogue and negotiation with the Soviet Union, particularly as regards nuclear armaments and security with less armaments and diminished cost.

I should wish, in conclusion, as Prime Minister of Canada, to say that we were very happy to be the host nation of this

Summit meeting. I am particularly grateful to all of those who have accepted the challenge for this great endeavor and have provided the maximum in assuring success. May I be permitted also to express deep gratitude to my colleagues at this table for having made my task so easy and to wish them Godspeed as they return to their own countries.

SOURCE: U.S., Department of State, *Bulletin,* No. 2053 (August 1981): 10–11.

Versailles

4–6 June 1982

VERSAILLES, 4–6 JUNE 1982

DELEGATIONS

Canada

Pierre Elliot Trudeau, *Prime Minister*
Mark MacGuigan, *Secretary of State for External Affairs*
Allan J. MacEachen, *Minister of Finance*
De Montigny Marchand, *Personal Representative (Sherpa)*

France

François Mitterand, *President*
Claude Cheysson, *Minister of External Relations*
Jacques Delors, *Minister for the Economy, Finance and Budget*
Jacques Attali, *Personal Representative (Sherpa)*

Germany (Federal Republic)

Helmut Schmidt, *Federal Chancellor*
Hans-Dietrich Genscher, *Federal Minister for Foreign Affairs*
Manfred Lahnstein, *Federal Minister of Finance*

Germany (Federal Republic) *continued*

Otto Lambsdorff, *Federal Minister of Economics*
Horst Schulmann, *Personal Representative (Sherpa)*

Italy

Giovanni Spadolini, *President of the Council of Ministers*
Emilio Colombo, *Minister for Foreign Affairs*
Beniamino Andreatta, *Minister of the Treasury*
Sergio Berlinguer, *Personal Representative (Sherpa)*

Japan

Zenko Suzuki, *Prime Minister*
Yoshio Sakurauchi, *Minister for Foreign Affairs*
Michio Watanabe, *Minister of Finance*
Shintaro Abe, *Minister of International Trade and Industry*
Nobuo Matsunaga, *Personal Representative (Sherpa)*

United Kingdom

Margaret Thatcher, *Prime Minister*
Francis Pym, *Secretary of State for Foreign and
    Commonwealth Affairs*
Geoffrey Howe, *Chancellor of the Exchequer*
Robert Armstrong, *Personal Representative (Sherpa)*

United States

Ronald Reagan, *President*
Alexander Haig, *Secretary of State*
Donald Regan, *Secretary of the Treasury*
Robert Hormats, *Personal Representative (Sherpa)*

European Communities

Wilfried Martens, *President of the European Council*
Gaston Thorn, *President of the Commission*
Jean Durieux, *Personal Representative (Sherpa)*

DECLARATION OF THE SEVEN HEADS OF STATE AND GOVERNMENT AND REPRESENTATIVES OF THE EUROPEAN COMMUNITIES

June 6, 1982

In the course of our meeting at Versailles we have deepened our mutual understanding of the gravity of the world economic situation, and we have agreed on a number of objectives for urgent action with a view to improving it.

We affirm that the improvement of the present situation, by a further reduction of inflation and by a return to steady growth and higher levels of employment, will strengthen our joint capacity to safeguard our security, to maintain confidence in the democratic values that we share, and to preserve the cultural heritage of our peoples in all their diversity. Full employment, price stability and sustained and balanced growth are ambitious objectives. They are attainable in the coming years only if we pursue policies which encourage productive investment and technological progress; if, in addition to our own individual efforts, we are willing to join forces, if each country is sensitive to the effects of its policies on others and if we collaborate in promoting world development.

In this spirit, we have decided to implement the following lines of action:

—Growth and employment must be increased. This will be attained on a durable basis only if we are successful in our continuing fight against inflation. That will also help to bring down interest rates, which are now unacceptably high, and to bring about more stable exchange rates. In order to achieve this essential reduction of real interest rates, we will as a matter of urgency pursue prudent monetary policies and achieve greater control of budgetary deficits. It is essential to intensify our economic and monetary cooperation. In this regard, we will work towards a constructive and orderly evolution of the international monetary system by a closer cooperation among the authorities representing the currencies of North America, of Japan and of the European Community in pursuing medium-term economic and monetary objectives. In this respect, we have committed ourselves to the undertakings contained in the attached statement.

—The growth of world trade in all its facets is both a necessary element for the growth of each country and a consequence of that growth. We reaffirm our commitment to strengthening the open multilateral trading system as embodied in the GATT [General Agreement on Tariffs and Trade] and to maintaining its effective operation. In order to promote stability and employment through trade and growth, we will resist protectionist pressures and trade-distorting practices. We are resolved to complete the work of the Tokyo Round and to improve the capacity of the GATT to solve current and future trade problems. We will also work towards the further opening of our markets. We will cooperate with the developing countries to strengthen and improve the multilateral system, and to expand trading opportunities in particular with the newly industrialized countries. We shall participate fully in the forthcoming GATT Ministerial Conference in order to take concrete steps towards these ends. We shall work for early agreement on the renewal of the OECD [Organisation for Economic Cooperation and Development] export credit consensus.[1]

—We agree to pursue a prudent and diversified economic approach to the USSR and Eastern Europe, consistent

---

[1]Twenty-two member countries of the OECD Trade Committee's Group on Export Credits and Credit Guarantees participate in the consensus known formally as Arrangement on Guidelines for Officially Supported Export Credits. The consensus (renewed approximately once a year) came into being in April 1978 in its present form. Its purpose is "to provide the institutional framework for an orderly export credit market and thus to prevent an export credit race." OECD, *The Export Credit Financing Systems in OECD Member Countries,* 3d ed. (Paris, 1981), p. 7.—ED.

with our political and security interests. This includes actions in three key areas. First, following international discussions in January, our representatives will work together to improve the international system for controlling exports of strategic goods to these countries and national arrangements for the enforcement of security controls. Second, we will exchange information in the OECD on all aspects of our economic, commercial and financial relations with the Soviet Union and Eastern Europe. Third, taking into account existing economic and financial considerations, we have agreed to handle cautiously financial relations with the USSR and other Eastern European countries in such a way as to ensure that they are conducted on a sound economic basis, including also the need for commercial prudence in limiting export credits. The development of economic and financial relations will be subject to periodic ex-post review.

—The progress we have already made does not diminish the need for continuing efforts to economize on energy, particularly through the price mechanism, and to promote alternative sources, including nuclear energy and coal, in a long-term perspective. These efforts will enable us further to reduce our vulnerability to interruptions in the supply of energy and instability of prices. Cooperation to develop new energy technologies, and to strengthen our capacity to deal with disruptions, can contribute to our common energy security. We shall also work to strengthen our cooperation with both oil-exporting and oil-importing developing countries.

—The growth of the developing countries and the deepening of a constructive relationship with them are vital for the political and economic well-being of the whole world. It is therefore important that a high level of financial flows and official assistance should be maintained and that their amount and their effectiveness should be increased as far as possible, with responsibilities shared broadly among all countries capable of making a contribution. The launching of global negotiations is a major political objective approved by all participants in the Summit. The latest draft resolution circulated by the Group of 77[2] is helpful, and the discussion at Versailles showed general acceptance of the view that it would serve as a basis for consultations with the countries concerned. We believe that there is now a good prospect for the early launching and success of the global negotiations, provided that the independence of the specialized agencies is guaranteed. At the same time, we are prepared to continue and develop practical cooperation with the developing countries through innovations within the World Bank, through our support of the work of the regional development banks, through progress in countering instability of commodity export earnings, through the encouragement of private capital flows, including international arrangements to improve the conditions for private investment, and through a further concentration of official assistance on the poorer countries. This is why we see a need for special temporary arrangements to overcome funding problems for IDA [International Development Association] VI, and for an early start to consideration of IDA VII. We will give special encouragement to programs or arrangements designed to increase food and energy production in developing countries which have to import these essentials, and to programs to address the implications of population growth.

In the field of balance-of-payments support, we look

---

[2]"A grouping of developing countries that [originated] in the 'Caucus of 75' developing countries organized preparatory to UNCTAD I in Geneva in 1964. By the [end of] UNCTAD I the group had expanded [to 77 members] and issued a 'Joint Declaration of the 77 Developing Countries.' This numerical designation for the group has persisted, although by 1985 membership had increased to more than 120 countries." —U.S. Department of State, *Dictionary of International Relations Terms (Washington, D.C., 1987)*, p. 47.

forward to progress at the September IMF [International Monetary Fund] annual meeting towards settling the increase in the size of the Fund appropriate to the coming eighth quota review.

—Revitalization and growth of the world economy will depend not only on our own efforts but also to a large extent upon cooperation among our countries and with other countries in the exploitation of scientific and technological development. We have to exploit the immense opportunities presented by the new technologies, particularly for creating new employment. We need to remove barriers to, and to promote, the development of the trade in new technologies both in the public sector and in the private sector. Our countries will need to train men and women in the new technologies and to create the economic, social and cultural conditions which allow these technologies to develop and flourish. We have considered the report presented to us on these issues by the President of the French Republic. In this context we have decided to set up promptly a working group of representatives of our governments and of the European Community to develop, in close consultation with the appropriate international institutions, especially the OECD, proposals to give help to attain these objectives. This group will be asked to submit its report to us by 31 December 1982. The conclusions of the report and the resulting action will be considered at the next economic Summit to be held in 1983 in the United States of America.

STATEMENT ON INTERNATIONAL MONETARY UNDERTAKINGS

1. We accept a joint responsibility to work for greater stability of the world monetary system. We recognize that this rests primarily on convergence of policies designed to achieve lower inflation, higher employment and renewed economic growth; and thus to maintain the internal and external values of our currencies. We are determined to discharge this obligation in close collaboration with all interested countries and monetary institutions.

2. We attach major importance to the role of the IMF as a monetary authority and we will give it our full support in its efforts to foster stability.

3. We are ready to strengthen our cooperation with the IMF in its work of surveillance; and to develop this on a multilateral basis taking into account particularly the currencies constituting the SDR [special drawing rights].[3]

4. We rule out the use of our exchange rates to gain unfair competitive advantages.

5. We are ready, if necessary, to use intervention in exchange markets to counter disorderly conditions, as provided for under Article IV of the IMF Articles of Agreement.

6. Those of us who are members of the EMS [European Monetary System] consider that these undertakings are complementary to the obligations of stability which they have already undertaken in that framework and recognize the role of the system in the further development of stability in the international monetary system.

---

[3]"International reserve units created by the International Monetary Fund in 1969 to supplement the limited supplies of gold and dollars which had been the prime stable monetary assets. By 1986, $342.1 billion worth of SDRs had been allocated by the IMF to member countries according to a formula based on their IMF assessments. . . . From 1974 to 1980, the SDR was pegged to a 16-currency basket. Since 1981, the value of the SDR has been based on a basket of currencies of the Group of 5, which comprises France, Japan, the United Kingdom, the United States, and Western Germany." —*Dictionary of International Relations Terms,* p. 93.

7. We are all convinced that greater monetary stability will assist freer flows of goods, services and capital. We are determined to see that greater monetary stability and freer flows of trade and capital reinforce one another in the interest of economic growth and employment.

SOURCE: France, Ministère des Relations extérieures, *La Politique étrangère de la France: textes et documents, avril–mai–juin 1982* (Paris: La Documentation française, 1982), pp. 124–25; U.S., Department of State, *Bulletin*, No. 2064 (July 1982): 5–7; Economic Summits, 1975–1986: Declarations (Rome: Istituto Affari Internazionali, 1987): 91–95; Great Britain, Foreign and Commonwealth Office, *Declarations of Annual Economic Summits, 1975–1986* (London, 198—): A8, Versailles, 1–4 [unpublished].

[STATEMENT ON LEBANON][4]

June 6, 1982

We are shocked by the news from Lebanon and the Lebanese–Israeli border area. We are deeply moved by the loss of human life, the suffering and destruction. We think that this new cycle of violence, if it were to continue, could have disastrous consequences for the whole area.

We have taken note of the unanimous adoption by the UN Security Council of a resolution expressing grave concern at the violation of the territorial integrity, independence and sovereignty of Lebanon and calling on all the parties to the conflict to cease immediately and simultaneously all military activities in Lebanon and across the Lebanese–Israeli border. We have also taken note of the appeal addressed to the parties by Mr. Pérez de Cuéllar, Secretary-General of the UN, and of a message sent by him to the President of the French Republic, as Chairman of this meeting.

We strongly endorse the urgent appeals by the Security Council and the Secretary-General for an immediate and simultaneous cessation of violence, and we call upon all the parties to heed these appeals, in order that peace and security throughout the area be safeguarded.

Each of our governments will use all the means at its disposal to achieve this objective.

SOURCE: France, Ministère des Relations extérieures, *La Politique étrangère de la France: textes et documents, avril–mai–juin 1982* (Paris: La Documentation française, 1982), p. 122; Great Britain, Foreign and Commonwealth Office, *Political Declarations and Statements of Annual Economic Summits, 1978–1986* (London, 198—) [unpublished].

---

[4]There is no official title in the English text.—ED.

RAPPORT DE M. LE PRESIDENT
DE LA REPUBLIQUE [FRANÇAISE]
AU SOMMET DES PAYS INDUSTRIALISES:
TECHNOLOGIE, EMPLOI ET CROISSANCE

5 juin 1982

Nous sommes réunis, ici, nous qui représentons sept pays parmi les plus riches de la planète pour réfléchir ensemble pendant deux jours à la situation économique et politique du moment. Nous n'avons pas à décider entre nous de l'avenir du monde, pas plus que nous n'avons à défendre nos intérêts aux dépens de ceux des absents. Mais les moyens que nous détenons nous donnent, à nos yeux et aux yeux des autres, une responsabilité collective pour le présent et l'avenir. Il importe d'y réfléchir, afin de définir ensemble les grandes lignes d'une action qui devrait nous rassembler pour la défense des valeurs qui nous sont communes.

Examinons d'abord les faits.

Dans le monde en crise, nos sept pays ne sont pas épargnés et la tendance n'est pas à l'amélioration: depuis le sommet d'Ottawa, cinq millions d'hommes et de femmes ont perdu leur emploi, chez l'un et l'autre d'entre nous. La production, l'investissement et les échanges stagnent, le protectionnisme menace, les monnaies s'installent dans le désordre, les taux d'intérêt atteignent des niveaux empêchant toute croissance créatrice d'emploi. L'égoïsme devient la règle.

Dans les pays du Sud, les conditions de survie se sont aggravées: près de 30 millions d'êtres humains sont morts de faim.

Mais, si l'on veut bien regarder, le bilan de cette année n'est pas entièrement négatif et des signes plus encourageants existent: l'inflation se ralentit, la productivité augmente; dans certains pays, dont le mien, la croissance a repris et le chômage a cessé d'augmenter.

Voyons maintenant plus loin: l'avenir dépend de notre volonté politique. La crise peut être dépassée si nous croyons en notre propre devenir, si nous refusons la fatalité qui stérilise les

134

innombrables talents et les capacités de création, si nous unissons nos efforts.

Mais l'ampleur de la transformation nécessaire doit aller bien au-delà de ce que chacun peut pour lui-même.

La crise dépasse le cadre des Etats: c'est donc seulement ensemble que nous pouvons maîtriser la mutation dont je parle, ensemble, que nous pouvons préparer l'avenir.

Si nous étions dans un monde idéal, le système monétaire international serait stable, le protectionnisme serait banni, chaque nation commercerait avec les autres sur une base équilibrée, aucun monopole ne s'opposerait à l'émulation de la concurrence, les taux d'intérêt seraient bas, le Nord et le Sud uniraient leurs efforts pour l'épanouissement de leurs cultures et des libertés. Ainsi seraient remplies les conditions économiques adaptées au développement d'une alliance forte. Notre action commune serait aisée à définir.

Tel n'est pas le cas aujourd'hui. C'est pourquoi nous réfléchirons aux moyens d'organiser une croissance équilibrée, de réduire le chômage, d'enrayer les protectionnismes, de construire un système monétaire stable et de donner au Sud les moyens de son développement.

En attendant d'y parvenir, faut-il se contenter d'un constat d'impuissance? Certainement pas. Ce serait une vue hâtive et fausse. Non seulement nous avons le devoir d'examiner ensemble, pour les résoudre, les problèmes posés par la crise et, pour cela de s'accorder sur sa nature et sur ses causes, mais encore il reste à explorer de vastes champs ouverts à nos efforts communs. Parmi eux, celui qu'offrent la science et la technologie, dont l'évolution rapide entraîne le bouleversement de nos sociétés et risque de se détourner contre l'homme lui-même dont pourtant elles procèdent, si celui-ci ne s'en assure pas la maitrîse.

Certes à cette interrogation se consacrent déjà nombre d'entreprises privées et publiques et chacun de nos pays. La France y a sa part. Mais si nous percevons les enjeux de la révolution industrielle qui commence sommes-nous sûrs d'avoir mis tous les atouts dans notre jeu? Il manque l'atout maître qui seul nous donnerait la cohérence et la solidarité de notre action. Je vous invite à y réfléchir.

UN ELAN VITAL PORTE L'HUMANITE
VERS DE NOUVEAUX CHAMPS DE DEVELOPPEMENT

Où en est aujourd'hui le progrès technique et que peut-il changer, dans les dix ans qui viennent, à la crise que nous traversons? Depuis cinq ans il s'est accéléré, dans la biotechnologie et dans l'électronique. Les domaines nouveaux apparaissent sans limite: le temps, l'espace, la matière vivante.

1. Les biotechnologies devraient faire reculer la faim, la maladie, la surpopulation.

Demain, l'utilisation conjointe de la biochimie, de la microbiologie et du génie génétique permettra l'exploitation industrielle des micro-organismes et transformera des secteurs économiques entiers: non seulement la chimie et le médicament, mais aussi l'alimentation et l'énergie.

C'est l'alimentation qui bénéficiera le plus, à moyen terme, des découvertes biologiques. Leur utilisation accroîtra, en effet, considérablement les rendements et économisera les engrais, dont la production est aujourd'hui coûteuse en énergie. Grâce à ces techniques, une nouvelle industrie agro-alimentaire est en train de naître. Elle transformera toutes les conditions de la production agricole.

La microbiologie économisera l'utilisation des protéines par l'agriculture. Une telle évolution, par laquelle les protéines seront prioritairement destinées aux besoins des hommes, autorisera de grandes espérances pour la sécurité alimentaire du Tiers Monde.

2. L'électronique multiplie les capacités de production et de création de nos économies.

La micro-électronique, les nouveaux matériaux composites, les fibres optiques, modifieront en profondeur d'anciennes industries (télécommunications, transports, mécanique) et en créeront de nouvelles (robotique, bureautique).

C'est déjà le cas: en dix ans, la capacité des circuits

électroniques intégrés à été multipliée par cent et leur coût divisé par mille; ce progrès va s'accélérer. Le développement des mémoires de masse, l'utilisation du vidéodisque à laser, augmentent la puissance de l'informatique, réduisent les coûts de production et créent de nouveaux biens de consommation, des produits qui n'existaient pas en 1975 deviennent accessibles à de plus en plus de personnes (ordinateurs personnels, magnétoscopes, vidéodisques) et leur marché sera décuplé d'ici en 1990.

La robotisation de l'industrie a commencé dans nos pays. Plusieurs milliers de robots sophistiqués sont disséminés dans le monde. Ils augmentent la productivité dans bien des secteurs d'activité (automobile, construction électrique et électronique, nucléaire . . .). Avant la fin de la décennie leur parc sera multiplié par dix à douze et ils accompliront des tâches de plus en plus complexes, changeant l'organisation du travail et posant d'une façon radicalement différente le problème de l'emploi.

3. Les moyens énergétiques évolueront rapidement au cours des deux prochaines décennies.

Les techniques telles que les bioénergies, la géothermie ou l'énergie solaire apporteront une importante contribution aux ressources déjà exploitées. L'énergie nucléaire bien maitrîsée modifiera le fonctionnement de plusieurs secteurs-clefs de nos économies et le progrès chimique les conditions d'exploration, d'extraction, de transport, de stockage et d'utilisation des hydrocarbures.

4. Enfin de nouvelles dimensions s'offrent à l'intelligence.

Je voudrais ne prendre ici que quelques exemples.

—L'exploration océanographique permettra d'exploiter des gisements encore mal connus de ressources naturelles, d'énergie et de minerais.

—L'exploration spatiale multipliera nos moyens de communication. Dans dix ans, plusieurs centaines de satellites permettront de constituer des grilles complètes d'observation de la terre et de développer des systèmes de communications évolués.

—Avec de nouvelles technologies de la communication une autre forme de civilisation s'instaure. La prolifération et l'interdépendance des systèmes d'information électroniques agiront sur notre univers quotidien, nos modes de relations, nos systèmes de valeurs: dans dix ans, il y aura plusieurs dizaines de millions d'ordinateurs personnels. Magnétoscope, caméra vidéo, télévision reliée par câble constitueront des objets familiers dans les foyers. Avec la «monnaie informatique», permettant l'achat et la vente à distance, ce seront les actes et les relations habituelles du consommateur qui se trouveront modifiés.

Déjà la communication se mondialise. Une même série télévisée, un même événement politique ou sportif, sont regardés dans plus de cent pays.

Déjà l'orientation moderne des voies traditionnelles de diffusion du savoir et de l'information modifie brusquement l'ensemble des relations entre personnes, entre groupes sociaux, entre nations, entre régions du monde.

En quoi ces changements, parmi d'autres, transforment-ils les enjeux auxquels nous avons à faire face?

En augmentant nos pouvoirs sur la matière, sur le temps, sur l'espace, la révolution technologique commande l'évolution de nos économies, de nos modes de vie et de pensée, de nos systèmes de référence.

Elle pèsera, de façon heureuse ou dangereuse, sur le chômage, l'inflation, la croissance selon la façon dont on la conduira.

Sans attendre, il importe de puiser pour la démocratie et pour la paix dans l'immense réservoir de la connaissance.

PUISER DANS L'IMMENSE RESERVOIR DE L'INTELLIGENCE HUMAINE

Face à ces bouleversements, l'attentisme ou l'égoïsme accentueraient les perturbations, les nuisances, les violences, les déséquilibres, les conflits. Tout doit être fait chez chacun d'entre nous et par une grande coopération économique pour que le progrès constitue un moyen de paix et de prospérité, pour éviter qu'il ne produise d'abord comme par le passé chômage et récession. Je vous propose cinq thèmes de réflexion et d'action.

1. Créer le plein emploi en maîtrisant le contenu du travail.

Le progrès technologique ne peut pas se diffuser dans un contexte de chômage, qui crée un environnement pessimiste, qui suscite des comportements de repli, qui détruit la confiance. C'est pourquoi la lutte contre ce fléau, par nos politiques économiques concertées, est une priorité.

Certains craignent que le progrès n'aggrave le chômage qui nous frappe. Ayant réfléchi à cela, je peux vous dire mon optimisme à moyen terme.

Le progrès n'est un danger que pour ceux qui ne savent pas maîtriser la transition qu'il impose entre des activités en déclin et des activités nouvelles. Pour les autres il est une chance.

Il est vrai que son effet sur l'emploi en termes quantitatifs est difficile à appréhender: la révolution technologique est à la fois créatrice d'emplois, par le développement de nouveaux secteurs, et destructrice d'emplois, par l'automatisation de certaines activités.

Dès 1990, 20% de la production de masse seront réalisés par des machines d'assemblage automatique, réduisant le nombre d'emplois et particulièrement les plus pénibles dans l'industrie. Les activités tertiaires telles que les banques et les assurances seront aussi touchées. Au total, une suppression de plusieurs millions de postes de travail pourrait en résulter d'ici à 1990, dans les seuls pays industrialisés.

Nous devons donc nous donner les moyens de gérer cette

mutation afin que les technologies ne suppriment pas plus vite les emplois qu'elles n'en créeront. Nous devons raccourcir les délais de cette inévitable transition.

Si l'on s'y prépare, les nouvelles technologies susciteront la création d'emplois autant sinon plus qu'elles n'en supprimeront, non seulement par la production de nouveaux biens industriels, mais également par les services associés (distribution, ingenierie, conseil, formation, activités de loisir . . .) à condition de savoir les organiser, et par les effets d'entraînement qui auront lieu dans des secteurs tels que la métallurgie, la sidérurgie, la mécanique, la chimie. . . .

Le problème qui nous est donc posé est celui d'une substitution ordonnée et rapide de nouveaux emplois aux anciens. Je ferai plus loin à ce sujet des suggestions.

Cette substitution ne pourra être seulement quantitative. Elle s'accompagnera d'une profonde évolution du contenu du travail et de son organisation. Elle donnera à la diminution du temps de travail une autre signification. Nécessité économique, sociale et culturelle, elle deviendra un des instruments de la politique économique en contrepoint des gains de productivité.

On sait que les risques de déqualification, d'uniformisation des tâches, d'isolement, inquiètent à juste titre les travailleurs. Faute de savoir comment nos sociétés s'adapteront aux mutations technologiques, nous risquons de maintenir nos nations dans un état de refus frileux du progrès ainsi qu'en témoigne le ralentissement de nos investissements.

C'est pourquoi nous devons ensemble investir dans tout ce qui touche à l'environnement du travail et à l'adaptation des connaissances pour que le progrès social accompagne le progrès technique.

Dans cette perspective, trois lignes d'action, me semble-t-il, s'imposent à chacun de nous:

—le soutien de la demande afin de favoriser le développement des marchés pour les nouveaux biens et services de consommation incorporant les progrès technologiques;

—la stabilisation des taux d'intérêt et des taux de change. Je n'y insisterai pas ici car ce sera l'objet essentiel du reste de nos discussions;

—un effort accru de formation et de mobilité professionnelles. L'organisation et le contenu du travail seront déterminés, je l'ai dit, par la diffusion des techniques nouvelles. L'exercice de plusieurs métiers au cours d'une vie de travail sera une des caractéristiques majeures de nos sociétés dans les années à venir.

Or à ce sujet tout reste à faire. Dans les pays les plus développés, la progression du nombre d'ingénieurs et de techniciens formés a été considérablement réduite. En 1980 les dépenses publiques et privées de formation professionnelle ne représentaient même pas 1% de notre PNB [produit national brut] commun. Ce qui paraissait suffisant dans un contexte d'expansion soutenue et de stabilité de l'organisation du travail devient impropre à l'organisation de la mobilité et à la diffusion des connaissances.

Un tel effort est une condition nécessaire pour que le progrès soit assumé et rendu acceptable pour toutes les forces du travail.

Sans cet immense effort de formation, dont doivent bénéficier les salariés de tous les secteurs, de tous les âges, hommes et femmes, du haut en bas de l'échelle des qualifications, seul un petit nombre de privilégiés sera à même de comprendre et d'agir sur le monde, aux dépens d'un gaspillage dramatique de la capacité créatrice des autres.

Il nous appartient dès lors de lancer une politique active de formation et d'adaptation de nos savoir-faire.

Le contenu du travail sera modifié en qualité et en quantité dans le sens de l'amélioration de la condition des travailleurs, si nous en prenons les moyens, notamment en assurant et en développant la concertation avec les intéressés et leurs organisations.

Ce mouvement n'est possible que si l'éducation, la culture et l'environnement accompagnent le progrès scientifique et économique, en lui donnant une âme, un projet, un sens.

2. Favoriser le dynamisme industriel.

Les bases de départ existent. Il devient possible de surmonter la récession, de rompre le mouvement de baisse des gains de productivité, et d'ouvrir de nouveaux marchés.

—En 1990 les activités situées au coeur de la révolution technologique (circuits intégrés, bureautique, robotique, nouvelles applications télématiques, nouveaux biens grand public, espace, génie biologique, offshore, énergie, nouveaux matériaux) auront triplé leur place relative dans la production de nos pays.

—A cette même date les industries à haut contenu technologique (télécommunications, aéronautique-espace, produits médicaux et pharmaceutiques, énergie, chimie, transport) représenteront près d'un tiers de la production industrielle des Sept; elles constitueront un facteur de croissance auquel s'ajoutera l'ensemble des activités servant au fonctionnement ou à l'utilisation des biens et services produits par ces secteurs (formation, recherche et développement, distribution, programme, etc.).

—L'automatisation rapide de la production industrielle devrait provoquer des gains de productivité de plus de 10% par an, condition indispensable au succès des politiques anti-inflationnistes.

Pour cela, les conditions d'un nouveau dynamisme industriel doivent être réunies: un effort d'investissement et une concurrence garantie.

(a) Relancer l'effort d'investissement industriel.

Les politiques dites d'austérité freinent le progrès technologique en décourageant les investissements à long terme créateurs d'une nouvelle demande, alors qu'il nous faut répondre à la révolution technologique en encourageant les investissements industriels privés et publics.

C'est une mobilisation sans précédent du capital vers l'industrie et la recherche que nous devrons réaliser. Cet effort d'investissement correspondra à un prélèvement supplémentaire annuel très important sur les ressources disponibles du marché international des capitaux. Nos marchés monétaires et financiers auront à y répondre. Aussi faut-il que les taux d'intérêt internationaux soient raisonnables afin de rendre possible ces investissements et que nos taux de change soient stabilisés, grâce à une coopération entre les principales monnaies permettant de reconstruire un système monétaire international ordonné. Cette question occupera assurément nos discussions et nous en reparlerons cet après-midi.

Les investissements et marchés publics (communications, transport, énergie. . .) par leur ampleur et parce qu'ils peuvent s'appuyer sur un projet global, ont un rôle moteur à jouer. Nous échangerons nos points de vue et pourrons amorcer une coopération sur ce thème.

(b) Garantir la concurrence.

La concurrence est un facteur essentiel de la croissance et du progrès technique. Or elle posera des problèmes très différents de ceux que nous connaissons aujourd'hui.

Dans le domaine des biotechnologies, par exemple, plus d'un tiers des produits étant fabriqué par des firmes en situation de monopole mondial, le déséquilibre va s'accentuer. De même, dans le domaine de l'électronique avancée, huit firmes contrôlent déjà 70% du marché des circuits intégrés. Cette concentration s'accentuera.

L'innovation technologique reste pourtant pour l'essentiel le fait de petites et moyennes entreprises privées et c'est heureux. Mais elle s'intègre dans un système de production de plus en plus complexe et, les conditions traditionnelles de la concurrence modifiées, les courants d'échanges deviennent source de plus grande tension, les rapports de force entre firmes, entre régions du monde, entre marchés s'exacerbent. Il nous faut y réfléchir. Je proposerai plus loin des voies d'action.

3. Lutter contre les déséquilibres Nord–Sud.

Enfin, il faut mettre les découvertes technologiques récentes au service des pays du Sud. Elles aideront concrètement, comme je l'ai déjà dit à propos des biotechnologies, à réduire leur dépendance énergétique et alimentaire.

Certes on ne peut se dissimuler qu'elles susciteront aussi, pour eux, des menaces nouvelles: instabilités et dépendances.

Par exemple, les biotechnologies développeront des substituts aux matières premières et aux énergies traditionnelles risquant d'aggraver l'état des pays pauvres producteurs de matières premières. La création de nouveaux matériaux, plus tard l'exploitation de nodules polymétalliques (cobalt, nickel, manganèse, cuivre), l'absence d'une répartition équitable des fonds marins menaceront les pays qui dépendent fortement des exportations de minerais. Nous devons donc accélérer les transferts de technologies vers le Sud, tout en développant l'organisation des marchés mondiaux.

On réfléchira non seulement aux moyens de transférer vers eux nos technologies en les adaptant, mais aussi de rassembler les conditions qui permettront la naissance de technologies directement centrées sur leurs réalités propres: c'est à cette condition que le développement autonome de leur agriculture, de leur industrie, de leurs services est possible.

Enfin, s'il est de l'intérêt des pays industrialisés que l'immense marché des pays du Sud s'ouvre à la révolution technologique, il faut que la science et la technique apportent à ces pays les conditions de la survie et de la dignité en protégeant et en mobilisant leurs ressources naturelles et leur environnement: augmenter les productions nationales d'énergie, arrêter l'extension des zones incultivables, arrêter la disparition d'espèces végétales et animales et la dégradation des sols, lutter contre les causes et les effets dramatiques d'une concentration urbaine, qui s'accroît à un rythme sans précédent.

Pour cela les moyens dont disposent les institutions multi-latérales d'aide à la recherche technologique devront être orientés vers les besoins du Sud.

Je proposerai des voies d'action permettant aux pays du Sud de maîtriser de nouvelles technologies.

Bref, il est possible de se servir de la recherche scientifique et technique pour la mise en valeur globale du patrimoine commun au pays du Nord et du Sud.

4. Vaincre les tentations de repli sur soi.

Alors que le commerce mondial s'est ralenti, les produits incluant de la haute technologie occupent une part croissante de son volume. Il nous faut surmonter cette contradiction.

Le progrès technique créera de nouvelles occasions d'échange. Mais le protectionnisme trouve, dans la nature même des produits hautement technologiques, des moyens nouveaux de s'exprimer (normes, procédures d'agrément . . .). Le développement technologique dans son ensemble peut provoquer à court terme des réactions de repli, des désirs d'isolement, contraires, à moyen terme, aux intérêts de tous les pays. Il convient de coopérer pour que le protectionnisme ne finisse pas par l'emporter.

5. Construire une nouvelle civilisation.

Une nouvelle civilisation commence là ou la multiplication des moyens aide à libérer les hommes de la double contrainte de la distance et du temps, à échanger, communiquer. L'inter-relation des réseaux conduit les sociétés les plus diverses à entrer en communication, à mieux se connaître, à mieux se comprendre.

L'impact des nouvelles technologies sur la civilisation de la ville est encore mal connu: on veillera à ce que le développement des moyens de transport, la prolifération et l'interdépendance des systèmes d'information, la mise en place des réseaux câbles, les nouvelles techniques de l'habitat, rendent les villes plus accueillantes pour tous et rompent l'isolement des campagnes.

L'enjeu est là, immense, car en l'absence d'un puissant mouvement d'échanges un risque d'uniformisation pèsera sur toutes les cultures et toutes les langues.

La communication se concentre en effet dans tous les pays. Quelques firmes s'approprient l'ensemble des réseaux nécessaires à la diffusion électronique. En les maîtrisant elles influencent en retour les média traditionnels: le cinéma, la presse ou la télévision. L'essentiel des nouvelles activités dans lesquelles s'engagent la plupart des firmes (production, stockage, traitement de l'information) suppose de très lourds investissements qui conduisent à une forte concentration.

Déjà, les deux premières banques d'images alimentent la quasi-totalité des stations de télévision dans le monde, plus de trois-quarts des informations de presse émanent de cinq agences. Généralisée, cette tendance naturelle conduira, dès la fin de la décennie, au contrôle de l'industrie mondiale de la communication par une vingtaine de firmes.

En coopérant, nous éviterons que l'information ne soit accumulée et traitée par un petit nombre de firmes et de nations disposant des systèmes de traitement et de stockage les plus rapidement mis au point.

Plus généralement, la diffusion d'informations élaborées et contrôlées par quelques pays dominant pourrait faire perdre leur mémoire ou leur souveraineté aux autres, remettant ainsi en cause les libertés de penser et de décider.

PROPOSITIONS POUR UN DEVELOPPEMENT CONCERTE DE L'ECONOMIE MONDIALE

Et maintenant que faire? Je souhaite que nous réfléchissions à un ensemble de mesures capables de mettre en oeuvre rapidement, chez chacun d'entre nous et en commun, les principes que je viens d'exposer.

Non que je vous demande d'en décider aujourd'hui; mais qu'au moins on puisse lancer, dans l'année qui vient, l'indispensable action commune.

Sans cela, chacun se repliera sur lui, les batailles commerciales s'aggraveront, les protectionnismes s'installeront. Nul n'y gagnera rien.

Le passé prouve la réalité de ces dangers. Lors de chacune des deux précédentes révolutions industrielles que l'Occident a connues, on a assisté dans un premier temps à la montée du chômage, du protectionnisme et de l'inflation.

Puis, en un second temps, dans les pays les mieux préparés, les forces sociales du changement l'ont emporté, la croissance et la stabilité sont revenues, les investissements ont repris.

Nous risquons aujourd'hui, si l'on n'y prend garde, d'assister à la même succession d'événements: la nouvelle révolution industrielle a commencé d'aggraver le chômage, l'inflation, les difficultés financières et les inégalités. Cela durera longtemps si nous ne décidons d'y mettre un terme.

Aucun de nous, malgré les différences de point de vue qui nous séparent, ne peut s'y résigner. Tous, avons le devoir de faire en sorte que la transition s'achève au plus tôt. Nous en avons les moyens car nous pouvons prévoir, organiser le changement, coordonner les mutations. C'est pourquoi j'ai tenu à aborder avec vous ce sujet.

Je vous propose:

—de lancer un programme concerté de croissance sélective par la technologie;

—d'accorder une priorité commune à l'emploi et aux conditions de travail;

—de favoriser ensemble l'épanouissement des cultures.

Première proposition: lancer un programme concerté de croissance par la technologie

Six grandes orientations constitueront une voie assez large pour que nous puissions nous y engager:

(1) Des objectifs globaux: les fixer en pourcentage du PNB pour 1985 et 1990 et échanger nos vues sur les politiques nationales de recherche–développement en complétant au besoin par des objectifs sectoriels et en tirant parti des travaux déjà entrepris dans les institutions internationales, notamment l'OCDE [Organisation de coopération et de développement économique].

(2) Des actions prioritaires de coopération technologique entre firmes privées et publiques et entre nations. Et ce dans les domaines suivants nécessitant de forts investissements de départ: énergies nouvelles, télécommunications, robotique, nouveaux matériaux, matériaux composites, électronique, intelligence artificielle, espace, biotechnologies, technologies agricoles plus particulièrement destinées au Tiers Monde.

Un comité de développement pour chaque projet retenu, pourrait être mis en place. Il comprendrait les organismes concernés des pays participants. Un effort minimum d'investissement par pays serait fixé.

(3) L'innovation: l'accélérer sous toutes ses formes en mettant au point les procédures utiles. Faciliter la création de nouvelles entreprises, la coopération entre les firmes des différents pays et définir les politiques communes contre les pratiques monopolistiques et les obstacles à la concurrence.

(4) Création progressive d'un marché mondial de technologie (normes, brevets).

(5) Initiatives conjointes pour assurer aux pays du Sud la maîtrise des nouvelles technologies. Accroissement de la recherche-développement dans les domaines intéressant particulièrement ces pays, essentiellement l'éducation, la formation, l'alimentation et la santé dans le cadre d'accords de co-développement; création de centres de recherches et promotion des échanges de chercheurs; croissance des énergies nationales par des organismes spécialisés au sein de la Banque mondiale. On accélérera enfin la mise en oeuvre des orientations définies par la conférence des Nations unies pour la science, la technique et le développement.

(6) Enfin, il conviendra, aussi vite que possible, de stabiliser le système monétaire international dont l'imprévisibilité freine les investissements. Pour cela il faut rechercher les voies et les moyens d'un renforcement de la coopération monétaire équilibrée entre les trois pôles européen, américain et japonais dans la perspective d'un retour à des taux de change stables et économiquement corrects.

La préparation de ce programme pourrait s'inspirer des méthodes utilisées dans diverses formules de coopération: réseaux de centres de recherches pour une large diffusion de l'information (météorologie, environnement, océanographie), établissement de règles et de normes communes, actions bilatérales dans le cadre d'un programme multilatéral (programme international de développement des télécommunications, programme météorologique mondial), formules de projet «à la carte» (programmes scientifiques de l'Unesco).

Deuxième proposition: mettre la technologie au service de l'emploi et des conditions de travail

1. Mettre en place un vaste dispositif de formation, pour la mutation des emplois dont j'ai parlé pour accélérer la transition de la révolution industrielle. A cette fin:

—organiser dès 1983, dans chacun de nos pays, avec les méthodes propres à chacun, un dispositif spécifique de formation aux nouvelles technologies telles l'informatique, la biologie, et les métiers nouveaux (télécommunications, sciences de la vie, ingenierie, loisirs) selon les trois axes suivants:

—priorité à la formation des ingénieurs et des techniciens; action de formation des jeunes chômeurs de 16 à 18 ans; action de conversion aux nouvelles technologies des travailleurs en cours de carrière;

—demander à l'OCDE de préparer dans les six prochains mois un programme spécial d'échanges et de coopération en matière de méthode de formation et de conversion;

—demander à l'OIT [Organisation internationale du travail] de mettre en place un observatoire afin de suivre l'évolution des métiers concernés par les nouvelles technologies.

2. Il faut également tirer parti des nouvelles technologies pour améliorer les conditions de travail et de vie. Je vous suggère de:

—développer la coopération et la recherche sur l'organisation du travail, les conditions de travail liées aux nouvelles technologies, et les effets des nouvelles technologies sur la durée du travail et sur sa possible réduction;

—établir avant le prochain sommet un programme d'évaluation des expériences positives et négatives menées dans les villes et des effets sur le mode de vie urbain de changements technologiques tels le câblage, les nouveaux modes de transport et d'habitat.

Troisième proposition: favoriser ensemble l'épanouissement des cultures, sur trois thèmes:

1. L'école.

Peu à peu, la révolution de l'informatique remonte aux sources de l'éducation aux premières années de la vie scolaire. Nos systèmes d'enseignement, tout en gardant les traditions qui leur sont propres, vont s'en trouver profondément bouleversés avec des menaces et des espérances. Pour mieux faire face à ces transformations il conviendra de:

—mener un effort conjoint en vue de définir les systèmes d'enseignement adaptés à chaque pays et de réfléchir ensemble aux moyens par lesquels nos systèmes scolaires seront en harmonie avec leur environnement;

—élaborer au niveau mondial une famille de langages informatiques simples;

—agir conjointement pour développer l'usage de l'ordinateur à l'école afin de former très vite les jeunes aux objets de leur vie quotidienne de demain et aux exigences de leur métier futur.

2. Les communications et les langages.

Le développement de l'enseignement et de la recherche dans le domaine des langues et de la communication est indispensable pour résister au puissant mouvement d'uniformisation que j'ai évoqué. Nous pourrions:

—instituer au sein de l'université des Nations unies un réseau mondial reliant tous les centres d'enseignement de formation et de recherche consacrés aux langues et à la communication. Ce réseau faciliterait le développement, dans les divers pays intéressés, des actions suivants: l'étude des langues, le rôle des langues nationales dans la diffusion des technologies, les lexiques multilingues sur ordinateurs, les programmes de traduction automatique pour les langues autres que les langues principales, la formation de spécialistes de la communication;

—lancer une grande encyclopédie de toutes les cultures du monde. On peut aujourd'hui envisager de créer des outils de diffusion à grande échelle des cultures fussent-elles très locales; chaque nation recueillant en son sein ce qui lui semble être l'essence de son (ou de ses) identité(s) culturelle(s); les moyens de diffusion seraient, outre les livres:

un ou plusieurs satellites, placés sous contrôle de l'Unesco, offrant une diffusion régionale d'émission TV;

un grand centre informatique, par exemple celui de l'Agence spatiale européenne, qui pourrait être le serveur d'une base de données bibliographique interrogeable sur les grands réseaux télématiques mondiaux.

3. Une charte de la communication.

Je pense qu'une négociation devrait être menée par étapes, dans les instances internationales, en vue de préparer une charte mondiale de la communication aujourd'hui si difficile. Elle pourrait s'organiser autour de cinq principes:

—affirmer le respect de la diversité des langues;

—promouvoir l'harmonisation des législations en matière d'information, de propriété intellectuelle, de droit contractuel, de protection des libertés individuelles;

—inciter à la détermination de règles communes pour les échanges internationaux de données;

—protéger la souveraineté des Etats et leur intégrité culturelle menacée par les nouvelles technologies;

—garantir aux pays du Sud les moyens de maîtriser leurs moyens de communications et les messages qu'ils véhiculent.

4. Une exposition mondiale «pour une image présente du futur».

Il s'agit d'illustrer le rôle du développement technologique comme facteur de rapprochement entre les peuples.
La France serait prête à organiser cette exposition en 1989.

Il me reste, avant de conclure, à préciser les conditions de la mise en oeuvre concertée des propositions que je viens de vous présenter:

—un groupe de travail de huit personnalités créé par nous dès le lendemain de ce sommet recevrait pour mission de dégager quelques priorités en s'inspirant des propositions contenues dans le présent rapport de votre discussion.

—Ce groupe travaillerait en consultation avec les institutions internationales compétentes, notamment l'OCDE, et présenterait son rapport avant le 31 décembre.

—Les conclusions du rapport et les actions qui en résulteraient seraient examinées au prochain sommet des pays industrialisés qui se tiendra en 1983 aux Etats-Unis d'Amérique.

Si nous réussissons, par notre action commune, à entreprendre ces projets, aurons-nous résolu les problèmes que nos sociétés affrontent? Assurément non: le progrès technique n'assure pas, par lui-même, le progrès économique et le progrès social. Il ne peut qu'y concourir, dans les sociétés qui sauront le mettre au service d'une volonté politique.

Il restera bien du chemin à faire, pour rétablir une croissance équilibrée et juste, pour en finir avec toutes les formes de misère et de servitude: il nous faudra reconstruire un système monétaire stable, procurer aux entreprises les moyens d'un financement peu coûteux, imaginer des rapports économiques et politiques équitables entre les continents, éliminer tous les obstacles au commerce. Il nous faudra enfin, et c'est l'essentiel, permettre à chaque homme d'utiliser librement le temps que le progrès dégagera.

Nous aurons alors rempli notre rôle de gouvernants.

Chacun aura ensuite plus de moyens matériels à sa disposition pour vivre à sa façon la condition humaine. Avec ce qu'elle a de limité et d'exaltant, d'inachevé et de grandiose, de fugitif et d'éternel.

Nous aurons seulement, pour ce qui nous concerne, en prenant à bras le corps les problèmes qui nous assaillent et en accélérant leurs solutions, assuré à nos nations l'essentiel: la confiance en elles-mêmes.

SOURCE: France, Ministère des Relations extérieures, *La Politique étrangère de la France: textes et documents, avril–mai–juin 1982* (Paris: La Documentation française, 1982), pp. 110–15.

[TRANSLATION]
TECHNOLOGY, EMPLOYMENT AND GROWTH: REPORT BY MR. FRANÇOIS MITTERRAND, PRESIDENT OF THE FRENCH REPUBLIC, AT THE SUMMIT OF THE INDUSTRIALIZED COUNTRIES

June 5, 1982

We, the representatives of seven of the richest countries in the world, find ourselves gathered here to examine together, over the next two days, the current economic and political situation. It is not our task to decide alone the future of the world, nor is it to defend our own interests at the expense of those not here among us. However, in our eyes and in the eyes of the world, the means that we possess vest in us a collective responsibility both for the present and for the future. It is incumbent on us to join in reflection in order to lay down the major lines of a concerted action in defense of the values we hold in common.

Let us first examine the facts.

Our seven countries have not been spared the consequences of the crisis from which the world is suffering. Moreover, the situation is not improving. Unemployment has touched all of our countries: since the Ottawa Summit, five million men and women have lost their jobs. Production, investment and trade are sluggish, protectionism poses a threat, currencies are falling into a state of near-permanent disorder and interest rates have reached levels that preclude any job-generating growth. Self-interest is becoming the rule.

In the countries of the South, conditions of survival have worsened: nearly thirty million human beings have died of starvation.

Yet, if we consider it closely, the balance sheet for the year is not entirely negative, and encouraging signs have appeared: inflation has slowed down, productivity has improved; in some countries, and France among them, growth has resumed and unemployment is no longer on the increase.

Let us now look ahead. The future hinges on our political

determination. We can surmount the crisis by having faith in our own future, by rejecting the inevitability of the crisis which stifles so many individuals of talent and creative capacity, and by uniting our efforts.

The scope of the transformation required, however, must exceed the individual efforts made by countries for themselves.

The crisis extends far beyond national borders: thus it is only through joint action that we shall be able to control this transformation, and prepare for the future.

In a perfect world, the international monetary system would be stable, protectionism would be banished, each nation would maintain balanced trade relations with others, no monopoly would interfere with the dynamic of the competitive market-place, interest rates would be low, and the North and South would unite in their efforts towards the mutual fulfillment of their cultures and liberties. In this manner, the economic requirements of the development of a strong alliance would be met. Our joint action would be easy to frame.

Such is not the case today. Thus, we must reflect on ways to organize balanced growth, reduce unemployment, stop protectionism, build a stable monetary system and provide the South with the means for its own development.

In the meantime, should we feel powerless to attain these goals? Certainly not. This would be a hasty and incorrect assessment of the situation. Our duty is not only to examine the global situation in order to resolve the problems created by the crisis, and, to this end, agree on its nature and causes, but to explore the vast fields of endeavor open to our common effort. Among the latter, science and technology, whose rapid development is revolutionizing our societies, threaten to turn against man, their creator, if he does not master them properly.

Undoubtedly, many private and public firms, and each of our countries, have already devoted time to this question, and France among them. But, although we are aware of what is at stake in the dawning industrial revolution, are we sure to have all the winning cards in our hand? We lack the master trump, which may only be had through coherent and concerted action. This is a subject worthy of your reflection.

MANKIND'S VITAL SPIRIT PROPELS IT TOWARDS NEW FIELDS OF DEVELOPMENT

Where does technological progress stand today, and in what ways will it be able, over the next ten years, to resolve the crisis we are experiencing? In the past five years it has accelerated rapidly in the fields of biotechnology and electronics. The new spheres seem limitless, and include time, space and organic matter.

1. Biotechnologies Should Succeed in Reducing Famine, Disease and Overpopulation.

Tomorrow, the combined use of biochemistry, microbiology and genetic engineering will open the way to industrial micro-organism production, and will transform entire economic sectors. The latter will include not only the chemistry and pharmaceutical sectors, but food and energy as well.

The food sector will derive the greatest benefits from biological discoveries in the medium term. Their application will increase yields considerably, and will save on fertilizers, which are costly to produce in terms of energy. Thanks to these technologies, a new agrofood industry is in the making, which will revolutionize all facets of agricultural production.

New microbiological techniques will allow for protein savings in agriculture. This development, which will allow proteins to be used primarily for human consumption, will furnish new hope for an assured food supply in the Third World.

2. Electronics is Multiplying Productive and Creative Capacities.

Micro-electronics, new composite materials and optical fibres will radically transform such established industries as telecommunications, transport and the mechanical industry, while creating new ones, such as robotics and office automation.

This is already a reality: in ten years, the capacity of integrated electronic circuits has increased a hundredfold, while their cost has dropped a thousandfold. This trend will continue to progress rapidly. The development of bulk storage and the use of laser videodiscs improve data processing performance, reduce production costs and create new consumer goods. Products which were non-existent in 1975 are now available to an increasing number of users (personal computers, videotape recorders, videodiscs) and their market will be ten times larger in 1990.

Industrial robotization has begun to be used in our countries. Thousands of highly sophisticated robots are in use throughout the world. They increase productivity in many operational sectors, including the automobile, electrical, electronics and nuclear industries. Before the end of this decade, robot inventory will increase ten- to twelvefold, and they will perform increasingly complex tasks, thus changing labor organization, and restating the employment question in radically different terms.

3. Energy Technologies Will Develop Rapidly Over the Next Twenty Years.

Technologies such as bioenergy, geothermal and solar energy, will contribute substantially to resources already in use. Nuclear energy, carefully controlled, will modify the operations of several key sectors in our economies, and progress made in the field of chemistry will alter techniques of exploration, extraction, transport, storage and use of hydrocarbons.

4. Lastly, New Spheres are Opening up to our Intelligence.

I shall limit myself to only a few examples here:

—Oceanographic exploration will allow us to discover and extract deposits of heretofore unknown natural resources, energy and minerals.

—Space exploration will multiply our means of communication. In ten years' time, several hundred satellites will permit a complete earth observation system to be established and advanced communications systems to be developed.

—These new communication technologies will usher in a new form of civilization. The proliferation and interdependence of electronic information systems will influence our everyday lives, ways of communicating and value systems. In ten years, tens of millions of personal computers will be in use. Videotape recorders, video-cameras and cable television will become familiar household objects. With "electronic banking" permitting long-distance transactions to be carried out, the everyday activities and traditional behavior patterns of the consumer will be modified.

—Communication is already becoming worldwide. The same television series, political and sports events, are viewed in hundreds of countries.

The modern orientation of the traditional means of knowledge and information dissemination is already precipitately changing inter-personal relations, as well as those between different social groups, nations and regions of the world.

How will these changes, among many others, transform the challenges facing us?

The technological revolution, by increasing our control over matter, time and space, shapes the evolution of our economics, life-styles, thought patterns and systems of reference.

It will have a positive or dangerous effect on unemployment, inflation and growth, according to the way in which it is managed.

Without further delay, and in the interests of democracy and peace, we must draw on the immense resources of knowledge.

DRAWING ON THE IMMENSE RESOURCES OF HUMAN INTELLIGENCE

Faced with these upheavals, wait-and-see attitudes and self-interest would only exacerbate the disturbances, hardships, violence, imbalances and dissensions. Each of us must do everything in his power, at home, and through broad economic cooperation, to guarantee that progress will be a factor for peace and prosperity, to avoid its producing, as the case has been in the past, unemployment and recession. I offer you five propositions for reflection and action.

1. Achieving Full Employment While Controlling the Content of Work.

Technological progress cannot spread in a context of high unemployment, which creates a pessimistic environment, incites isolationist patterns, and destroys confidence. This is why the fight against this scourge, by our concerted economic policies, is a top priority matter.

Many fear that progress only aggravates the unemployment that assails us. After due consideration, I can assure you of my medium-term optimism.

Progress is only a danger for those who cannot dominate the transition which it implies between declining activities and new ones. For those who can, it is an opportunity.

It is certainly true that the quantitative effect of progress on employment is difficult to assess. The technological revolution, which creates jobs through the development of new sectors and the preservation of older ones, also destroys jobs, through the automation of certain activities.

By 1990, twenty percent of mass production will be carried out by automatic assembly machines, eliminating many industrial tasks, especially the most tiresome. Tertiary activities such as banking and insurance will also be affected. On the whole, several million jobs could be destroyed by 1990 in the industrialized countries alone.

We must therefore devise the means to manage this transformation, to make sure that technology will not destroy jobs at a faster rate than it can create them. We must reduce the period necessary for that unavoidable transition.

If we are prepared, the new technologies will induce the creation of as many jobs, if not more, than they eliminate, not only by the production of new industrial goods, but also by related services (marketing, engineering, consulting, training, leisure activities, etc.), provided we succeed in organizing them, and through the repercussions which they undoubtedly will have in sectors such as metallurgy, iron and steel, mechanical engineering and chemicals.

Therefore the problem we face is the orderly and rapid substitution of new jobs for old. I shall make a number of suggestions about this matter.

This substitution cannot be only quantitative. It will be accompanied by sweeping changes in the substance and organization of work. It will impart a new meaning to the reduction of the workweek. An economic, social and cultural need, this reduction will become one of the instruments of economic policy, a counterpart to the gains in productivity.

We know that the risks of a loss in professional qualifications, of a uniformization of the tasks, of isolation, are worrying the workers, and these fears are quite well-founded. Should we fail to elucidate the means by which our societies will adapt to the technological transformations, we risk keeping our nations in a state of chilled rejection of progress, as shown by the slowdown in our investments.

This is why we must invest together in anything that affects the work environment and the adaptation of knowledge, in order that social progress can accompany technological progress.

In this perspective, I feel that each of us should observe three guidelines.

—Sustaining demand to stimulate the growth of markets for the new consumer goods and services incorporating these technological advances.

—Stabilizing interest rates and exchange rates. I shall not dwell on this, because this will be the essential subject of the rest of our discussions.

—A greater effort for professional training and mobility. The organization and content of work will, as I have said, be determined by the spread of new technologies. The practice of several occupations during a working life will be one of the salient features of our future societies.

On this level, however, nothing has yet been accomplished. In the most developed countries, the growth of the number of trained engineers and specialists has declined considerably. In 1980, public and private professional training expenditures failed to account for even one percent of our joint Gross National Product. What seemed adequate in a context of sustained expansion and of steady work organization is now unsuitable for organizing the mobility of the work force and the spread of knowledge.

This effort is a prerequisite for the undertaking and acceptance of progress by all the working categories.

Without this immense training effort, from which wage-earners of every sector, of every age group, men and women alike, from the top to the bottom of the scale of professional qualifications, must benefit, only a select few will be able to understand and influence the world, at the cost of a prodigal waste of the creative capacities of the rest.

We must therefore launch a vigorous policy of training and adaptation of our know-how.

The content of work will change qualitatively and quantitatively, in the direction of improved working conditions, provided we develop the means to achieve this, especially by furthering and developing cooperative action with the workers and their organizations.

This movement is only feasible if education, culture and the environment accompany scientific and economic progress, by giving it a soul, a plan, a meaning.

2. Stimulating the Dynamics of Industry.

The basic foundations exist. It is becoming possible to overcome the recession, to staunch the loss of productivity, and to open new markets.

—In 1990, the central activities in the technological revolution (integrated circuits, office automation, robotics, new telematics applications, new mass consumer goods, space, biological engineering, offshore [sic], energy and new materials) will treble their relative share of production in our countries.

—Simultaneously, the high technology industries (telecommunications, aerospace, medical and pharmaceutical products, energy, chemicals, transport) will account for nearly a third of the industrial production of the Seven. They will constitute an important growth factor, together with all the activities involved in the operation or utilization of the goods and services produced by these sectors (training, research and development, marketing, planning, etc.).

—The rapid automation of industrial production should help to achieve productivity gains of over ten percent per year. These gains are a prerequisite for the success of anti-inflationist policies.

—To accomplish this, the conditions for a new industrial dynamism must be satisfied: an investment effort and guaranteed competition.

(a) Revitalizing the industrial investment effort.

Whereas the so-called austerity policies hinder technological progress by discouraging long-term investments that generate new demand, we must now respond to the technological revolution by encouraging private and public industrial investments.

—We have to bring about an unprecedented mobilization of capital for industry and research; this investment effort will mean a very large additional annual levy on the available resources of the international capital market. Our monetary and financial markets will have to comply. It is therefore essential for international interest rates to be reasonable in order to allow this investment to take place, and for our exchange rates to be stabilized by cooperation between the chief currencies, so that an orderly international monetary system can be rebuilt. This matter will certainly occupy our discussions, and we shall deal with it again this afternoon.

—Owing to their scale and the fact that they can rely on a national plan, public investments and contracts (communications, transport, energy) will play a driving role. We shall exchange our points of view and can set up a cooperative scheme on this subject.

(b) Ensuring competition.

Competition is an essential factor for growth and technical progress. However, the problems it will raise are quite different from those with which we are familiar today.

In the field of biotechnologies, for example, since more than one-third of products are manufactured by firms enjoying a world monopoly, the imbalance will become more pronounced.

Similarly, in the field of advanced electronics, eight firms control seventy percent of the integrated circuits market. This concentration is to be intensified.

Technological innovations are nevertheless essentially produced by small and medium-sized companies, and this is a good thing. But they fit into an increasingly complex production system, and since the traditional conditions of competition are altered, the flow of trade becomes a source of greater stresses, and power relationships between companies, between regions of the world, and between markets, are exacerbated. We must consider this matter closely, and I shall volunteer a number of proposals for action.

3. Fighting Against North–South Imbalances.

The latest technological discoveries must serve the nations of the South. Like the biotechnologies, which I dealt with earlier, they will help materially to reduce their energy and food dependence.

We certainly cannot hide the fact that they will also raise new dangers in these countries, generating other forms of instability and dependence.

Biotechnologies, for example, will develop substitutes for traditional raw materials and energies, incurring the risk of aggravating the condition of poor commodity-producing countries. The development of new materials, and the future mining of polymetallic nodules (cobalt, nickel, manganese, copper), in the absence of a fair distribution of the seabed, will threaten counties which are heavily dependent on ore exports. We must therefore accelerate the transfer of technologies to the countries of the South, while perfecting the organization of world markets.

We must consider not only the means to transfer our technologies to them by suitably adapting them, but also the creation of conditions to encourage the development of technologies that focus directly on their own realities; it is on this condition that the independent development of their agriculture, their industry and their services is possible.

Lastly, although it is in the interest of the industrialized nations for the immense markets of the countries of the South to open up to the technological revolution, science and technology must provide these countries with the conditions for survival in dignity: by protecting and mobilizing their natural resources and their environment; by boosting national energy output; by halting the spread of untillable zones; by stopping the disap-

165

pearance of plant and animal species and soil depletion; and by fighting against the dramatic causes and effects of an urban concentration which is accelerating at an unprecedented rate.

To achieve this, the resources of the multilateral agencies for aid to technological research must be oriented towards the needs of the South.

I shall suggest the means to enable the countries of the South to accommodate new technologies.

In brief, it is possible for us to make use of scientific and technological research for the full and global utilization of the common heritage of the nations of the North and South.

4. Overcoming Isolationist Temptations.

As world trade slows down, products incorporating high technology are occupying a growing share of this trade. We must overcome this contradiction.

Technical progress will offer new opportunities for trade. However, the very nature of high technology products affords protectionism new forms of expression (standards, licensing procedures). Technological development as a whole could, in the short term, trigger withdrawal and isolationism, which oppose the medium-term interests of all countries. It is essential to cooperate to guarantee that protectionism will not eventually triumph.

5. Building a New Civilization.

A new civilization begins at the point where the greater availability of resources serves to liberate mankind from the twofold constraint of time and distance, affecting interchange and communication. The interrelationship of networks will lead the most diverse societies to communicate with each other, to know and to understand each other better.

The impact of new technologies on urban civilization is still unclear. We shall ensure that the expansion of the means of transport, the proliferation and interdependence of information systems, the laying of cable networks and the implementation of new housing techniques, will make the cities more attractive for all and break the isolation of the countryside.

Herein lies the great adventure, because in the absence of a powerful current of interchange and communication, all cultures and languages will be threatened with uniformity.

In actual fact, communications are becoming more concentrated in all countries. A handful of firms have taken possession of the electronic distribution infrastructures. By dominating them, they influence the traditional media, cinema, press and television. The major part of the new activities in which most of the firms are engaged (information production, storage and processing) implies very large investments, and therefore encourages intense concentration. Already, the two leading image banks supply nearly all the television stations worldwide, more than three quarters of all press news is supplied by five agencies. If this natural tendency spreads further, by the end of the decade it will mean the control of the world communication industry by some twenty firms.

By cooperating, we can prevent the accumulation and processing of information by a small number of firms and nations possessing the most highly and rapidly developed processing and storage systems.

More generally speaking, the dissemination of information processed and largely controlled by a small number of dominant countries could cause the rest to lose their memory and sovereignty, thus jeopardizing their freedom of thought and decision.

This is why I should like us to reflect on a possible Charter of Communication.

PROPOSALS FOR A CONCERTED DEVELOPMENT OF THE WORLD ECONOMY

What remains for us to do? I would like for us to reflect on a comprehensive set of measures capable of rapidly implementing the principles I have just outlined, for each of our countries individually, and as a group.

I do not ask that you decide upon such a set of measures today, but that at least this indispensable joint action be launched in the coming year.

Barring this, each one of us will withdraw into himself, trade conflicts will worsen, and protectionist practices will establish themselves. No one has anything to gain by this.

The past bears witness to the reality of these dangers. The first phase of each of the two previous industrial revolutions in the West was characterized by rising unemployment, protectionism, and inflation.

During a second phase, in the better prepared countries, the social forces of change prevailed; growth and stability returned, and investment rose.

Today, if we are not careful, we run the risk of witnessing the same sequence of events; the new industrial revolution has already begun to intensify unemployment, inflation, financial problems and inequalities. This trend may last if we do not decide to put an end to it.

Not one of us, despite the differences of opinion dividing us, can resign himself to this. We are all responsible for ensuring that the transition is carried out as soon as possible. We are equipped to do so, as we can anticipate and organize change, and coordinate the transformation. It is for this reason that I wished to approach this subject with you.

I propose:

—that we launch a concerted programme of selective growth through technology;

—that we grant equal priority to employment and working conditions;

—that together we foster the fulfillment of cultures.

First Proposal: Launching a Concerted Programme of Growth Through Technology.

The broad field of action open to us may be organized into six major branches:

1. Global targets: fixing them in percentage of GNP for 1985 and 1990 and exchanging our views on national research and development policies, completing this action, if necessary, with sectoral objectives and drawing upon work already completed by international institutions such as the OECD.

2. Setting a few priority measures for technological cooperation between private and public companies and between nations, in the following areas requiring heavy initial investment: new energy sources, telecommunications, robotics, new materials, composite materials, electronics, artificial intelligence, space, biotechnologies and agricultural technologies specifically designed for the Third World.

   An Implementation Committee could be appointed for each project adopted, which would include relevant public agencies from the participating countries. A minimal financial contribution from each country would be established.

3. Innovation should be stepped up in all of its forms by determining useful procedures. This should entail the creation of new firms, cooperation between firms in different countries and the framing of joint policies in opposition to monopolistic practices and to hindrances to competition.

4. Establishing gradually a world technology market (standards, patents).

5. Taking a number of joint initiatives in order to enable the countries of the South to master new technologies. Increasing research and development in areas of particular interest to these countries, essentially education, training, nutrition and health, within the framework of co-development agreements; creating research centres and promoting research personnel exchanges; ensuring the growth of national energy sources through specialized subsidiaries of the World Bank. Finally, the implementation of the guidelines established by the United Nations Conference on Science and Technology for Development will be accelerated.

6. Finally, we should stabilize as quickly as possible the international monetary system, the impredictability of which is curbing investment. In order to achieve this, we have to search for the ways and means of reinforcing a balanced monetary cooperation between the three monetary poles—Europe, America, and Japan—with a view to returning to stable and economically correct exchange rates.

Preparation for this programme could be based on the methods already used in different cooperation formulae: the setting up of networks of research centers allowing for wide distribution of information (weather, environmental and oceanographic data), the establishment of common rules and standards, bilateral action within the framework of a multilateral program (international telecommunications development program, world weather program) and "custom-built" project models (Unesco science programs).

Second Proposal: Placing Technology at the Service of Employment and of Working Conditions.

1. By establishing a vast training system designed to manage the job transformations which I discussed, in order to speed up

the transition of the industrial revolution. To this end, we should:

—Begin in 1983, in each of our countries, using our own methods, a specific system for training in the new technologies, such as data processing, biology and the new jobs (telecommunications, biological sciences, engineering, leisure activities), in the following three directions:

—priority for the training of engineers and specialists;

—training programs for the young jobless aged 16 to 18;

—a program for the conversion of workers in mid-career to the new technologies.

—Request the OECD to prepare, in the forthcoming six months, a special exchange and cooperation program concerning training and conversion methods.

—Request the International Labour Organisation to set up an observation post to follow the evolution of the occupations concerned with the new technologies.

2. We must also draw on the new technologies to improve living and working conditions. I suggest the following:

—To intensify cooperation and research on the organization and conditions of work associated with the new technologies, and on the effects of the new technologies on the duration of the workweek and its possible reduction.

—To set up, prior to the next Summit, a program to evaluate the experiments—both positive and negative—conducted in the cities, and the effects of the technological changes on urban living patterns, pertaining to cabled cities, new modes of transport and housing.

Third proposal: Fostering Together the Fulfillment of Cultures.

I suggest directing our efforts at three matters:

1. The School.

The computer revolution is gradually working its way back to the wellsprings of education, to the earliest years of schooling. While they maintain their standard traditions, our teaching systems are in for some rude shocks, and this implies hopes and fears. To cope with these transformations, we should:

—mount a joint effort in order to develop new teaching systems adapted to each country, and elucidate together the means to enable our school systems to keep pace with their environment;

—develop a family of simple data-processing languages for worldwide use;

—act jointly to expand the use of computers in the classroom, in order to familiarize young people very rapidly with the tools of their future everyday life and with the requirements of their future jobs.

2. Communication and Language.

The development of teaching and research in the field of

linguistics and communication is indispensable to withstand the powerful trend towards uniformity which I discussed earlier. We could do the following:

—Set up, within the United Nations University, a world network linking all the teaching, training and research centers devoted to languages and communication. This network should facilitate the development of the following activities in the different countries concerned: the study of languages, the elevation of the role of national languages in the spread of technologies, the proliferation of multilingual computer glossaries, the setting up of programs of mechanical translation for languages other than the major ones, and the training of specialists in communication.

—Compile a great encyclopedia of all the cultures of the world. It is conceivable today to create the tools for the mass dissemination of cultures, even isolated ones. For each nation, this means gathering together all the essential components of its cultural identity or identities. Apart from books, the means of dissemination could be:

—one or more satellites, placed under the control of Unesco, designed for regional television broadcasts;

—a major computer center, such as that of the European Space Agency, which could be the server of a bibliographic data base that could be consulted via the world's leading telematics networks.

3. Charter of Communication.

I feel that negotiations should be carried out in stages, in the international bodies concerned, for the preparation of a World

Charter of Communication, which is so difficult nowadays. The Charter could be based on five principles:

—affirming the respect for the diversity of languages;

—promoting the harmonization of legislations governing information, intellectual property, contract law and the protection of individual liberties;

—instigating the determination of common rules for international data exchanges;

—protecting the sovereignty of States and their cultural integrity, which is threatened by the new technologies;

—guaranteeing the countries of the South the means to control their communications and the messages of which they are the vehicles.

4. A World Exhibition "For a Present Image of the Future."

This would illustrate the role of technological development in bringing nations closer together. France would be ready to organize this exhibition in 1989.

Before concluding, I should like to clarify the conditions for the joint implementation of the proposals that I have presented to you:

—we will set up a working group of eight personalities immediately after this Summit, with the mission of identifying a number of priorities based on the proposals contained in this report and on your discussions;

—the group would work in consultation with the competent international institutions, including the OECD, and would be required to prepare a report, by the end of this year;

—the report's conclusions and the resulting projects would be examined at the next Summit of the industrialized countries, to be held in 1983 in the United States of America.

If, through our concerted action, we succeed in launching these projects, will we have resolved the problems facing our societies? Certainly not. Technological progress does not in itself ensure economic and social progress. It can only contribute to the resolution of these problems in those societies able to incorporate it into coherent policy. Much remains to be done in order to re-establish balanced and equitable growth, and in order to abolish misery and servitude in all of their guises. We must rebuild a stable monetary system, provide low-cost financing for companies, devise equitable economic and political relations between continents, and do away with all trade barriers. Finally, and most importantly, we must make it possible for each individual to freely use the time made available to him by progress.

We will in this way have accomplished our role as leaders.

Each individual will thus have more material means at his disposal to live the human experience as he sees fit. The human experience: both limited and exalting, incomplete and grandiose, fleeting and eternal.

For our part, by tackling the problems that beset us, and finding rapid solutions to them, we will have secured for our nations the most important element of all: self-confidence.

SOURCE: France, Ministère des relations extérieures, Service d'information et de presse, *France Information* 117 (1982): insert.

DECLARATION A LA PRESSE
DE M. LE PRESIDENT DE LA REPUBLIQUE
[FRANÇAISE] A L'ISSUE DU SOMMET DES PAYS
INDUSTRIALISES
6 juin 1982

La conférence au sommet des sept pays conviés à Versailles avec les représentants des Communautés européennes a tenu ses séances de travail et vient de les achever par l'adoption d'une déclaration.

Cette déclaration a, bien entendu, été adoptée par tous et représente donc un consentement général. Ce document vous sera distribué, si ce n'est déjà fait, dans les langues correspondantes, et pour vos travaux de commentateurs, vous pourrez les consulter et vous reporter au texte lui-même afin d'en apprécier la teneur.

Nous sommes venus ici vous rencontrer, chefs d'Etat, chefs de gouvernement, autorités des Communautés européennes, non pas pour engager un dialogue—cela sera fait par chacun d'entre nous devant la presse qui souhaiterait nous entendre—mais vous faire comprendre par la déclaration que je fais devant vous, que je vous adresse et au-delà à ceux qui, dans mon pays et dans les autres, nous entendent, que ce sommet s'est déroulé dans un climat de travail, de coopération, de compréhension et, je crois pouvoir le dire, de relations d'amitié indispensables pour qui dispose d'une responsabilité aussi étendue que la nôtre.

Nous avons successivement examiné les problèmes que vous savez, inscrits à l'ordre du jour—nous sommes restés fidèles à l'ordre du jour—lors des séances plénières. Nous avons étudié ce que l'on appelle l'état du monde, certaines zones sensibles où se jouent la paix et la guerre, nous avons étudié les relations entre l'Est et l'Ouest, nous avons étudié les relations entre le Nord et le Sud et nous avons débattu des problèmes qui nous sont propres, problèmes économiques, financiers, commerciaux touchant particuliérement aux domaines de la monnaie et du commerce.

A l'intérieur de ces discussions, de nombreux points ont été précisés. Par exemple, dans les relations entre l'Est et l'Ouest, la manière dont nous concevons le déroulement des relations commerciales; par exemple, lorsque dans les relations Nord–Sud, nous envisageons la relance prochaine des négociations globales, nous précisons, comme nous l'avons toujours fait, que doivent être préservés les droits, les obligations des institutions spécialisées. Mais enfin, tout cela vous le trouverez au détour de ce texte.

Sur chacun des points examinés en séance plénière, l'accord a été obtenu de telle sorte que les textes dans les différentes langues, ont été exactement précisés afin qu'aucune interprétation divergente ne puisse prévaloir.

J'ai dit que notre souci principal, sur le plan économique, était de parvenir à harmoniser nos actions dans la lutte contre l'inflation, dans la lutte contre le chômage et pour le développement de la croissance. A cette fin, nous nous imposons un certain nombre de règles ou de lignes de conduite. Nous ne voulons pas que l'attitude de l'un puisse nuire aux autres, et nous avons besoin de coopérer pour réussir ensemble.

Nous n'avons pas prétendu décider pour les autres, c'est-à-dire pour ceux qui ne participaient pas au sommet; cela n'était pas dans notre esprit ni dans nos intentions, mais nous connaissions l'importance de nos choix et nous avons veillé à ce que ces choix s'inscrivent dans un développement de progrès pour tous et dans la finalité et le respect des principes de la paix.

Nous n'avons d'intentions agressives à l'égard de personne. Nous voulons protéger ce que nous appelons certaines valeurs de civilisation qui nous sont communes et, particulièrement, sur le plan des régimes politiques, les traditions, les moeurs et les institutions démocratiques qui caractérisent les pays participant à cette réunion.

En dehors des séances plénières, nous avons beaucoup discuté, échangé nos points de vue lors des repas qui étaient, certes des repas amicaux, mais aussi des repas de travail et nous avons occupé nos soirées à nous entretenir de tous les problèmes qui sollicitent notre attention. Aucun n'était interdit. Ce qui est le propre de ce type de réunion, c'est que les chefs d'Etat et de gouvernement ainsi que les représentants des Communautés font prévaloir le dialogue direct, l'échange de vues sur le côté rituel ou rigoureux des ordres du jour des assemblées internationales ou des confrontations administratives.

ILES MALOUINES

C'est ainsi que nous avons abordé, dès le premier soir, la préoccupante affaire, disons les actes de guerre des Falklands dus malheureusement à l'initiative violente de l'Argentine qui a entraîné toute une série de conséquences dans la logique de cette situation. Et nous avons à nouveau répété notre condamnation des initiatives ou instigations violentes préférées par certains à la discussion dans le cadre des règles internationales, d'où notre soutien à la résolution 502 du Conseil de sécurité et notre souhait de voir, le plus tôt qu'il sera possible, triompher un cessez-le-feu, c'est-à-dire les termes d'un armistice s'appliquant à l'ensemble du conflit ou plutôt à l'ensemble des deux pays directement en cause.

Mais, nous avons tenu à affirmer notre solidarité entière à l'égard de la Grande-Bretagne agressée en la circonstance dans ses intérêts nationaux et dans sa fierté nationale, solidarité qui est naturelle, la Grande-Bretagne doit retrouver son droit étant entendu que nous ferons tout pour que, ce droit reconnu, la paix l'emporte sur la guerre.

LIBAN

Nous avons évoqué l'affaire du Liban qui est intervenue pendant la durée de notre conférence. Un texte a été diffusé. Ce texte a été élaboré et adopté, à peine savions-nous les premiers déroulements de cette affaire. Il n'a donc pas l'intention de recouvrir les événements qui se déroulent actuellement sinon qu'il y a intervention des armées israéliennes sur le sol du Liban et que ce pays, le Liban, a droit comme tout autre à l'indépendance, à la liberté, à l'unité et à sa souveraineté sur son territoire national, souveraineté bafouée souvent et par beaucoup, mais en la circonstance, de telle sorte que nous avons marqué notre réprobation vigoureuse des événements en question.

Quant au corps du texte, je l'ai là, vous ne l'avez pas tous, et comme nous n'en discuterons pas, ceci n'est pas une conférence de presse, mais une déclaration, c'est à l'intérieur des autres conférences de presse que l'on pourra entrer dans le vif du sujet, répondre à vos questions, dialoguer avec vous.

Nous avons voulu procéder de la sorte, qui est un peu différente de celle d'Ottawa, pour éviter déclarations successives un peu artificielles, c'est la loi du genre, et qui n'apportaient pas grand chose au débat.

Comme ce n'était pas non plus un concours d'éloquence, à quoi cela servait-il?

Nous avons donc décidé de confier au Président du sommet le soin de faire, devant la presse, la déclaration terminale, c'est ce que je fais au nom du sommet et en ma qualité de président, achevant son mandat, du sommet de Versailles. Il n'y aura donc pas d'autre déclaration que celle que j'énonce.

J'avais pris le relais du Premier ministre du Canada, M. Pierre Elliot Trudeau, je le repasse à M. le Président des Etats-Unis d'Amérique puisque c'est dans son pays que se tiendra le sommet de 1983.

Je dois dire, avant d'en terminer, qu'en tant que président, mais plutôt alors cette fois-ci faisant prévaloir ma qualité de Français et de Président de la République française, je me suis réjouis de pouvoir me concerter avec les chefs d'Etat et de gouvernement des principaux pays alliés et amis, de pouvoir entretenir la même nature de liens avec les Communautés européennes, de leur offrir l'hospitalité que nous avons essayé de leur rendre agréable. Nous avons le sentiment d'avoir avancé.

C'est aussi un appel au progrès, au développement, à la capacité pour nos sociétés de maîtriser la situation difficile dans laquelle nous sommes . . . pas nous, le monde entier!

Nous sommes assurés que notre responsabilité, nous sommes capables de l'assumer; c'est l'impression qui domine dans mon esprit, au moment où j'achève mon mandat. Mais je le répète, en tant que Français, cela a été, c'est encore, pour nous, un honneur que d'avoir reçu et que de recevoir les représentants des peuples amis, comme de recevoir en ce moment la presse internationale qui, je l'espère, s'est estimée en mesure de faire correctement son travail et qui, sans aucun doute, nous a beaucoup honorés en retransmettant avec beaucoup de célérité et, j'espère aussi, d'exactitude, l'ensemble de nos travaux.

Je n'ai rien d'autre à ajouter. Cette image derrière cette tribune sera donc éphémère; il y a peu de chance qu'elle se reconstitue d'ici quelque temps, sinon dans d'autres lieux, c'est-à-dire aux Etats-Unis d'Amérique où nous nous rendrons avec plaisir et intérêt l'année prochaine. Je vous remercie.

SOURCE: France, Ministère des Relations extérieures, *La Politique étrangère de la France: textes et documents, avril–mai–juin 1982* (Paris: La Documentation française, 1982), pp. 122–24.

[TRANSLATION]
PRESIDENT MITTERAND'S STATEMENT TO THE PRESS AT THE CONCLUSION OF THE VERSAILLES SUMMIT

6 June 1982

We, Heads of State, Heads of Government and Authorities of the European Communities, have come to meet you here, not in order to engage in a dialogue but to let it be known by this statement I am making to you—and to those who in my country and the other countries are listening to us—that this Summit has taken place in an atmosphere of work, cooperation, understanding and, I think I can say, of the relations of friendship essential for anyone bearing such broad responsibilities as we do.

We examined successively the problems which you know to be on the agenda—we kept to the agenda—during the plenary meetings. We examined what is called the state of the world, certain sensitive areas where war and peace are at stake, we studied the relations between East and West, we studied the relations between North and South, and we discussed problems specific to ourselves, economic, financial and commercial problems affecting in particular the areas of currency and trade.

During the discussions many points were cleared up. For example, in regard to East–West relations the manner in which we conceive the development of trade relations; for example, in North–South relations, when we envisage the early launching of global negotiations, we specify, as we have always done, that the rights and obligations of the specialized agencies must be preserved. However, all that you will find in a reading of the text itself.

On each of the points examined at the plenary meetings agreement was arrived at in such a way that the texts in the different languages were made with complete precision so that there can be no divergent interpretation of them.

I said that our main economic concern was to succeed in coordinating our action in the combat against inflation, in the combat against unemployment and for promoting growth. To that end we are imposing on ourselves a number of rules or lines of conduct. We are against anyone's behaving in a manner that is detrimental to others, to succeed together we must cooperate with one another.

We did not presume to take decisions for others, that is for those who were not participating in the Summit; nothing could have been further from our minds, but we were aware of the importance of our options and saw to it that these options were in line with the fostering of progress for all and wholly consonant with respect for the principles of peace as the ultimate objective.

We have no aggressive intentions against anyone. We want to safeguard certain common values of civilization, as we call them, and especially, as regards political systems, to preserve the democratic traditions, practices and institutions that are characteristics of the countries participating in this meeting.

Outside the plenary sessions, we discussed many things and exchanged our points of view during meals which, to be sure, were friendly occasions, but at the same time working dinners; and we spent all our evenings discussing all those problems that required our attention. No problem was taboo. The thing that is distinctive about a meeting of this kind is that it provides the Heads of State and Government and Representatives of the [European] Communities with a special opportunity for engaging in direct dialogue and an exchange of views outside of the ceremonial constraints of the agendas of international assemblies or business meetings.

THE FALKLANDS

It was in this spirit that from the first evening we tackled the alarming event, that of the act of war in the Falklands due unfortunately to the violent action initiated by Argentina which resulted in a chain of consequences that grew naturally out of that situation. And we reiterated our condemnation of the violent actions or incitements to violence that were preferred by some to discussion within the framework of international procedures, whence our support of resolution 502 of the Security Council and our desire to see as soon as possible the conclusion of a cease-fire, that is, armistice terms applicable to the conflict or, rather, to the two countries directly involved.

But we wished to make a point of affirming our full solidarity with Great Britain whose national interests and national pride have been violated, such solidarity being natural. Great Britain's rights must be preserved, it being understood that we shall do all we can to ensure that, while these rights are recognized, peace proves stronger than war.

LEBANON

We have discussed the situation which developed in Lebanon during the Conference. A text has been distributed. This text was drawn up and adopted almost immediately after we heard of the beginning of the affair. It does not therefore cover the events taking place now—except that since the Israeli forces have intervened on Lebanese soil and that this country, Lebanon, like every other country, has the right to independence, freedom, unity and sovereignty over its national territory, sovereignty which is often flouted, and by many, but in the circumstances in such a way that we have made known our strong disapproval of what is taking place.

As for the text itself, I have it here, you have not all got it, and since we shall not be discussing it, it is not a press communiqué but a statement, it is in other press conferences that we could go into this subject in details [sic], reply to your questions and discuss it with you.

We have adopted the procedure we are now following, a little different from that of Ottawa, to avoid having eight consecutive somewhat artificial statements as used to be the case and which added little to our proceedings.

Since it was not a contest of eloquence either, what purpose did it serve?

We have therefore decided to entrust the task of making the

183

final statement to the press to the President of the Conference. And that is what I am now doing on behalf of the Summit in my capacity as President, on completing my term of office, of the Versailles Summit. Mine will therefore be the only statement.

I took up this office after the Prime Minister of Canada, Mr. Pierre Elliot Trudeau, and I shall be ceding it to the President of the United States of America, since the 1983 Summit is to be held in his country.

Before concluding, I should like to say, in my capacity as President, but this time speaking more as a Frenchman and the President of the French Republic, that I greatly appreciated the opportunity of consulting the Heads of State and Government of our principal allied and friendly countries, of having similar links with the European Communities and of extending our hospitality, which we have done our best to make enjoyable, to them. We have the impression that we have moved forward.

This Conference is also an appeal for progress, for development, for our societies to be able to control the difficult situation we are in—not that we are in, but that the whole world is in!

We are aware of our responsibility, we are capable of shouldering it—that is my dominant impression when I am on the point of completing my term of office. But I must repeat that, as a Frenchman, it has been and still is an honor for us to have welcomed and to welcome the representatives of friendly peoples, as it is at the moment to welcome the international press which, I hope, found itself in a position to carry out its work in satisfactory conditions and which has certainly greatly honored us by transmitting very rapidly and, I also hope, correctly all our discussions.

I have nothing else to add. The image behind this tribune [sic] will therefore be ephemeral. There is very little chance that it will appear again for some time, if not in another place, that is to say the United States of America, where we shall go with pleasure and interest next year.

Thank you very much.

SOURCE: France, Ministère des relations extérieures, Service d'information et de presse, *France Information* 117 (1982): 30–31.

CONFÉRENCE DE PRESSE
DE M. LE PRÉSIDENT DE LA REPUBLIQUE
[FRANÇAISE] A L'ISSUE DU SOMMET DES PAYS
INDUSTRIALISES
6 juin 1982

Nous allons, si vous le voulez bien, commencer cette conférence de presse qui a été précédée comme vous le savez d'une déclaration que j'ai faite en ma qualité de président du sommet des pays industrialisés, qui se bornait à une déclaration unilatérale sans discussion, sans dialogue. Je m'exprimais au nom des huit, mais je n'ai pu entrer dans le détail des discussions. C'est l'occasion, ce n'est pas une invite à ce qu'on ne discute plus qu'il ne faut, ce n'est pas un encouragement, ce n'est pas une incitation à la débauche de dialogue, car je ne dispose au maximum que de 3/4 d'heure, mais je me contenterai de deux quarts d'heure, si vous le voulez bien, cela dépend de vous.

Quels sont les textes?

Une déclaration.

Cette déclaration s'appelle «déclaration des 7 chefs d'Etat et de gouvernement, et des représentants des Communautés européennes». Vous savez de quoi il s'agit.

Cette déclaration, qui touche à beaucoup de sujets, est suivie d'une pièce jointe qui s'appelle: «engagement monétaire international».

Un autre texte, mais qui a déjà été diffusé et qui n'est pas lié à celui-ci, porte sur le Liban. Vous devez le connaître.

D'autres questions n'ont pas fait l'objet de communiqués, notamment l'affaire des Falklands ou Malouines; des discussions ont eu lieu entre ministres compétents, Affaires étrangères d'une part, Economie et Finances de l'autre, parfois ensemble.

Certaines des délibérations de ces réunions éclairent les textes en question. C'est le tout qui fait foi pour apprecier les résultats du sommet de Versailles.

Je vais, si vous le voulez bien, faire très rapidement l'inventaire des questions traitées dans la déclaration.

Elle commence par des affirmations générales, essentiellement centrées sur la lutte contre l'inflation et le chômage et sur
le développement de la croissance, croissance durable, sur la
nécessité de sauvegarder la sécurité du monde occidental et du
Japon, sur la confiance dans les valeurs démocratiques.

Il est bien entendu que sont menées de pair les actions pour
la lutte contre l'inflation, pour les niveaux d'emploi et pour la
croissance.

Un certain nombre de résolutions s'ensuivent, sur la croissance et l'emploi, pour réaliser ces objectifs: lutte contre
l'inflation, je viens de vous le dire, afin de faire baisser les taux
d'intérêts aujourd'hui insupportables, et de réaliser des taux de
change plus stables . . . c'est l'entrée en matière, nous en
parlerons davantage tout à l'heure.

Pour réaliser cette réduction essentielle des taux d'intérêt
élevés, la déclaration prévoit un ensemble de moyens: une
politique monétaire prudente et la maîtrise des déficits budgétaires, l'intensification de la coopération économique et monétaire, en particulier entre les monnaies d'Amérique du Nord, du
Japon et de la Communauté européenne.

Ensuite la croissance du commerce mondial; nous réaffirmons
notre engagement de renforcer le système ouvert de commerce
multilatéral représenté par le GATT et de maintenir son rôle
effectif.

Refus des mesures protectionnistes: donc l'ouverture des
marchés. Une participation active à la prochaine conférence
ministérielle, fin août ou début septembre, du GATT.

Pour en revenir aux considérations générales: nous sommes
convenus de conserver à l'égard de l'URSS [Union des répub-
liques socialistes soviétiques] et des pays de l'Europe de l'Est une
approche prudente et diversifiée compatible avec nos intérêts
politiques et de sécurité.

D'où une action dans trois secteurs clés: amélioration du
système international des exportations de biens stratégiques,
échanges d'informations économiques commerciales, financières,
gestion prudente des relations financières avec l'URSS et les
pays de l'Est, de manière à assurer qu'elles soient conduites de
façon économiquement saine en tenant compte de la prudence

que requièrent les relations commerciales, dans le cadre des relations économiques et financières en général, en limitant aussi les crédits à l'exportation, en procédant à un examen périodique du développement de ces relations, etc.

Les progrès que nous avons déjà accompli ne diminuent pas le besoin de poursuivre la politique d'économie d'énergie; là nous sommes allés plus loin que lors des conférences précédentes.

Toute une partie de la déclaration vise les pays en voie de développement, avec quelques notations majeures. Il faut maintenir un niveau élevé de flux financier d'aides publiques et même accroître leur montant et leur efficacité. Lancement de négociations globales: c'est l'objectif majeur, en référence au récent projet de résolution du groupe des 77, reconnu comme constructif. A Versailles un accord général a été atteint sur le fait que cet accord peut servir de base de consultation avec les pays du Tiers Monde.

Perspective positive pour le lancement prochain de négociations globales et leur succès, sous réserve que l'indépendance des institutions spécialisées soit garantie, thème que connaissent déjà les spécialistes mais qu'il n'était pas mauvais d'écrire noir sur blanc.

Coopération, innovation au sein de la Banque mondiale, soutien aux banques de développement régional, progrès à faire pour lutter contre l'instabilité des recettes issues des matières premières. Encouragement, parallèlement, au développement des aides publiques, encouragement aux aides et aux capitaux privés. Vous pourrez noter que nous reconnaissons également la nécessité des dispositifs temporaires spéciaux pour surmonter les problèmes de financement de l'AID [Association internationale de développement] VI et un démarrage rapide de l'AID VII.

Ceux qui sont suivi ces problèmes savent de quoi il s'agit: la plupart des pays ont réduit leur contribution à l'AID. Seuls, quelques pays ont résisté à l'entraînement: les pays scandinaves, la France et, en partie, la Grande-Bretagne vis-à-vis de pays comme l'Inde, et nous avons demandé que ces contributions maintenues puissent être gérées de façon particulière. C'est ce qui fait ici évoquer les possibilités de dispositifs temporaires spéciaux.

Production alimentaire et énergétique dans les pays en développement, balance des paiements: nous souhaitons donc vivement, pour la balance des paiements, un progrès à l'occasion de la réunion annuelle du Fonds monétaire international qui, lui, se réunit en septembre, pour régler la question de l'accroissement des quotas du Fonds.

Le dernier paragraphe exploite les propositions que j'ai été amené à faire sur le plan technologique: technologie, croissance, emploi, avec une référence explicite à mon rapport et la volonté clairement expliquée de poursuivre de façon concrète les différentes directions que j'avais proposées; un groupe de travail est déjà constitué; il devra soumettre son rapport avant le 31 décembre 1982.

Les conclusions du rapport, les actions qui en résulteront seront examinées, donc suivies, au prochain sommet, en 1983, aux Etats-Unis d'Amérique.

Enfin, pour ce qui est de l'engagement monétaire international si vous me posez des questions, je vous en donnerai lecture.

Je pense que j'ai assez monologué.

Auriez-vous l'obligeance de me poser des questions . . . pas tous à la fois. . . .

Q: A Ottawa, vous aviez considéré comme un point positif que les 7 acceptent de combattre conjointement l'inflation et le chômage. Depuis Ottawa, quels progrès avez-vous noté et, au-delà, par rapport à cette conférence, quels succès ou quels échecs, quelle avancée ou quel recul?

R: Il n'y a pas du tout de recul, il y a une avancée entre Ottawa et Versailles.

Quant à la conception selon laquelle sont liées les différentes formes de lutte contre l'inflation, contre le chômage et la solution des problèmes de croissance, sont apparues de plus en plus dans nos textes et, j'espère, dans notre action, des notions d'emploi, de plein emploi et de croissance, auparavant souvent absentes. J'ai déjà eu l'occasion de l'expliquer hier.

C'est une dispute vaine que de croire que certains veulent

lutter contre l'inflation mais pas contre le chômage, tandis que d'autres combattent le chômage et non l'inflation!

Mais, comme il s'agit des deux termes d'un couple infernal, selon qu'on met l'accent sur l'un ou sur l'autre, on semble délaisser celui qu'on ne cite pas en premier, et c'est là que s'intercalent les différences de politique, non pas quant aux objectifs—l'objectif politique d'un responsable ne peut être que la réduction de l'inflation et du chômage pour la reprise de la croissance—mais selon quel rythme?

C'est là qu'interviennent les différences: certains pays veulent écraser l'inflation, quel qu'en soit le risque du côté de l'emploi. D'autres veulent combattre l'inflation sans amonceler les décombres du côté de l'emploi.

Alors, c'est un choix difficile à faire, d'ailleurs, qui aboutit à ce que, dans certains pays, les taux d'inflation ont beaucoup baissé—c'est le cas des Etats-Unis d'Amérique, et puis c'est le cas de l'Allemagne—ils ont d'ailleurs baissé partout, mais très sensiblement tandis que le chômage s'accroît très vite. Ou bien on aboutit au cas d'un pays comme la France, dont l'inflation a baissé, mais à un rythme moins rapide que dans ceux dont j'ai parlé, mais qui a par contre considérablement limité l'accroissement continu du chômage constaté depuis huit ans, c'est-à-dire à un tassement de la courbe d'augmentation.

Nous ne sommes pas encore parvenus à renverser la tendance, c'est-à-dire à diminuer l'accroissement du chômage.

Je suis obligé de parler avec précision, pour qu'il n'y ait pas d'ambiguïté entre nous.

Donc, les résultats de l'inflation ont été plus sensibles là où l'on a moins tenu compte des problèmes de l'emploi; ils sont moins sensibles là où la priorité de la lutte contre le chômage a été reconnue dans les faits.

Mais partout l'inflation a baissé, partout le chômage a augmenté, ici il est considérablement augmenté suivant une courbe continue, ailleurs—ce qui est notre cas—la courbe a commencé à fléchir. C'est donc une indication de tendance intéressante, étant bien entendu qu'au bout du compte, seuls les pays qui seront capables de produire disposeront de l'arme déterminante contre toute forme de chômage.

Q: Monsieur le Président, vous l'avez signalé, le texte mis au point par les Sept sur le Liban l'a été avant que l'on connaisse les derniers développements.

On vient de signaler l'approche de deux brigades syriennes dans la zone des combats.

Est-ce que, depuis le communiqué qui a été lu dernièrement, il y a eu un nouveau communiqué des Sept, une nouvelle déclaration des Sept, et quelles vont être les actions de la France dans cette région?

R: Nous sommes, à l'évidence, dans une situation constamment évolutive. L'action des troupes israéliennes au Liban, se dirigeant dans deux directions différentes, en particulier le long de la côte, et dans la zone contrôlée par la Syrie, n'était sans doute pas faite pour s'arrêter tout aussitôt. A compter du moment où elle se poursuit, les développements sont, eux aussi, continus et nous ne pouvons pas publier un communiqué par quart d'heure.

Par contre, et vous avez eu raison de le dire, il y a des événements repères, et, autant on peut déplorer, nous déplorons et je le déplore, l'intervention israélienne sur le territoire du Liban, pays qui, en dépit de ses déchirements, reste un pays souverain, autant nous déplorons et donc nous reprochons, le choix de la violence comme moyen de résoudre le problème en question, autant nous savons bien que c'est un événement nouveau si un tiers pays est amené à intervenir.

Mais, vous me le dites . . . moi, je ne le savais pas au moment où je m'exprime. Je savais qu'il y avait des mouvements de troupes à l'intérieur de la Syrie, je n'avais pas encore entendu parler de mouvements à l'extérieur de la Syrie. Je me contenterai donc de commenter cet événement, s'il se produit, quand il se sera produit.

Les chefs d'Etat et de gouvernement seront réunis, non pas en séance, mais quand même réunis, à Versailles, jusqu'à 21 h, 22 h, pour Mme Thatcher, et 23 h, 23 h 30 pour les autres; nous aurons encore le temps, s'il le faut, de réagir à un événement de ce calibre.

Pour le reste, je le répète, malheureusement ce n'est qu'une évolution prévisible dans les relations directes d'Israël et du Liban.

Q: Monsieur le Président, à ce propos, quels sont les moyens à la disposition de la France auxquels vous àvez fait allusion à la fin de la déclaration lorsqu'il est dit que chaque pays se réserve d'utiliser les moyens à sa disposition pour rétablir la paix et la sécurité?

Est-ce que vous en avez parlé à sept? Quels sont les moyens de la France?

R: Non, non. . . . Les moyens de la France sont de plusieurs ordres. Ils sont de l'ordre diplomatique, avec le rôle de la France dans le domaine international. Nous sommes membres du Conseil de sécurité, nous avons donc une responsabilité particulière dans le cadre de l'Organisation des Nations unies. Là, nous pouvons agir conformément à nos conceptions, qui ont toujours tendu, vous le savez, à défendre l'intégrité d'Israël, et qui ont également toujours tendu à reconnaître le droit des autres à disposer d'une patrie, enfin à la solution pacifique du conflit et non pas à sa résolution violente.

Nous pouvons adapter constamment, par nos actions au sein des Nations unies, notre pratique à cette définition.

Et puis, sur le terrain, la France n'est pas mêlée en tant que telle aux événements du Liban. Elle y est représentée par des soldats, mais ces soldats ne sont pas sous commandement français, ils sont là en tant qu'éléments d'une force internationale. C'est donc une question qu'il faut poser aux Nations unies et non pas à la France.

La présence de soldats français signifie quoi?

D'une part, que la France est presque toujours volontaire lorsqu'il s'agit de remplir une mission pacifique dans le cadre des Nations unies.

Cela veut dire ensuite que le problème du Liban nous intéresse au premier chef, car il y a des relations traditionnelles d'amitié entre le Liban et la France.

Mais, c'est le point sur lequel j'insiste, nous ne voulons pas, nous n'avons pas l'intention de nous substituer à la décision souveraine du Liban lui-même, qui dispose d'un gouvernement légitime. Il appartient à ce gouvernement de prendre les initiatives, de faire les démarches, que nous examinerons si elles nous sont faites. Nous n'avons pas du tout d'intention interventionniste. Nous voulons simplement—le Premier ministre l'a dit au cours d'un voyage récent à Beyrouth—que le Liban sache que la France fait partie du cercle des pays amis, mais est respectueuse avant tout de la souveraineté de ce pays.

Q: Monsieur le Président, vous avez dit tout à l'heure au Palais des congrès que la déclaration commune avait été rédigée de telle façon qu'elle ne pouvait pas prêter à des interprétations divergentes.

Alors, vous pourriez sans doute nous aider à dissiper une double ambiguïté qui a régné dans cette conférence depuis deux jours.

La première concerne les affaires monétaires. La délégation française, par la bouche des différents ministres qui ont pris la parole, peut-être par vous-mêmes, avait dit que le principe d'intervention sur le marché, avait été accepté d'un commun accord. Les Américains, eux disent: oui, intervention dans le cas de mouvements erratiques—«disorderly conditions»—et ils ajoutent: ceci est conforme à notre doctrine constante, conforme aussi à l'article 4 du Fonds monétaire, donc rien de fondamentalement nouveau dans notre disposition, ajoutant même que le groupe d'étude qui doit se réunir devra trancher la question de savoir s'il faut intervenir plus ou moins.

Par conséquent, la question reste ouverte.

Le deuxième malentendu portait sur l'affaire du commerce avec l'Est, la délégation française insistant surtout sur le fait que la déclaration ne comporte pas de restriction particulière à l'octroi de crédits, alors que les Américains insistent sur le fait qu'il est fait état de limitations—«to limit», je crois que le verbe a le même sens en anglais et en français—à l'octroi des crédits.

Pourriez-vous, sur ces deux points, nous éclairer?

R: D'abord, moi, je sais généralement ce que je dis, et je porte la responsabilité de ce que je dis. Je ne sais pas ce que sont les «on dit», et je n'ai pas observé dans votre première remarque une telle différence entre ce qu'auraient dit les Américains—dans votre première remarque sur le sujet monétaire, pas dans la deuxième sur le sujet commercial—et ce que j'ai dit. Je n'ai jamais dit autre chose, j'ai même employé l'expression, elle était sur le papier, je n'ai pas eu grand mérite hier soir, «à moyen terme».

Le texte qui s'est ajouté—après tout, c'est vous qui commentez, donc je vais vous en donner lecture, et puis vous verrez bien ce que vous avez à en penser—dit en effet: «. . . interventions, si nécessaire . . . » le «si nécessaire» comportant naturellement des fluctuations insupportables, ce qui, pour l'instant, n'a pas lieu. La dernière fois que cela a eu lieu, c'est lorsque la Communauté européenne est venue au secours du dollar, il y a quelques années. En sens contraire, cela ne s'est pas produit.

Alors, comme il serait vain d'en discuter, je vais essayer de vous retrouver le texte, d'abord celui de la déclaration générale, et ensuite celui de la pièce jointe. Puis j'y ajouterai un élément qui n'est ni dans l'une ni dans l'autre de ces pièces.

Nous sommes convenus de conserver à l'égard de l'URSS et de l'Europe orientale une approche prudente et diversifiée.

M. Fabra parle du passage où il est dit: «En troisième lieu et compte tenu des considérations économiques et financières existantes, nous sommes convenus de gérer avec prudence les relations financières avec l'URSS et les autres pays d'Europe orientale, de manière à s'assurer qu'elles sont conduites de manière économiquement saine, y compris la nécessité de la prudence que requièrent les relations commerciales en limitant aussi les crédits à l'exportation».

Le développement des relations sera périodiquement examiné, c'est une autre affaire, ce n'est pas là-dessus que vous m'interrogez.

Donc, vous voulez savoir s'il y a limitation; limitation de quoi?

La limitation, ou la prudence devant tendre à la limitation, s'applique à l'ensemble des relations économiques et financières avec l'Union soviétique et les pays d'Europe orientale.

Voilà le premier point.

Deuxièmement, puisque l'on veut une précision, c'était là-dessus que devait porter la discussion, il y avait la difficulté sur les crédits à l'exportation. Si vous avez suivi de près cette discussion, ce dont je ne doute pas, vous savez qu'il s'agissait initialement de demander la limitation des aides publiques à l'exportation considérées comme des subsides accordées à l'Union soviétique. Aides publiques accordées par qui? Par deux pays: l'Italie et la France.

Oui, j'avoue que j'ai refusé cette vue un peu étroite des choses.

Remuer un troupeau d'éléphants pour écraser cette puce qui s'appelle les crédits publics à l'exportation italiens et français en direction de l'Union soviétique et des Pays de l'Est, cela me paraissait disproportionné.

J'ai donc fait valoir que cela devait s'appliquer avec la même prudence partout. La prudence, chaque pays en est juge. Cela devait s'appliquer aux crédits à l'exportation. S'agira-t-il des crédits privés, alors vous seriez fondés à dire: cela ne s'applique-t-il pas non plus aux crédits publics?

Pour les crédits à l'exportation, je vais prendre un exemple: le Japon a un important mouvement de crédits privés par ses banques, sans contrôle d'Etat, sans intervention de l'Etat, à 8%. L'aide publique française, qui a été considérablement élevée au cours de ces derniers mois, est à 12%.

Faudrait-il donc permettre l'aide privée à 8% et interdire une aide publique à 12%? Les uns aident-ils par des subsides l'Union soviétique, tandis que les autres ne le feraient pas?

Je vous donne ces éléments d'appréciation, qui expliquent cette phrase, dont je ne sais si elle est ambiguë; mais, si elle l'est, alors elle est permissive, et si elle est permissive, elle l'est à l'égard de chacun, et pas simplement à l'égard des deux pays qui pratiquent une aide publique, je le répète, l'Italie et la France.

Voilà l'explication qui paraîtra simple à ceux qui suivent de très près ces problèmes, qui peut paraître compliquée à ceux qui ne sont pas des spécialistes. Ils n'auront qu'à se reporter au texte, que je vais compléter par la lecture du document suivant qui s'appelle: «engagement monétaire international».

[1]. Primo, nous acceptons la responsabilité conjointe qui est la nôtre de travailler à une plus grande stabilité du système monétaire mondial. Là, je réponds déjà à la deuxième question, j'en termine avec l'affaire des crédits à l'exportation (et non pas des aides publiques à l'exportation) et j'en arrive au système monétaire, à l'ébauche du système monétaire ou à la réalité: celle sur laquelle vous vous interrogez.

S'agit-il de mouvements erratiques?

Je reprends mon discours de tout à l'heure, mais en l'éclairant

par le langage monétaire international et, plutôt que commenter:
il vaut mieux que je vous lise le texte, que vous avez peut-être déjà

«[1.] Nous acceptons la responsabilité conjointe qui est la
nôtre de travailler à une plus grande stabilité du système
monétaire mondial. Nous reconnaissons que les progrès de
la stabilité reposent en premier sur la convergence de
politiques destinées à réduire l'inflation, à développer
l'emploi, à faire redémarrer la croissance et à maintenir de
la sorte la valeur interne et externe de nos monnaies.

Nous sommes déterminés à nous acquitter de cette
obligation en collaboration étroite avec tous les pays et
toutes les institutions monétaires concernées.

2. Nous attachons une importance majeure au rôle du FMI
[Fonds monétaire international] en tant qu'institution
monétaire et nous lui apporterons notre plein appui dans
ses efforts pour promouvoir la stabilité.

3. Nous sommes prêts à renforcer notre coopération avec le
Fonds monétaire international dans l'exercice de sa surveillance et à développer cette surveillance sur une base
multilatérale en prenant particulièrement en compte les
monnaies qui composent le droit de tirage spécial.

4. Nous excluons l'utilisation de nos taux de change pour
obtenir des avantages indûs de compétitivité.

5. Nous sommes prêts, si nécessaire, à procéder à des
interventions sur les marchés des changes pour contrecarrer des situations de désordre selon les dispositions de
l'article 4 des statuts du Fonds monétaire international».

Ceci se relie à ce qui se trouve énoncé dans la première page de
la déclaration générale où il est dit:

Pour réaliser cette réduction—cela aidera à faire baisser les taux d'intérêt aujourd'hui insupportables et à réaliser des taux de change plus stables—nous appliquerons d'urgence des politiques monétaires prudentes et maîtriserons davantage les déficits budgétaires.

A cet égard, nous travaillerons à une évolution constructive et ordonnée du système monétaire international par une coopération plus étroite entre les autorités représentant les monnaies d'Amérique du Nord, du Japon et des Communautés européennes, en vue de poursuivre des objectifs économiques et monétaires à moyen terme. A cet effet, nous avons pris l'engagement contenu dans le texte ci-joint que je viens de vous lire.

On doit en conclure que l'idée de coordonner, par une évolution constructive, ce qui est appelé ici le système monétaire international, bien qu'il n'y en ait pas, en précisant la coopération des monnaies d'Amérique du Nord, du Japon et des Communautés européennes, en vue de poursuivre les objectifs économiques et monétaires à moyen terme, c'est, monsieur Fabra, ce que je vous ai dit hier soir. Donc, je n'ai pas dit: «c'est tout de suite, c'est demain matin»; j'ai dit: «à moyen terme».

Le texte sur l'engagement monétaire international peut comporter à court terme, si nécessaire, des interventions sur les marchés des changes.

Enfin, il existe un troisième document, qui, lui, n'est pas un document du même niveau, c'est le document qui lie les ministres des Finances des sept pays en cause, et je vois: groupe de travail, suite à donner (c'est le titre de cette note) au texte précédent:

«1. Nos représentants se réuniront d'ici, aujourd'hui et demain pour nous proposer la manière dont il convient de coopérer avec le FMI, mettre en oeuvre la décision qui sera adoptée au titre du paragraphe 3 de la déclaration monétaire internationale».

Le paragraphe 3, c'est ce que je viens de vous lire.

«2. Dès le mois de juin, nos représentants au sein d'un groupe de travail présidé par un Français, prendront les mesures appropriées pour définir le champ et la forme de l'étude sur les interventions.

«3. Les ministres et les représentants de la Communauté économique européenne, qui assistent au sommet se réuniront à Toronto à l'occasion de l'assemblée du Fonds monétaire international pour examiner les progrès accomplis en ce qui concerne cette étude. . . .»

Bref, le principe de la coordination et de l'ordonnancement: ordonner, ce n'est pas seulement coordonner un système monétaire international (expression qu'on n'avait pas retrouvée depuis très longtemps dans une déclaration de ce type), c'est prévoir un système efficace à moyen terme.

La déclaration ci-jointe précise qu'on pourra procéder, si nécessaire, à des interventions sur le marché des changes pour contrecarrer les situations de désordre.

Enfin, les ministres des Finances se sont déjà réunis pour se mettre immédiatement à l'oeuvre.

Alors, bien entendu, je ne veux pas maintenant forcer l'interprétation, tout cela part d'une divergence de points de vue, j'estime qu'on est arrivé, par rapport à la situation antérieure, où l'on évitait même de parler de ces choses, à un réel progrès. Est-il suffisant pour estimer que l'on va demain contrôler les mouvements désordonnés? Cela correspond à un engagement que nous avons pris. Quant au rythme et à l'ampleur de ces décisions, seule la pratique vous en fera juge.

Je me suis attardé sur ce sujet, non seulement parce que le journaliste qui m'a posé cette question méritait que je lui réponde de cette façon, mais aussi parce que je sais que vous êtes nombreux à vous interroger là-dessus et que cela m'évitera d'avoir à me répéter, du moins je le suppose.

Q: Le Liban est victime d'un conflit international. Ne mérite-t-il pas la convocation d'une conférence internationale pour y rétablir la paix et l'indépendance? Là France ferait-elle une proposition pareille?

R: C'est certainement une idée qui en vaut bien d'autres. Vous avez peut-être trouvé la clé, moi, je la cherche encore. Tout ce qui permettra à la société internationale de préserver ou plutôt de rétablir l'indépendance et l'unité du Liban, et ce par des moyens pacifiques et non par des actions violentes, sera le bienvenu. Mais cela suppose toujours que le «top» soit donné par le gouvernement du Liban.

Quant au Conseil de sécurité, vous savez que le secrétaire général des Nations unies a déjà, depuis ce matin, réuni ou appelé à se réunir à diverses reprises les responsables qui se trouvent actuellement présents à New York. C'est donc une affaire à suivre.

Q: Puis je vous demander, monsieur le Président, en revenant un peu à la question antérieure, de nous dire dans quels domaines vous estimez avoir le plus progressé et ceux dans lesquels vous estimez avoir le moins avancé durant ce sommet.

R: Vous savez, ce n'était pas du tout une course où l'on s'acharnait à savoir lequel était arrivé avec une poitrine d'avance sur l'autre. Aucun d'entre nous ne s'est trouvé dans la situation de Sébastien Coen hier soir en train de battre le record du monde à Bordeaux du 2 000 m, avec plusieurs longueurs d'avance sur ses concurrents.

Donc, les choses ne se font pas tout à fait comme cela, ce n'est pas une épreuve sportive. Disons que personnellement, je reste sur ma faim pour les taux d'intérets. . . .

Q: Monsieur le Président . . .

R: Je n'avais pas tout à fait fini, monsieur. Je répondais à M. Vernay. . . . Je reste sur ma faim en ce qui concerne les taux d'intérêts, bien qu'il y ait une référence explicite aux taux d'intérêt réels dans un cadre d'action qui, tout de même, commence à marquer la volonté que je signalais tout à l'heure à M. Fabra, d'ordonner cette situation dommageable.

Je considère que c'est une avancée sur le plan des relations avec le Tiers Monde, par rapport à ce qui s'est produit au cours de ces six derniers mois, que l'on reparle de l'AID, que l'on reparle des négociations globales, que l'on approuve la résolution des 77. Faut-il insister pour remarquer que ce n'était pas le langage entendu depuis de longs mois, peut-être depuis le retour de Cancun.

Sur le plan du système monétaire international, je ne vais pas me répéter, mais je le dis pour M. Vernay, il y a une terminologie qui était abandonnée. Elle est reprise et, la pratique faisant foi—là-dessus, je ne suis pas le seul maître—le seul fait de pouvoir examiner les interventions sur le marché des changes, alors qu'il n'en était pas question, marque pour moi une satisfaction. Autant que je l'aurais voulu, non, puisque moi je désire la mise en place la plus rapide possible d'un système monétaire international; donc, cela va moins vite que je ne le voudrais mais cela va beaucoup plus vite que d'autres le souhaiteraient.

Je ne veux pas faire preuve d'amour-propre d'auteur, mais je pense que la dimension procurée au sommet par nos propositions à caractère technologique pour lutter en faveur de l'emploi, pour la croissance et, surtout, pour donner un nouvel élan à nos sociétés dès maintenant et pour les années à venir, a été introduite d'une façon très claire dans un texte; c'est nouveau et c'est important.

Quant aux relations avec les pays de l'Est, disons que la situation est à peu près égale. On a sans doute précisé davantage la volonté commune de ne pas disposer des marchandises de haute valeur technologique pouvant avoir des applications militaires. Le texte est plus clair qu'il ne l'était auparavant. Ou plutôt, disons que la volonté est plus grande.

Sur les crédits, je m'en suis expliqué. Je serais très intéressé de savoir quel est le premier de nos pays qui annoncera qu'il a réduit ses crédits.

A cet égard, j'espère que ce sera clair pour tout le monde. Je suis toujours favorable à des mesures de coopération dans ce domaine, mais ce commerce entre l'Union soviétique et le monde occidental est tellement faible—cela représente une somme inférieure à 1% du produit intérieur brut de l'Union soviétique—que vivre dans l'idée qu'une action sur ce moins de 1% pourrait modifier la politique russe et diminuer son potentiel militaire, moi, personnellement, je ne vais pas jusque-là, en contre-partie, on risque de se lancer dans une forme au demeurant très partielle de blocus économique, dont deux seuls pays—l'Italie et la France—auraient seuls été comptables si l'on avait suivi les propositions initiales.

S'il s'agit de dire qu'on n'aide plus l'Union soviétique, il faut aussi supprimer tout commerce, toute exportation. Que signifie le fait de parler de «subsides» parce qu'il y a une aide publique, si l'on subventionne des agriculteurs pour vendre du blé? Je veux dire par là que c'est une mesure générale, et que s'il s'agit de mesures particulières, leur effet sera très réduit.

Mais enfin, je veux être honnête jusqu'au bout, de même que je me réjouis de l'idée du système monétaire international, de même que je me réjouis de l'idée de négociations globales, de même j'accepte l'idée que si les efforts sont communs à tous, il puisse y avoir, selon les circonstances, limitation. Voilà ce que je veux dire à ce sujet.

Q: Monsieur le Président, je pense que c'est dans le domaine monétaire que les plus grandes précisions ont été données. C'est la première fois depuis que le FMI existe qu'il a obtenu le droit de regard sur les économies nationales occidentales. Je trouve que ceci est extrêmement grave car, comme l'a dit Michel Jobert, hier, le FMI dépend pour 85% des Etats-Unis et, moi, j'ajouterai des anglo-américains.

Donc, cette décision-là constitue une attitude à la sûreté nationale.

D'autre part, je m'étonne aussi qu'on parle de développement pour le Tiers-Monde, en même temps qu'on ouvre les portes de nos économies au FMI qui est précisément l'institution qui a posé des conditions d'austérité atroces aux pays en voie de développement.

Je voudrais que vous nous éclaircissiez cette question.

R: C'est un angle de vue romanesque: il n'est pas dit que les formes romanesques soient détestables, mais en l'occurence, il s'agit d'un roman d'imagination car je ne vois pas quel est le quart de phrase, la moitié de mot, les deux lettres réunies, qui permettent de penser qu'on vient de donner au FMI des attributions nouvelles. Je ne vois pas du tout, absolument pas. J'ajoute que pour ce qui concerne le FMI, il faudrait être à ma place pour connaître les démarches que je fais au nom des peuples d'Afrique ou de Madagascar pour obtenir du FMI qu'il adopte telle ou telle mesure qui contribuera au développement des économies des pays en question.

Certes, ces pays se plaignent souvent de ce que le FMI ait des conceptions soit un peu archaïques, soit trop conformes à la manière dont on considère un budget équilibré dans un pays capitaliste avancé . . . bien qu'aucun des pays capitalistes avancés n'ait de budget en équilibre. Celui qui est le plus en équilibré du monde, c'est le nôtre . . . et si je vous lis bien, ce n'est pas peu dire.

Donc, premièrement, le FMI n'a obtenu aucun droit de regard supplémentaire qui puisse faire dire qu'il y ait perte ou danger pour l'indépendance nationale. Il n'y a rien de nouveau. S'il s'agit de préserver l'indépendance nationale, c'est autant mon affaire que la vôtre et vous pouvez compter sur moi autant que sur vous. Je n'aperçois rien, rien qui permette d'affirmer ce que vous venez de dire, et que par déduction vous disiez que puisque le FMI vient altérer notre indépendance nationale, il empiètera plus encore sur les pays en voie de développement: c'est le dernier chapitre de cette version romancée d'une déclaration qui ne permet aucune de ces conclusions.

Si l'on considère que le FMI pèse trop sur les économies nationales, alors il faut s'en prendre aux gouvernements qui ont accepté la création du FMI qui, selon moi, autant que je me souvienne, a dépendu des accords de Bretton Woods, c'est-à-dire en 1945. . . . C'est bien cela, non? Et tous les gouvernements, depuis cette époque, ont continué de l'accepter, ce qui recouvre à peu près la totalité de l'horizon politique français, en dehors de ceux qui n'ont pas pour vocation de gouverner, même s'ils ont vocation naturelle à participer au débat politique.

Q: Monsieur le Président, concernant la guerre Irak–Iran, vous avez abordé le sujet mais dans quel sens l'avez-vous abordé et pourquoi n'y a-t-il pas eu de communiqué en ce qui concerne le Liban, par exemple?

R: Nous en avons parlé, Monsieur, en effet, nous considérons, d'une façon générale—mais là je ne suis pas chargé d'interpréter une résolution qui n'a pas été prise—que l'ampleur de ce conflit apparaît de plus en plus. Longtemps, on l'a contenu dans des considérations, disons localisées, on s'aperçoit aujourd'hui que ses conséquences en sont beaucoup plus vastes.

Nous en avons parlé mais nous n'avons pas présentement une possibilité réelle de paix sur la décision de l'un ou de l'autre et, en tout cas, des deux à la fois.

De telle sorte qu'en général, on prend garde à ne pas prendre des résolutions totalement inopérantes ou vaines.

Ce que je veux dire, c'est que nous en sommes très préoccupés, pour ce qui touche la France. Le jour où on en parlera d'une façon plus complète, vous saurez que nous n'avons pas été absents dans les démarches faites pour parvenir à un arrêt des hostilités.

Q: Si vous permettez, monsieur le Président, je ne voudrais pas évoquer la question du Liban, quoiqu'il s'agisse de ma propre mère, de mes huit frères et soeurs qui sont coincés, à cette heure-ci entre l'artillerie, les blindés, l'aviation, à quelques kilomètres à l'est, mais, tout en reconnaissant votre générosité je dois voir aussi les limites des pouvoirs de votre fonction et je poserai donc une question sur les taux de chômage.

Je crois comprendre que vos partenaires ont admis l'évidence, qui a toujours été prônée par la délégation française, qu'il y a un seuil, qu'il y a des frontières au-delà desquelles le chômage ne serait pas tolérable.

Est-ce qu'il n'y a pas aussi un seuil pour l'assassinat et la mort, ou doit-on faire confiance à la précision, à la sophistication du matériel américain qui saura distinguer cette fois-ci entre objectifs civils ou non civils, comme cela des gens comme les miens seront épargnés ou auront plus de chance que d'autres?

Je m'excuse d'avoir introduit cette question, c'est le général Haig qui nous a ouvert la route, puisqu'il s'est déclaré réjouit hier de se retrouver de nouveau à Cancún, et lorsqu'il s'agit de Cancún. . . .

R: Monsieur, vous avez fait des considérations sur le Liban avec émotion. Je le comprends; nous sommes quelques-uns à beaucoup aimer le Liban, je suis de ceux-là et à souhaiter participer le plus possible au rétablissement d'une situation juste pour ce pays, à la sauvegarde de vies humaines, à la sauvegarde des biens, à la sauvegarde de ce peuple et de cette nation.

Mais, vous avez mêlé à ces considérations des propos sur le chômage en France qui ont beaucoup altéré, je vous prie de le croire, la qualité de votre intervention car elle prenait une couleur de petite attaque politique sur un sujet qui ne le méritait pas.

Je n'ai pas compris ce que vous attendiez de la France, sinon qu'elle vous aide davantage.

Je vous répète que la France n'hésite pas à condamner l'intervention israélienne, pas plus qu'elle n'a hésité à condamner les autres interventions militaires sur le territoire du Liban, dès lors qu'elles se faisaient contre la volonté des dirigeants légitimes du Liban.

Nous n'avons jamais cessé, par notre diplomatie, de contribuer à défendre ces principes d'unité, d'indépendance, de souveraineté, d'aide. Nous nous sommes bornés aux actions diplomatiques parce que tel est notre rôle.

Si nous sommes mêlés militairement, c'est dans le cadre des forces internationales et non pas au titre de la France.

Enfin, si cela devait être au titre de la France, cela ne serait pas possible par l'initiative de la France, seul le gouvernement libanais a autorité dans ce domaine.

Nous examinerons les propositions du gouvernement libanais s'il en fait, et quand il en fera.

Voilà tout ce que je peux dire à ce sujet.

Q: Je reviens sur votre commentaire sur les crédits de l'URSS; comment expliquez-vous que les Américains soient si contents

qu'ils aient dit: c'est la première fois que les nations industrial-
isées ont accepté de limiter le «package deal», c'est-à-dire les
relations commerciales avec l'URSS.
Est-ce qu'il n'y a pas une source de malentendus?

R: C'est possible, pour l'instant il est admis que c'est tout le
monde ou personne. Moi je suis tout prêt, s'il y a danger pour la
paix, à considérer que les restrictions pourraient être nécessaires.

Comme le commerce américain est beaucoup plus important
que le commerce français, j'agirais certainement dans ce cas là
comme ils le feront eux-mêmes, en cas de danger naturellement.
. . . Bref, c'est tout le monde, ou c'est personne. . . . Pour l'instant,
c'est personne.

Ce sera peut-être tout le monde, mais chaque pays restera
souverainement juge de la prudence que requièrent les relations
commerciales, expression qui figure en toutes lettres dans ce
texte, que vous n'aviez peut-être pas remarquées.

Q: Excusez-moi, monsieur le Président, mais je voudrais revenir
encore sur le Liban.

Dans le communiqué du sommet à propos des derniers
développements vous dites, dans la dernière phrase, que «chacun
de nos gouvernements utilisera tous les moyens à sa disposition
pour atteindre ce but».

Je voudrais savoir si les mesures et les moyens que vous
autoriserez seront semblables à ceux que vous avez pris déjà à
l'égard de l'Argentine?

R: C'est possible, comme il est possible que non. Ce qui est
certain c'est qu'il faut que les nations responsables soient un peu
plus logiques avec elles-mêmes, c'est-à-dire que la violence doit
être refusée partout. Lorsque le délégué de la France s'ex-
primera à ce sujet, il estimera sans aucun doute que la violence
doit être rejetée également ici et là.

Dans l'affaire argentine, la grande difficulté tient au fait que,
l'initiative de l'agression étant de la responsabilité de l'Argentine, si l'on condamne la violence, on commence par condamner

l'Argentine. Ensuite, c'est l'enchaînement des circonstances, qu'il est difficile d'éviter.

Mais comme l'objectif—de la France, en tout cas—(je ne peux, sur ce terrain là, engager que moi-même, que mon pays) c'est d'affirmer sa solidarité avec la Grande-Bretagne contre cette violation du droit, et de préserver autant que faire se peut les relations très importantes qui unissent la France, l'Europe occidentale, aussi, et l'Amérique latine, cela signifie qu'au cours des jours qui vont venir, toute une série d'actions seront rendues nécessaires.

Q: Monsieur le Président, ma question précédente. J'aimerais vous demander si la déclaration des chefs d'Etat et de gouvernement va plus loin dans le sens de la solidarité avec la Grande-Bretagne que les positions qui avaient été prises jusqu'ici, et d'autre part si les chefs d'Etat et de gouvernement se sont mis d'accord, non seulement sur la nécessité d'un cessez-le-feu local, mais sur celle d'un cessez-le-feu qui engloberait toutes les nations qui sont parties prenantes du conflit actuel, autrement dit sur le fait que l'Argentine ne puisse plus continuer à harceler les positions britanniques dans les Malouines lorsque le droit aura été rétabli?

R: Ecoutez, soyons simples. Il n'y a pas eu de texte adopté sur l'affaire des Falklands-Malouines. . . . Je dis Falklands-Malouines, parce que si je dis Malouines, vous traduirez Falklands, et si je dis Falklands, d'autres traduiront Malouines! Mais il s'agit de la même chose. Donc, je ne vais pas faire de discours inutile à ce sujet.

Ce qui est vrai, c'est que l'Argentine a préféré régler par la force un vieux débat qui l'opposait à la Grande-Bretagne. Ce qui est vrai aussi, c'est que nombre de pays n'ont jamais reconnu ni défini le droit de souveraineté de la Grande-Bretagne, et pourtant nous sommes aux côtés de la Grande-Bretagne.

Pourquoi? Parce qu'elle a été agressée, parce qu'elle est notre amie et notre alliée et qu'à partir du moment où l'agression a eu lieu, s'est engagé un engrenage d'événements dont nous ne sommes pas maîtres.

Nous avons soutenu dès l'abord la résolution 502 des Nations unies. Nous nous en tenons là. Nous avons d'autre part, adopté au sein de la Communauté européenne un embargo sur les échanges commerciaux avec l'Argentine, qui nous paraissait la conséquence normale de notre condamnation de la violence.

Ce qui s'est produit depuis lors, et notamment l'avance britannique sur le sol des Falklands-Malouines, fait partie d'un événement sur lequel la France n'a pas prise, sinon indirectement par le fait qu'elle participe à cet embargo, c'est vrai. Simplement, nous considérons que ce que l'on pourrait appeler un événement nouveau, dans ce jeu de la fatalité, serait constitué par le fait que la Grande-Bretagne aurait récupéré le sol qui lui était contesté.

A partir de là, une nouvelle phase commencera—ce n'est pas un principe que j'émets, c'est une évidence politique—qui, je l'espère, se terminera dans le délai le plus bref par un cessez-le-feu ou un armistice, appelez-le comme vous voudrez, et la France sera naturellement du côté de ceux qui plaideront ce dossier là.

SOURCE: France, Ministère des Relations extérieures, *La Politique étrangère de la France: textes et documents, avril–mai–juin 1982* (Paris: La Documentation française, 1982), pp. 126–33.

[UNOFFICIAL TRANSLATION]
PRESIDENT MITTERAND'S PRESS CONFERENCE
AT THE CONCLUSION OF
THE SUMMIT OF INDUSTRIALIZED COUNTRIES
June 6, 1982

We shall now, if you wish, start this press conference which was preceded, as you know, by a declaration that I made as president of the Summit of Industrialized Nations. That declaration was unilateral, with no discussion and no dialogue. I was speaking on behalf of the Eight, but I was not able to give a detailed account of the discussions. Now is the time to do that—though this is not an invitation to discuss more than necessary, it is not an encouragement, it is not an incitement to excessive dialogue; I have, at the most, three quarters of an hour, but I would be satisfied with half an hour, if you are willing. It depends on you.

What are the texts?

A declaration.

That declaration is called "Declaration of the Seven Heads of State and Government, and Representatives of the European Communities." You know what it is about.

This declaration, which covers many topics, is followed by an attached document called "Statement on International Monetary Undertakings."

Another text, which has already been released and is not linked to this one, is about Lebanon. You must be familiar with this one.

Other questions were not the subjects of communiqués, among them the matter of the Falklands or Malvinas; discussions were held among concerned ministers, Foreign Ministers on the one hand, those for Economy and Finance on the other, sometimes together.

Some of the debates from these meetings explain the texts in question. Everything must be examined to judge the results of the Versailles Summit.

If you don't mind, I will quickly go over the issues covered in the declaration.

It starts with general affirmations, mostly centered on the fight against inflation and unemployment and on the development of growth, lasting growth, on the necessity to safeguard the security of the Western world and of Japan, and on the confidence in democratic values.

It is clearly understood that the actions in the fight against inflation, for [higher] levels of employment and for growth go hand in hand.

A certain number of resolutions, on growth and employment, follow to realize these objectives: control of inflation, as I just mentioned, to bring down the interest rates that are nowadays unacceptably high, and to achieve more stable exchange rates . . . that's the introduction, we will talk more about it later.

To realize this essential reduction of the high interest rates, the Declaration provides a series of means: prudent monetary policies and control of budget deficits, intensification of economic and monetary cooperation, particularly among the currencies of North America, Japan, and the European Community.

Then comes the growth of world trade; we reaffirm our commitment to strengthen the open multilateral trading system as embodied in the GATT and to maintain its effective role.

Refusal of protectionist measures: thus opening of the markets. An active participation in the forthcoming GATT ministerial conference, late August or early September.

To come back to general considerations: we have agreed to maintain toward the USSR and the Eastern European countries a prudent and diversified approach, consistent with our political and security interests.

Therefore, action in three key areas: improvement of the international system of exports of strategic goods, exchange of economic, commercial and financial information, and cautious handling of the financial relations with the USSR and the Eastern [European] countries, so as to insure that they are conducted on a sound economic basis taking into account the caution required by trade relations, within the general framework of economic and financial relations, also limiting export credits and proceeding to a periodic examination of the development of these relations, and so forth.

The progress we have already made does not diminish the need to pursue policies for economizing on energy; there, we went further than during the previous conferences.

A whole section of the Declaration is concerned with developing countries, with a few major points. We must maintain a high level of financial flows of public assistance and even increase its amount and effectiveness. Launching of global negotiations: it's the major objective, referring to the recent draft resolution of the Group of 77, recognized as constructive. At Versailles, a general agreement was reached on the fact that this agreement can serve as the basis of consultation with the Third World countries.

A positive perspective for the forthcoming start of global negotiations and their success, provided that the independence of the specialized agencies is guaranteed, a theme that is already known by the specialists, but one that isn't bad to set down in black and white.

Cooperation, innovation within the World Bank, support to the regional development banks, progress to be made in the struggle against instability of raw-material export earnings. At the same time, encouragement for the development of public assistance, encouragement for private assistance and capital. You will note that we also recognize the necessity of special temporary arrangements to overcome funding problems for IDA VI and for an early start of IDA VII.

Those who followed these problems know what I am talking about: most countries have reduced their contribution to IDA. Only a few resisted the trend: the Scandinavian countries, France, and, partly, Great Britain in relation to countries like India; and we have requested that the contributions which were maintained be managed in a particular way. That is what brings up the possibility of special temporary arrangements.

Food and energy production in developing countries, balance of payments: we strongly wish, regarding the balance of payments, that progress be made at the annual meeting of the International Monetary Fund in September to settle the question of the increase in the Fund's quotas.

The last paragraph exploits the propositions that I made on the technological level: technology, growth, employment, with an explicit reference to my report and the clearly stated will to pursue concretely the different directions that I had proposed. A working group has already been formed; it will submit its report before 31 December 1982.

The conclusions of the report, the resulting actions, will be examined and followed up at the next Summit, in 1983, in the United States of America.

Finally, on the issue of the international monetary undertakings, if you ask me questions, I will read the statement to you.

I think that I have talked enough.

Would you please ask me questions . . . not all at once. . . .

Q: At Ottawa, you considered it a plus that the Seven accepted to fight inflation and unemployment together. Since Ottawa, what progress have you noted and, in particular, in relation to that Conference, what successes or what failures, what steps forward or backward?

A: There is no step backward, there is a step forward between Ottawa and Versailles.

As for the idea that the different ways of fighting inflation and unemployment, and the solution to the growth problems are linked: concepts of employment, full employment and growth, previously often missing, now appear more and more in our texts and, I hope, in our action. I explained this yesterday.

It is an empty debate to believe that some want to fight inflation but not unemployment while others fight unemployment but not inflation!

But, as they are the two parts of an abominable couple, depending on whether the stress is placed on one or the other, the one that is not cited first seems to be neglected, and that's where political differences appear, not in the objectives—the political objective of a responsible authority can only be reduction of inflation and unemployment for a resumption of growth—but at what rate?

That is where the differences intervene: some countries want to crush inflation, whatever the risk to employment. Others want to fight inflation without piling up debris on the side of employment.

So, it is a difficult choice. As a result, in some countries, inflation rates have decreased a great deal—such as in the U.S. and also in Germany—they have in fact decreased everywhere, but very noticeably when unemployment increased very rapidly. And then, there is the case of a country like France, where inflation has decreased, though at a less rapid rate than in the countries I mentioned, but which, on the other hand, has considerably limited the continued growth of unemployment that has existed for the last eight years, in other words, where there is a flattening of the curve of increase.

We have not yet managed to reverse the trend, that is to diminish the rise of unemployment.

I have to speak precisely to avoid any ambiguities.

So, the results on inflation were more apparent where unemployment problems were considered to a lesser extent; they were less apparent where the priority of fighting unemployment was recognized.

But everywhere inflation decreased, everywhere unemployment increased; there it increased considerably following a continued curve; elsewhere—as in our case—the curve has begun to flatten. It is an interesting indication of a trend, but of course, in the end, only the countries that will be able to produce will dispose of the determining factor against any form of unemployment.

Q: Mr. President, as you mentioned, the text on Lebanon agreed upon by the Seven was finalized before the last developments were known.

It has just been announced that two Syrian brigades have approached into the combat zone.

Since the last communiqué, have the Seven issued a new communiqué, a new declaration, and what will France do in that region?

A: Evidently, we are faced with a constantly changing situation. The action of the Israeli troops in Lebanon, going in two different directions, in particular along the coast and in the area controlled by Syria, was probably not meant to stop immediately. As long as it goes on, the developments are constant and we cannot publish a communiqué every fifteen minutes.

Nonetheless, and you were right to say so, some events are landmarks and, although one deplores, we deplore and I deplore it, the Israeli intervention on the territory of Lebanon, a country which, despite its conflicts, remains a sovereign county, although we deplore and thus reproach the choice of violence as a way to solve the problem in question, we know that it is a new event if a third country intervenes.

But you are telling me . . . I didn't know about it. I knew that there were troop movements within Syria, I hadn't heard about any outside of Syria. I will thus comment on that event, if it occurs, after it has occurred.

The Heads of State and Government will be gathered, not in session but nonetheless gathered, in Versailles until 9, 10 PM for Mrs. Thatcher, 11, 11:30 PM for the others; we will still have time, if necessary, to react to an event of that importance.

For the rest, I repeat, unfortunately, it is an evolution of the direct relations of Israel and Lebanon that could be foreseen.

Q: Mr. President, on that subject, what are the means at France's disposal, means to which you alluded at the end of the Declaration, where it says that each country reserves the right to use the means at its disposal to reestablish peace and security?

Did the Seven talk about it? What are France's means?

A: No, no. . . . The means of France are of several kinds. They are diplomatic, with the role of France in the international arena. We are members of the Security Council and thus have a particular responsibility within the framework of the United Nations. There, we can act in conformity with our ideas which have always aimed, as you know, at defending Israel's integrity and which have also always aimed at recognizing the right of others to a homeland, and to a peaceful solution of the conflict, not to a violent one.

By our actions within the United Nations, we can constantly adapt our practice to this definition.

And then, on site, France is not directly involved in the events in Lebanon. It is represented there by soldiers, but those soldiers are not under French command, they are there as part of an international force. It is thus a question that must be asked of the United Nations, not of France.

What does the presence of French soldiers mean?

First of all, that France almost always volunteers when a peace-keeping mission must be carried out within the framework of the United Nations.

It also means that the problem of Lebanon is of prime interest to us because there are traditional friendly relations between Lebanon and France.

But, I must insist, we do not want to, we have no intention of substituting ourselves for the sovereign decision of Lebanon itself, which has a legitimate government. It is up to that government to take initiatives, to make advances, that we will examine if they are made toward us. We have no interventionist intentions. We simply want Lebanon to know—the Prime Minister said so during a recent trip to Beirut—that France is part of its circle of friendly countries, but is respectful, above all, of the sovereignty of that country.

Q: Mr. President, you said earlier at the Palais des congrès that the common Declaration had been drafted so it could not lend itself to divergent interpretations.

So, you will doubtless be able to help us dissipate a double ambiguity that has reigned in this Conference for two days.

The first concerns monetary affairs. The French delegation, in the words of the different ministers who have spoken, perhaps even yourself, said that the principle of intervention in the market had been unanimously accepted. The Americans, for their part, say: yes, intervention in the case of erratic movements— "disorderly conditions"—and they add: this conforms to our constant doctrine, conforms also to article IV of the [International] Monetary Fund, thus nothing is fundamentally new in our measure, even adding that the study group that will meet will have to decide whether there should be more or less intervention.

Consequently the question remains open.

The second misunderstanding had to do with the matter of trade with the East, the French delegation insisting especially on the fact that the Declaration does not include any particular restriction to the granting of credits, while the Americans insist on the fact that there are limitations—"to limit," I think the verb has the same meaning in English and in French— to credit grants.

Could you enlighten us on those two points?

A: First of all, I generally know what I say, and I am responsible for what I say. I don't know about the "it was said," and in your first remark I did not observe such a difference between what the Americans would have said—in your first remark on the monetary subject, not in the second one on trade—and what I said. I never said anything else. I even used the expression—it was in the paper, I didn't make up anything new last night—"at medium-term."

The text that was added—after all, you are the commentator, so I will read it to you, and then you will see what you think of it—the text says: "interventions, if necessary . . .," the "if necessary" including of course unacceptable fluctuations, which at present are not occurring. The last time it happened was when the European Community came to the assistance of the dollar, a few years ago. It hasn't happened the other way around.

So, as it would be useless to discuss it, I will try to find you the text, first the text of the general Declaration, then the attached document. Then I will add an element that is in neither of them.

We have agreed to maintain a prudent and diversified approach toward the USSR and Eastern Europe.

Mr. Fabra is talking about the section which says: "Third, taking into account existing economic and financial considerations, we have agreed to handle cautiously financial relations with the USSR and other Eastern European countries in such a way as to ensure that they are conducted on a sound economic basis, including also the need for commercial prudence in limiting export credits. The development of . . . relations will be subject to periodic ex-post review";—that is another story, you are not questioning me on that.

So, you want to know if there is a limitation; limitation of what?

The limitation, or the caution tending toward limitation, applies to all the economic and financial relations with the Soviet Union and the Eastern European countries.

That is the first point.

Secondly, since you asked for clarification (the discussion was supposed to be on that point), there was the difficulty of the export credits. If you followed that discussion closely, and I am sure you did, you know that initially the purpose was to ask for the limitation of public assistance to exports considered as subsidies to the Soviet Union. Public assistance given by whom? By two countries, Italy and France.

Yes, I admit that I refused that rather limited view of things. To me, it seemed out of proportion—moving a herd of elephants to squash that flea called "Italian or French public export credits to the Soviet Union and the Eastern Countries."

I emphasized that it should be applied with the same caution everywhere. Each country must exercise caution. It had to be applied to export credits. If it were private credits, then you would be justified in saying: isn't it applicable to public credits as well?

For export credits, I will give an example: Japan has a significant movement of private credits through its banks, without any State control, without any State intervention, at eight percent. French public assistance, which has been very high in the last months, is at twelve percent.

Should private aid at eight percent be allowed and public aid at twelve percent be forbidden? Do some help the Soviet Union by subsidies while the others don't?

I offer you these elements of clarification that explain this sentence, which I don't know is ambiguous or not; but if it is, then it is permissive, and if it permissive, it is so for each of us, and not only for the two countries that practice public aid, I repeat, Italy and France.

That is the explanation which will appear simple to those who follow these problems very closely, and which might appear complicated to those who are not specialists. All they have to do is refer to the text, which I will accomplish by reading the following document that is called: "International Monetary Undertakings."

"1. We accept a joint responsibility to work for greater stability of the world monetary system." There, I am already answering the second question; I am finished with the issue of the export credits (and not of public assistance to exports) and I am getting to the monetary system, to the outline of the monetary system or to the real thing: the one on which you are questioning me.

Is it a question of disorderly conditions?

I am going back to my earlier speech, but clarifying it through international monetary language and, rather than to comment, it might be better if I read you the text; perhaps you already have it.

1. We accept a joint responsibility to work for greater stability of the world monetary system. We recognize that this rests primarily on convergence of policies designed to achieve lower inflation, higher employment and renewed economic growth; and thus to maintain the internal and external values of our currencies. We are determined to discharge this obligation in close collaboration with all interested countries and monetary institutions.

2. We attach major importance to the role of the IMF as a monetary authority and we will give it our full support in its efforts to foster stability.

3. We are ready to strengthen our cooperation with the IMF in its work of surveillance; and to develop this on a multilateral basis taking into account particularly the currencies constituting the SDR [special drawing rights].

4. We rule out the use of our exchange rates to gain unfair competitive advantages.

5. We are ready, if necessary, to use intervention in exchange markets to counter disorderly conditions, as provided for under Article IV of the IMF Articles of Agreement.

This is linked to what is said in the first page of the general Declaration:

In order to achieve this essential reduction of real interest rates,

—it will help to bring down interest rates which are now unacceptably high and to bring about more stable exchange rates—

we will as a matter of urgency pursue prudent monetary policies and achieve greater control of budgetary deficits. . . . In this regard, we will work towards a constructive and orderly evolution of the international monetary system by a closer cooperation among the authorities representing the currencies of North America, of Japan and of the European Community in pursuing medium-term economic and monetary objectives. In this respect, we have committed ourselves to the undertakings contained in the attached statement

that I just read to you.

One must conclude that the idea of coordinating, by a constructive evolution, what is called here the international monetary system—although there is no such thing—by specifying the cooperation among the currencies of North America, Japan and the European Communities in pursuing the medium-term economic and monetary objectives is, Mr. Fabra, what I told you last night. Thus, I did not say: "it's right away, it's tomorrow morning," I said "at medium-term."

The statement on the international monetary undertakings can include in the short term, if necessary, interventions in foreign exchange markets.

Finally, there is a third document, which is not a document of the same level, it is the document that links the Finance Ministers of the seven countries—and I see: "working group, to be followed up" (it is the title of this note)—to the preceding text:

1. Our representatives will meet here, today and tomorrow, to propose to us the manner in which we should cooperate with the IMF, to implement the decision that will be adopted in accordance with the third paragraph of the international monetary declaration.

The third paragraph is what I read to you earlier.

2. As early as June our representatives within a working group, presided over by a French national, will take the appropriate measures to define the field and form of the study on the interventions.

3. The ministers and the representatives of the European Economic Community who are participating in the Summit will meet in Toronto on the occasion of the meeting of the International Monetary Fund to examine the progress accomplished in regard to this study. . . .

Briefly, the principle of coordination and of regulation: to regulate is not only to coordinate an international monetary system (an expression that had not been seen for a long time in this type of declaration), it is to foresee an effective system in the medium term.

The joint declaration specifies that, if necessary, interventions could be made in the foreign exchange markets to counteract disorderly situations.

Lastly, the Finance Ministers have already met to start their work immediately.

So, of course, I do not want now to force this interpretation upon you. All this starts from diverging points of view. I believe that we have achieved real progress in relation to the previous situation in which even speaking about these things was avoided. Is the progress sufficient to consider that disorderly movements will be controlled tomorrow? It corresponds to a commitment that we made. As to the rate and the extent of these decisions, only practice will answer that for you.

I lingered on this subject, not only because the reporter who asked me that question deserved to be answered this way, but also because I know that many of you have questions about that and it will save me having to repeat myself, at least I hope so.

Q: Lebanon is the victim of an international conflict. Doesn't it deserve the convocation of an international conference to reestablish peace and independence? Will France make such a proposal?

A: It's certainly as good an idea as any other. You might have found the key, I'm still looking for it. Anything that will allow international society to preserve or rather to reestablish the independence and the unity of Lebanon, and by peaceful means and not by violent actions, will be welcome. But that always supposes that the Lebanese government gives the go-ahead.

As to the Security Council, you know that this morning the Secretary-General of the United Nations convened or called for the convening of the responsible people who are currently in New York. It is thus a matter to follow.

Q: May I ask you, Mr. President, going back to the previous question, to tell us in which areas you think you have progressed the most and those in which you think you have progressed the least during this Summit?

A: You know, it wasn't a race where one worked unceasingly to know who had arrived one length ahead of the other. None of us was in the situation of Sébastien Coen who last night was trying to break the world record of 2000 meters in Bordeaux, with several lengths on his competitors.

So, it doesn't happen that way, it's not a sporting event. Let's say that personally I have a slight sense of frustration about the interest rates. . . .

Q: Mr. President . . .

A: I haven't finished yet. I was answering Mr. Vernay. . . . I have a slight sense of frustration concerning interest rates, although there is an explicit reference to real interest rates in a framework of action that, nonetheless, is starting to mark the willingness, which I was mentioning earlier to Mr. Fabra, to regulate this detrimental situation.

On the level of relations with the Third World, I consider that, in relation to what happened during these last six months, it is a step forward that we are talking again about the IDA, that we are talking again about global negotiations, and that the resolution of the 77 is approved. It is hardly necessary to note that this wasn't the language heard for many months, maybe since the return from Cancún.

On the level of the international monetary system, I will not repeat myself, but I will say this to Mr. Vernay: there is a terminology that had been abandoned. It is used once again and, practice will attest to it—I am not the only one who controls it—the mere fact of being able to examine interventions on the foreign exchange market, while there previously had been no question of it, is for me a source of satisfaction. Not as far as I would have liked, since I desire the establishment, as quickly as possible, of an international monetary system; so it isn't going as fast I would wish, but it's going much faster than others would like.

I do not want to show an author's pride but I believe that the dimension brought to the Summit by our technological proposals to fight for employment, for growth and, especially, to give a new impetus to our societies, now and in the coming years, was introduced very clearly in the text; it's new and it's important.

As for the relations with the Eastern countries, let us say that the situation is about the same. We were undoubtedly more specific in the common will not to make available goods of high technological value that could have military applications. The text is clearer that it was previously. Or rather, let us say that the will is greater.

As for credits, I have explained myself. I would be very interested to know which one of our countries will be the first to announce that it has reduced its credits.

In that regard, I hope that it will be clear to everyone. I always favor measures of cooperation in that area, but the trade between the Soviet Union and the Western world is so low—it represents less than one percent of the gross domestic product of the Soviet Union—that to think that an action on that trade of less than one percent could change the policies of Russia and diminish its military potential, personally, I don't go that far. On the other hand, we run the risk of starting an economic blockade, albeit a very partial form of it, for which two countries—Italy and France—would have been solely responsible if the initial proposals had been followed.

If the idea is not to help the Soviet Union anymore, then all trade, all exports, should also be stopped. What does it mean to speak of "subsidies" because there is public assistance, if one subsidizes the farmers to sell wheat? I mean by that that it is a general measure, and that if it is a matter of particular measures, their effect will be very reduced.

But still, I want to be totally honest. Just as I welcome the idea of the international monetary system, just as I welcome the idea of global negotiations, I accept the idea that if efforts are common to all, there might be a limitation, depending on the circumstances. That is all I have to say on this subject.

Q: Mr. President, I think that it is in the monetary area that the most precise language is found. For the first time since the IMF was established, it has obtained a right of surveillance of the Western national economies. I find this extremely serious because, as Michel Jobert said yesterday, the IMF depends on 85 percent [of its funds] from the United States and, I will add personally, on the Anglo-Americans.

So, that decision has a bearing on national security.

On the other hand, I am surprised that development of the Third World is discussed at the same time as the doors of our economies are opened to the IMF, which is precisely the institution that set atrocious conditions of austerity for the developing countries.

I would like you to clarify this question.

A: That's an imaginative point of view: this is not to say that all forms of imagination are necessarily detestable, but in this case, it really strains credibility. For I don't see where is the quarter of a sentence, the half word, the two joined letters that allow one to think that we have just given new prerogatives to the IMF. I absolutely do not see that. I add in regard to the IMF that one would have to be in my place to know the steps I am taking in the name of the peoples of Africa or of Madagascar to get the IMF to adopt such and such a measure that will contribute to the development of the economies of the countries in question.

Indeed, those countries often complain that the IMF has conceptions that are either slightly archaic, or conform too closely to the manner in which one considers a balanced budget in an advanced capitalist country . . . although none of the advanced capitalist countries has a balanced budget. The most balanced one is ours . . . and if I understand you correctly, that is saying a lot.

So, first of all, the IMF has not obtained a new right of surveillance that might allow one to say that there is a loss or a danger for national independence. There is nothing new. If it is a question of preserving national independence, it's as much my problem as yours and you can count on me as much as on yourself. I can't see anything, anything, that allows you to affirm what you just said, and that by deduction you say that since the IMF has just altered our national independence, it will encroach even more on the developing countries: it is the last chapter of this fictitious version of a declaration that does not allow for any of these conclusions.

If one considers that the IMF weighs too heavily on the national economies, then one should blame the governments that accepted the creation of the IMF which, to me, as far as I remember, depended on the Bretton Woods agreements, and that was in 1945. . . . Isn't that so? And all governments, since that time, have continued to accept it, and that covers about the totality of the French political horizon, apart from those who do not have an aptitude to govern, even if they have a natural aptitude to participate in the political debate.

Q: Mr. President, concerning the Iraq-Iran war, you dealt with the subject, but in which sense did you deal with the conflict and why wasn't there a communiqué about Lebanon, for example?

A: Indeed, we talked about it. We generally consider—but there I am not in charge of interpreting a resolution that was not adopted—that the extent of the conflict is becoming more and more apparent. For a long time, it was contained regionally, let us say locally, but today its consequences appear to be much wider.

We talked about it but we don't have at present a real possibility of peace based on the readiness of one or the other belligerents and certainly not on the readiness of both at the same time.

So, in general, we try not to make any resolutions that are totally ineffective or empty.

What I mean is that as far as France is concerned, we are very preoccupied by it. The day when it will be discussed at length, you will know that we were not absent when steps were taken to reach a cessation of the hostilities.

Q: If you will allow me, Mr. President, I do not wish to bring up the question of Lebanon—although my own mother and my eight brothers and sisters are stuck right now between the artillery, the tanks, and the air force a few kilometers east—but, while recognizing your generosity, I must also see the limits of the powers of your position; so I will therefore ask a question about the unemployment rate.

I understand that your partners have admitted the evidence, which was always defended by the French delegation, that there is a threshold, there are limits beyond which unemployment would not be tolerated.

Isn't there also a threshold for assassination or death, or must one set one's faith in the precision and the sophistication of the American matériel that will be able to distinguish this time between civilian and noncivilian objectives, so that people like mine will be spared or will have more chance than others.

I am sorry to have introduced this question, but it is General Haig who opened the way, since he rejoiced yesterday to be back in Cancún, and when it comes to Cancún. . . .

A: Sir, you made some emotional observations about Lebanon. I understand; we are among those who love Lebanon, I am among those and I wish to participate as much as possible in the reestablishment of a just situation for that country, to safeguard human lives, to safeguard goods, to safeguard that people and that nation.

But you mixed with those considerations words about unemployment in France that have much altered, you will know, the quality of your intervention because it took on the color of a little political attack on a subject that did not deserve it.

I did not understand what you were expecting from France except that it should do more to help you.

I repeat that France does not hesitate to condemn the Israeli intervention, any more than it did not hesitate to condemn the other military interventions on Lebanese territory, as long as they were made against the wishes of the legitimate leaders of Lebanon.

We have never ceased by our diplomacy to contribute to defending those principles of unity, independence, sovereignty, and assistance. We restricted ourselves to diplomatic actions because such is our role.

If we are involved militarily, it is within the framework of the international forces and not in the name of France. In any case, if it were in the name of France, it would not be possible by French initiative; only the Lebanese government has authority in that area.

We will examine the proposals of the Lebanese government if it makes any and when it makes them.

That is all I can say on the subject.

Q: I am going back to your comment on credits to the USSR; how do you explain that the Americans are so satisfied that they said: it is the first time that the industrialized nations have accepted to limit the "package deal," that is, the commercial relations with the USSR.

Isn't there a source of misunderstanding?

A: It's possible, right now it is admitted that it is everyone or no one. I am ready, if there is any danger to peace, to consider that restrictions might be necessary.

As American trade is much more important than French trade, I would certainly act in that case as they would, in case of danger, naturally. . . . In sum, it is everyone or no one. . . . Right now, it's no one.

It will perhaps be everyone, but each country will remain sovereign judge of the caution required by commercial relations; that is expressed in every letter of the text, perhaps you didn't notice.

Q: Excuse me, Mr. President, but I would like to get back to Lebanon.

In the communiqué of the summit on the latest developments, you say in the last sentence that "each of our governments will use all the means at its disposal to achieve this objective."

I would like to know if the measures and the means that you will authorize will be similar to those that you already took toward Argentina.

A: Maybe yes, maybe no. What is certain is that the responsible nations have to be a little more logical with themselves, that is, violence must be refused everywhere. When the delegate of France expresses himself on that subject, he will no doubt consider that violence must be rejected equally everywhere.

In the Argentina matter, the great difficulty derives from the fact that Argentina initiated the aggression. If one condemns violence, one starts by condemning Argentina. Then, it is the chain of circumstances that is difficult to avoid.

But as the purpose—of France in any case (in that area, I can only commit myself, my country)—is to affirm its solidarity with Great Britain against that violation of right and to preserve as much as possible the very important relations that unite France, also Western Europe, and Latin America, that means that, in the coming days, a whole series of actions will be necessary.

Q: Mr. President, my previous question. I would like to ask you if the declaration of the Heads of State and Government goes further in the direction of solidarity with Great Britain than the positions that had been taken until now, and also if the heads of State and Government have agreed not only on the necessity of a local cease-fire, but also of a cease-fire that would include all nations that are engaged in the present conflict—in other words, that Argentina cannot continue to harass the British positions in the Falklands when law will have been reestablished?

A: Listen, let's keep it simple. No text has been adopted on the matter of the Falklands-Malvinas . . . I say Falklands-Malvinas because if I say Malvinas, you will translate Falklands and if I say Falklands, others will translate Malvinas. But it is the same thing. So, I will not make any unnecessary speech on that subject.

What is true is that Argentina preferred to solve by violence an old debate with Great Britain. What is also true is that many countries never recognized or defined the sovereignty of Great Britain, and still we have sided with Great Britain.

Why? Because it was attacked, because it is our friend and our ally and that from the moment when the aggression occurred, a set of events started which we cannot control.

We supported Resolution 502 of the United Nations from the beginning. We stand by that. On the other hand, we adopted within the European Community an embargo on trade exchanges with Argentina, which seemed to us the normal consequence of our condemnation of violence.

What has happened since then, particularly in the British advance on the Falklands-Malvinas, is part of an event in which France has no influence, except, it is true, indirectly, due to the fact that it participates in the embargo. Simply stated, we consider that what one could call a new event in this game of fate will be constituted by the fact that Great Britain will have recovered the land to which its right was disputed.

From then on, a new phase will begin—this is not a principle, it is a political fact—that, I hope, will result as soon as possible in a cease-fire or an armistice, call it what you will, and France will naturally be on the side of those who will plead that case.

Williamsburg

28–30 May 1983

WILLIAMSBURG, VIRGINIA, 28–30 MAY 1983

DELEGATIONS

Canada

Pierre Elliot Trudeau, *Prime Minister*
Allan J. MacEachen, *Secretary of State for External Affairs*
Marc Lalonde, *Minister of Finance*
De Montigny Marchand, *Personal Representative (Sherpa)*

France

François Mitterand, *President*
Claude Cheysson, *Minister of External Relations*
Jacques Delors, *Minister for the Economy, Finance and Budget*
Jacques Attali, *Personal Representative (Sherpa)*

Germany (Federal Republic)

Helmut Kohl, *Federal Chancellor*
Hans-Dietrich Genscher, *Federal Minister for Foreign Affairs*
Gerhard Stoltenberg, *Federal Minister of Finance*

Germany (Federal Republic) *continued*

Otto Lambsdorff, *Federal Minister of Economics*
Hans Tietmeyer, *Personal Representative (Sherpa)*

Italy

Amintore Fanfani, *President of the Council of Ministers*
Emilio Colombo, *Minister for Foreign Affairs*
Giovanni Goria, *Minister of the Treasury*
Remo Paolini, *Personal Representative (Sherpa)*

Japan

Yasuhiro Nakasone, *Prime Minister*
Shintaro Abe, *Minister for Foreign Affairs*
Noboru Takeshita, *Minister of Finance*
Sadanori Yamanaka, *Minister of International Trade and Industry*
Moriyuki Motono, *Personal Representative (Sherpa)*

United Kingdom

Margaret Thatcher, *Prime Minister*
Francis Pym, *Secretary of State for Foreign and Commonwealth Affairs*
Geoffrey Howe, *Chancellor of the Exchequer*
Robert Armstrong, *Personal Representative (Sherpa)*

United States

Ronald Reagan, *President*
George P. Shultz, *Secretary of State*
Donald Regan, *Secretary of the Treasury*
W. Allen Wallis, *Personal Representative (Sherpa)*

European Communities

Gaston Thorn, *President of the Commission*
Jean Durieux, *Personal Representative (Sherpa)*

DECLARATION ON ECONOMIC RECOVERY
(Read by President Reagan)

May 30, 1983

It is my duty and pleasure to read the Williamsburg Declaration on Economic Recovery.

Our nations are united in their dedication to democracy, individual freedom, creativity, moral purpose, human dignity, and personal and cultural development. It is to preserve, sustain, and extend these shared values that our prosperity is important.

The recession has put our societies through a severe test, but they have proved resilient. Significant success has been achieved in reducing inflation and interest rates; there have been improvements in productivity; and we now clearly see signs of recovery.

Nevertheless, the industrialized democracies continue to face the challenge of ensuring that the recovery materializes and endures, in order to reverse a decade of cumulative inflation and reduce unemployment. We must all focus on achieving and maintaining low inflation, and reducing interest rates from their present too-high levels. We renew our commitment to reduce structural budget deficits, in particular, by limiting the growth of expenditures.

We recognize that we must act together and that we must pursue a balanced set of policies that take into account and exploit relationships between growth, trade, and finance in order that recovery may spread to all countries, developed and developing alike.

In pursuance of these objectives, we have agreed as follows:

1. Our governments will pursue appropriate monetary and budgetary policies that will be conducive to low inflation, reduced interest rates, higher productive investment and greater employment opportunities, particularly for the young.

2. The consultation process initiated at Versailles will be enhanced to promote convergence of economic performance in our economies and greater stability of exchange rates, on the lines indicated in an annex to this declaration. We agree to pursue closer consultations on policies affecting exchange markets and on market conditions. While retaining our freedom to operate independently, we are willing to undertake coordinated intervention in exchange markets in instances where it is agreed that such intervention would be helpful.

3. We commit ourselves to halt protectionism and as recovery proceeds to reverse it by dismantling trade barriers. We intend to consult within appropriate existing fora on ways to implement and monitor this commitment. We shall give impetus to resolving current trade problems. We will actively pursue the current work programs in the General Agreement on Tariffs and Trade (GATT) and Organisation for Economic Co-operation and Development, including trade in services and in high-technology products. We should work to achieve further trade liberalization negotiations in the GATT, with particular emphasis on expanding trade with and among developing countries. We have agreed to continue consultations on proposals for a new negotiating round in the GATT.

4. We view with concern the international financial situation, and especially the debt burdens of many developing nations. We agree to a strategy based on: effective adjustment and development policies by debtor nations; adequate private and official financing; more open markets; and worldwide economic recovery. We will seek early ratification of the increases in resources for the International Monetary Fund and the General Arrangements to Borrow. We encourage closer cooperation and timely sharing of information

among countries and the international institutions, in particular between the International Monetary Fund (IMF), the International Bank for Reconstruction and Development (IBRD), and the GATT.

5. We have invited Ministers of Finance, in consultation with the Managing Director of the IMF, to define the conditions for improving the international monetary system and to consider the part which might, in due course, be played in this process by a high-level international monetary conference.

6. The weight of the recession has fallen very heavily on developing countries, and we are deeply concerned about their recovery. Restoring sound economic growth while keeping our markets open is crucial. Special attention will be given to the flow of resources, in particular official development assistance, to poorer countries, and for food and energy production, both bilaterally and through appropriate international institutions. We reaffirm our commitments to provide agreed funding levels for the International Development Association. We welcome the openness to dialogue which the developing countries evinced at the recent conferences of the Non-Aligned Movement in New Delhi and the Group of 77 in Buenos Aires, and we share their commitment to engage with understanding and cooperation in the forthcoming meeting of the United Nations Conference on Trade and Development in Belgrade.

7. We are agreed upon the need to encourage both the development of advanced technology and the public acceptance of its role in promoting growth, employment, and trade. We have noted with approval the report of the Working Group on Technology, Growth and Employment which was set up at Versailles last year, and commend the progress made in the 18

cooperative projects discussed in that report. We will follow the implementation and coordination of work on these projects, and look forward to receiving a further report at our next meeting.

8. We all share the view that more predictability and less volatility in oil prices would be helpful to world economic prospects. We agree that the fall in oil prices in no way diminishes the importance and urgency of efforts to conserve energy, to develop economic alternative energy sources, to maintain and, where possible, improve contacts between oil-exporting and importing countries, and to encourage the growth of indigenous energy production in developing countries which at present lack it.

9. East–West economic relations should be compatible with our security interests. We take note with approval of the work of the multilateral organizations which have in recent months analyzed and drawn conclusions regarding the key aspects of East–West economic relations. We encourage continuing work by these organizations, as appropriate.

10. We have agreed to strengthen cooperation in protection of the environment, in better use of natural resources, and in health research.

Our discussions here at Williamsburg give us new confidence in the prospects for a recovery. We have strengthened our resolve to deal cooperatively with continuing problems so as to promote a sound and sustainable recovery, bringing new jobs and a better life for the people of our own countries and of the world.

We have agreed to meet again next year, and have accepted the British Prime Minister's invitation to meet in the United Kingdom.

Annex: Strengthening Economic Cooperation for Growth and Stability

[The Annex is part of the Declaration but was not read by the President.—Ed.]

I. We have examined, in the light of our experience, the procedures outlined in the undertakings agreed at Versailles last year which seek to ensure greater monetary stability in the interest of balanced growth and progress of the world economy.

II. We reaffirm the objectives of achieving non-inflationary growth of income and employment, and promoting exchange market stability through policies designed to bring about greater convergence of economic performance in this direction.

III. We are reinforcing our multilateral cooperation with the International Monetary Fund in its surveillance activities, according to the procedures agreed at Versailles, through the following approach:

A. We are focusing on near-term policy actions leading to convergence of economic conditions in the medium term. The overall medium-term perspective remains essential, both to ensure that short-term policy innovations do not lead to divergence and to reassure business and financial markets.

B. In accordance with the agreement reached at Versailles, we are focusing our attention on issues in the monetary and financial fields including interaction with policies in other areas. We shall take fully into account the international implications of our own policy decisions. Policies and objectives that will be kept under review include:

(1) Monetary Policy. Disciplined non-inflationary growth of monetary aggregates, and appropriate interest rates, to avoid subsequent resurgence of inflation and rebound in interest rates, thus allowing room for sustainable growth.

(2) Fiscal Policy. We will aim, preferably through discipline over government expenditures, to reduce structural budget deficits and bear in mind the consequences of fiscal policy for interest rates and growth.

(3) Exchange Rate Policy. We will improve consultations, policy convergence, and international cooperation to help stabilize exchange markets, bearing in mind our conclusions on the Exchange Market Intervention Study.

(4) Policies Toward Productivity and Employment. While relying on market signals as a guide to efficient economic decisions, we will take measures to improve training and mobility of our labor forces, with particular concern for the problems of youth unemployment, and promote continued structural adjustment, especially by:

—Enhancing flexibility and openness of economies and financial markets;

—Encouraging research and development as well as profitability and productive investment; and

—Continued efforts in each country, and improved international cooperation, where appropriate, on structural adjustment measures (e.g., regional, sectoral, energy policies).

IV. We shall continue to assess together regularly in this framework the progress we are making, consider any corrective action which may be necessary from time to time, and react promptly to significant changes.

*[Text of Annex ends here.—*ED.*]*

It has been inspiring to meet with the leaders of the seven major industrial nations in this beautifully restored village of the past. Here we have tried to shape the positive and common approach to our economic future. These democracies feel special responses for, or responsibility for, the world economy and for the democratic values we all share.

And so, we came together determined to do something about some of the world's toughest problems. Our meeting has shown a spirit of confidence, optimism, and certainty—confidence that recovery is under way, optimism that it will be durable, and certainty that economic policy and security ties among us will be strengthened in the future.

The United States has been privileged to host this meeting from which a message of hope can be sent to the people of the world and to future generations. Together the Summit partners are facing today's enormous challenges head on and not settling for quick fixes. We are the guardians of fundamental democratic values that have always united us.

We will only be satisfied when we have restored durable economic growth that offers our people an opportunity for the better future that they deserve.

The meeting will conclude with tonight's dinner and may I just add a heartfelt thank you to the wonderful people of

Williamsburg who have been so warm in their greeting to us, so gracious and so kind, and that have made this, in addition to a hard-working session, a distinct pleasure. And I think I speak for all of us in saying this. Thank you all.

SOURCE: U.S., Department of State, *Bulletin,* No. 2076 (July 1983): 13–15; *Economic Summits, 1975–1986: Declarations* (Rome: Istituto Affari Internazionali, 1987): 99–104; Great Britain, Foreign and Commonwealth Office, *Declarations of Annual Economic Summits, 1975–1986* (London, 198—): A9, Williamsburg, 1–5 [unpublished].

STATEMENT AT WILLIAMSBURG
[DECLARATION ON SECURITY]

May 29, 1983

1. As leaders of our seven countries, it is our first duty to defend the freedom and justice on which our democracies are based. To this end, we shall maintain sufficient military strength to deter any attack, to counter any threat, and to ensure the peace. Our arms will never be used except in response to aggression.

2. We wish to achieve lower levels of arms through serious arms control negotiations. With this statement, we reaffirm our dedication to the search for peace and meaningful arms reductions. We are ready to work with the Soviet Union to this purpose and call upon the Soviet Union to work with us.

3. Effective arms control agreements must be based on the principle of equality and must be verifiable. Proposals have been put forward from the Western side to achieve positive results in various international negotiations: on strategic weapons, the START talks [Strategic Arms Reduction Talks]; on intermediate-range nuclear missiles, the INF [Intermediate-range Nuclear Forces] talks; on chemical weapons; on reduction of forces in Central Europe, the MBFR [Mutual and Balanced Force Reductions] talks; and a Conference on Disarmament in Europe [CDE].

4. We believe that we must continue to pursue these negotiations with impetus and urgency. In the area of INF, in particular, we call upon the Soviet Union to contribute constructively to the success of the negotiations. Attempts to divide the West by proposing inclusion of the deterrent forces of third countries, such as those of France and the United Kingdom, will fail. Consideration of these systems has no place in the INF negotiations.

5. Our nations express the strong wish that a balanced INF agreement be reached shortly. Should this occur, the negotiations will determine the level of deployment. It is well-known that should this not occur, the countries concerned will proceed with the planned deployment of the U.S. systems in Europe beginning at the end of 1983.

6. Our nations are united in efforts for arms reductions and will continue to carry out thorough and intensive consultations. The security of our countries is indivisible and must be approached on a global basis. Attempts to avoid serious negotiation by seeking to influence public opinion in our countries will fail.

7. We commit ourselves to devote our full political resources to reducing the threat of war. We have a vision of a world in which the shadow of war has been lifted from all mankind, and we are determined to pursue that vision.

SOURCE: U.S., Department of State, *Bulletin,* No. 2076 (July 1983): 4–5; *Economic Summits, 1975–1986: Declarations* (Rome: Istituto Affari Internazionali, 1987): 104–105; Great Britain, Foreign and Commonwealth Office, *Political Declarations and Statements of Annual Economic Summits, 1978–1986* (London, 198—) [unpublished].

PRESIDENT REAGAN'S DINNER TOAST, ROCKEFELLER FOLK ART CENTER

May 30, 1983

It is a pleasure to see all of you and to tell you that our discussions over the last few days have been as fruitful and as useful and enjoyable as we had all hoped. As I noted at the outset—that our countries were linked by a multitude of mutual interests and by a shared commitment to freedom and democracy.

Williamsburg, as a site, was the site of the first representative assembly and the second university in the Colonies which then became the United States. It has been a particularly appropriate place in which to rededicate ourselves to these principles.

The preservation of the values we share must strengthen our domestic economies, seek advantages of vigorous international trade, and deal intelligently with the problems of crises in the developing world. And while doing this, we must also give appropriate attention to our security interests. These objectives are complex, sometimes seemingly contradictory, and always difficult to achieve.

Our individual perceptions about particular issues may sometimes differ, but gatherings such as this give us an opportunity to work together on a regular basis to address the problems we share. This meeting has, in my judgment, achieved that objective. It has left me more confident than ever of the basic health of our free way of life and our ability and cooperation to lay a sound foundation for our children and our children's children.

In that spirit, I want to toast all of you, who in the last few days have participated in this chapter of a vital and unceasing effort. And so, therefore, I think we can drink to the causes that have brought us here, to the success we've had, and to our dream of continuing on this road as far as we all can see.

And for some of us here, there is great gratitude to many of you for all that you have done to contribute to these meetings.

SOURCE: U.S., Department of State, *Bulletin,* No. 2076 (July 1983): 20.

INTERVIEW WITH PRESIDENT REAGAN

May 31, 1983

Q: You had said before this Summit that you wanted it structured in this way because you'd have a frank discussion with other leaders. Did you learn anything from that? Did your views change in any way because of what was said to you here in that format?

A: Actually, not in any major way because you would be amazed at how much our thinking was alike on so many of the things discussed.

But in connection with the question also on structure, the difference was that the summits that I've been to before, each head of state would make a statement and that would be it then. Whether they agreed, disagreed, or not, they had made their statement.

The difference was here, you'd open up a subject—let us say that the subject had to do with trade—we'd open up the subject and everyone could express their views and so forth and then we kept going and discussing to see that we could all agree on a consensus of what we would do with this in the area of this subject that would further benefit, not only us, but the world.

Q: Do you feel that you persuaded anybody to some view that they didn't have before they came here?

A: Not really. The whole idea of convergence—the answer is that you can't have one nation recover without the others, that this is a world recession, what we do affects each other, and that, therefore, we must have more surveillance, more constant communication, particularly at our ministerial level, on the progress that we're all making. And this included the developing countries also, that they cannot be out there on the other side of a door that their good economic situation, their prosperity is as vital to us as ours is to them. And, as I say, there was great agreement on this.

246

But what then did happen was you had the thoughts of others that contributed to come into a consensus as to how we were going to go about this, what we were going to do. And remember that the idea of the subjects wasn't just chaos of anyone coming with what they thought. A lot of this was based on the fact that at the ministerial level, OECD [Organisation for Economic Co-operation and Development], the NATO [North Atlantic Treaty Organization] summit, in the discussions on international monetary funds [*sic*] and all, we were well prepared in advance of knowing what was on the minds of each other.

Q: If I may, this was a Summit designed so that those of you who met privately could, on several occasions, have a frank exchange, candid exchange of views—candid, personal. And yet you're saying that there were diverse views in here. And yet you're saying in spite of all of that, nobody's views changed very much—

A: As I interpreted the question there, was there any sudden situation where you had just diametrically opposed ideas, say, a way to bring about prosperity. No, everyone recognized that—for example, in our own problems of deficits and interest rates and the bad effect that they have had on the economy. There was general agreement on all of these things. And then the thing was how, for example—it's in the statement that came out, differing from some conferences where the statement was written in advance and before you'd had the discussions. That statement was the result of the discussions.

Q: Let me give you a for instance. You said in your personal addendum to the statement that the world now recognizes there should be no quick fixes which as you mentioned in the United States [sic]. But I know you were told by some of the leaders in there that despite the best expected performance of the economy, unemployment is going to remain high for some time to come, recession may even deepen in some countries, and there are people who are concerned about the political and social upheaval that this can cause and, therefore, might favor some kind of quick fix, at least to avert the kind of crisis the United States faces. Did that

247

discussion not temper your views about at least some quick fixes some way?

A: No, as a matter of fact, one of the participants referred to quick fixes as "quack medicine" and that we've proven by experience they don't work. They only worsen the situation. There is great willingness on the part of all of them, that they realized that they had to face up to some social changes in order to get control of excessive spending. And, as I say, the document attests that—the statement to the outcome. We didn't leave any subject up in the air and say, "Well, you know, we're differing on this. Let's move on to something else." No. We stayed until we'd worked out what we all felt was a way to go on the particular subject. And there was no vote taken. There were no winners or losers. There wasn't any case in which five said, "Well, to two, you're out-voted and this is what we're going to say." No, before we settled it, all seven were in agreement.

Q: It's well known that your Administration wasn't enthusiastic about an international monetary conference. Did you modify your views during the Summit?

A: The funny thing was in the conversations, it isn't so much a modifying of views as it is a learning of what the views really were. For example, the principal proponent of such a conference opened by making it plain that he had not meant in any way that we go back 40 years and follow a pattern of something that was adopted 40 years ago—the world has changed—but that it was something to be looked at. We ourselves had come with the idea that just as out of the Versailles Summit—and while many people have been quick to say that nothing good came out of that, a lot did. We have had since the Versailles Summit a relationship at the ministerial level on several subjects that has been ongoing and that has made great progress with regard to trade, the East–West situation, all of these things.

And so the idea that these same ministers will now, as they go forward in this surveillance—mutual surveillance to make sure that we're not getting off the track in some country or other that might set back for all of us the recovery, that this they will look at very closely and see if such a conference would be a help in what we're trying to do. It's going to depend on what they all decide and what they recommend.

Q: The dollar is reaching record highs against other currencies. Do you think that is a positive development for the world economy and for the American recovery?

A: There's no question about the value of the dollar, that it results from our success with reducing inflation. And, of course, we want to go on reducing inflation.

But we also want to see as the others progress that this levels off, because, remember, the high dollar is not an unmitigated blessing for us. We will have a trade deficit this year of probably $60 billion simply because the high value of the dollar has priced us out of many foreign markets.

We'd like to see a better balance. But we believe the better balance will come through convergence. And so, here again, out of this has come the decision that we're going to monitor each other closely on how we're progressing on this.

Q: You indicated in an interview last week that the Soviets were stepping up their aid to Nicaragua. I wondered whether you see the possibility of a superpower confrontation developing in Central America, and whether increased Soviet aid requires an increased response from the United States.

A: It is a little off the Summit. I did, in one session, simply explain as well as I could the entire situation in Central America. And many of them admitted that they had not been clear on some of what was going on. There has been a step-up in Soviet activity as to bringing in supplies. But we still believe that our plan of economic aid and such military assistance as we think is needed there in the line of supplies—training, mainly—should go forward.

But again, call attention to the fact that our economic aid is three to one in value over the military aid. We want, indeed, a political settlement if it can be reached.

Q: Did you ask your allies for help on that question—I mean, did you ask them to—

A: No. On this one, this was just one where I gave them a report and—

Q: From a very general point of view, now that you have heard the opinion of all the other leaders at the same time, what is your feeling on the future of relations with Russia? Is it going to be an ever-increasing tension and hostility, or will there be a point where there will be a thaw? I'm not asking about your hopes, but about your gut feeling of what actually is going to happen.

A: If there is an increase of tension, it will be the Soviet Union that causes it. Let me just quickly—because I know time is important—point something out. Sitting at that table in this Summit were the representatives—the heads of state—of nations that not too many years ago were deeply engaged in a hatred-filled war with each other. And here we were, sitting as closely as we're sitting with a really warm, personal friendship that had developed among us, but more than that, with a friendship between our peoples. And, what is the cause of disarray in the world—if we had been able to do this with our erstwhile enemies, doesn't it sort of follow that we are the ones who want a peaceful world? I don't mean when I say "we" the United States, I mean all of us—the people who were around that table—that we are the ones who are striving for peace and have been successful in healing those terrible, deep wounds. But that one country that was an ally in that great war is the cause of tension in the world and that the things that we had to think about with regard to our national security, all dealt with our national security vis-à-vis that particular country.

Over and over again in talking trade we stressed that we don't want a trade war with the Soviet Union. We've been forced into having to view our relationship with our own security in mind. But, I couldn't help but think several times, why in the world isn't that other so-called superpower—why didn't they have someone sitting at that table able to get along with the rest of us?

Q: But do you see better or worse relations? If you were to predict today, is it better or worse relations with the Soviet Union?

A: I see better, because I think all of us together have a more realistic view of them. This may not be visible in the rhetoric in the immediate future, because there's an awful lot of rhetoric that is delivered for home consumption.

Q: They've accused you of wrecking détente—with the INF statement.

A: Détente, as it existed, was only a cover under which the Soviet Union built up the greatest military power in the world. I don't think we need that kind of a détente. But, all of us, we're ready—at any time—if they want to make it plain by deed, not word, that they want to join in the same things that are of concern to all of us—the betterment of life for our peoples.

Q: You spent some time in the last couple of evenings talking about the Middle East as well, I understand, with your partners. And, most recently, there has been an increasing tension between both Syrian and Israeli forces in Lebanon right now. You have an agreement between Lebanon and Israel for a troop withdrawal, but the Syrians are not cooperating. Really, without their cooperation, you have very little. What is the next step? And, can you tell me, with the increased tensions, have you been in contact with the Soviet Union to get the Syrians to cool it?

A: This is hardly a Summit meeting thing, but let me say we're continuing what we've been doing all the time and that is trying to persuade the Syrians who had made a statement in the very beginning of all these talks that they would withdraw when the others did. And we're talking to their Arab friends and allies about this, I think making some progress. So this does not require any new course.

And as to whether there were several meetings, there was just one meeting in which I summed up and gave my—well, no, I didn't. I'm sorry, I was thinking there—I was talking about something else. No, on the Middle East, we did have one session and a dinner session and, actually, there was no quarrel with what we're doing. It was total support; but there was more a report on some of those who had been closer to the situation back over the years, our European neighbors, giving their views on some of the things that were at issue there and some of the problems.

Q: Just in light of the INF declaration, can you envision an outcome—an interim solution in Geneva which would delay the stationing of the missiles in Europe?

A: I don't think you can predict on anything there without getting into the dangerous field of discussing strategy.

Frankly, my own opinion is that the negotiations won't really get down to brass tacks until they see that we are going forward with the scheduled deployment.

Q: Does that mean that the negotiations won't go forward until after you deploy?

A: Oh, no. We're going to try. The meetings are on now. We're going to try to negotiate. I am just anticipating from the Soviet side; they have based their entire propaganda campaign, everything they've been doing, on seeking to prevent the beginning deployment. And we have a schedule of deployment, the request of our NATO allies, and we're going to follow that.

SOURCE: U.S., Department of State, *Bulletin*, No. 2076 (July 1983): 20–22.

London

7–9 June 1984

LONDON (UNITED KINGDOM), 7–9 JUNE 1984

DELEGATIONS

Canada

Pierre Elliot Trudeau, *Prime Minister*
Allan J. MacEachen, *Secretary of State for External Affairs*
Marc Lalonde, *Minister of Finance*
Sylvia Ostry, *Personal Representative (Sherpa)*

France

François Mitterand, *President*
Claude Cheysson, *Minister of External Relations*
Jacques Delors, *Minister for the Economy, Finance and Budget*
Jacques Attali, *Personal Representative (Sherpa)*

Germany (Federal Republic)

Helmut Kohl, *Federal Chancellor*
Hans-Dietrich Genscher, *Federal Minister for Foreign Affairs*
Gerhard Stoltenberg, *Federal Minister of Finance*

Germany (Federal Republic) *continued*

Otto Lambsdorff, *Federal Minister of Economics*
Hans Tietmeyer, *Personal Representative (Sherpa)*

Italy

Bettino Craxi, *President of the Council of Ministers*
Giulio Andreotti, *Minister for Foreign Affairs*
Giovanni Goria, *Minister of the Treasury*
Renato Ruggiero, *Personal Representative (Sherpa)*

Japan

Yasuhiro Nakasone, *Prime Minister*
Shintaro Abe, *Minister for Foreign Affairs*
Noboru Takeshita, *Minister of Finance*
Moriyuki Motono, *Personal Representative (Sherpa)*

United Kingdom

Margaret Thatcher, *Prime Minister*
Geoffrey Howe, *Secretary of State for Foreign and
   Commonwealth Affairs*
Nigel Lawson, *Chancellor of the Exchequer*
Robert Armstrong, *Personal Representative (Sherpa)*

United States

Ronald Reagan, *President*
George P. Shultz, *Secretary of State*
Donald Regan, *Secretary of the Treasury*
W. Allen Wallis, *Personal Representative (Sherpa)*

European Communities

Gaston Thorn, *President of the Commission*
François Xavier Ortoli, *Vice-President of the Commission*
Jean Durieux, *Personal Representative (Sherpa)*

THE LONDON ECONOMIC DECLARATION

June 9, 1984

1. We, the Heads of State or Government of seven major industrialized countries and the President of the Commission of the European Communities, have gathered in London from 7 to 9 June 1984 at the invitation of the Rt. Hon. Margaret Thatcher, FRS MP, the Prime Minister of the United Kingdom, for the tenth annual Economic Summit.

2. The primary purpose of these meetings is to enable Heads of State or Government to come together to discuss economic problems, prospects and opportunities for our countries and for the world. We have been able to achieve not only closer understanding of each other's positions and views but also a large measure of agreement on the basic objectives of our respective policies.

3. At our last meeting, in Williamsburg in 1983, we were already able to detect clear signs of recovery from world recession. That recovery can now be seen to be established in our countries. It is more soundly based than previous recoveries in that it results from the firm efforts made in the Summit countries and elsewhere over recent years to reduce inflation.

4. But its continuation requires unremitting efforts. We have to make the most of the opportunities with which we are now presented to reinforce the basis for enduring growth and the creation of new jobs. We need to spread the benefits of recovery widely, both within the industrialized countries and also to the developing countries, especially the poorer countries who stand to gain more than any from a sustainable growth of the world economy. High interest rates, and failure to reduce inflation further and dampen down inflationary expectations, could put recovery at risk. Prudent monetary and budgetary policies of the kind that have brought us so far will have to be sustained and where necessary strengthened. We reaffirm the commitment of our Governments to those objectives and policies.

5. Not the least of our concerns is the growing strain of public expenditure in all our countries. Public expenditure has to be kept within the limits of what our national economies can afford. We welcome the increasing attention being given to these problems by national governments and in such international bodies as the Organisation for Economic Co-operation and Development (OECD).

6. As unemployment in our countries remains high, we emphasize the need for sustained growth and creation of new jobs. We must make sure that the industrial economies adapt and develop in response to demand and to technological change. We must encourage active job training policies and removal of rigidities in the labor market, and bring about the conditions in which more new jobs will be created on a lasting basis, especially for the young. We need to foster and expand the international trading system and liberalize capital markets.

7. We are mindful of the concerns expressed by the developing countries, and of the political and economic difficulties which many of them face. In our discussion of each of the issues before us we have recognized the economic interdependence of the industrialized and developing countries. We reaffirm our willingness to conduct our relations with them in a spirit of goodwill and cooperation. To this end we have asked Ministers of Finance to consider the scope for intensified discussion of international financial issues of particular concern to developing countries in the IBRD [International Bank for Reconstruction and Development] Development Committee, an appropriate and broadly representative forum for this purpose.

8. In our strategy for dealing with the debt burdens of many developing countries, a key role has been played by the International Monetary Fund (IMF), whose resources have been strengthened for the purpose. Debtor countries have been

increasingly ready to accept the need to adjust their economic policies, despite the painful and courageous efforts it requires. In a climate of world recovery and growing world trade, this strategy should continue to enable the international financial system to manage the problems that may still arise. But continuously high or even further growing levels of international interest rates could both exacerbate the problems of the debtor countries and make it more difficult to sustain the strategy. This underlines the importance of policies which will be conducive to lower interest rates and which take account of the impact of our policies upon other countries.

9. We have therefore agreed:

(1) To continue with and where necessary strengthen policies to reduce inflation and interest rates, to control monetary growth and where necessary reduce budgetary deficits;

(2) To seek to reduce obstacles to the creation of new jobs:

—by encouraging the development of industries and services in response to demand and technological change, including in innovative small and medium-sized businesses;

—by encouraging the efficient working of the labor market;

—by encouraging the improvement and extension of job training;

—by encouraging flexibility in the patterns of working time;

—and by discouraging measures to preserve obsolescent production and technology.

(3) To support and strengthen work in the appropriate international organizations, notably the OECD, on increasing understanding of the sources and patterns of economic change, and on improving economic efficiency and promoting growth, in particular by encouraging innovation and working for a more widespread acceptance of technological change, harmonizing standards and facilitating the mobility of labor and capital;

(4) To maintain and wherever possible increase flows of resources including official development assistance and assistance through the international financial and development institutions, to the developing countries and particularly to the poorest countries; to work with the developing countries to encourage more openness towards private investment flows; and to encourage practical measures in those countries to conserve resources and enhance indigenous food and energy production. Some of us also wish to activate the Common Fund for Commodities;

(5) In a spirit of cooperation with the countries concerned, to confirm the strategy on debt and continue to implement and develop it flexibly case by case; we have reviewed progress and attach particular importance to:

—helping debtor countries to make necessary economic and financial policy changes, taking due account of political and social difficulties;

—encouraging the IMF in its central role in this process, which it has been carrying out skillfully;

—encouraging closer cooperation between the IMF and the International Bank for Reconstruction and Development (IBRD), and strengthening the role of the IBRD in fostering development over the medium and long term;

—in cases where debtor countries are themselves making successful efforts to improve their position, encouraging more extended multi-year rescheduling of commercial debts and standing ready where appropriate to negotiate similarly in respect of debts to governments and government agencies;

—encouraging the flow of long-term direct investment; just as there is need for industrial countries to make their markets more open for the exports of developing countries, so these countries can help themselves by encouraging investment from the industrial countries;

—encouraging the substitution of more stable long-term finance, both direct and portfolio, for short-term bank lending.

(6) To invite Finance Ministers to carry forward, in an urgent and thorough manner, their current work on ways to improve the operation of the international monetary system, including exchange rates, surveillance, the creation, control and distribution of international liquidity and the role of the IMF; and to complete the present phase of their work in the first half of 1985 with a view to discussion at an early meeting of the IMF Interim Committee. The question of a further allocation of Special Drawing Rights is to be reconsidered by the IMF Interim Committee in September 1984;

(7) To carry forward the procedures agreed at Versailles and at Williamsburg for multilateral monitoring and surveillance of convergence of economic performance toward lower inflation and higher growth;

(8) To seek to improve the operation and stability of the international financial system, by means of prudent policies among the major countries, by providing an adequate flow of funding to the international financial institutions, and by improving international access to capital markets in industrialized countries;

(9) To urge all trading countries, industrialized and developing alike, to resist continuing protectionist pressures, to reduce barriers to trade and to make renewed efforts to liberalize and expand international trade in manufactures, commodities and services;

(10) To accelerate the completion of current trade liberalization programs, particularly the 1982 GATT [General Agreement on Tariffs and Trade] work program, in cooperation with other trading partners; to press forward with the work on trade in services in the international organizations; to reaffirm the agreement reached at the OECD Ministerial Meeting in May 1984 on the important contribution which a new round of multilateral trade negotiations would make to strengthening the open multilateral trading system for the mutual benefit of all economies, industrial and developing; and, building on the 1982 GATT work program, to consult partners in the GATT with a view to decisions at an early date on the possible objectives, arrangements and timing for a new negotiating round.

10. We are greatly concerned about the acute problems of poverty and drought in parts of Africa. We attach major importance to the special action program for Africa which is being prepared by the World Bank and should provide renewed impetus to the joint efforts of the international community to help.

11. We have considered the possible implications of a further deterioration of the situation in the Gulf for the supply of oil. We are satisfied that, given the stocks of oil presently available in the world, the availability of other sources of energy, and the scope for conservation in the use of energy, adequate supplies could be maintained for a substantial period of time by international cooperation and mutually supportive action. We will continue to act together to that end.

12. We note with approval the continuing consensus on the security and other implications of economic relations with Eastern countries, and on the need to continue work on this subject in the appropriate organizations.

13. We welcome the further report of the Working Group on Technology, Growth and Employment created by the Versailles Economic Summit, and the progress made in the eighteen areas of cooperation, and invite the Group to pursue further work and to report to Personal Representatives in time for the next Economic Summit. We also welcome the invitation of the Italian Government to an international conference to be held in Italy in 1985 on the theme of technological innovation and the creation of new jobs.

14. We recognize the international dimension of environmental problems and the role of environmental factors in economic development. We have invited Ministers responsible for environmental policies to identify areas for continuing cooperation in this field. In addition we have decided to invite the Working Group on Technology, Growth and Employment to consider what has been done so far and to identify specific areas for research on the causes, effects and means of limiting environmental pollution of air, water and ground where existing knowledge is inadequate, and to identify possible projects for industrial cooperation to develop cost-effective techniques to reduce environmental damage. The Group is invited to report on these matters by 31 December 1984. In the meantime we welcome the invitation from the Government of the Federal

Republic of Germany to certain Summit countries to an international conference on the environment in Munich on 24–27 June 1984.

15. We thank the Prime Minister of Japan for his report on the Hakone Conference of Life Sciences and Mankind, organized by the Japan Foundation in March 1984, and welcome the intention of the French Government to sponsor a second conference in 1985.

16. We believe that manned space stations are the kind of program that provides a stimulus for technological development leading to strengthened economies and improved quality of life. Such stations are being studied in some of our countries with a view to their being launched in the framework of national or international programs. In that context each of our countries will consider carefully the generous and thoughtful invitation received from the President of the United States to other Summit countries to participate in the development of such a station by the United States. We welcome the intention of the United States to report at the next Summit on international participation in their program.

17. We have agreed to meet again next year and have accepted the Federal Chancellor's invitation to meet in the Federal Republic of Germany.

SOURCE: U.S., Department of State, *Bulletin*, No. 2089 (August 1984): 2–4; *Economic Summits, 1975–1986: Declarations* (Rome: Istituto Affari Internazionali, 1987): 109–16; Great Britain, Foreign and Commonwealth Office, *Declarations of Annual Economic Summits, 1975–1986* (London, 198—): A10, London, 1–6 [unpublished].

DECLARATION ON DEMOCRATIC VALUES

June 8, 1984

1. We, the Heads of State or Government of seven major industrial democracies with the President of the Commission of the European Communities, assembled in London for the Tenth Economic Summit meeting, affirm our commitment to the values which sustain and bring together our societies.

2. We believe in a rule of law which respects and protects without fear or favor the rights and liberties of every citizen, and provides the setting in which the human spirit can develop in freedom and diversity.

3. We believe in a system of democracy which ensures genuine choice in elections freely held, free expression of opinion and the capacity to respond and adapt to change in all its aspects.

4. We believe that, in the political and economic systems of our democracies, it is for Governments to set conditions in which there can be the greatest possible range and freedom of choice and personal initiative; in which the ideals of social justice, obligations and rights can be pursued; in which enterprise can flourish and employment opportunities can be available for all; in which all have equal opportunities of sharing in the benefits of growth and there is support for those who suffer or are in need; in which the lives of all can be enriched by the fruits of innovation, imagination and scientific discovery; and in which there can be confidence in the soundness of the currency. Our countries have the resources and will jointly to master the tasks of the new industrial revolution.

5. We believe in close partnership among our countries in the conviction that this will reinforce political stability and economic growth in the world as a whole. We look for cooperation with all countries on the basis of respect for their independence and territorial integrity, regardless of differences between political, economic and social systems. We respect genuine non-alignment. We are aware that economic strength places special moral responsibilities upon us. We reaffirm our determination to fight hunger and poverty throughout the world.

6. We believe in the need for peace with freedom and justice. Each of us rejects the use of force as a means of settling disputes. Each of us will maintain only the military strength necessary to deter aggression and to meet our responsibilities for effective defense. We believe that in today's world the independence of each of our countries is of concern to us all. We are convinced that international problems and conflicts can and must be resolved through reasoned dialogue and negotiation and we shall support all efforts to this end.

7. Strong in these beliefs, and endowed with great diversity and creative vigor, we look forward to the future with confidence.

SOURCE: U.S., Department of State, *Bulletin,* No. 2089 (August 1984): 1–2; *Economic Summits, 1975–1986: Declarations* (Rome: Istituto Affari Internazionali, 1987): 116–117; Great Britain, Foreign and Commonwealth Office, *Political Declarations and Statements of Annual Economic Summits, 1978– 1986* (London, 198—) [unpublished].

DECLARATION ON INTERNATIONAL TERRORISM

June 9, 1984

1. The Heads of State and Government discussed the problem of international terrorism.

2. They noted that hijacking and kidnapping had declined since the Declarations of Bonn (1978), Venice (1980) and Ottawa (1981) as a result of improved security measures, but that terrorism had developed other techniques, sometimes in association with traffic in drugs.

3. They expressed their resolve to combat this threat by every possible means, strengthening existing measures and developing effective new ones.

4. They were disturbed to note the ease with which terrorists move across international boundaries, and gain access to weapons, explosives, training and finance.

5. They viewed with serious concern the increasing involvement of states and governments in acts of terrorism, including the abuse of diplomatic immunity. They acknowledged the inviolability of diplomatic missions and other requirements of international law; but they emphasized the obligations which that law also entails.

6. Proposals which found support in the discussion included the following:

—closer cooperation and coordination between police and security organizations and other relevant authorities, especially in the exchange of information, intelligence and technical knowledge;

—scrutiny by each country of gaps in its national legislation which might be exploited by terrorists;

—use of the powers of the receiving State under the Vienna Convention in such matters as the size of diplomatic missions, and the number of buildings enjoying diplomatic immunity;

—action by each country to review the sale of weapons to States supporting terrorism;

—consultation and as far as possible cooperation over the expulsion or exclusion from their countries of known terrorists, including persons of diplomatic status involved in terrorism.

7. The Heads of State and Government recognized that this is a problem which affects all civilized States. They resolved to promote action through competent international organizations and among the international community as a whole to prevent and punish terrorist acts.

SOURCE: U.S., Department of State, *Bulletin,* No. 2089 (August 1984): 4–5; *Economic Summits, 1975–1986: Declarations* (Rome: Istituto Affari Internazionali, 1987): 117–118; Great Britain, Foreign and Commonwealth Office, *Political Declarations and Statements of Annual Economic Summits, 1978–1986* (London, 198—) [unpublished].

DECLARATION ON EAST–WEST RELATIONS AND ARMS CONTROL

June 9, 1984

1. We had a substantial discussion of East–West relations. We stressed that the first need is for solidarity and resolve among us all.

2. At the same time, we are determined to pursue the search for extended political dialogue and long-term cooperation with the Soviet Union and her allies. Contacts exist and are being developed in a number of fields. Each of us will pursue all useful opportunities for dialogue.

3. Our aim is security and the lowest possible level of forces. We wish to see early and positive results in the various arms control negotiations and the speedy resumption of those now suspended. The United States has offered to re-start nuclear arms control talks anywhere, at any time, without preconditions. We hope that the Soviet Union will act in a constructive and positive way. We are convinced that this would be in the common interest of both East and West. We are in favor of agreements which would build confidence and give concrete expression, through precise commitments, to the principle of the non-use of force.

4. We believe that East and West have important common interests: in preserving peace; in enhancing confidence and security; in reducing the risks of surprise attack or war by accident; in improving crisis management techniques; and in preventing the spread of nuclear weapons.

SOURCE: U.S., Department of State, *Bulletin,* No. 2089 (August 1984): 4; *Economic Summits, 1975–1986: Declarations* (Rome: Istituto Affari Internazionali, 1987): 118–119; Great Britain, Foreign and Commonwealth Office, *Political Declarations and Statements of Annual Economic Summits, 1978–1986* (London, 198—) [unpublished].

THE IRAQ–IRAN CONFLICT
(STATEMENT BY THE CHAIR)

June 9, 1984

1. We discussed the Iraq–Iran conflict in all its various aspects.

2. We expressed our deep concern at the mounting toll in human suffering, physical damage and bitterness that this conflict has brought; and at the breaches of international humanitarian law that have occurred.

3. The hope and desire of us all is that both sides will cease their attacks on each other and on the shipping of other States. The principle of freedom of navigation must be respected. We are concerned that the conflict should not spread further and we shall do what we can to encourage stability in the region.

4. We encourage the parties to seek a peaceful and honorable settlement. We shall support any efforts designed to bring this about, particularly those of the United Nations Secretary-General.

5. We also considered the implications for world oil supplies on the lines set out in the Economic Declaration. We noted that the world oil market has remained relatively stable. We believe that the international system has both the will and the capacity to cope with any foreseeable problems through the continuation of the prudent and realistic approach that is already being applied.

SOURCE: U.S., Department of State, *Bulletin,* No. 2089 (August 1984): 5; *Economic Summits, 1975–1986: Declarations* (Rome: Istituto Affari Internazionali, 1987): 119–120; Great Britain, Foreign and Commonwealth Office, *Political Declarations and Statements of Annual Economic Summits, 1978–1986* (London, 198—) [unpublished].

PRESS CONFERENCE GIVEN BY
PRIME MINISTER MRS. MARGARET THATCHER
AT THE END OF THE ECONOMIC SUMMIT IN
LONDON

June 9, 1984

Question: Prime Minister, one of the agreements today in the final communiqué says: "to work with the developing countries, to encourage more openness towards private investment flows." That seems to be much less forceful than your statement on the same subject yesterday.

Do you think this final conclusion was a watering down of what you were proposing yesterday?

Prime Minister: No, I think it was a slightly briefer version perhaps of what I said yesterday. We were talking about the debtor countries, the countries that have a serious international debt position. One of the ways of dealing with that debt is obviously either sale of assets or equity investment. It is not a path which a lot of them take because somehow some of them have either laws against it or do not wish to take that path. But it is one which is a method of dealing with their debt and if they made certain changes, they could follow.

I think it would help if we had a code for international investment, but if you are dealing with the problem of international debt, it is a path that must be considered. After all, some of the countries that have welcomed external equity investment have been those which have recovered fast and also those which have developed their economies fast.

So it is a shorthand version of what we discussed.

Question: Prime Minister, I wonder which came first, the chicken or the egg?

Prime Minister: Don't ask me!

Question: Inasmuch whether it is a reflection of what the international institutions and the banks in Great Britain are thinking about the measures for the international indebtedness and also seeing it is being considered on more of a technical approach as a strategy, I wonder what you think are the international political consequences of the indebtedness of our countries?

Prime Minister: We now have a problem and we have to deal with it as it is. If you look back, you can have several different analyses and two points in the analysis would be that perhaps some of the developing countries borrowed more than they could properly service and some of the lending banks lent more than it was wise to lend to those countries.

Be that as it may, we actually have the existing problem to deal with and we had to set out a framework of how to deal with it. We have done that. I think there are about five or six points in that section. They do not all apply to each country. Some of them will apply to every country, but we have set out that framework and then said, really rather for the political reason which indicated that each country is different and you have to look at it for what that country is and the problems it has, and you have to look at it in the light of its own specific problems. Mexico ... Are you from Mexico?

Questioner: Yes, I am.

Prime Minister: Yes. Well, you know, Mexico has made enormous strides in tackling her underlying problems with great courage and I believe just two days ago she did get a longer-term rescheduling of debt which we hope helps her. It will take a longer time to repay, but it is partly because she has done so much herself to restore confidence.

So what we have tried to lay out is a framework and some criteria which will apply to those developing countries and then they are applied according to the specific circumstances of that country. They recognize two factors: that the debtor country has to make considerable efforts, as Mexico is doing, to solve its

273

problems, and then also, of course, the banks have their problems to deal with, and in my speech yesterday I said that they would have to look at ways of strengthening their balance sheet.

So I hope we have got an economic framework and criteria and that the application of those criteria will take into account the political difficulties, circumstances, problems of the countries to which the framework applies.

Question: Prime Minister, are you at all disappointed with the statement on terrorism? It seems to be more an expression of concern, with proposals instead of firm action or mechanisms to combat terrorism.

Prime Minister: No, I am not disappointed with it. I know all of the problems, but I know that above all we have to have a much closer exchange of information and a much closer cooperation between countries and that, I think, is what this sets out to achieve.

Question: Prime Minister, you refer in the communiqué by Heads of Government that you should strengthen the role of the IBRD [International Bank for Reconstruction and Development] in fostering the development over the medium and long term. I was just wondering how you intend to strengthen the role of the IBRD and if you or the Chancellor [of the Exchequer Nigel Lawson] could perhaps be more specific in explaining that.

Prime Minister: I think in one's earlier speech one pointed out that you could use some of the public money as a catalyst to stimulate private investment as well and that that might in fact get larger amounts of help to some of those countries who need it.

To some extent, that is already done, but not sufficiently, and we believe that that aspect of its work could be strengthened.

Question: Prime Minister, the communiqué refers to the need to reduce federal deficits where necessary. My question is: is the

United States one of the places where that is necessary and is the United States taking adequate steps to do that?

Prime Minister: I think you should address that question to the United States. I think, if you look at the percentage of GDP [gross domestic product] which is represented by the deficit, you will find quite a number of countries may wish to reduce their deficit, so it does not necessarily apply only to one country but to quite a number.

We have, after all, taken strenuous steps to reduce our own deficit, thank goodness, so we are not in an acute position and we will go on trying to hold down our deficit, but it is done, really, by a variety of ways: trying to hold your public expenditure and then trying to cover a reasonable amount of it by taxation so that your borrowing—that is, your actual deficit—is kept to fairly low percentage terms of your GDP.

I am not going to mention any countries. You must ask each of them.

Question: Prime Minister, I would like to follow up on the subject of terrorism. American officials have said that they felt that private agreements were more important than public statements. Really, a two-part question:

First of all, what do you think you have achieved by the public statement, and secondly, have there been the kinds of private agreements on concrete action that may be more important in the long run?

Prime Minister: Well, if there are private agreements on concrete action, by definition a private agreement is a private agreement and I will not refer to it. What I think we have done publicly is to show our joint concern about this and willingness, indeed determination, to do as much jointly as we possibly can to defeat this thing, which is the scourge of many people's lives.

Question: Prime Minister, are you not a little disappointed with the statement on the Iran–Iraq gulf war? Does it not mean that the seven leading statesmen of the world cannot find a solution or impose a solution on these two countries? Surely there must be some way round this particular problem?

Prime Minister: Really, your last sentence illustrates what is the answer to your own question. I do not find it surprising that you cannot impose a solution on two countries. Nor, I think, on reflection, would you. I think it is a matter of great concern; it is a matter of great sorrow. The loss of life, particularly of young people there, is enormous, but you cannot impose a settlement on those two countries. There is no way in which you can do it, anymore than we were ever able to avoid the terrible slaughter that took place in Cambodia. Many of us felt deeply concerned and with all the international institutions we could not stop that.

One is deeply concerned, but it is in fact a fact of life and it is a realistic fact which I am sure you face just as much as we have to. We still continue to do everything we can, but it is not enough to stop the hostilities and conflict between those two countries. That will only come when they themselves are prepared to negotiate to stop it and have the will to stop it.

Question: Prime Minister, in the section dealing with the problems of the debtor nations ...

Prime Minister: You have come a long way since education, haven't you?

Questioner: I could return the compliment.

Prime Minister: Yes, indeed! We were both together on education. Ten years ago.

Question: On the section dealing with international debt, in paragraph 5 of the communiqué, you left out the section about the multi-year rescheduling of official debt when you were reading it out. Was there any significance in that? It seems to be rather an important part of the communiqué.

Prime Minister: No, I am sure I read out multi-year rescheduling, but I might have cut it down. Frankly, when you are reading this thing through, you realize how long it is. When you are going through it, everyone is straining to get their bits in and to get a complete section. When you are reading it through you realize that you are going to be there rather long if you read out absolutely everything. But I am sure that I did read out. Yes, I read out the first part of that and then I just dropped. The last three lines were not absolutely vital to the reading out of it, but the communiqué stands. But I think I saved people at least five minutes of listening time by doing some quick editing as I was going through, but the communiqué stands as a whole even though I did not read out each and every word. Trust an education correspondent to pick that up.

Question: Prime Minister, perhaps Chancellor Lawson will want to answer this as well. I am wondering if there was a sense of whether the IMF is currently adequately funded or whether, particularly with a large number of debt repayments coming due in a bunch in 1986/87, whether there will have to be more money put into that agency.

Prime Minister: That, as you know, is being reconsidered in September 1984. It is not long since we increased the funds available to the IMF by fifty percent.

Chancellor: That was in February 1983. There is no need for additional funds at the present time. The [IMF] Managing Director is not asking the countries to put up extra funds at the present time. There will obviously come a time, as you look ahead, when there will be a need for further funds, but that time is not yet.

Question: Prime Minister, you will probably like this question. A very distinguished writer, one of the most distinguished writers in the world, Lev Kopelev, who was born in the Soviet Union, has expressed considerable disgust at the fact that the West does not seem to care for Sakharov. Why was not Andrei Sakharov mentioned in that statement so that his treatment should have been exposed to a little more contempt than it already has?

Prime Minister: I do not think we need to mention Andrei Sakharov in a statement to give greater exposure to his case, because we all of us frequently mentioned it and have done everything we can to make representations that he should be properly treated and his wife should have the requisite medical treatment. So I do not think we needed to deal with it in this statement. This, after all, is an economic statement and it did not seem appropriate to mention specific cases in one on East-West relations without also mentioning many other cases.

Question: Prime Minister, what is the basic objective of the declaration on East–West relations? One accepts your good intentions but is it realistic to expect the Soviet Union to come back to the negotiating table before November?

Prime Minister: Whether it is realistic or not, we meet once a year and we have to express our views as they are and the views really are threefold. One, the total unity and solidarity and determination of the Western countries; the wish, nevertheless, to have dialogue across the East–West divide, believing that the avoidance of conflict is in the interests both of East and West. That is absolutely clear; and the third one that it was the Soviet Union that walked out of the nuclear disarmament talks. The United States has indicated that she will go back to the table without pre-conditions and we hope to get some response before very long to return to the negotiating table. Whether that is before or after November, your views may well be the realistic ones.

Question: Prime Minister, what is going to happen to interest rates and unemployment?

Prime Minister: It would be a very unwise Prime Minister who would say anything about interest rates. As you know, it is always asked and never answered.

On unemployment, we seek to do as much as we can for job creation. You will know that we have to create quite a lot of jobs even to stand still on unemployment, because the demographic curve in this country is such that in the last six years we have had one million more people of working age in the population than previously, and the increase of numbers of people in the working population will continue until 1989. It is because of the extra numbers of children leaving school compared with those who are retiring. So we have to go as fast as we can on trying to create extra jobs and having the kind of financial system and help which enables genuine jobs to be created. We had quite a long discussion about this in the Summit. Indeed, a very long and interesting one, and most people find that their extra jobs are coming really from two sources; to some extent the two sources overlap. One is small businesses, and among the small businesses in particular it is businesses in services.

So we shall go as fast as we can.

Question: Prime Minister, was it the sense of the nations meeting here in the discussion on East–West that deployment of missiles will continue in Europe if the Soviets do not return to the bargaining table to negotiate an agreement?

Prime Minister: It is the anticipation that we shall complete the dual-track decision of NATO [North Atlantic Treaty Organization] and deploy the missiles which we agreed to deploy.

Question: Prime Minister, you told us before the Summit began that we would be blessed if we expected nothing. Now, you are trying to tell us in fact that the Summit accomplished a very great deal. Are we wrong now or were we misguided earlier?

Prime Minister: No. You had such enormous expectations of brand new, magic solutions that I had to damp those down and therefore I hope, having damped those down you might really be very, very pleased with what you actually find in the communiqué. I had a pretty good idea of what it would be and we managed to deliver it, so I hope you are quite pleased.

It would have been terrible if we had delivered all this and you had been disappointed. It is much better to have you pleased, I trust.

Question: Prime Minister, which subjects generated the most argument and disagreement?

Prime Minister: Oh goodness me! Genuine debate, I think, is the appropriate term. It is not so much the actual discussion of the subjects which generates the debate. It is when you translate what you think you have agreed to precise language in a communiqué. Then you will find very considerable debate over two or three words and certainly there was quite a debate on the precise wording we should use in East–West. And that was not a fundamental debate. They were really debates on emphasis, rather more than fundamentals.

Question: Why were the specific references to the U.S. budget deficit and to a specific time-table for GATT that were evident in the draft communiqué dropped from the final communiqué and were you at all disappointed by that?

Prime Minister: No, we have not made any reference to the financial affairs of any particular country at all and I think that that was the best way to take, and on GATT there was a difference of opinion as to whether we should set some kind of time in which the decision should be taken or we should say it should be effected as soon as possible, and some felt it would be wise to set a target for the decision and others were not prepared to do that. They wanted to complete the GATT work program first and they thought that if we set a target for a decision, some of the other GATT countries might think we were trying to impose one upon them, and of course, we are only a very small part of the GATT apparatus. That was the reason.

SOURCE: Great Britain, British Information Services, *Economic Summit: Press Conference, 9 June 1984 (Ottawa)* [unpublished].

Bonn

2–4 May 1985

BONN, 2–4 MAY 1985

DELEGATIONS

Canada

Brian Mulroney, *Prime Minister*
Joe Clark, *Secretary of State for External Affairs*
Michael H. Wilson, *Minister of Finance*
Sylvia Ostry, *Personal Representative (Sherpa)*

France

François Mitterand, *President*
Roland Dumas, *Minister of External Relations*
Pierre Bérégovoy, *Minister for the Economy, Finance and the Budget*
Jacques Attali, *Personal Representative (Sherpa)*

Germany (Federal Republic)

Helmut Kohl, *Federal Chancellor*
Hans-Dietrich Genscher, *Vice-Chancellor and Federal Foreign Minister*
Gerhard Stoltenberg, *Federal Minister of Finance*

Germany (Federal Republic) *continued*

Martin Bangemann, *Federal Minister of Economics*
Hans Tietmeyer, *Personal Representative (Sherpa)*

Italy

Bettino Craxi, *President of the Council of Ministers*
Giulio Andreotti, *Minister for Foreign Affairs*
Giovanni Goria, *Minister of the Treasury*
Renato Ruggiero, *Personal Representative (Sherpa)*

Japan

Yasuhiro Nakasone, *Prime Minister*
Shintaro Abe, *Minister for Foreign Affairs*
Noboru Takeshita, *Minister of Finance*
Reishi Teshima, *Personal Representative (Sherpa)*

United Kingdom

Margaret Thatcher, *Prime Minister*
Geoffrey Howe, *Secretary of State for Foreign and
    Commonwealth Affairs*
Nigel Lawson, *Chancellor of the Exchequer*
Robert Armstrong, *Personal Representative (Sherpa)*

United States

Ronald Reagan, *President*
George P. Shultz, *Secretary of State*
James A. Baker, *Secretary of the Treasury*
W. Allen Wallis, *Personal Representative (Sherpa)*

European Communities

Jacques Delors, *President of the Commission*
Willy De Clercq, *Member of the Commission*
Alois Pfeiffer, *Member of the Commission*
Pascal Lamy, *Personal Representative (Sherpa)*

THE BONN ECONOMIC DECLARATION: TOWARDS SUSTAINED GROWTH AND HIGHER EMPLOYMENT

May 4, 1985

1. Conscious of the responsibility which we bear, together with other governments, for the future of the world economy and the preservation of natural resources, we, the Heads of State or Government of seven major industrial nations and the President of the Commission of the European Communities, meeting in Bonn from 2 to 4 May 1985, have discussed the economic outlook, problems, and prospects for our countries and the world.

2. World economic conditions are better than they have been for a considerable time. Since we last met, further progress has been achieved in bringing down inflation and strengthening the basis for growth. The recovery in the industrial countries has begun to spread to the developing world. The debt problems of developing countries, though far from solved, are being flexibly and effectively addressed.

3. Nevertheless, our countries still face important challenges. Above all, we need:

—to strengthen the ability of our economies to respond to new developments;

—to increase job opportunities;

—to reduce social inequalities;

—to correct persistent economic imbalances;

—to halt protectionism; and

—to improve the stability of the world monetary system.

4. Our discussions of these challenges have led us to the following conclusions:

(a) The best contribution we can make to a lasting new prosperity in which all nations can share is unremittingly to pursue, individually in our own countries and cooperatively together, policies conducive to sustained growth and higher employment.

(b) The prosperity of developed and developing countries has become increasingly linked. We will continue to work with the developing countries in a spirit of true partnership.

(c) Open multilateral trade is essential to global prosperity and we urge an early and substantial reduction of barriers to trade.

(d) We seek also to make the functioning of the world monetary system more stable and more effective.

(e) Economic progress and the preservation of the natural environment are necessary and mutually supportive goals. Effective environmental protection is a central element in our national and international policies.

GROWTH AND EMPLOYMENT

5. In order to sustain non-inflationary growth and higher employment, we have agreed that:

—We will consolidate and enhance the progress made in bringing down inflation.

—We will follow prudent, and where necessary strengthened monetary and budgetary policies with a view to stable prices, lower interest rates and more productive investment. Each of our countries will exercise firm control over public spending in order to reduce budget deficits, when excessive, and, where necessary, the share of public spending in Gross National Product.

—We will work to remove obstacles to growth and encourage initiative and enterprise so as to release the creative energies of our peoples, while maintaining appropriate social policies for those in need.

—We will promote greater adaptability and responsiveness in all markets, particularly the labor market.

—We will encourage training to improve occupational skills, particularly for the young.

—We will exploit to the full the opportunities for prosperity and the creation of permanent jobs, provided by economic change and technological progress.

6. Building on these common principles, each of us has indicated the specific priorities for national policies.

—The President of the United States considers it essential to achieve a rapid and appreciable cut in public expenditures and thus a substantial reduction in the budget deficit. He stresses also the need for further deregulation and for a reform of the tax system aimed at encouraging the efficient use of resources and stimulating new saving and investment.

—The President of the French Republic stresses the need to continue bringing down inflation, to modernize the means of production and to improve employment, to control public spending and to combat social inequality. In that context he attaches high priority to education, research and investment in high technologies with a view to sustained growth.

—The Government of the United Kingdom will continue to work to reduce inflation and to create the conditions for sustained growth. It will continue to keep public spending under strict control and maintain monetary discipline. It will promote the development of small and medium-sized businesses and advanced technological industries, and encourage initiative and enterprise and the creation of new job opportunities.

—The Government of the Federal Republic of Germany attaches high priority to strengthening the flexibility and vigor of the economy in order to achieve a lasting improvement in growth and to create new jobs. Small and medium-sized businesses should be especially encouraged as well as high technologies. It will continue to reduce the claims of the public sector on the economy, the budget deficit and the burden of taxation.

—The Government of Japan considers it essential to persevere with its policy of budgetary discipline and strengthening market functions, particularly with a view to fostering investment. It intends to achieve further progress in deregulating financial markets, promoting the international role of the yen, facilitating access to markets and encouraging growth in imports.

—The Italian Government gives priority to the further reduction of inflation and of the public deficit, while sustaining growth and investment. Particular emphasis will be put on incentives to create small and medium-sized industries, especially in the field of high technology, and to promote employment, especially for young people.

—The Government of Canada will focus on promoting investment and creating jobs in the private sector, on removing obstacles to sustained non-inflationary growth, on reducing the budget deficit and on restraining government expenditure. It will encourage entrepreneurial activities, with emphasis on the small and medium-sized business sectors.

—The Commission of the European Communities attaches high priority to completing a genuine internal market without barriers, which will eliminate rigidities and generate fresh economic growth on a Community-wide scale. A strengthened European Monetary System and closer economic convergence will further serve this end.

By pursuing these policies we will not only address our domestic problems, but at the same time contribute to an enduring growth of the world economy and a more balanced expansion of international trade.

RELATIONS WITH DEVELOPING COUNTRIES

7. Sustained growth in world trade, lower interest rates, open markets and continued financing in amounts and on terms appropriate to each individual case are essential to enable developing countries to achieve sound growth and overcome their economic and financial difficulties. Flows of resources, including official development assistance, should be maintained and,

wherever possible, increased, especially to the poorer countries. In particular, more stable long-term finance, such as direct investment from industrial countries, should be encouraged. We welcome longer-term debt restructuring agreements between debtor countries and commercial banks. We continue to stand ready, where appropriate, to negotiate further multi-year reschedulings of debts to governments and government agencies.

8. We continue to encourage the constructive dialogue with the developing countries in the existing international institutions with a view to promoting their economic development and thereby their social and political stability. We emphasize the crucial role of, and the improved cooperation between, the International Monetary Fund and the World Bank Group in supporting policies by debtor countries necessary to strengthen the confidence of domestic and foreign creditors and investors, to mobilize domestic savings and to ensure efficient use of resources and sound long-term development. We agree to work to ensure that these institutions are equipped with the necessary resources and instruments, and we stand ready to discuss an increase in the resources available to the World Bank which may be necessary in the coming years. We remain concerned over the particular problems facing a number of developing countries that are neither among the poorest nor foremost among the group of major debtors. We agree that consideration should be given to easing the financial constraints of these countries on a case-by-case basis.

9. We are deeply concerned about the plight of African peoples who are suffering from famine and drought. We welcome the positive response from our citizens and from private organizations, as well as the substantial assistance provided by the governments of many countries and the establishment by the World Bank of the Special Facility for Sub-Saharan Africa. We shall continue to supply emergency food aid. In addition, we shall intensify our cooperation with African countries to help them develop their economic potential and a long-term food strategy, based on their own agricultural programs. We are

prepared to promote increases in food production by supplying agricultural inputs such as seed, pesticides and fertilizers, within the framework of agricultural development projects. We agree upon the need to improve the existing early warning systems and improve transportation arrangements. Political obstacles in the countries concerned should not be allowed to stand in the way of the delivery of food to the hungry. We emphasize the need to examine the establishment of a research network on dry zone grains. We shall strengthen our cooperation with African countries in fighting against desertification. Continued efforts are needed by all countries in a position to contribute to any or all of this work. We call upon the Soviet Union and other Communist countries to assume their responsibilities in this regard. We have set up an expert group to prepare proposals for follow-up measures to be reported to Foreign Ministers by September 1985.

MULTILATERAL TRADING SYSTEM AND INTERNATIONAL MONETARY SYSTEM

10. Protectionism does not solve problems; it creates them. Further tangible progress in relaxing and dismantling existing trade restrictions is essential. We need new initiatives for strengthening the open multilateral trading system. We strongly endorse the agreement reached by the OECD [Organisation for Economic Co-operation and Development] Ministerial Council that a new GATT [General Agreement on Tariff and Trade] round should begin as soon as possible. Most of us think that this should be in 1986. We agree that it would be useful that a preparatory meeting of senior officials should take place in the GATT before the end of the summer to reach a broad consensus on subject matter and modalities for such negotiations. We also agree that active participation of a significant number of developed and developing countries in such negotiations is essential. We are looking to a balanced package for negotiation.

11. It is also essential to improve the functioning of the international monetary system. We take note that the Finance Ministers of the Group of Ten,[1] at their meeting in Tokyo in June, intend to complete their current work on ways to improve the functioning of the monetary system and to put forward proposals, to be discussed at the next meeting of the Interim Committee of the International Monetary Fund in Seoul in October, with a view to making the international monetary system more stable and more effective.

ENVIRONMENTAL POLICIES

12. New approaches and strengthened international cooperation are essential to anticipate and prevent damage to the environment, which knows no national frontiers. We shall cooperate in order to solve pressing environmental problems such as acid deposition and air pollution from motor vehicles and all other significant sources. We shall also address other concerns such as climatic change, the protection of the ozone layer and the management of toxic chemicals and hazardous wastes. The protection of soils, fresh water and the sea, in particular of regional seas, must be strengthened.

13. We shall harness both the mechanisms of governmental vigilance and the disciplines of the market to solve environmental problems. We shall develop and apply the "polluter pays" principle more widely. Science and technology must contribute to reconciling environmental protection and economic growth.

14. Improved and internationally harmonized techniques of environmental measurement are essential. We invite the environmental experts of the Technology, Growth and Employment

---

[1]See Editor's note, page 113.

Working Group to consult with the appropriate international bodies about the most efficient ways for achieving progress in this field.

15. We welcome the contribution made by the Environment Ministers to closer international cooperation on environmental concerns. We shall focus our cooperation within existing international bodies, especially the OECD. We shall work with developing countries for the avoidance of environmental damage and disasters worldwide.

COOPERATION IN SCIENCE AND TECHNOLOGY

16. We are convinced that international cooperation in research and technology in major projects should be enhanced to make maximum use of our scientific potential. We recognize that such projects require appropriately shared participation and responsibility as well as adequate rules concerning access to the results achieved, the transfer of technology and the use of technologies involved.

17. We welcome the positive responses of the Member States of the European Space Agency (ESA), Canada and Japan to the invitation of the President of the United States to cooperate in the United States Manned Space Station Program on the basis of a genuine partnership and a fair and appropriate exchange of information, experience and technologies. Discussions on intergovernmental cooperation in development and utilization of permanently manned space stations will begin promptly. We also welcome the conclusions of the ESA Council on the need for Europe to maintain and expand its autonomous capability in space activity, and on the long-term European Space Plan and its objectives.

18. We welcome the report from the Technology, Growth and

Employment Working Group on the work done in the eighteen areas of cooperation and invite the Group to complete its review by the end of the year. We welcome the positive contribution which the Ministerial Conference on "Technological Development and Employment" held in Venice has made towards wider acceptance of the role of technological change in promoting growth and employment. We also welcome the results of the Rambouillet Conference on Bioethics and thank the Federal Republic of Germany for its willingness to host a symposium on neurobiology in 1986.

19. We have agreed to meet again next year and have accepted the Japanese Prime Minister's invitation to meet in Japan.

SOURCE: U.S., Department of State, *Bulletin,* No. 2100 (July 1985): 3–6; *Economic Summits, 1975–1986: Declarations* (Rome: Istituto Affari Internazionali, 1987): 123–131; Great Britain, Foreign and Commonwealth Office, *Declarations of Annual Economic Summits, 1975–1986* (London, 198—): A11 Bonn, 1–7 [unpublished]; Germany (West), Presse- und Informationsamt der Bundesregierung, *Bulletin,* No. 48 (May 7, 1985): 410–15; Germany (West), Presse- und Informationsamt der Bundesregierung, *Pressemitteilung: Bonn Economic Summit 1985: Final Communiqué (Bonn).*

POLITICAL DECLARATION ON THE 40TH ANNIVERSARY OF THE END OF THE SECOND WORLD WAR

May 3, 1985

The Heads of State or Government of Canada, the French Republic, the Federal Republic of Germany, the Republic of Italy, Japan, the United Kingdom and the United States, with the President of the Commission of the European Communities, meeting together in Bonn on the eve of the fortieth anniversary of the end of the Second World War, remember in grief all those who lost their lives in that time, whether by acts of war or as victims of inhumanity, repression and tyranny. We acknowledge the duty we owe to their memories, and to all those who follow after them, to uphold peace, freedom and justice in our countries and in the world.

We have learned the lessons of history. The end of the war marked a new beginning. As the sounds of battle ceased, we tackled the tasks of moral and spiritual renewal and physical reconstruction. Transcending the hostilities which had once divided us we initiated on the basis of common values a process for reconciliation and cooperation amongst us. Today, linked in a peaceful, secure and lasting friendship, we share in all our countries a commitment to freedom, democratic principles and human rights. We are proud that the governments of our countries owe their legitimacy to the will of our people, expressed in free elections. We are proud that our people are free to say and write what they will, to practice the religions they profess, and to travel where they will. We are committed to assuring the maintenance of societies in which individual initiative and enterprise may flourish and the ideals of social justice, obligations and rights may be pursued.

We recognize that we can secure those aims, and meet both the opportunities and the challenges presented by technological and industrial change, more effectively in partnership than on our own. In Europe, the Community, the embodiment of reconciliation and common purpose, is growing in membership, strength and prosperity. The nations of the dynamic Pacific region are drawing ever closer together. The partnership of North America, Europe and Japan is a guarantee of peace and stability in the world.

Other nations that shared with ours in the agonies of the Second World War are divided from us by fundamental differences of political systems. We deplore the division of Europe. In our commitment to the ideals of peace, freedom and democracy we seek by peaceful means to lower the barriers that have arisen within Europe. We believe that the CSCE [Conference on Security and Co-operation in Europe] process with its promise of enhancing human rights provides an opportunity to increase confidence, cooperation and security in Europe.

Considering the climate of peace and friendship which we have achieved among ourselves forty years after the end of the war we look forward to a state of peace in Europe in which the German people will regain their unity through free self-determination; and in Asia we earnestly hope that a political environment will be created which permits the parties to overcome the division of the Korean peninsula in freedom.

As recognized in the Charter of the United Nations, all countries have a joint responsibility to maintain international peace and security and to this end refrain from the threat and the use of force. We for our part share a determination to preserve the peace while protecting our democratic freedoms. To that end, each of us will work to maintain and strengthen a stable military balance at the lowest possible levels of forces, neither seeking superiority for ourselves nor neglecting our defenses. We are prepared to pursue a high-level dialogue to deal with the profound differences dividing East and West. We strongly support endeavors to strengthen the peace and enhance deterrence through the negotiation of meaningful reductions in existing levels of nuclear arms, limitations on conventional arms, the banning of chemical weapons and lessening the risks of conflict. We welcome the opening of negotiations in Geneva. We appreciate the positive proposals of the United States of America. We urge the Soviet Union to act positively and constructively in order to achieve significant agreements there.

We shall continue to seek to work with the developing

countries, so as to help them to fight hunger and disease, to build free and prosperous societies, and to take their part in the community of nations committed to peace and freedom. We respect genuine non-alignment as an important contribution to international security and peace.

So, as we look back to the terrible suffering of the Second World War and the common experience of forty years of peace and freedom, we dedicate ourselves and our countries anew to the creation of a world in which all peoples enjoy the blessings of peace, of justice, and of freedom from oppression, want and fear; a world in which individuals are able to fulfill their responsibilities for themselves, to their families and to their communities; a world in which all nations, large and small, combine to work together for a better future for all mankind.

SOURCE:: U.S., Department of State, *Bulletin,* No. 2100 (July 1985): 1–3; *Economic Summits, 1975–1986: Declarations* (Rome: Istituto Affari Internazionali, 1987): 131–33; Great Britain, Foreign and Commonwealth Office, *Political Declarations and Statements of Annual Economic Summits, 1978– 1986* (London, 198—): [unpublished]; Germany (West), Presse- und Informationsamt der Bundesregierung, *Bulletin,* No. 48 (May 7, 1985): 409–10.

STATEMENT DES BUNDESKANZLERS

4. Mai 1985

Bundeskanzler Dr. Helmut Kohl hatte vor Bekanntgabe des Schlussdokuments des Wirtschaftsgipfels Bonn, "Wirtschaftserklärung von Bonn—Für dauerhaftes Wachstum und höhere Beschäftigung" am 4. Mai 1985 im Plenarsaal des Deutschen Bundestages folgendes einleitendes Statement abgegeben:

Meine Herren Präsidenten, verehrte Kolleginnen und Kollegen, Exzellenzen, meine sehr verehrten Damen und Herren!

Es ist mir eine grosse Ehre und eine grosse Freude, dass ich zum Abschluss dieses Bonner Gipfels hier vor Ihnen unseren Bericht über zwei Tage intensiver Gespräche und Arbeit erstatten darf.

Wir hatten sehr offene, sehr freundschaftliche, gelegentlich auch kontroverse Diskussionen, aber das Wichtige war und ist, dass auch gegensätzliche Meinungen im Geiste der Partnerschaft und der Freundschaft ausgetragen wurden.

Wir haben bereits gestern eine Politische Erklärung verabschiedet und sie der ffentlichkeit übergeben. Sie werden verstehen, dass gerade ich als Kanzler der Bundesrepublik Deutschland diese Politische Erklärung ganz besonders würdige und begrüsse.

Die gestern verabschiedete Politische Erklärung zum 40. Jahrestag des Kriegsendes ist für uns alle ein politisches Dokument von hohem Rang. Wir gedenken darin der Opfer des Krieges und der Gewaltherrschaft, und gleichzeitig blicken wir auf das, was in 40 Jahren gemeinsamer Arbeit aus dem Geist der Versöhnung geschaffen wurde, mit Stolz zurück.

Wir bekennen uns zu den Grundlagen unserer Freundschaft, zu unseren gemeinsamen Wertvorstellungen, zu Frieden und Freiheit, zu Demokratie und Menschenrechten.

Diese Politische Erklärung ist ein Dokument der politischen und geistigen Übereinstimmung unserer Länder. Die Partnerschaft zwischen Nordamerika, Europa und Japan ist ein Garant für Frieden und Stabilität in der Welt. Wir wollen unsere

Erfahrungen aus 40 Jahren in Frieden und Freiheit für die Schaffung einer besseren Zukunft für die ganze Menschheit einsetzen.

Wir haben verständlicherweise—die Staats- und Regierungschefs, die Finanz- und Wirtschaftsminister, die Aussenminister—in diesen vielen Stunden über zahlreiche Themen gesprochen. Ich kann diese Themen in meiner Zusammenfassung, bevor ich das eigentliche Dokument zum Abschluss verlese, natürlich nicht alle ansprechen. Ich will zwei Ausnahmen machen.

Wir sind im Rahmen unseres Meinungsaustausches über West–Ost-Fragen auch auf die Frage der Strategischen Verteidigungsinitiative des amerikanischen Präsidenten eingegangen. Der Präsident hat sein langfristiges Forschungsprogramm erläutert. Die Vereinigten Staaten sind zu intensiven Konsultationen auch für die Zukunft bereit. Ich will dies ausdrücklich unterstreichen und begrüssen.

Der Präsident hat betont, dass die Vereinigten Staaten nicht das Ziel verfolgen, Überlegenheit zu erlangen, sondern strategische Stabilität zu festigen. Die Strategie des Bündnisses bleibt erhalten, solange es keine für das Ziel der Kriegsverhinderung wirksamere Alternative gibt.

In Genf geht es darum, die nuklearen strategischen und Mittelstreckenwaffen drastisch zu reduzieren und frühzeitig damit zu beginnen, das Verhältnis zwischen Offensiv- und Defensivwaffen im Hinblick auf künftige kooperative Lösungen zu erörtern.

Wir haben unter anderem auch ein Problem angesprochen, das in vielen Ländern der Welt vor allem junge Menschen betrifft und nicht zuletzt ihre Eltern, das viel Elend in viele Familien gebracht hat: das Drogenproblem. Wir haben uns damit befasst, weil wir wissen, dass gerade viele junge Leute tragische Opfer dieses Drogenproblems sind.

Wir sind entschlossen, es entschieden zu bekämpfen. Wir sind übereingekommen, neben den bereits getroffenen Massnahmen eine möglichst umfassende und wirksame Strategie, unter Inanspruchnahme der Dienste bestehender Stellen, zu entwerfen, um die Drogenherstellung, den Drogenhandel und die damit im Zusammenhang stehenden Verbrechen wirksamer bekämpfen zu können.

Wir werden Sachverständige beauftragen, diese Strategie und wirksame Massnahmen zu erörtern und zu prüfen, welche zusätzlichen Initiativen getroffen werden können. Wir haben vereinbart, dass die notwendigen Vorschläge bis Ende dieses Jahres vorgelegt werden, damit wir daraus so bald wie möglich die notwendigen Konsequenzen ziehen können.

SOURCE: Germany (West), Presse- und Informationsamt der Bundesregierung, *Bulletin,* No. 48 (May 7, 1985): 415–16.

[UNOFFICIAL TRANSLATION]
CHANCELLOR HELMUT KOHL'S
CONCLUDING STATEMENT
May 4, 1985

Federal Chancellor Dr. Helmut Kohl made the following statement in the German Bundestag [Parliament] on May 4, 1985, before the release of the final document of the Bonn Economic Summit, the *Bonn Economic Declaration: Towards Sustained Growth and Higher Employment:*

Presidents, Colleagues, Excellencies, Ladies and Gentlemen:

It is a great honor and a great pleasure for me to be able to submit to you at the conclusion of the Bonn Summit our report on two days of intensive talks and work.

We had very open, very friendly, occasionally also controversial discussions, but the important thing was and is that even differences of opinion were dealt with in the spirit of partnership and friendship.

Yesterday we approved and released a political declaration. You will understand that as Chancellor of the Federal Republic of Germany I welcome and value very highly this political declaration.

The political declaration approved yesterday on the occasion of the fortieth anniversary of the end of the war is for all of us a political document of great importance. We remember thus the victims of war and tyranny, and at the same time we look back with pride on what we accomplished in forty years of joint effort in the spirit of conciliation.

We affirm our faith in the bases of our friendship, our common values, in peace and freedom, in democracy, and in human rights.

This political declaration is a document of the political and spiritual togetherness of our countries. The partnership of North America, Europe and Japan guarantees peace and stability in the world. We want to make use of our experiences of the last forty years of peace and freedom for the creation of a better future for all mankind.

It is understandable that we—the Heads of State and Government, the finance and economic ministers, the foreign ministers—talked about numerous subjects during these many hours. Naturally, I cannot refer to all those subjects in this summary statement, before reading the actual document at the conclusion. I will make two exceptions.

We took up the question of the Strategic Defense Initiative of the American President within the framework of our exchange of opinions on East–West questions. The President clarified his long-term research project. The United States is ready for intensive consultations even in the future. I will make a special point of emphasizing and welcoming this.

The President stressed that the United States does not aim at achieving superiority, but at strengthening strategic stability. The strategy of the alliance will remain preserved as long as there is no effective alternative for the prevention of war.

The task in Geneva is to reduce drastically strategic and medium-range nuclear weapons and to start early discussions on the relationship between offensive and defensive weapons with a view to achieving cooperative solutions in the future.

We also talked, *inter alia,* about a problem that affects, in many countries of the world, young people especially, and ultimately their parents: the drug problem. We have dealt with this matter for we know that many young people particularly are tragic victims of the drug problem.

We are determined to fight it resolutely. We have agreed to develop—in addition to measures already in place—a most comprehensive and effective strategy by relying on the services of existing agencies in order to fight the drug manufacture, the drug trade, and related crimes more effectively.

We will charge experts to discuss and evaluate this strategy as well as effective measures which might be adopted through supplementary initiatives. We have agreed that the necessary proposals will be submitted by the end of this year to enable us as soon as possible to draw the necessary conclusions.

Tokyo

4–6 May 1986

TOKYO, 4–6 MAY 1986

DELEGATIONS

Canada

Brian Mulroney, *Prime Minister*
Joe Clark, *Secretary of State for External Affairs*
Michael H. Wilson, *Minister of Finance*
Sylvia Ostry, *Personal Representative (Sherpa)*

France

François Mitterand, *President*
Jacques Chirac, *Prime Minister*
Jean-Bernard Raimond, *Minister of External Affairs*
Jacques Attali, *Personal Representative (Sherpa)*

Germany (Federal Republic)

Helmut Kohl, *Federal Chancellor*
Hans-Dietrich Genscher, *Vice-Chancellor and Federal Foreign Minister*
Gerhard Stoltenberg, *Federal Minister of Finance*

Germany (Federal Republic) *continued*

Martin Bangemann, *Federal Minister of Economics*
Hans Tietmeyer, *Personal Representative (Sherpa)*

Italy

Bettino Craxi, *President of the Council of Ministers*
Giulio Andreotti, *Minister for Foreign Affairs*
Giovanni Goria, *Minister of the Treasury*
Renato Ruggiero, *Personal Representative (Sherpa)*

Japan

Yasuhiro Nakasone, *Prime Minister*
Shintaro Abe, *Minister for Foreign Affairs*
Noboru Takeshita, *Minister of Finance*
Michio Watanabe, *Minister of International Trade and Industry*
Reishi Teshima, *Personal Representative (Sherpa)*

United Kingdom

Margaret Thatcher, *Prime Minister*
Geoffrey Howe, *Secretary of State for Foreign and Commonwealth Affairs*
Nigel Lawson, *Chancellor of the Exchequer*
Robert Armstrong, *Personal Representative (Sherpa)*

United States

Ronald Reagan, *President*
George P. Shultz, *Secretary of State*
James A. Baker, *Secretary of the Treasury*
W. Allen Wallis, *Personal Representative (Sherpa)*

European Communities

Jacques Delors, *President of the Commission*
Ruud Franciscus Maria Lubbers, *Prime Minister of the Netherlands and President of the European Council*
Hans van den Broek, *Minister of External Affairs of the Netherlands*
Willy De Clercq, *Member of the Commission*
Pascal Lamy, *Personal Representative (Sherpa) (for Mr. Delors)*
H. C. Posthumus Meyes, *Personal Representative (Sherpa) (for Mr. Lubbers)*

TOKYO ECONOMIC DECLARATION

May 6, 1986

1. We, the Heads of State or Government of seven major industrialized countries and the representatives of the European Community, meeting in Tokyo for the twelfth Economic Summit, have reviewed developments in the world economy since our meeting in Bonn a year ago, and have reaffirmed our continuing determination to work together to sustain and improve the prosperity and well-being of the peoples of our own countries, to support the developing countries in their efforts to promote their economic growth and prosperity, and to improve the functioning of the world monetary and trading systems.

2. Developments since our last meeting reflect the effectiveness of the policies to which we have committed ourselves at successive Economic Summits in recent years. The economies of the industrialized countries are now in their fourth year of expansion. In all our countries, the rate of inflation has been declining. With the continuing pursuit of prudent fiscal and monetary policies, this has permitted a substantial lowering of interest rates. There has been a significant shift in the pattern of exchange rates which better reflects fundamental economic conditions. For the industrialized countries, and indeed for the world economy, the recent decline in oil prices will help to sustain non-inflationary growth and to increase the volume of world trade, despite the difficulties which it creates for certain oil-producing countries. Overall, these developments offer brighter prospects for, and enhance confidence in, the future of the world economy.

3. However, the world economy still faces a number of difficult challenges which could impair sustainability of growth. Among these are high unemployment, large domestic and external imbalances, uncertainty about the future behavior of exchanges rates, persistent protectionist pressures, continuing difficulties of many developing countries and severe debt problems for some, and uncertainty about medium-term prospects for the levels of energy prices. If large imbalances and other distortions are allowed to persist for too long, they will present an increasing threat to world economic growth and to the open multilateral trading system. We cannot afford to relax our efforts. In formulating our policies, we need to look to the medium and longer term, and to have regard to the interrelated and structural character of current problems.

4. We stress the need to implement effective structural adjustment policies in all countries across the whole range of economic activities to promote growth, employment and the integration of domestic economies into the world economy. Such policies include technological innovation, adaptation of industrial structure and expansion of trade and foreign direct investment.

5. In each of our own countries, it remains essential to maintain a firm control of public spending within an appropriate medium-term framework of fiscal and monetary policies. In some of our countries there continue to be excessive fiscal deficits which the governments concerned are resolved progressively to reduce.

6. Since our last meeting we have had some success in the creation of new jobs to meet additions to the labor force, but unemployment remains excessively high in many of our countries. Non-inflationary growth remains the biggest single contributor to the limitation and reduction of unemployment, but it needs to be reinforced by policies which encourage job creation, particularly in new and high-technology industries, and in small businesses.

7. At the same time, it is important that there should be close and continuous coordination of economic policy among the seven Summit countries. We welcome the recent examples of improved coordination among the Group of Five Finance Ministers and Central Bankers, which have helped to change the pattern of exchange rates and to lower interest rates on an orderly and

non-inflationary basis. We agree, however, that additional measures should be taken to ensure that procedures for effective coordination of international economic policy are strengthened further. To this end, the Heads of State or Government:

—Agree to form a new Group of Seven Finance Ministers, including Italy and Canada, which will work together more closely and more frequently in the periods between the annual Summit meetings;

—Request the seven Finance Ministers to review their individual economic objectives and forecasts collectively at least once a year, using the indicators specified below, with a particular view to examining their mutual compatibility;

With the representatives of the European Community:

—State that the purposes of improved coordination should explicitly include promoting non-inflationary economic growth, strengthening market-oriented incentives for employment and productive investment, opening the international trading and investment system, and fostering greater stability in exchange rates;

—Reaffirm the undertaking at the 1982 Versailles Summit to cooperate with the IMF in strengthening multilateral surveillance, particularly among the countries whose currencies constitute the SDR [Special Drawing Rights], and request that, in conducting such surveillance and in conjunction with the Managing Director of the IMF, their individual economic forecasts should be reviewed, taking into account indicators such as GNP growth rates, inflation rates, interest rates, unemployment rates, fiscal deficit ratios, current account and trade balances, monetary growth rates, reserves, and exchange rates;

—Invite the Finance Ministers and Central Bankers in conducting multilateral surveillance to make their best efforts to reach an understanding on appropriate remedial measures whenever there are significant deviations from an intended course; and recommend that remedial efforts focus first and foremost on underlying policy fundamentals, while reaffirming the 1983 Williamsburg commitment to intervene in exchange markets when to do so would be helpful.

The Heads of State or Government:

—Request the Group of Five Finance Ministers to include Canada and Italy in their meetings whenever the management or the improvement of the international monetary system and related economic policy measures are to be discussed and dealt with;

—Invite Finance Ministers to report progress at the next Economic Summit meeting.

These improvements in coordination should be accompanied by similar efforts within the Group of Ten.

8. The pursuit of these policies by the industrialized countries will help the developing countries in so far as it strengthens the world economy, creates conditions for lower interest rates, generates the possibility of increased financial flows to the developing countries, promotes transfer of technology and improves access to the markets of the industrialized countries. At the same time, developing countries, particularly debtor countries, can fit themselves to play a fuller part in the world economy by adopting effective structural adjustment policies,

coupled with measures to mobilize domestic savings, to encourage the repatriation of capital, to improve the environment for foreign investment, and to promote more open trading policies. In this connection, noting in particular the difficult situation facing those countries highly dependent on exports of primary commodities, we agree to continue to support their efforts for further processing of their products and for diversifying their economies, and to take account of their export needs in formulating our own trade and domestic policies.

9. Private financial flows will continue to play a major part in providing for their development needs. We reaffirm our willingness to maintain and, where appropriate, expand official financial flows, both bilateral and multilateral, to developing countries. In this connection, we attach great importance to an early and substantial eighth replenishment of the International Development Association (IDA) and to a general capital increase of the World Bank when appropriate. We look for progress in activating the Multilateral Investment Guarantee Agency.

10. We reaffirm the continued importance of the case-by-case approach to international debt problems. We welcome the progress made in developing the cooperative debt strategy, in particular building on the United States initiative. The role of the international financial institutions, including the multilateral development banks, will continue to be central, and we welcome moves for closer cooperation among these institutions, and particularly between the IMF and the World Bank. Sound adjustment programs will also need resumed commercial bank lending, flexibility in rescheduling debt and appropriate access to export credits.

11. We welcome the improvement which has occurred in the food situation in Africa. Nonetheless a number of African countries continue to need emergency aid, and we stand ready to assist. More generally, we continue to recognize the high priority to be given to meeting the needs of Africa. Measures identified in the Report on Aid to Africa adopted and forwarded to us by our

Foreign Ministers should be steadily implemented. Assistance should focus in particular on the medium- and long-term economic development of these countries. In this connection we attach great importance to continued cooperation through the Special Facility for Sub-Saharan African countries, early implementation of the newly established Structural Adjustment Facility of the IMF and the use of the IDA. We intend to participate actively in the forthcoming United Nations Special Session on Africa to lay the foundation for the region's long-term development.

12. The open multilateral trading system is one of the keys to the efficiency and expansion of the world economy. We reaffirm our commitment to halting and reversing protectionism, and to reducing and dismantling trade restrictions. We support the strengthening of the system and functioning of the GATT [General Agreement on Tariffs and Trade], its adaptation to new developments in world trade and to the international economic environment, and the bringing of new issues under international discipline. The new round should, inter alia, address the issues of trade in services and trade-related aspects of intellectual property rights and foreign direct investment. Further liberalization of trade is, we believe, of no less importance for the developing countries than for ourselves, and we are fully committed to the preparatory process in the GATT with a view to the early launching of the new round of multilateral trade negotiations. We shall work at the September Ministerial meeting to make decisive progress in this direction.

13. We note with concern that a situation of global structural surplus now exists for some important agricultural products, arising partly from technological improvements, partly from changes in the world market situation, and partly from long-standing policies of domestic subsidy and protection of agriculture in all our countries. This harms the economies of certain developing countries and is likely to aggravate the risk of wider protectionist pressures. This is a problem which we all share and can be dealt with only in cooperation with each other.

We all recognize the importance of agriculture to the well-being of rural communities, but we are agreed that, when there are surpluses, action is needed to redirect policies and adjust structure of agricultural production in the light of world demand. We recognize the importance of understanding these issues and express our determination to give full support to the work of the OECD [Organisation for Economic Co-operation and Development] in this field.

14. Bearing in mind that the recent oil price decline owes much to the cooperative energy policies which we have pursued during the past decade, we recognize the need for continuity of policies for achieving long-term energy market stability and security of supply. We note that the current oil market situation enables countries which wish to do so to increase stock levels.

15. We reaffirm the importance of science and technology for the dynamic growth of the world economy and take note, with appreciation, of the final report of the Working Group on Technology, Growth and Employment. We welcome the progress made by the United States Manned Space Program and the progress made by the autonomous work of the European Space Agency (ESA). We stress the importance for genuine partnership of appropriate exchange of information, experience and technologies among the participating States. We also note with satisfaction the results of the Symposium on Neuroscience and Ethics, hosted by the Federal Republic of Germany, and we appreciate the decision of the Canadian Government to host the next meeting.

16. We reaffirm our responsibility, shared with other governments, to preserve the natural environment, and continue to attach importance to international cooperation in the effective prevention and control of pollution and natural resources management. In this regard, we take note of the work of the environmental experts on the improvement and harmonization of the techniques and practices of environmental measurement, and ask them to report as soon as possible. We also recognize the

316

need to strengthen cooperation with developing countries in the area of the environment.

17. We have agreed to meet again in 1987 and have accepted the invitation of the President of the Council of the Italian Government to meet in Italy.

SOURCE: U.S., Department of State, *Bulletin,* No. 2112 (July 1986): 8–10; *Economic Summits, 1975–1986: Declarations* (Rome: Istituto Affari Internazionali, 1987): 137–143; Great Britain, Foreign and Commonwealth Office, *Declarations of Annual Economic Summits, 1975–1986* (London, 198—): A12 Tokyo, 1–6 [unpublished].

STATEMENT ON INTERNATIONAL TERRORISM

May 5, 1986

1. We, the Heads of State or Government of seven major democracies and the representatives of the European Community, assembled here in Tokyo, strongly reaffirm our condemnation of international terrorism in all its forms, of its accomplices and of those, including governments, who sponsor or support it. We abhor the increase in the level of such terrorism since our last meeting, and in particular its blatant and cynical use as an instrument of government policy. Terrorism has no justification. It spreads only by the use of contemptible means, ignoring the values of human life, freedom and dignity. It must be fought relentlessly and without compromise.

2. Recognizing that the continuing fight against terrorism is a task which the international community as a whole has to undertake, we pledge ourselves to make maximum efforts to fight against that scourge. Terrorism must be fought effectively through determined, tenacious, discreet and patient action combining national measures with international cooperation. Therefore, we urge all like-minded nations to collaborate with us, particularly in such international fora as the United Nations, the International Civil Aviation Organization and the International Maritime Organization, drawing on their expertise to improve and extend countermeasures against terrorism and those who sponsor or support it.

3. We, the Heads of State or Government, agree to intensify the exchange of information in relevant fora on threats and potential threats emanating from terrorist activities and those who sponsor or support them, and on ways to prevent them.

4. We specify the following as measures open to any government concerned to deny to international terrorists the opportunity and the means to carry out their aims, and to identify and deter those who perpetrate such terrorism. We have decided to apply these measures within the framework of international law and in our own jurisdictions in respect of any State which is clearly involved in sponsoring or supporting international terrorism, and in particular of Libya, until such time as the State concerned abandons its complicity in, or support for, such terrorism. These measures are:

—Refusal to export arms to States which sponsor or support terrorism;

—Strict limits on the size of the diplomatic and consular missions and other official bodies abroad of States which engage in such activities, control of travel of members of such missions and bodies, and, where appropriate, radical reductions in, or even the closure of, such missions and bodies;

—Denial of entry to all persons, including diplomatic personnel, who have been expelled or excluded from one of our States on suspicion of involvement in international terrorism or who have been convicted of such a terrorist offence;

—Improved extradition procedures within due process of domestic law for bringing to trial those who have perpetrated such acts of terrorism;

—Stricter immigration and visa requirements and procedures in respect of nationals of States which sponsor or support terrorism;

—The closest possible bilateral and multilateral cooperation between police and security organizations and other relevant authorities in the fight against terrorism.

Each of us is committed to work in the appropriate international bodies to which we belong to ensure that similar measures are accepted and acted upon by as many other governments as possible.

5. We will maintain close cooperation in furthering the objectives of this statement and in considering further the measures. We agree to make the 1978 Bonn Declaration more effective in dealing with all forms of terrorism affecting civil aviation. We are ready to promote bilaterally and multilaterally further actions to be taken in international organizations or for a competent to fight against international terrorism in any of its forms.

SOURCE: U.S., Department of State, *Bulletin,* No. 2112 (July 1986): 5; *Economic Summits, 1975–1986: Declarations* (Rome: Istituto Affari Internazionali, 1987): 143–45; Great Britain, Foreign and Commonwealth Office, *Political Declarations and Statements of Annual Economic Summits, 1978–1986* (London, 198—) [unpublished]; Embassy of Japan, Ottawa, Canada.

STATEMENT ON THE IMPLICATIONS OF THE CHERNOBYL NUCLEAR ACCIDENT

May 5, 1986

1. We, the Heads of State or Government of seven major industrial nations and the Representatives of the European Community, have discussed the implications of the accident at the Chernobyl nuclear power station. We express our deep sympathy for those affected. We remain ready to extend assistance, in particular medical and technical, as and when requested.

2. Nuclear power is and, properly managed, will continue to be an increasingly widely used source of energy. For each country the maintenance of safety and security is an international responsibility, and each country engaged in nuclear power generation bears full responsibility for the safety of the design, manufacture, operation and maintenance of its installations. Each of our countries meets exacting standards. Each country, furthermore, is responsible for prompt provision of detailed and complete information on nuclear emergencies and accidents, in particular those with potential transboundary consequences. Each of our countries accepts that responsibility, and we urge the Government of the Soviet Union, which did not do so in the case of Chernobyl, to provide urgently such information, as our [countries] and other countries have requested.

3. We note with satisfaction the Soviet Union's willingness to undertake discussions this week with the Director-General of the International Atomic Energy Agency (IAEA). We expect that these discussions will lead to the Soviet Union's participation in the desired post-accident analysis.

4. We welcome and encourage the work of the IAEA in seeking to improve international cooperation on the safety of nuclear installations, the handling of nuclear accidents and their consequences, and the provision of mutual emergency assistance. Moving forward from the relevant IAEA guidelines, we urge the early elaboration of an international convention committing the parties to report and exchange information in the event of nuclear emergencies or accidents. This should be done with the least possible delay.

SOURCE:: U.S., Department of State, *Bulletin,* No. 2112 (July 1986): 4–5; *Economic Summits, 1975–1986: Declarations* (Rome: Istituto Affari Internazionali, 1987): 145–46; Great Britain, Foreign and Commonwealth Office, *Political Declarations and Statements of Annual Economic Summits, 1978–1986* (London, 198—) [unpublished]; Embassy of Japan, Ottawa, Canada.

TOKYO DECLARATION: LOOKING FORWARD TO A BETTER FUTURE

May 5, 1986

1. We, the Heads of State or Government of seven major industrial nations and the representatives of the European Community, with roots deep in the civilizations of Europe and Asia, have seized the opportunity of our meeting at Tokyo to raise our sights not just to the rest of this century but into the next as well. We face the future with confidence and determination, sharing common principles and objectives and mindful of our strengths.

2. Our shared principles and objectives, reaffirmed at past Summits, are bearing fruit. Nations surrounding the Pacific are thriving dynamically through free exchange, building on their rich and varied heritages. The countries of Western Europe, the Community members in particular, are flourishing by raising their cooperation to new levels. The countries of North America, enriched by European and Asian cultures alike, are firm in their commitment to the realization in freedom of human potential. Throughout the world we see the powerful appeal of democracy and growing recognition that personal initiative, individual creativity and social justice are main sources of progress. More than ever we have all to join our energies in the search for a safer and healthier, more civilized and prosperous, free and peaceful world. We believe that close partnership of Japan, North America and Europe will make a significant contribution toward this end.

3. We reaffirm our common dedication to preserving and strengthening peace, and as part of that effort, to building a more stable and constructive relationship between East and West. Each of us is ready to engage in cooperation in fields of common interest. Within existing alliances, each of us is resolved to maintain a strong and credible defense that can protect freedom and deter aggression, while not threatening the security of others. We know that peace cannot be safeguarded by military strength alone. Each of us is committed to addressing East–West differences through high-level dialogue and negotiation. To that end, each of us supports balanced, substantial and verifiable reductions in the level of arms; measures to increase confidence and reduce the risks of conflicts; and the peaceful resolution of disputes. Recalling the agreement between the United States and the Soviet Union to accelerate work at Geneva, we appreciate the United States' negotiating efforts and call on the Soviet Union also to negotiate positively. In addition to these efforts, we shall work for improved respect for the rights of individuals throughout the world.

4. We proclaim our conviction that in today's world, characterized by ever increasing interdependence, our countries cannot enjoy lasting stability and prosperity without stability and prosperity in the developing world and without the cooperation among us which can achieve these aims. We pledge ourselves afresh to fight against hunger, disease and poverty, so that developing nations can also play a full part in building a common, bright future.

5. We owe it to future generations to pass on a healthy environment and a culture rich in both spiritual and material values. We are resolved to pursue effective international action to eliminate the abuse of drugs. We proclaim our commitment to work together for a world which respects human beings in the diversity of their talents, beliefs, cultures and traditions. In such a world based upon peace, freedom and democracy, the ideals of social justice can be realized and employment opportunities can be available for all. We must harness wisely the potential of science and technology, and enhance the benefits through cooperation and exchange. We have a solemn responsibility so to educate the next generation as to endow them with the

creativity befitting the twenty-first century and to convey to them the value of living in freedom and dignity.

SOURCE: U.S., Department of State, *Bulletin,* No. 2112 (July 1986): 3–4; *Economic Summits, 1975–1986: Declarations* (Rome: Istituto Affari Internazionali, 1987): 146–48; Great Britain, Foreign and Commonwealth Office, *Political Declarations and Statements of Annual Economic Summits, 1978–1986* (London, 198—) [unpublished]; Embassy of Japan, Ottawa, Canada.

Venice

8–10 June 1987

VENICE, 8–10 JUNE 1987

DELEGATIONS

Canada

Brian Mulroney, *Prime Minister*
Joe Clark, *Secretary of State for External Affairs*
Michael H. Wilson, *Minister of Finance*
Sylvia Ostry, *Personal Representative (Sherpa)*

France

François Mitterand, *President*
Jacques Chirac, *Prime Minister*
Jean-Bernard Raimond, *Minister of External Affairs*
Jacques Attali, *Personal Representative (Sherpa)*

Germany (Federal Republic)

Helmut Kohl, *Federal Chancellor*
Hans-Dietrich Genscher, *Vice-Chancellor and Federal Foreign Minister*
Gerhard Stoltenberg, *Federal Minister of Finance*

Germany (Federal Republic) *continued*

Martin Bangemann, *Federal Minister of Economics*
Hans Tietmeyer, *Personal Representative (Sherpa)*

Italy

Amintore Fanfani, *President of the Council of Ministers*
Giulio Andreotti, *Minister for Foreign Affairs*
Giovanni Goria, *Minister of the Treasury*
Renato Ruggiero, *Personal Representative (Sherpa)*

Japan

Yasuhiro Nakasone, *Prime Minister*
Tadashi Kuranari, *Minister for Foreign Affairs*
Kiichi Miyazawa, *Minister of Finance*
Hajime Tamura, *Minister of International Trade and Industry*
Hiroshi Kitamura, *Personal Representative (Sherpa)*

United Kingdom

Margaret Thatcher, *Prime Minister*
Geoffrey Howe, *Secretary of State for Foreign and Commonwealth Affairs*
Nigel Lawson, *Chancellor of the Exchequer*
Robert Armstrong, *Personal Representative (Sherpa)*

United States

Ronald Reagan, *President*
George P. Shultz, *Secretary of State*

United States *continued*

James A. Baker, *Secretary of the Treasury*
W. Allen Wallis, *Personal Representative (Sherpa)*

European Communities

Jacques Delors, *President of the Commission*
Wilfried Martens, *President of the European Council*
Leo Tindemans, *Minister of Foreign Affairs of Belgium*
Willy De Clercq, *Commissioner for External Relations*
Pascal Lamy, *Personal Representative (Sherpa) (for Mr. Delors)*
Alphons Verplaese, *Personal Representative (Sherpa) (for Mr. Martens)*

VENEZIA ECONOMIC DECLARATION

June 10, 1987

INTRODUCTION

1. We, the Heads of State or Government of the seven major industrialized countries and the representatives of the European Community, have met in Venice from 8 to 10 June 1987, to review the progress that our countries have made, individually and collectively, in carrying out the policies to which we committed ourselves at earlier Summits. We remain determined to pursue these policies for growth, stability, employment and prosperity for our own countries and for the world economy.

2. We can look back on a number of positive developments since we met a year ago. Growth is continuing into its fifth consecutive year, albeit at lower rates. Average inflation rates have come down. Interest rates have generally declined. Changes have occurred in relationships among leading currencies which over time will contribute to a more sustainable pattern of current account positions, and have brought exchange rates within ranges broadly consistent with economic fundamentals. In volume terms, the adjustment of trade flows is under way, although in nominal terms imbalances so far remain too large.

MACROECONOMIC POLICIES AND EXCHANGE RATES

3. Since Tokyo, the Summit countries have intensified their economic policy coordination with a view to ensuring internal consistency of domestic policies and their international compatibility. This is essential to achieving stronger and sustained global growth, reduced external imbalances and more stable exchange rate relationships. Given the policy agreements reached at the Louvre and in Washington, further substantial shifts in exchange rates could prove counterproductive to efforts to increase growth and facilitate adjustment. We reaffirm our commitment to the swift and full implementation of those agreements.

4. We now need to overcome the problems that nevertheless remain in some of our countries: external imbalances that are still large; persistently high unemployment; large public sector deficits; and high levels of real interest rates. There are also continuing trade restrictions and increased protectionist pressures; persistent weakness of many primary commodity markets; and reduced prospects for developing countries to grow, find the markets they need and service their foreign debt.

5. The correction of external imbalances will be a long and difficult process. Exchange rate changes alone will not solve the problem of correcting these imbalances while sustaining growth. Surplus countries will design their policies to strengthen domestic demand and reduce external surpluses while maintaining price stability. Deficit countries, while following policies designed to encourage steady low-inflation growth, will reduce their fiscal and external imbalances.

6. We call on other industrial countries to participate in the effort to sustain economic activity worldwide. We also call on newly industrialized economies with rapid growth and large external surpluses to assume greater responsibility for preserving an open world trading system by reducing trade barriers and pursuing policies that allow their currencies more fully to reflect underlying fundamentals.

7. Among the Summit countries, budgetary discipline remains an important medium-term objective and the reduction of existing public sector imbalances a necessity for a number of them. Those Summit countries which have made significant progress in fiscal consolidation and have large external sur-

pluses remain committed to following fiscal and monetary policies designed to strengthen domestic growth, within a framework of medium-term fiscal objectives. Monetary policy should also support non-inflationary growth and foster stability of exchange rates. In view of the outlook for low inflation in many countries, a further market-led decline of interest rates would be helpful.

STRUCTURAL POLICIES

8. We also agree on the need for effective structural policies especially for creating jobs. To this end we shall:

—Promote competition in order to speed up industrial adjustment;

—Reduce major imbalances between agricultural supply and demand;

—Facilitate job-creating investment;

—Improve the functioning of labor markets;

—Promote the further opening of internal markets; and

—Encourage the elimination of capital market imperfections and restrictions and the improvement of the functioning of international financial markets.

MULTILATERAL SURVEILLANCE AND POLICY COORDINATION

9. We warmly welcome the progress achieved by the Group of Seven Finance Ministers [G-7] in developing and implementing strengthened arrangements for multilateral surveillance and economic coordination as called for in Tokyo last year. The new process of coordination, involving the use of economic indicators, will enhance efforts to achieve more consistent and mutually compatible policies by our countries.

10. The Heads of State or Government reaffirm the important policy commitments and undertakings adopted at the Louvre [1987] and Washington meetings of the Group of Seven,[1] including those relating to exchange rates. They agree that, if in the future world economic growth is insufficient, additional actions will be required to achieve their common objectives. Accordingly, they call on their Finance Ministers to develop, if necessary, additional appropriate policy measures for this purpose and to continue to cooperate closely to foster stability of exchange rates.

11. The coordination of economic policies is an ongoing process which will evolve and become more effective over time. The Heads of State or Government endorse the understandings reached by the Group of Seven Finance Ministers to strengthen, with the assistance of the International Monetary Fund (IMF), the surveillance of their economies using economic indicators including exchange rates, in particular by:

—The commitment by each country to develop medium-term objectives and projections for its economy, and for the group to develop objectives and projections that are mutually consistent both individually and collectively; and

—The use of performance indicators to review and assess current economic trends and to determine whether there are significant deviations from an intended course that require consideration of remedial actions.

---

[1]See page 312.

12. The Heads of State or Government consider these measures important steps towards promoting sustained non-inflationary global growth and greater currency stability. They call upon the Group of Seven Finance Ministers and Central Bank governors to:

—Intensify their coordination efforts with a view to achieving prompt and effective implementation of the agreed policy undertakings and commitments;

—Monitor economic developments closely in cooperation with the Managing Director of the IMF; and

—Consider further improvements as appropriate to make the coordination process more effective.

TRADE

13. We note rising protectionist pressures with grave concern. The Uruguay Round can play an important role in maintaining and strengthening the multilateral trading system, and achieving increased liberalization of trade for the benefit of all countries.[2] Recognizing the interrelationship among growth, trade and development, it is essential to improve the multilateral system based on the principles and rules of the General Agreement on Tariffs and Trade (GATT) and bring about a wider coverage of world trade under agreed, effective and enforceable multilateral discipline. Protectionist actions would be counterproductive, would increase the risk of further ex-

---

[2]The Uruguay round (the eighth round of multilateral trade negotiations held under the auspices of GATT) is so named becaused agreement to launch it was reached by trade ministers of GATT countries meeting in September 1986 at Punta del Este, Uruguay.—ED.

change rate instability and would exacerbate the problems of development and indebtedness.

14. We endorse fully the commitment to adopt appropriate measures in compliance with the principles of stand-still and rollback which have been reaffirmed in the Ministerial Declaration on the Uruguay Round. It is important to establish in the GATT a multilateral framework of principles and rules for trade in services, trade-related investment measures and intellectual property rights. This extension of the multilateral trading system would also be beneficial to developing countries in fostering growth and enhancing trade, investment and technology transfers.

15. Basing ourselves on the Ministerial Declaration on the Uruguay Round and on the principles of the GATT, we call on all Contracting Parties to negotiate comprehensively, in good faith and with all due dispatch, with a view to ensuring mutual advantage and increased benefits to all participants. Canada, Japan, the United States and the European Community will table a wide range of substantive proposals in Geneva over the coming months. Progress in the Uruguay Round will be kept under close political review. In this context the launching, the conduct and the implementation of the outcome of the negotiations should be treated as parts of a single undertaking; however, agreements reached at an early stage might be implemented on a provisional or definitive basis by agreement prior to the formal conclusion of the negotiations, and should be taken into account in assessing the overall balance of the negotiations.

16. A strong, credible, working GATT is essential to the well-being of all trading countries and is the best bulwark against mounting bilateral protectionist pressures. The functioning of the GATT should be improved through enhancing its role in maintaining an open multilateral system and its ability to manage disputes; and through ensuring better coordination between the GATT and the IMF and the World Bank. We consider that it would be useful to have, as appropriate, in the course of the negotiations, a meeting of the Trade Negotiating Committee at the ministerial level.

AGRICULTURE

17. At Tokyo we recognized the serious nature of the agricultural problem. We agreed that the structure of agricultural production needed to be adjusted in the light of world demand, and expressed our determination to give full support to the work of the OECD [Organisation for Economic Co-operation and Development] in this field. In doing so, we all recognized the importance of agriculture to the well-being of our rural communities. In the past year, we have actively pursued the approach outlined at Tokyo, and we take satisfaction from the agreement in the Ministerial Declaration adopted in Punta del Este on the objectives for the negotiations on agriculture in the Uruguay Round.

18. We reaffirm our commitment to the important agreement on agriculture set out in the OECD ministerial communiqué of May 13, 1987; in particular, the statement of the scope and urgency of the problem which require that a concerted reform of agricultural policies be implemented in a balanced and flexible manner; the assessment of the grave implications, for developed and developing countries alike, of the growing imbalances in supply of and demand for the main agricultural products; the acknowledgment of shared responsibility for the problems as well as for their equitable, effective and durable resolution; the principles of reform and the action required. The long-term objective is to allow market signals to influence the orientation of agricultural production, by way of a progressive and concerted reduction of agricultural support, as well as by all other appropriate means, giving consideration to social and other concerns, such as food security, environmental protection and overall employment.

19. We underscore our commitment to work in concert to achieve the necessary adjustments of agricultural policies, both at home and through comprehensive negotiations in the Uruguay Round. In this as in other fields, we will table comprehensive proposals for negotiations in the coming months to be conducted in accordance with the mandate in the Ministerial Declaration, and we intend to review at our next meeting the progress achieved and the tasks that remain.

20. In the meantime, in order to create a climate of greater confidence which would enhance the prospect for rapid progress in the Uruguay Round as a whole, and as a step towards the long-term result to be expected from those negotiations, we have agreed, and call upon other countries to agree, to refrain from actions which, by further stimulating production of agricultural commodities in surplus, increasing protection or destabilizing world markets, would worsen the negotiating climate and, more generally, damage trade relations.

DEVELOPING COUNTRIES AND DEBT

21. We attach particular importance to fostering stable economic progress in developing countries, with all their diverse situations and needs. The problems of many heavily indebted developing countries are a cause of economic and political concern and can be a threat to political stability in countries with democratic regimes. We salute the courageous efforts of many of these countries to achieve economic growth and stability.

22. We underline the continuing importance of official development assistance and welcome the increased efforts of some of our countries in this respect. We recall the target already established by international organizations (0.7 percent) for the future level of official development assistance, and we take note that overall financial flows are important to development. We

339

strongly support the activities of international financial institutions, including those regional development banks which foster policy reforms by borrowers and finance their programs of structural adjustment. In particular:

—We support the central role of the IMF through its advice and financing and encourage closer cooperation between the IMF and the World Bank, especially in their structural adjustment lending;

—We note with satisfaction the contribution made by the eighth replenishment of the International Development Association (IDA);

—We support a general capital increase of the World Bank when justified by increased demand for quality lending, by its expanded role in the debt strategy and by the necessity to maintain the financial stability of the institution; and

—In the light of the difference of contributions of our countries to official development assistance, we welcome the recent initiative of the Japanese Government in bringing forward a new scheme which will increase the provision of resources from Japan to developing countries.

23. For the major middle-income debtors, we continue to support the present growth-oriented case-by-case strategy. Three elements are needed to strengthen the growth prospects of debtor countries: the adoption of comprehensive macroeconomic and structural reforms by debtor countries themselves; the enhancement of lending by international financial institutions, in particular the World Bank; and adequate commercial bank lending in support of debtor country reforms. We shall play our part by helping to sustain growth and expand trade. A number of debt agreements have allowed some resumption of growth, correction of imbalances, and significant progress in restoring the creditworthiness of some countries. But some still lack

adequate policies for structural adjustment and growth designed to encourage the efficient use of domestic savings, the repatriation of flight capital, increased flows of foreign direct investment and, in particular, reforms of financial markets.

24. There is equally a need for timely and effective mobilization of lending by commercial banks. In this context, we support efforts by commercial banks and debtor countries to develop a "menu" of alternative negotiating procedures and financing techniques for providing continuing support to debtor countries.

25. Measures should be taken, particularly by debtor countries, to facilitate non-debt-creating capital flows, especially direct investment. In this connection, the Multilateral Investment Guarantee Agency (MIGA) should begin to serve its objectives as soon as possible. It is important to maintain flexibility on the part of export credit agencies in promptly resuming or increasing cover for countries that are implementing comprehensive adjustment programs.

26. We recognize the problems of developing countries whose economies are solely or predominantly dependent on exports of primary commodities, the prices of which are persistently depressed. It is important that the functioning of commodity markets should be improved, for example, through better information and greater transparency. Further diversification of these economies should be encouraged, with the help of the international financial institutions, through policies to support their efforts for improved processing of their products, to expand opportunities through market access liberalization and to strengthen the international environment for structural change.

27. We recognize that the problems of some of the poorest countries, primarily in Sub-Saharan Africa, are uniquely difficult and need special treatment. These countries are characterized by such features as acute poverty, limited resources to invest in their own development, unmanageable debt burdens, heavy reliance on one or two commodities, and the fact that their debt is owed for the most part to governments of industrialized countries themselves or to international financial institutions. For those of the poorest countries that are undertaking adjustment effort, consideration should be given to the possibility of applying lower interest rates to their existing debt, and agreement should be reached, especially in the Paris Club,[3] on longer repayment and grace periods to ease the debt service burden. We welcome the various proposals made in this area by some of us, and also the proposal by the Managing Director of the IMF for a significant increase in the resources of the Structural Adjustment Facility over the three years from January 1, 1988. We urge a conclusion on [sic] discussions on these proposals within this year.

28. We note that UNCTAD VII [UN Conference on Trade and Development, Seventh Session] provides an opportunity for a discussion with developing countries with a view to arriving at a common perception of the major problems and policy issues in the world economy.

ENVIRONMENT

29. Further to our previous commitment to preserve a healthy environment and to pass it on to future generations, we welcome the report by the environment experts on the improvement and harmonization of techniques and practices of environmental measurement. Accordingly, we encourage the United Nations Environment Programme (UNEP) to institute a forum for information exchange and consultation in cooperation with the

---

[3]The Paris Club is an informal group of the finance ministers of the ten wealthiest member states of the IMF (the "Group of Ten"): Belgium, Canada, the Federal Republic of Germany, France, Italy, Japan, The Netherlands, Sweden, the United Kingdom, and the United States. In recent years the Paris Club has been meeting monthly, under the chairmanship of the French treasury.—ED.

International Organization for Standardization (ISO) and the International Council of Scientific Unions (ICSU), assisted by other interested international organizations and countries, so that continuing progress in this important field can be ensured. The priority environmental problems identified by the environmental experts in their report should receive full attention.

30. We underline our own responsibility to encourage efforts to tackle effectively environmental problems of worldwide impact such as stratospheric ozone depletion, climate change, acid rains, endangered species, hazardous substances, air and water pollution, and destruction of tropical forests. We also intend to examine further environmental issues such as stringent environmental standards as an incentive for innovation and for the development of clean, cost-effective and low-resource technology; as well as promotion of international trade in low-pollution products, low-polluting industrial plants and other environmental protection technologies.

31. We welcome the important progress achieved since Tokyo, particularly in the International Atomic Energy Agency, in enhancing effective international cooperation with regard to safety in the management of nuclear energy.

OTHER ISSUES

32. We welcome the initiative of the Human Frontier Science Program (HFSP) presented by Japan, which is aimed at promoting, through international cooperation, basic research on biological functions. We are grateful for the informal opportunities our scientists have had to take part in some of the discussions of the feasibility study undertaken by Japan. We note that this study will be continued, and we would be pleased to be kept informed about its progress.

33. We welcome the positive contribution made by the Confer-

ence of High Level Experts on the Future Role of Education in Our Society, held in Kyoto in January 1987.

34. We shall continue to review the ethical implications of developments in the life sciences. Following the conferences sponsored by Summit governments—by Japan in 1984, by France in 1985, by the Federal Republic of Germany in 1986 and by Canada in 1987—we welcome the Italian Government's offer to host the next bioethics conference in Italy in April 1988.

NEXT ECONOMIC SUMMIT

35. We have agreed to meet again next year and have accepted the invitation of the Canadian Prime Minister to meet in Canada.

SOURCE: U.S., Department of State, *Bulletin,* No. 2125 (August 1987): 11–14; Canada, Department of External Affairs, *Economic Summits, 1975–1987: Declarations* (Ottawa, 198—): Tab 31, 1–8 [unpublished]; Canada, Department of External Affairs, *Toronto Economic Summit, June 19–21, 1988 (Ottawa, 1988), pp. 46–50.*

STATEMENT ON EAST–WEST RELATIONS

June 9, 1987

1. We, the Heads of State or Government of seven major industrial nations and the Representatives of the European Community, have discussed East-West relations. We reaffirm our shared principles and objectives, and our common dedication to preserving and strengthening peace.

2. We recognize with pride that our shared values of freedom, democracy and respect for human rights are the source of the dynamism and prosperity of our societies. We renew our commitment to the search for a freer, more democratic and more humane world.

3. Within existing alliances, each of us is resolved to maintain a strong and credible defense which threatens the security of no one, protects freedom, deters aggression and maintains peace. We shall continue to consult closely on all matters affecting our common interest. We will not be separated from the principles that guide us all.

4. Since we last met, new opportunities have opened for progress in East-West relations. We are encouraged by these developments. They confirm the soundness of the policies we have each pursued in our determination to achieve a freer and safer world.

5. We are following with close interest recent developments in the internal and external policies of the Soviet Union. It is our hope that they will prove to be of great significance for the improvement of political, economic and security relations between the countries of East and West. At the same time, profound differences persist; each of us must remain vigilantly alert in responding to all aspects of Soviet policy.

6. We reaffirm our commitment to peace and increased security

345

at lower levels of arms. We seek a comprehensive effort to lower tensions and to achieve verifiable arms reductions. While reaffirming the continuing importance of nuclear deterrence in preserving peace, we note with satisfaction that dialogue on arms control has intensified and that more favorable prospects have emerged for the reduction of nuclear forces. We appreciate U.S. efforts to negotiate balanced, substantial and verifiable reductions in nuclear weapons. We emphasize our determination to enhance conventional stability at a lower level of forces and achieve the total elimination of chemical weapons. We believe that these goals should be actively pursued and translated into concrete agreements. We urge the Soviet Union to negotiate in a positive and constructive manner. An effective resolution of these issues is an essential requirement for real and enduring stability in the world.

7. We will be paying close attention not only to Soviet statements but also to Soviet actions on issues of common concern to us. In particular:

—We call for significant and lasting progress in human rights, which is essential to building trust between our societies. Much still remains to be done to meet the principles agreed and commitments undertaken in the Helsinki Final Act and confirmed since;

—We look for an early and peaceful resolution of regional conflicts, and especially for a rapid and total withdrawal of Soviet forces from Afghanistan so that the people of Afghanistan may freely determine their own future; and

—We encourage greater contacts, freer interchange of ideas and more extensive dialogue between our people and the people of the Soviet Union and Eastern Europe.

8. Thus, we each seek to stabilize military competition between East and West at lower levels of arms; to encourage stable political solutions to regional conflicts; to secure lasting im-

provements in human rights; and to build contacts, confidence and trust between governments and peoples in a more humane world. Progress across the board is necessary to establish a durable foundation for stable and constructive relationships between the countries of East and West.

SOURCE: U.S., Department of State, *Bulletin*, No. 2125 (August 1987): 3; Canada, Department of External Affairs, *Economic Summits, 1975–1987: Declarations* (Ottawa, 198—): Tab 32, 1–2 [unpublished]; Embassy of Italy, Ottawa, Canada; Canada, Department of External Affairs, *Toronto Economic Summit, June 19–21, 1988* (Ottawa, 1988), p. 52.

STATEMENT ON TERRORISM

June 9, 1987

We, the Heads of State or Government of seven major democracies and the Representatives of the European Community assembled here in Venice, profoundly aware of our peoples' concern at the threat posed by terrorism:

—Reaffirm our commitment to the statements on terrorism made at previous Summits in Bonn, Venice, Ottawa, London and Tokyo;

—Resolutely condemn all forms of terrorism, including aircraft hijackings and hostage-taking, and reiterate our belief that whatever its motives, terrorism has no justification;

—Confirm the commitment of each of us to the principle of making no concessions to terrorists or their sponsors;

—Remain resolved to apply, in respect of any State clearly involved in sponsoring or supporting international terrorism, effective measures within the framework of international law and in our own jurisdictions;

—Welcome the progress made in international cooperation against terrorism since we last met in Tokyo in May 1986, and in particular the initiative taken by France and Germany to convene in May in Paris a meeting of Ministers of nine countries who are responsible for counter-terrorism;

—Reaffirm our determination to combat terrorism both through national measures and through international cooperation among ourselves and with others, when appropriate, and therefore renew our appeal to all like-minded countries to consolidate and extend international cooperation in all appropriate fora;

—Will continue our efforts to improve the safety of travelers. We welcome improvements in airport and maritime security, and encourage the work of ICAO [International Civil Aviation Organization] and IMO [International Maritime Organization] in this regard. Each of us will continue to monitor closely the activities of airlines which raise security problems. The Heads of State or Government have decided on measures, annexed to this statement, to make the 1978 Bonn Declaration more effective in dealing with all forms of terrorism affecting civil aviation;

—Commit ourselves to support the rule of law in bringing terrorists to justice. Each of us pledges increased cooperation in the relevant fora and within the framework of domestic and international law on the investigation, apprehension and prosecution of terrorists. In particular, we reaffirm the principle established by relevant international conventions of trying or extraditing, according to national laws and those international conventions, those who have perpetrated acts of terrorism.

ANNEX

The Heads of State or Government recall that in their Tokyo Statement on international terrorism they agreed to make the 1978 Bonn Declaration more effective in dealing with all forms of terrorism affecting civil aviation. To this end, in cases where a country refuses extradition or prosecution of those who have committed offences described in the Montreal Convention for the Suppression of Unlawful Acts against the Safety of Civil Aviation and/or does not return the aircraft involved, the Heads of State or Government are jointly resolved that their Governments shall take immediate action to cease flights to that country as stated in the Bonn Declaration.

At the same time, their Governments will initiate action to halt incoming flights from that country or from any country by the airlines of the country concerned as stated in the Bonn Declaration.

The Heads of State or Government intend also to extend the Bonn Declaration in due time to cover any future relevant amendment to the above Convention or any other aviation conventions relating to the extradition or prosecution of the offenders.

The Heads of State or Government urge other governments to join them in this commitment.

SOURCE: U.S., Department of State, *Bulletin*, No. 2125 (August 1987): 3–4; Canada, Department of External Affairs, *Economic Summits, 1975–1987: Declarations* (Ottawa, 198—): Tab 33, 3–5 [unpublished]; Embassy of Italy, Ottawa, Canada; Canada, Department of External Affairs, *Toronto Economic Summit, June 19–21, 1988* (Ottawa, 1988), p. 53.

STATEMENT ON IRAQ-IRAN WAR AND FREEDOM OF NAVIGATION IN THE GULF

June 9, 1987

We agree that new and concerted international efforts are urgently required to help bring the Iraq–Iran war to an end. We favor the earliest possible negotiated end to the war with the territorial integrity and independence of both Iraq and Iran intact. Both countries have suffered grievously from this long and tragic war. Neighboring countries are threatened with the possible spread of the conflict. We call once more upon both parties to negotiate an immediate end of the war. We strongly support the mediation efforts of the United Nations Secretary-General and urge the adoption of just and effective measures by the UN Security Council. With these objectives in mind, we reaffirm that the principle of freedom of navigation in the Gulf is of paramount importance for us and for others, and must be upheld. The free flow of oil and other traffic through the Strait of Hormuz must continue unimpeded.

We pledge to continue to consult on ways to pursue these important goals effectively.

SOURCE: U.S., Department of State, *Bulletin*, No. 2125 (August 1987): 4; Canada, Department of External Affairs, *Economic Summits, 1975–1987: Declarations* (Ottawa, 198—): Tab 34 [unpublished]; Embassy of Italy, Ottawa, Canada; Canada, Department of External Affairs, *Toronto Economic Summit, June 19–21, 1988* (Ottawa, 1988), p. 54.

CHAIRMAN'S SUMMARY ON POLITICAL ISSUES

June 10, 1987

The Venice Summit has provided us with the opportunity for a useful exchange of views on the main international political issues of the moment. Our discussions took place in the same spirit of constructive cooperation which inspired yesterday's statements on East-West relations, the Gulf conflict, and terrorism and confirmed a significant unity of approaches.

In the field of East-West relations, particular attention was paid to a number of regional issues.

On the subject of Afghanistan, emphasis was placed once again on the need to keep up pressure so that the Afghan people can very soon determine their own future in a country no longer subject to external military occupation.

It was noted that the presence in Kampuchea of foreign troops continues to be an obstacle to the peace and tranquility of South-East Asia.

In the Pacific, newly independent island States are faced with difficult economic situations. We have stressed the need to support their development process in conditions of complete freedom from outside political interference.

In Asia, we agreed that particular attention should be paid to the efforts for economic reform undertaken by China. We reviewed the situation in the Korean Peninsula, in the belief that the next Olympic Games may create a climate favorable to the development of a more open dialogue between North and South. In the Philippines, the democratic government is involved in a courageous attempt at economic and social renewal which deserves our support.

As regards Africa—a continent with enormous potentialities but facing extremely serious economic, social and political problems—we viewed the situation in South Africa with particular concern. We agreed that a peaceful and lasting solution can only be found to the present crisis if the apartheid regime is dismantled and replaced by a new form of democratic, non-racial government. There is an urgent need, therefore, to begin a genuine dialogue with the representatives of all the components of South African society. At the same time we noted the importance of humanitarian assistance initiatives for the victims of apartheid and of supporting the efforts by SADCC (Southern African Development Coordination Conference) member States to develop and strengthen their own economies.

Serious concern was expressed at the continuing dangerous tensions and conflicts in the Near and Middle East and at the absence of concrete progress toward a solution to the Arab–Israeli dispute. The need for action to create conditions for a just, global and lasting peace was reaffirmed.

Concern was also expressed at the situation in the occupied territories.

The situation in Lebanon, with its serious internal tensions and the persisting problem of the Palestinian camps, continues to give cause for concern. In this connection, we reaffirmed our hope that genuine efforts be made towards national reconciliation.

With regard to Latin America, the discussion highlighted the need to promote appropriate initiatives aimed at supporting democratic governments and encouraging the return to democracy and its consolidation throughout the continent. There was also agreement that efforts toward regional integration will help open up a fruitful and constructive dialogue with the West; they, therefore, deserve support.

With regard to developments in Central America, it is hoped that the forthcoming Summit to be held in Guatemala can play a positive role in paving the way to peace and stability.

Finally, we turned to the problems of the United Nations Organizations [sic] and, in particular, to its current financial difficulties, and considered possible ways of overcoming them.

SOURCE: U.S., Department of State, *Bulletin*, No. 2125 (August 1987): 10; Canada, Department of External Affairs, *Economic Summits, 1975–1987: Declarations* (Ottawa, 198—): Tab 35, 1–2 [unpublished].

CHAIRMAN'S STATEMENT ON AIDS

June 10, 1987

On the basis of the concern already shown in the past for health problems (London Chairman's oral statement on cancer and Bonn Chairman's oral statement on drugs), the Heads of State or Government and the representatives of the European Community affirm that AIDS [Acquired Immune Deficiency Syndrome] is one of the biggest potential health problems in the world. National efforts need to be intensified and made more effective by international cooperation and concerted campaigns to prevent AIDS from spreading further, and will have to ensure that the measures taken are in accordance with the principles of human rights. In this connection, they agree that:

—International cooperation will not be improved by duplication of effort. Priority will have to be given to strengthening existing organizations by giving them full political support and by providing them with the necessary financial, personnel and administrative resources. The World Health Organization (WHO) is the best forum for drawing together international efforts on a worldwide level to combat AIDS, and all countries should be encouraged fully to cooperate with the WHO and support its special program of AIDS-related activities;

—In the absence of a vaccine or cure, the best hope for the combat and prevention of AIDS rests on a strategy based on educating the public about the seriousness of the AIDS epidemic, the ways the AIDS virus is transmitted and the practical steps each person can take to avoid acquiring or spreading it. Appropriate opportunities should be used for exchanging information about national education campaigns and domestic policies. The Heads of State or Government and the representatives of the European Community welcome the proposal by the United Kingdom government to co-sponsor, with the

WHO, an international conference at ministerial level on public education about AIDS; and

—Further cooperation should be promoted for basic and clinical studies on prevention, treatment and the exchange of information (as in the case of the EC program). The Heads of State or Government and the representatives of the European Community welcome and support joint action by researchers in the seven countries (as in the case of the joint program of French and American researchers, which is being enlarged, and similar programs) and all over the world for the cure of the disease, clinical testing on components of the virus and the development of a successful vaccine. The Heads of State or Government and the representatives of the European Community welcome the proposal by the president of the French Republic aiming at the creation of an international committee on the ethical issues raised by AIDS.

SOURCE: U.S., Department of State, *Bulletin*, No. 2125 (August 1987): 10–11; Canada, Department of External Affairs, *Economic Summits, 1975–1987: Declarations* (Ottawa, 198—): Tab 36 [unpublished]; Canada, Department of External Affairs, *Toronto Economic Summit, June 19–21, 1988* (Ottawa, 1988), p. 51.

CHAIRMAN'S STATEMENT ON DRUGS

June 10, 1987

The Heads of State or Government have examined the drug abuse problem, which causes a tragic loss of human life and now affects people all over the world, especially the young and their families. They emphasize the importance of undertaking a strategy in support of national, regional and multilateral campaigns in order to overcome this problem. They intend to continue their fight against illegal production and distribution of drugs and to create all necessary conditions for more effective international cooperation. They will also work for the eradication of illegal cultivation of natural drugs and for its replacement with other types of production which will further the aims of social and economic development. The leaders welcome the agreements already reached on bilateral and multilateral bases, and look forward with confidence to a successful International Conference on Drug Abuse and Illicit Trafficking, which the United Nations is convening next week in Vienna.

SOURCE: U.S., Department of State, *Bulletin*, No. 2125 (August 1987): 11; Canada, Department of External Affairs, *Economic Summits, 1975–1987: Declarations* (Ottawa, 198—): Tab 37 [unpublished]; Canada, Department of External Affairs, *Toronto Economic Summit, June 19–21, 1988* (Ottawa, 1988), p. 51.

Toronto

19–21 June 1988

TORONTO, 19–21 JUNE 1988

DELEGATIONS

Canada

Brian Mulroney, *Prime Minister*
Joe Clark, *Secretary of State for External Affairs*
Michael H. Wilson, *Minister of Finance*
Sylvia Ostry, *Personal Representative (Sherpa)*

France

François Mitterand, *President*
Roland Dumas, *Minister of External Affairs*
Pierre Bérégovoy, *Minister for Economics, Finance and Privatization*
Jacques Attali, *Personal Representative (Sherpa)*

Germany (Federal Republic)

Helmut Kohl, *Federal Chancellor*
Hans-Dietrich Genscher, *Federal Minister for Foreign Affairs*

359

Germany (Federal Republic) *continued*

Gerhard Stoltenberg, *Federal Minister of Finance*
Martin Bangemann, *Federal Minister of Economics*
Hans Tietmeyer, *Personal Representative (Sherpa)*

Italy

Ciriaco de Mita, *President of the Council of Ministers*
Giulio Andreotti, *Minister for Foreign Affairs*
Giuliano Amato, *Minister of Finance*
Mario Sarcinelli, *Personal Representative (Sherpa)*

Japan

Noboru Takeshita, *Prime Minister*
Sousuke Uno, *Minister for Foreign Affairs*
Kiichi Miyazawa, *Minister of Finance*
Hajime Tamura, *Minister of International Trade and
    Industry*
Hiroshi Kitamura, *Personal Representative (Sherpa)*

United Kingdom

Margaret Thatcher, *Prime Minister*
Geoffrey Howe, *Secretary of State for Foreign and
    Commonwealth Affairs / Minister of Overseas Development*
Nigel Lawson, *Chancellor of the Exchequer*
Nigel Wicks, *Personal Representative (Sherpa)*

United States

Ronald Reagan, *President*
George P. Shultz, *Secretary of State*

United States *continued*

James A. Baker, *Secretary of the Treasury*
W. Allen Wallis, *Personal Representative (Sherpa)*

European Communities

Jacques Delors, *President of the Commission*
Willy De Clercq, *Commissioner, Foreign Affairs*
Peter M. Schmidhuber, *Commissioner, Monetary Affairs*
Pascal Lamy, *Personal Representative (Sherpa)*

TORONTO ECONOMIC SUMMIT
ECONOMIC DECLARATION

June 21, 1988

1. We, the Heads of State or Government of seven major industrial nations and the President of the Commission of the European Communities, have met in Toronto for the fourteenth annual Economic Summit. We have drawn lessons from the past and looked ahead to the future.

2. Over the past fourteen years, the world economy and economic policy have undergone profound changes. In particular, the information-technology revolution and the globalization of markets have increased economic interdependence, making it essential that governments consider fully the international dimensions of their deliberations.

3. We observed a sharp contrast between the 1970s and 1980s. The former was a decade of high and rising inflation, declining productivity growth, policies dominated by short-term considerations, and frequently inadequate international policy cooperation. In the 1980s inflation has been brought under control, laying the basis for sustained strong growth and improved productivity. The result has been the longest period of economic growth in post-war history. However, the 1980s have seen the emergence of large external imbalances in the major industrial economies, greater exchange rate volatility, and debt-servicing difficulties in a number of developing countries. Our response to these developments has been an increased commitment to international cooperation, resulting in the intensified process of policy coordination adopted at the 1986 Tokyo Summit and further strengthened at the Venice Summit and in the Group of Seven.

4. Summits have proven an effective forum to address the issues facing the world economy, promote new ideas and develop a common sense of purpose. Especially in the 1980s they have helped bring about an increasing recognition that the eradication of inflation and of inflationary expectations is fundamental to sustained growth and job creation. That recognition has been underpinned by a shift from short-term considerations to a medium-term framework for the development and implementation of economic policies, and a commitment to improve efficiency and adaptability through greater reliance on competitive forces and structural reform. Over this period we have also singled out for concerted attention a number of other issues of decisive importance: the overriding need to resist protectionism and strengthen the open, multilateral trading system; to maintain and strengthen an effective strategy to address the challenge of development and alleviate the burden of debt; and to deal with the serious nature of the world agricultural problem.

5. Since we last met, our economies have kept up the momentum of growth. Employment has continued to expand generally, inflation has been restrained, and progress has been made toward the correction of major external imbalances. These encouraging developments are cause for optimism, but not for complacency. To sustain non-inflationary growth will require a commitment to enhanced cooperation. This is the key to credibility and confidence.

INTERNATIONAL ECONOMIC POLICY COOPERATION

Macroeconomic Policies and Exchange Rates

6. The Tokyo and Venice Summits have developed and strengthened the process of coordination of our economic policies. Developments in the wake of the financial strains last October demonstrate the effectiveness and resilience of the arrangements that have emerged. The policies, the short-term prospects, and the medium-term objectives and projections of our econo-

mies are being discussed regularly in the Group of Seven. The policies and performance are assessed on the basis of economic indicators. We welcome the progress made in refining the analytical use of indicators, as well as the addition to the existing indicators of a commodity-price indicator. The progress in coordination is contributing to the process of further improving the functioning of the international monetary system.

7. Fiscal, monetary and structural policies have been undertaken to foster the adjustment to more sustainable economic and financial positions in the context of non-inflationary growth. Efforts in those directions, including continued reduction of budgetary deficits, will continue. We need to maintain vigilance against any resurgence of inflation. We reaffirm our determination to follow and, wherever feasible, strengthen our agreed strategy of coordinated efforts to reduce the growth of spending in countries with large external deficits and to sustain the momentum of domestic demand in those with large external surpluses. The reduction of large external imbalances, however, will require not only our cooperative efforts, but also those of smaller economies, including newly industrializing economies, with large external surpluses.

8. The exchange rate changes in the past three years, especially the depreciation of the U.S. dollar against the Japanese yen and the major European currencies, have played a major role in the adjustment of real trade balances. We endorse the Group of Seven's conclusion that either excessive fluctuation of exchange rates, a further decline of the dollar, or a rise in the dollar to an extent that becomes destabilizing to the adjustment process, could be counterproductive by damaging growth prospects in the world economy.

Structural Reforms

9. International cooperation involves more than coordination of

macroeconomic policies. Structural reforms complement macro-economic policies, enhance their effectiveness, and provide the basis for more robust growth. We shall collectively review our progress on structural reforms and shall strive to integrate structural policies into our economic coordination process.

10. We will continue to pursue structural reforms by removing barriers, unnecessary controls and regulations; increasing competition, while mitigating adverse effects on social groups or regions; removing disincentives to work, save, and invest, such as through tax reform; and by improving education and training. The specific priorities that each of us has identified are outlined in the attached Annex on Structural Reforms.

11. We welcome the further development of the OECD's surveillance of structural reforms. Such surveillance would be particularly useful in improving public understanding of the reforms by revealing their impact on government budgets, consumer prices, and international trade.

12. One of the major structural problems in both developed and developing countries is in the field of agricultural policies. It is essential that recent significant policy reform efforts undertaken by a number of parties be continued through further positive action by all Summit participants. More market-oriented agricultural policies should assist in the achievement of important objectives such as preserving rural areas and family farming, raising quality standards and protecting the environment. We welcome the OECD's increased emphasis on structural adjustment and development in the rural economy.

13. Financial and technological innovations are rapidly integrating financial markets internationally, contributing to a better allocation of capital but also increasing the speed and extent to which disturbances in one country may be transmitted to other countries. We will continue to cooperate with other countries in the examination of the functioning of the global financial system, including securities.

MULTILATERAL TRADING SYSTEM/URUGUAY ROUND

14. A successful Uruguay Round will assure the integrity of an open, predictable multilateral trading system based on clear rules, and will lead to trade expansion and enhanced economic growth. At Punta del Este, Ministers committed themselves to further trade liberalization across the wide range of goods and services, including such new areas as trade-related intellectual property and trade-related investment measures, to strengthen the multilateral trading system, and to allow for early agreements where appropriate. Countries must continue to resist protectionism and the temptation to adopt unilateral measures outside the framework of GATT rules. In order to preserve a favorable negotiating climate, the participants should conscientiously implement the commitments to standstill and rollback that they have taken at Punta del Este and subsequent international meetings.

15. We strongly welcome the Free Trade Agreement between Canada and the USA, and the steady progress towards the target of the European Community to complete the internal market by 1992. It is our policy that these developments, together with other moves towards regional cooperation in which our countries are involved, should support the open, multilateral trading system and catalyze the liberalizing impact of the Uruguay Round.

16. We attach major importance to strengthening the GATT itself. It is vital that the GATT become a more dynamic and effective organization, particularly in regard to the surveillance of trade policies and dispute settlement procedures, with greater ministerial involvement, and strengthened linkages with other international organizations. GATT disciplines must be improved so that members accept their obligations and ensure that disputes are resolved speedily, effectively and equitably.

17. Trade plays a key role in development. We encourage the

developing countries, especially the newly industrializing economies, to undertake increased commitments and obligations and
a greater role in the GATT, commensurate with their importance in international trade and in the international adjustment
process, as well as with their respective stages of development.
Equally, developed countries should continue to strive to ensure
more open markets for the exports of developing countries.

18. In agriculture, continued political impetus is essential to
underpin the politically difficult efforts at domestic policy
reform and to advance the equally difficult and related process
of agricultural trade reform. Although significant progress was
made in 1987 in the Uruguay Round negotiations, with the
tabling of major proposals, it is necessary to ensure that the
Mid-Term Review in Montreal in December 1988 adds impetus
to the negotiations in this as in other fields. We support efforts
to adopt a framework approach, including short- as well as
long-term elements which will promote the reform process as
launched last year and relieve current strains in agricultural
markets. This would be facilitated by a device for the measurement of support and protection. Also, ways should be developed
to take account of food security and social concerns. To move the
issue forward, and noting among other things the diversity of
our agricultural situations, our negotiators in Geneva must
develop a framework approach which includes short-term options in line with long-term goals concerning the reduction of all
direct and indirect subsidies and other measures affecting
directly or indirectly agricultural trade. The objective of the
framework approach would be to make the agricultural sector
more responsive to market signals.

19. As the Uruguay Round enters a more difficult phase, it is
vital to ensure the momentum of these ambitious negotiations.
The Mid-Term Review will provide a unique opportunity to send
a credible political signal to the trading world. The greatest
possible advance must be made in all areas of the negotiations,
including, where appropriate, decisions, so as to reach before the
end of the year the stage where tangible progress can be

registered. To this end, we support efforts to adopt a framework approach on all issues in the negotiations, i.e., reform of the GATT system and rules, market access, agriculture and new issues (such as trade in services, trade-related intellectual property rights, and trade-related investment measures). For our part, we are committed to ensure that the Mid-Term Review establishes a solid base for the full and complete success of the negotiations, in accordance with the Punta del Este Declaration.

20. We all recognize the critical and expanding role of international investment in the world economy, and share a deep concern that increased protectionism would undermine the benefits of open investment policies. We resolve to progressively liberalize international investment policies and urge other countries to do likewise.

NEWLY INDUSTRIALIZING ECONOMIES

21. Certain newly-industrializing economies (NIEs) in the Asia-Pacific region have become increasingly important in world trade. Although these economies differ in many important respects, they are all characterized by dynamic, export-led growth which has allowed them to treble their share of world trade since 1960. Other outward-oriented Asian countries are also beginning to emerge as rapidly-growing exporters of manufactures. With increased economic importance come greater international responsibilities and a strong mutual interest in improved constructive dialogue and cooperative efforts in the near term between the industrialized countries and the Asian NIEs, as well as the other outward-oriented countries in the region. The dialogue and cooperative efforts could center on such policy areas as macroeconomic, currency, structural and trade to achieve the international adjustment necessary for sustained, balanced growth of the world economy. We encourage the development of informal processes which would facilitate multilateral discussions of issues of mutual concern and foster the necessary cooperation.

DEVELOPING COUNTRIES AND DEBT

22. The performance of developing countries is increasingly important to the world economy. Central to the prospects of the developing countries are a healthy global economic environment and an open trading system, adequate financial flows and, most important, their commitment to appropriate economic reform. The problems of many heavily-indebted developing countries are a cause of economic and political concern and can be a threat to political stability in developing countries. Several countries find themselves in that situation in various regions of the world: Latin America, Africa and the Pacific, particularly the Philippines, and that merits our special attention.

Middle-Income Countries

23. A number of highly-indebted middle-income countries continue to have difficulties servicing their external debt and generating the investment necessary for sustainable growth. The market-oriented, growth-led strategy based on the case-by-case approach remains the only viable approach for overcoming their external debt problems.

24. We are encouraged that many indebted countries have begun the difficult process of macroeconomic adjustment and structural reform necessary for sustained progress, encouraging the return of flight capital and new investment flows. The success of these efforts is essential for improving the economic performance and strengthening the creditworthiness of these countries.

25. Official financing has played a central role in the debt strategy through the Paris Club (U.S. $73 billion of principal and interest have been consolidated since 1983) and the flexible policies of export credit agencies. The international financial institutions will continue to have a pivotal role. We endorse the recent initiatives taken by the International Monetary Fund to strengthen its capacity to support medium-term programs of macroeconomic adjustment and structural reform, and to provide greater protection for adjustment programs from unforeseen external developments. We strongly support the full implementation of the World Bank's U.S. $75 billion General Capital Increase to strengthen its capacity to promote adjustment in middle-income countries. We also support greater awareness by international financial institutions of the environmental impact of their development programs.

26. Commercial banks have played an important role in supporting debtor countries' reform efforts through an expanded menu of financing options which has facilitated the channeling of commercial bank lending into productive uses. Their continued involvement is indispensable to the debt strategy. In this regard, the World Bank and IMF can play an important catalytic role in mobilizing additional financing from private (and official) sources in support of debtor countries' adjustment programs.

27. We note that in recent years there has been increasing recourse to innovative financing techniques. The important characteristics of these techniques are that they are voluntary, market-oriented, and applied on a case-by-case basis. The 'menu approach' has engendered new financial flows and, in some cases, reduced the existing stock of debt. The flexibility of the present strategy would be enhanced by the further broadening of the menu approach and the encouragement of innovative financing techniques to improve the quality of new lending, but particular initiatives would have to be carefully considered.

28. International direct investment plays an important role in spurring economic growth and structural adjustment in developing countries. Thus it contributes to alleviating debt problems. Developing countries should welcome and encourage such investment by creating a favorable investment climate.

Debt of the Poorest

29. An increase in concessional resource flows is necessary to help the poorest developing countries resume sustained growth, especially in cases where it is extremely difficult for them to service their debts. Since Venice, progress in dealing with the debt burden of these countries has been encouraging. Paris Club creditors are rescheduling debt at extended grace and repayment periods. In addition, the recent enhancement of the IMF's Structural Adjustment Facility; the World Bank and Official Development Assistance (ODA) agencies' enhanced program of co-financing; and the fifth replenishment of the African Development Fund will mobilize a total of more than U.S. $18 billion in favor of the poorest and most indebted countries undertaking adjustment efforts over the period 1988/90. Out of this total, U.S. $15 billion will be channeled to Sub-Saharan African countries.

30. We welcome proposals made by several of us to ease further the debt service burdens of the poorest countries that are undertaking internationally-approved adjustment programs. We have achieved consensus on rescheduling official debt of these countries within a framework of comparability that allows official creditors to choose among concessional interest rates usually on shorter maturities, longer repayment periods at commercial rates, partial write-offs of debt service obligations during the consolidation period, or a combination of these options. This approach allows official creditors to choose options consistent with their legal or budgetary constraints. The Paris Club has been urged to work out necessary technicalities to ensure comparability by the end of this year at the very latest. This approach will provide benefits over and above the impressive multilateral agreements to help the poorest countries over the past year. We also welcome the action taken by a number of creditor governments to write-off or otherwise remove the burden of ODA loans, and also urge countries to maintain a high grant element in their future assistance to the poorest.

ENVIRONMENT

31. We agree that the protection and enhancement of the environment is essential. The report of the World Commission on Environment and Development has stressed that environmental considerations must be integrated into all areas of economic policy-making if the globe is to continue to support humankind.[1] We endorse the concept of sustainable development.

32. Threats to the environment recognize no boundaries. Their urgent nature requires strengthened international cooperation among all countries. Significant progress has been achieved in a number of environmental areas. The Montreal Protocol on Substances that Deplete the Ozone Layer is a milestone. All countries are encouraged to sign and ratify it.

33. Further action is needed. Global climate change, air, sea and fresh water pollution, acid rain, hazardous substances, deforestation, and endangered species require priority attention. It is, therefore, timely that negotiations on a protocol on emissions of nitrogen oxides within the framework of the Geneva Convention on Long-range Transboundary Air Pollution be pursued energetically. The efforts of the United Nations Environment Programme (UNEP) for an agreement on the transfrontier shipment of hazardous wastes should also be encouraged as well as the establishment of an inter-governmental panel on global

---

[1]World Commission on Environment and Development, *Our Common Future* (New York: Oxford University Press, 1987) [Brundtland Report].—ED.

climate change under the auspices of UNEP and the World Meteorological Organization (WMO). We also recognize the potential impact of agriculture on the environment, whether negative through over-intensive use of resources or positive in preventing desertification. We welcome the Conference on the Changing Atmosphere to be held in Toronto next week.

FUTURE SUMMITS

34. We, the Heads of State or Government, and the representatives of the European Community, believe that the Economic Summits have strengthened the ties of solidarity, both political and economic, that exist between our countries and that thereby they have helped to sustain the values of democracy that underlie our economic and political systems. Our annual meetings have provided the principal opportunity each year for the governments of the major industrialized countries to reflect, in an informal and flexible manner, upon their common responsibility for the progress of the world economy and to resolve how that responsibility should have practical manifestation in the years ahead. We believe that the mutual understanding engendered in our meetings has benefited both our own countries and the wider world community. We believe, too, that the opportunities afforded by our meetings are becoming even more valuable in today's world of increasing interdependence and increasing technological change. We have therefore agreed to institute a further cycle of Summits by accepting the invitation of the President of the French Republic to meet in France, July 14-16, 1989.

OTHER ISSUES

Human Frontier Science Program

1. We note the successful conclusion of Japan's feasibility study on the Human Frontier Science Program and are grateful for the opportunities our scientists were given to contribute to the study. We look forward to the Japanese Government's proposal for the implementation of the program in the near future.

Bioethics

2. We note that, as part of the continuing review of the ethical implications of developments in the life sciences, the Italian Government hosted the fifth conference on bioethics in April 1988, and we welcome the intention of the European Communities to host the sixth conference in the spring of 1989.

ANNEX ON STRUCTURAL REFORMS

—Europe is pursuing structural reforms to complement macroeconomic policies in order to spur job creation, enhance growth potential, and achieve a sustainable pattern of external balances. Structural reform measures are being put into place in the framework of the Communities' program for a unified internal market by 1992; including full liberalization of capital movements; removal of physical, administrative and technical barriers to allow the full mobility of persons, goods and services, and an improvement of competition policy. However, full achievement will depend on complete and timely implementation of the measures and on complementary policies including those in the fields of regional, social and environmental policies and of technological co-operation.

—The main elements of Germany's structural reforms are tax reform and reduction, deregulation and privatization, reform of the postal and telecommunications system, increased flexibility in the labor market, and reform of the social security system.

—In France, the main structural reforms will deal with improving the level of education and professional training and development for workers, and with major improvements in the functioning of financial markets in order to facilitate the financing of the economy at the lowest possible cost.

—Italy will seek to promote training and education, increase the flexibility of the labor market to spur employment, improve the functioning of financial markets, revise the tax system to promote efficiency and eliminate distortions, and enhance public sector efficiency.

—In the United Kingdom, there has already been a substantial program of tax reform, trade union law reform, deregulation, opening up of markets and privatization of state industries. This will continue. Further measures are being introduced to improve both the quality of education and the flexibility of the housing market.

—Japan will pursue further structural reforms to support and sustain the greater reliance on domestic demand-led growth which has quickened remarkably. Japan will promote reform of government regulations in key sectors including land use policies and the distribution system, and reform of the tax system.

—For the United States, where recent indications that the declining trend in private savings may have bottomed out are encouraging, it is nonetheless a priority to increase incentives to save. Also, the United States will strengthen the international competitiveness of its industrial sector.

—The most promising areas of structural reform in Canada are implementation of the second stage of tax reform, the proposed liberalization of the financial services sector, and, most important, the implementation of the Free Trade Agreement with the United States.

SOURCE: U.S., Department of State, *Bulletin,* No. 2137 (August 1988): 49–52; Canada, Department of External Affairs, *Toronto Economic Summit Economic Declaration* (Ottawa, 1988) [unpublished].

POLITICAL DECLARATION

June 20, 1988

EAST–WEST

1. We the leaders of our seven countries, and the representatives of the European Community, uphold common principles of freedom, respect for individual rights, and the desire of all men to live in peace under the rule of law. Our peoples stand in solidarity within the framework of our existing alliances for the cause of freedom, to safeguard democracy and the prosperity which it has produced. In our discussions we considered how these goals and values could be pursued in the field of foreign affairs, particularly with regard to East-West relations.

2. We discussed a wide range of regional questions and these discussions are continuing throughout the Summit.

3. We confirmed our belief in constructive and realistic dialogue and cooperation, including arms control, human rights, and regional issues, as the way to build stability between East and West and enhance security at lower levels of arms. We also reaffirmed that for the foreseeable future nuclear deterrence and adequate conventional strength are the guarantees of peace in freedom.

4. In several important respects changes have taken place in relations between Western countries and the Soviet Union since we last met. For our part this evolution has come about because the industrialized democracies have been strong and united. In the Soviet Union greater freedom and openness will offer opportunities to reduce mistrust and build confidence. Each of us will respond positively to any such developments.

5. We welcome the beginning of the Soviet withdrawal of its occupation troops from Afghanistan. It must be total and apply to the entire country. The Afghan people must be able to choose their government freely. Each of us confirms our willingness to make our full contribution to the efforts of the international community to ensure the return of the refugees to their homeland, their resettlement, and the reconstruction of their country. We now look to the Soviet Union to make a constructive contribution to resolving other regional conflicts as well.

6. Since our last meeting, progress has been made between the United States and the Soviet Union in agreeing to reduce nuclear weapons in a manner which accords fully with the security interests of each of our countries. The INF [Intermediate-Range Nuclear Forces] Treaty, the direct result of Western firmness and unity, is the first treaty ever actually to reduce nuclear arms. It sets vitally important precedents for future arms control agreements: asymmetrical reductions and intrusive verification arrangements. We now look for deep cuts in U.S. and Soviet strategic offensive arms. We congratulate President Reagan on what he has already accomplished, along with General Secretary Gorbachev, towards this goal.

7. Nonetheless, the massive presence of Soviet conventional forces in Eastern Europe, the ensuing conventional superiority of the Warsaw Pact, and its capacity to launch surprise attacks and large-scale offensive operations, lie at the core of the security problem in Europe. The Soviet military buildup in the Far East is equally a major source of instability in Asia. These threats must be reduced. Our goal is enhanced security and stability at lower levels of forces, after having eliminated the present asymmetries. We seek the early establishment of a comprehensive, effectively verifiable, and truly global ban on chemical weapons.

8. Genuine peace cannot be established solely by arms control. It must be firmly based on respect for fundamental human rights. We urge the Soviet Union to move forward in ensuring

378

human dignity and freedoms and to implement fully and strengthen substantially its commitments under the Helsinki process. Recent progress must be enshrined in law and practice, the painful barriers that divide people must come down, and the obstacles to emigration must be removed.

9. We pay special attention to the countries in Eastern Europe. We encourage them to open up their economies and societies, and to improve respect for human rights. In this context we support the continuation and strengthening of the Helsinki process.

10. We take positive note of Eastern countries' growing interest in ending their economic isolation, for example in the establishment and development of relations with the European Community. East-West economic relations can be expanded and serve our common interests so long as the commercial basis is sound, they are conducted within the framework of the basic principles and the rules of the international trade and payments system, and are consistent with the security interests of each of our countries.

TERRORISM

11. We strongly reaffirm our condemnation of terrorism in all its forms, including the taking of hostages. We renew our commitment to policies and measures agreed at previous Summits, in particular those against state-sponsored terrorism.

12. We strongly condemn recent threats to air security, in particular the destruction of a Korean airliner and the hijacking of a Kuwaiti airliner. We recall the principle affirmed in previous declarations that terrorists must not go unpunished. We appeal to all countries who are not party to the international conventions on civil aviation security, in particular the Hague Convention, to accede to those conventions.

13. We express support for work currently under way in the International Civil Aviation Organization aimed at strengthening international protection against hijackings. We welcome the most recent declaration adopted by the ICAO Council which endorses the principle that hijacked aircraft should not be allowed to take off once they have landed, except in circumstances as specified in the ICAO declaration.

14. We welcome the adoption this year in Montreal and Rome of two international agreements on aviation and maritime security to enhance the safety of travelers.

15. We reaffirm our determination to continue the fight against terrorism through the application of rule of law, the policy of no concessions to terrorists and their sponsors, and international cooperation.

NARCOTICS

16. The illegal use of drugs and the illicit trafficking in them poses grave risks to the peoples of Summit countries as well as the peoples of source and transit countries. There is an urgent need for improved international cooperation in all appropriate fora on programs to counter all facets of the illicit drug problem, in particular production, trafficking, and financing of the drug trade. The complexity of the problem requires additional international cooperation, in particular to trace, freeze, and confiscate the proceeds of drug traffickers, and to curb money laundering.

17. We look forward to the successful negotiation in Vienna in November of a United Nations Convention on illicit trafficking.

18. We supported the initiative of the Government of the United States for a special task force to be convened to propose methods of improving cooperation in all areas including national, bilateral and multilateral efforts in the fight against narcotics.

SOURCE: U.S., Department of State, *Bulletin,* No. 2137 (August 1988): 47–49; Canada, Department of External Affairs, *[Toronto Economic Summit] Political Declaration* (Ottawa, 1988) [unpublished].

CHAIRMAN'S SUMMARY OF POLITICAL ISSUES

June 20, 1988

The following represents an agreed summary of the discussions on the Middle East, South Africa, and Cambodia.

MIDDLE EAST

We express our deep concern at the increasing instability in the Near East. The current violence in the Occupied Territories is a clear sign that the status quo is not sustainable. An early negotiated settlement to the underlying Arab-Israeli dispute is essential. We declare our support for the convening of a properly structured international conference as the appropriate framework for the necessary negotiations between the parties directly concerned. In this perspective we salute current efforts aimed at achieving a settlement, particularly the initiative pursued by Mr. Shultz since February. We urge the parties to cooperate fully in the search for a solution.

We have pursued our consultations about the continuing war between Iran and Iraq, which remains a source of profound concern to us. We reaffirm our support for Security Council Resolution 598, which was adopted unanimously. We express our warm appreciation for the efforts of the Secretary-General to work for a settlement on this basis and reiterate our firm determination to ensure implementation of this mandatory resolution by a follow-up resolution. We condemn the use of chemical weapons by either party, deplore proliferation of ballistic missiles in the region, and renew our commitment to uphold the principle of freedom of navigation in the Gulf.

SOUTH AFRICA

We declare our abhorrence of apartheid, which must be replaced through a process of genuine national negotiations by a non-racial democracy.

We expressed our urgent opinion on three particular matters:

(1) All legal options available in South Africa should be used to secure clemency for the Sharpeville Six;

(2) The enactment of legislation designed to deprive anti-apartheid organizations of overseas aid would place severe strain on the relations each of us has with South Africa;

(3) We strongly support the current negotiations seeking national reconciliation within Angola, an end to the Angola-Namibia conflict, and early implementation of UN Security Council Resolution 435.

CAMBODIA

As the recent message from Prince Sihanouk has reminded us, the continuing Cambodian conflict and the suffering of the Cambodian people is of deep concern. We join the vast majority of the nations of the world in calling for the prompt withdrawal of all Vietnamese troops. We support a political settlement in Cambodia which will provide for Cambodian self-determination and lead to the re-emergence of a free and independent Cambodia.

SOURCE: U.S., Department of State, *Bulletin,* No. 2137 (August 1988): 49; Canada, Department of External Affairs, *[Toronto Economic Summit] Chairman's Summary of Political Issues* (Ottawa, 1988) [unpublished].

Paris

14–16 July 1989

PARIS, 14–16 JULY 1989

"SUMMIT OF THE ARCH"[1]

DELEGATIONS

Canada

Brian Mulroney, *Prime Minister*
Joe Clark, *Secretary of State for External Affairs*
Michael H. Wilson, *Minister of Finance*
James H. Taylor, *Personal Representative (Sherpa)*

France

François Mitterand, *President*
Roland Dumas, *Minister of State, Minister for Foreign Affairs*
Pierre Bérégovoy, *Minister of State, Minister for the Economy,*
    Finance and the Budget
Jacques Attali, *Personal Representative (Sherpa)*

---

[1]So named because most meetings were held at l'Arche de la Défense [the Arch of la Défense] in Paris.—ED.

Germany (Federal Republic)

Helmut Kohl, *Federal Chancellor*
Hans-Dietrich Genscher, *Federal Minister for Foreign Affairs*
Theo Waigel, *Federal Minister of Finance*
Helmut Hausmann, *Federal Minister for Economic Affairs*
Hans Tietmeyer, *Personal Representative (Sherpa)*

Italy

Ciriaco de Mita, *President of the Council of Ministers*
Giulio Andreotti, *Minister of External Affairs*
Giuliano Amato, *Minister of the Treasury*
Umberto Vattani, *Personal Representative (Sherpa)*

Japan

Sousuke Uno, *Prime Minister*
Hiroshi Mitzuzuka, *Minister for Foreign Affairs*
Tatsuo Murayama, *Minister of Finance*
Seiroku Kajiyama, *Minister of International Trade and Industry*
Michihiko Kunihiro, *Personal Representative (Sherpa)*

United Kingdom

Margaret Thatcher, *Prime Minister*
Geoffrey Howe, *Secretary of State for Foreign and Commonwealth Affairs*
Nigel Lawson, *Chancellor of the Exchequer*
Nigel Wicks, *Personal Representative (Sherpa)*

United States

George Bush, *President*
James A. Baker, *Secretary of State*
Nicholas J. Brady, *Secretary of the Treasury*
Richard T. McCormack, *Personal Representative (Sherpa)*

European Communities

Jacques Delors, *President of the Commission*
Frans Andriessen, *Vice-President, External Relations*
Honning Christophersen, *Vice-President, Economic and Financial Affairs*
Pascal Lamy, *Personal Representative (Sherpa)*

ECONOMIC DECLARATION

July 16, 1989

1. We, the Heads of State or Government of seven major industrial nations and the President of the Commission of the European Communities, have met in Paris for the fifteenth annual Economic Summit. The Summit of the Arch initiates a new round of Summits to succeed those begun at Rambouillet in 1975 and at Versailles in 1982. The round beginning in 1982 has seen one of the longest periods of sustained growth since the Second World War. These Summits have permitted effective consultations and offered the opportunity to launch initiatives and to strengthen international cooperation.

2. This year's world economic situation presents three main challenges:

—The choice and the implementation of measures needed to maintain balanced and sustained growth, counter inflation, create jobs and promote social justice. These measures should also facilitate the adjustment of external imbalances, promote international trade and investment, and improve the economic situation of developing countries.

—The development and the further integration of developing countries into the world economy. Whilst there has been substantial progress in many developing countries, particularly those implementing sound economic policies, the debt burden and the persistence of poverty, often made worse by natural disasters affecting hundreds of millions of people, are problems of deep concern which we must continue to face in a spirit of solidarity.

—The urgent need to safeguard the environment for future generations. Scientific studies have revealed the existence of serious threats to our environment such as the depletion of the stratospheric ozone layer and excessive emissions of carbon dioxide and other greenhouse gases which could lead to future climate changes. Protecting the environment calls for a determined and concerted international response and for the early adoption, worldwide, of policies based on sustainable development.

INTERNATIONAL ECONOMIC SITUATION

3. Growth has been sustained by focusing policies on improving the efficiency and flexibility of our economies and by strengthening our cooperative efforts and the coordination process. In the medium term, the current buoyant investment seen during this period should pave the way for an increased supply of goods and services and help reduce the dangers of inflation. The outlook is not, however, without risks.

4. Until now, the threat of inflation in many countries has been contained, thanks to the concerted efforts of governments and monetary authorities. But continued vigilance is required and inflation, where it has increased, will continue to receive a firm policy response so that it will be put on a downward path.

5. While some progress has been made in reducing external imbalances, the momentum of adjustment has recently weakened markedly. There needs to be further progress in adjusting external imbalances through cooperation.

6. In countries with fiscal and current account deficits, including the United States of America, Canada and Italy, further reductions in budget deficits are needed. Action will be taken to bring them down. This may help reduce the saving-investment gap and external imbalances, contribute to countering inflation and encourage greater exchange rate stability in a context of decreasing interest rates.

7. Countries with external surpluses, including Japan and Germany, should continue to pursue appropriate macroeconomic policies and structural reforms that will encourage noninflationary growth of domestic demand and facilitate external adjustment.

8. All our countries share the responsibility for the sound development of the world economy. Over the medium term, deficit countries have to play a key role in global adjustment through their external adjustment and increased exports; surplus countries have to contribute to sustaining global expansion through policies providing favorable conditions for growth of domestic demand and imports.

9. The emergence of the newly industrializing economies and the initiation of a dialogue with them are welcome. We call on those with substantial surpluses to contribute to the adjustment of external imbalances and the open trade and payments system. To that end, they should permit exchange rates to reflect their competitive position, implement GATT [General Agreement on Tariffs and Trade] commitments and reduce trade barriers.

INTERNATIONAL MONETARY DEVELOPMENTS AND COORDINATION

10. Under the Plaza and Louvre agreements, our countries agreed to pursue, in a mutually reinforcing way, policies of surveillance and coordination aimed at improving their economic fundamentals and at fostering stability of exchange rates consistent with those economic fundamentals.

There has been progress in the multilateral surveillance and coordination of economic policies with a view to ensuring internal consistency of domestic policies and their international compatibility. The procedures to be used have been more clearly defined and improved in cooperation with the International Monetary Fund.

11. The coordination process has made a positive contribution to world economic development and it has also contributed greatly to improving the functioning of the International Monetary System. There has also been continued cooperation in exchange markets.

It is important to continue, and where appropriate, to develop this cooperative and flexible approach to improve the functioning and the stability of the International Monetary System in a manner consistent with economic fundamentals. We therefore ask the Finance Ministers to continue to keep under review possible steps that could be taken to improve the coordination process, exchange market cooperation, and the functioning of the International Monetary System.

12. We welcome the decision to complete the work on the ninth review of the International Monetary Fund quotas with a view to a decision on this matter before the end of the year.

We note that the question of a resumption of SDR [Special Drawing Rights] allocation remains under consideration in the Executive Board of the International Monetary Fund.

13. Within the European Community, the European Monetary System has contributed to a significant degree of economic policy convergence and monetary stability.

IMPROVING ECONOMIC EFFICIENCY

14. We will continue to promote measures in order to remove inefficiencies in our economies. These inefficiencies affect many aspects of economic activity, reduce potential growth rates and the prospects for job creation, diminish the effectiveness of macroeconomic policies and impede the external adjustment process. In this context, tax reforms, modernization of financial markets, strengthening of competition policies and reducing rigidities in all sectors including energy, industry and agriculture are necessary. So are the improvement of education and vocational training, transportation and distribution systems and further policies aimed at giving more flexibility and mobility to the labor market and reducing unemployment. Within the European Community, the steady progress towards the completion by the end of 1992 of the program contained in the Single European Act has already given a strong momentum to economic efficiency.

15. The decline of saving in some of our countries in this decade is a cause for concern. This lower level of saving can contribute to high real interest rates and therefore hamper growth. Inadequate saving and large fiscal deficits are associated with large external deficits. We recommend, within the framework of policy coordination, policies to encourage saving and remove hindrances where they exist.

16. Financial activities are being increasingly carried out with new techniques on a worldwide basis. As regards insider trading, which could hamper the credibility of financial markets, regulations vary greatly among our countries. These regulations have been recently, or are in the process of being, strengthened. International cooperation should be pursued and enhanced.

TRADE ISSUES

17. World trade developed rapidly last year. Yet protectionism remains a real threat. We strongly reaffirm our determination to fight it in all its forms. We shall fulfill the Punta del Este standstill and rollback commitments which, inter alia, require the avoidance of any trade restrictive or distorting measure inconsistent with the provisions of the General Agreement and its instruments. We agree to make effective use of the improved

GATT dispute settlement mechanism and to make progress in negotiations for further improvements. We will avoid any discriminatory or autonomous actions, which undermine the principles of the GATT and the integrity of the multilateral trading system. We also are pledged to oppose the tendency towards unilateralism, bilateralism, sectoralism and managed trade which threatens to undermine the multilateral system and the Uruguay Round negotiations.

18. The successful negotiation of the Trade Negotiations Committee of the Uruguay Round in Geneva last April, thereby completing the mid-term review, is a very important achievement. It gives a clear framework for future work in all sectors including the pursuit of agricultural reform in the short term as well as in the long term. It also gives the necessary framework for substantive negotiations in important sectors not yet fully included in GATT disciplines, such as services, trade-related investment measures and intellectual property.

Developing countries participated actively in these negotiations and contributed to this success. All countries should make their most constructive contribution possible.

We express our full commitment to making further substantive progress in the Uruguay Round in order to complete it by the end of 1990.

19. We note with satisfaction the entry into force of the Free Trade Agreement between Canada and the United States, as well as more recent initiatives to intensify the close economic relations between the European Community and EFTA [European Free Trade Association] countries. It remains our policy that these and other developments in regional cooperation, should be trade-creating and complementary to the multilateral liberalization process.

20. It is the firm intention of the European Community that the trade aspects of the single market program should also be trade-creating and complementary to the multilateral liberalization process.

21. We note with satisfaction the progress that has been made in strengthening the multilateral disciplines on trade and aid distorting export credit subsidies. This effort must be pursued actively and completed in the competent bodies of the OECD [Organisation for Economic Co-operation and Development] with a view to improving present guidelines at the earliest possible date.

GENERAL PROBLEMS OF DEVELOPMENT

22. Development is a shared global challenge. We shall help developing countries by opening the world trading system and by supporting their structural adjustment. We shall encourage, too, economic diversification in commodity dependent countries and the creation of a favorable environment for transfers of technology and capital flows.

We underline the continuing importance of official development assistance and welcome the increased efforts of Summit participants in this respect. We note the targets already established by international organizations for the future level of official development assistance and stress the importance of overall financial flows to development.

We underline simultaneously the importance attached to the quality of the aid and to the evaluation of the projects and the programs financed.

23. We urge developing countries to implement sound economic policies. A vital factor will be the adoption of financial and fiscal policies which attract inward investment and encourage growth and the return of flight capital.

24. We note with satisfaction that there has been substantial progress in the multilateral aid initiative for the Philippines that was given special attention in the Toronto economic declaration.

25. Faced with the worrying economic situation of Yugoslavia, we encourage its government to implement a strong economic reform program that can command bilateral and multilateral support.

THE SITUATION IN THE POOREST COUNTRIES

26. The enhancement of the International Monetary Fund Structural Adjustment Facility, the World Bank special program of assistance for the poorest and most indebted countries and the fifth replenishment of the African Development Fund are all important measures benefiting those countries having embarked upon an adjustment process. We stress the importance attached to a substantial replenishment of International Development Association resources.

27. As we urged last year in Toronto, the Paris Club reached a consensus in September 1988 on the conditions of implementation of significant reduction of debt service payments for the poorest countries. Thirteen countries have already benefited by this decision.

28. We welcome the increasing grant element in the development assistance as well as the steps taken to convert loans into grants and we urge further steps to this end. Flexibility in development aid as much as in debt rescheduling is required.

29. We attach great importance to the efficient and successful preparation of the next general conference of the United Nations on the least developed countries, which will take place in Paris in 1990.

STRENGTHENED DEBT STRATEGY FOR THE HEAVILY INDEBTED COUNTRIES

30. Our approach to the debt problems has produced significant results, but serious challenges remain: in many countries the

ratio of debt service to exports remains high, financing for growth promoting investment is scarce, and capital flight is a key problem. An improvement in the investment climate must be a critical part of efforts to achieve a sustainable level of growth without excessive levels of debt. These improvements of the current situation depend above all on sustained and effective adjustment policies in the debtor countries.

31. To address these challenges, we are strongly committed to the strengthened debt strategy. This will rely, on a case-by-case basis, on the following actions:

—borrowing countries should implement, with the assistance of the Fund and the Bank, sound economic policies, particularly designed to mobilize savings, stimulate investment and reverse capital flight;

—banks should increasingly focus on voluntary, market-based debt and debt service reduction operations, as a complement to new lending;

—the International Monetary Fund and the World Bank will support significant debt reduction by setting aside a portion of policy-based loans;

—limited interest support will be provided, through additional financing by the International Monetary Fund and the World Bank, for transactions involving significant debt and debt service reduction. For that purpose the use of escrow accounts is agreed;

—continued Paris Club rescheduling and flexibility of export-credit agencies;

—strengthening of the international financial institutions' capability for supporting medium-term macroeconomic and structural adjustment programs and for compensating the negative effects of export shortfalls and external shocks.

32. In the framework of this strategy:

—we welcome the recent decisions taken by the two institutions to encourage debt and debt service reduction which provide adequate resources for these purposes;

—we urge debtor countries to move ahead promptly to develop strong economic reform programs that may lead to debt and debt service reductions in accordance with the guidelines defined by the two Bretton Woods institutions;

—we urge banks to take realistic and constructive approaches in their negotiations with the debtor countries and to move promptly to conclude agreements on financial packages including debt reduction, debt service reduction and new money. We stress that official creditors should not substitute for private lenders. Our governments are prepared to consider as appropriate tax, regulatory and accounting practices with a view to eliminating unnecessary obstacles to debt and debt service reductions.

ENVIRONMENT

33. There is growing awareness throughout the world of the necessity to preserve better the global ecological balance. This includes serious threats to the atmosphere, which could lead to future climate changes. We note with great concern the growing pollution of air, lakes, rivers, oceans and seas; acid rain, dangerous substances; and the rapid desertification and deforestation. Such environmental degradation endangers species and undermines the well-being of individuals and societies.

Decisive action is urgently needed to understand and protect the earth's ecological balance. We will work together to achieve the common goals of preserving a healthy and balanced global environment in order to meet shared economic and social objectives and to carry out obligations to future generations.

34. We urge all countries to give further impetus to scientific research on environmental issues, to develop necessary technologies and to make clear evaluations of the economic costs and benefits of environmental policies.

The persisting uncertainty on some of these issues should not unduly delay our action.

In this connection, we ask all countries to combine their efforts in order to improve observation and monitoring on a global scale.

35. We believe that international cooperation also needs to be enhanced in the field of technology and technology transfer in order to reduce pollution or provide alternative solutions.

36. We believe that industry has a crucial role in preventing pollution at source, in waste minimization, in energy conservation, and in the design and marketing of cost-effective clean technologies. The agricultural sector must also contribute to tackling problems such as water pollution, soil erosion and desertification.

37. Environmental protection is integral to issues such as trade, development, energy, transport, agriculture, and economic planning. Therefore, environmental considerations must be taken into account in economic decision-making. In fact good economic policies and good environmental policies are mutually reinforcing.

In order to achieve sustainable development, we shall ensure the compatibility of economic growth and development with the protection of the environment. Environmental protection and related investment should contribute to economic growth. In this respect, intensified efforts for technological breakthrough are important to reconcile economic growth and environmental policies.

Clear assessments of the costs, benefits and resource implications of environmental protection should help governments to take the necessary decisions on the mix of price signals (e.g., taxes or expenditures) and regulatory actions, reflecting where possible the full value of natural resources.

We encourage the World Bank and regional development banks to integrate environmental considerations into their activities. International organizations such as the OECD and the United Nations and its affiliated organizations, will be asked to develop further techniques of analysis which would help governments assess appropriate economic measures to promote the quality of the environment. We ask the OECD, within the context of its work on integrating environment and economic decision-making, to examine how selected environmental indicators could be developed. We expect the 1992 UN Conference on Environment and Development to give additional momentum to the protection of the global environment.

38. To help developing countries deal with past damage and to encourage them to take environmentally desirable action, economic incentives may include the use of aid mechanisms and specific transfer of technology. In special cases, ODA [Official Development Assistance] debt forgiveness and debt for nature swaps can play a useful role in environmental protection.

We also emphasize the necessity to take into account the interests and needs of developing countries in sustaining the growth of their economies and the financial and technological requirements to meet environmental challenges.

39. The depletion of the stratospheric ozone layer is alarming and calls for prompt action.

We welcome the Helsinki conclusions related, among other issues, to the complete abandonment of the production and consumption of chloro-fluorocarbons covered by the Montreal protocol as soon as possible and not later than the end of the century. Specific attention must also be given to those ozone-depleting substances not covered by the Montreal protocol. We shall promote the development and use of suitable substitute substances and technologies. More emphasis should be placed on projects that provide alternatives to chloro-fluorocarbons.

40. We strongly advocate common efforts to limit emissions of carbon dioxide and other greenhouse gases, which threaten to induce climate change, endangering the environment and ultimately the economy. We strongly support the work undertaken by the Intergovernmental Panel on Climate Change on this issue.

We need to strengthen the worldwide network of observatories for greenhouse gases and support the World Meteorological Organization initiative to establish a global climatological reference network to detect climate changes.

41. We agree that increasing energy efficiency could make a substantial contribution to these goals. We urge international organizations concerned to encourage measures, including economic measures, to improve energy conservation and, more broadly, efficiency in the use of energy of all kinds and to promote relevant techniques and technologies.

We are committed to maintaining the highest safety standards for nuclear power plants and to strengthening international cooperation in safe operation of power plants and waste management, and we recognize that nuclear power also plays an important role in limiting output of greenhouse gases.

42. Deforestation also damages the atmosphere and must be reversed. We call for the adoption of sustainable forest management practices, with a view to preserving the scale of world forests. The relevant international organizations will be asked to complete reports on the state of the world's forests by 1990.

43. Preserving the tropical forests is an urgent need for the world as a whole. While recognizing the sovereign rights of developing countries to make use of their natural resources, we encourage, through a sustainable use of tropical forests, the protection of all the species therein and the traditional rights to land and other resources of local communities. We welcome the German initiative in this field as a basis for progress.

To this end, we give strong support to rapid implementation of the Tropical Forest Action Plan which was adopted in 1986 in the framework of the Food and Agriculture Organization [of the United Nations]. We appeal to both consumer and producer countries, which are united in the International Tropical Timber Organization, to join their efforts to ensure better conservation of the forests. We express our readiness to assist the efforts of nations with tropical forests through financial and technical cooperation, and in international organizations.

44. Temperate forests, lakes and rivers must be protected against the effects of acid pollutants such as sulphur dioxide and nitrogen oxides. It is necessary to pursue actively the bilateral and multilateral efforts to this end.

45. The increasing complexity of the issues related to the protection of the atmosphere calls for innovative solutions. New instruments may be contemplated. We believe that the conclusion of a framework or umbrella convention on climate change to set out general principles or guidelines is urgently required to mobilize and rationalize the efforts made by the international community. We welcome the work under way by the United Nations Environment Programme, in cooperation with the World Meteorological Organization, drawing on the work of the Intergovernmental Panel on Climate Change and the results of other international meetings. Specific protocols containing concrete commitments could be fitted into the framework as scientific evidence requires and permits.

46. We condemn indiscriminate use of oceans as dumping grounds for polluting waste. There is a particular problem with the deterioration of coastal waters. To ensure the sustainable management of the marine environment, we recognize the importance of international cooperation in preserving it and conserving the living resources of the sea. We call for relevant bodies of the United Nations to prepare a report on the state of the world's oceans.

We express our concern that national, regional and global capabilities to contain and alleviate the consequences of maritime oil spills be improved. We urge all countries to make better use of the latest monitoring and clean-up technologies. We ask all countries to adhere to and implement fully the international conventions for the prevention of oil pollution of the oceans. We also ask the International Maritime Organization to put forward proposals for further preventive action.

47. We are committed to ensuring full implementation of existing rules for the environment. In this respect, we note with interest the initiative of the Italian government to host in 1990 a forum on international law for the environment with scholars, scientific experts and officials, to consider the need for a digest of existing rules and to give in-depth consideration to the legal aspects of environment at the international level.

48. We advocate that existing environment institutions be strengthened within the United Nations system. In particular, the United Nations Environment Programme urgently requires strengthening and increased financial support. Some of us have agreed that the establishment within the United Nations of a new institution may also be worth considering.

49. We have taken note of the report of the sixth conference on bioethics held in Brussels which examined the elaboration of a universal code of environmental ethics based upon the concept of the "human stewardship of nature."

50. It is a matter of international concern that Bangladesh, one of the poorest and most densely populated countries in the world, is periodically devastated by catastrophic floods.

We stress the urgent need for effective, coordinated action by the international community, in support of the Government of Bangladesh, in order to find solutions to this major problem which are technically, financially, economically and environmentally sound. In that spirit, and taking account of help already given, we take note of the different studies concerning flood alleviation, initiated by France, Japan, the United States and the United Nations Development Programme, which have been reviewed by experts from all our countries. We welcome the

World Bank's agreement, following those studies, to coordinate the efforts of the international community so that a sound basis for achieving a real improvement in alleviating the effects of flood can be established. We also welcome the agreement of the World Bank to chair, by the end of the year, a meeting to be held in the United Kingdom by invitation of the Bangladesh Government, of the countries willing to take an active part in such a program.

51. We give political support to projects such as the joint project to set up an observatory of the Saharan areas, which answers the need to monitor the development of that rapidly deteriorating, fragile, arid region, in order to protect it more effectively.

DRUG ISSUES

52. The drug problem has reached devastating proportions. We stress the urgent need for decisive action, both on a national and an international basis. We urge all countries, especially those where drug production, trading and consumption are large, to join our efforts to counter drug production, to reduce demand, and to carry forward the fight against drug trafficking itself and the laundering of its proceeds.

53. Accordingly, we resolve to take the following measures within relevant fora:

—Give greater emphasis on [sic] bilateral and United Nations programs for the conversion of illicit cultivation in the producer countries. The United Nations Fund for Drug Abuse Control (UNFDAC), and other United Nations and multilateral organizations should be supported, strengthened and made more effective. These efforts could include particular support for the implementation of effective programs to stop drug cultivation and trading as well as developmental and technical assistance.

—Support the efforts of producing countries who ask for assistance to counter illegal production or trafficking.

—Strengthen the role of the United Nations in the war against drugs through an increase in its resources and through reinforced effectiveness of its operation.

—Intensify the exchange of information on the prevention of addiction, and rehabilitation of drug addicts.

—Support the international conference planned by 1990 on cocaine and drug demand reduction.

—Strengthen the efficiency of the cooperative and mutual assistance on these issues, the first steps being a prompt adhesion to, ratification and implementation of the Vienna Convention on illicit traffic in narcotic drugs and psychotropic substances.

—Conclude further bilateral or multilateral agreements and support initiatives and cooperation, where appropriate, which include measures to facilitate the identification, tracing, freezing, seizure and forfeiture of drug crime proceeds.

—Convene a financial action task force from Summit participants and other countries interested in these problems. Its mandate is to assess the results of cooperation already undertaken in order to prevent the utilization of the banking system and financial institutions for the purpose of money laundering, and to consider additional preventive efforts in this field, including the adaptation of the legal and regulatory systems so as to enhance multilateral judicial assistance. The first meeting of this task force will be called by France and its report will be completed by April 1990.

INTERNATIONAL COOPERATION AGAINST AIDS

54. We take note of the creation of an International Ethics Committee on AIDS which met in Paris in May 1989, as decided at the Summit of Venice (June 1987). It assembled the Summit participants and the other members of the EC, together with the active participation of the World Health Organization.

---

55. We take note of the representations that we received from various Heads of State or Government and organizations and we will study them with interest.

NEXT ECONOMIC SUMMIT

56. We have accepted the invitation of the President of the United States to meet next year in the United States of America.

SOURCE: Released by the Summit of the Arch, July 16, 1989.

DECLARATION ON CHINA

July 15, 1989

We have already condemned the violent repression in China in defiance of human rights. We urge the Chinese authorities to cease action against those who have done no more than claim their legitimate rights to democracy and liberty.

This repression has led each of us to take appropriate measures to express our deep sense of condemnation to suspend bilateral Ministerial and high-level contacts, and also to suspend arms-trade with China, where it exists. Furthermore, each of us has agreed that, in view of current economic uncertainties, the examination of new loans by the World Bank be postponed. We have also decided to extend the stays of those Chinese students who so desire.

We look to the Chinese authorities to create conditions which will avoid their isolation and provide for a return to cooperation based upon the resumption of movement towards political and economic reform, and openness. We understand and share the grave concern felt by the people of Hong Kong following these events. We call on the Government of the People's Republic of China to do what is necessary to restore confidence in Hong Kong. We recognize that the continuing support of the international community will be an important element in the maintenance of confidence in Hong Kong.

SOURCE: Released by the Summit of the Arch, July 15, 1989.

DECLARATION ON EAST–WEST RELATIONS

July 15, 1989

1. We, the leaders of our seven countries and the representatives of the European Community, reaffirm the universal and supreme importance which we attach to freedom, democracy and the promotion of human rights.

2. We see signs of this same desire for greater freedom and democracy in the East. The people there, including the young people, are reasserting these values and calling for a pluralist democratic society. Some of their leaders are aware of the positive contribution that greater freedom and democracy can make to the modernization of their countries and are starting to make changes to their laws, practices and institutions. Others are still endeavoring to resist this movement by taking repressive measures which we strongly condemn.

3. We hope that freedom will be broadened and democracy strengthened and that they will form the basis, after decades of military confrontation, ideological antagonism and mistrust, for increased dialogue and cooperation. We welcome the reforms underway and the prospects of lessening the division of Europe.

4. We call upon the Soviet Government to translate its new policies and pronouncements into further concrete action at home and abroad. Military imbalances favoring the Soviet Union, both in Europe and in Asia, remain an objective threat to each of us. Our Governments must therefore continue to be vigilant and maintain the strength of our countries. For the foreseeable future, there is no alternative for each of us, within existing alliances, to maintaining a strategy of deterrence based upon an appropriate mix of adequate and effective nuclear and conventional forces. In order to hasten the advent of a world in which the weight of arms and military strength is reduced, we recommit ourselves to the urgent pursuit of a global ban on chemical weapons, a conventional forces balance in Europe at the lowest possible level consistent with our security requirements, and a substantial reduction in Soviet and American strategic nuclear arms.

5. We offer the countries of the East the opportunity to develop balanced economic cooperation on a sound commercial basis consistent with the security interests of each of our countries and with the general principles of international trade. We have noted developments of relations between the EEC and countries of the East, in particular the conclusion of an agreement with Hungary, the progress already achieved during the current discussions with Poland and the opening of negotiations with the Soviet Union.

6. We welcome the process of reform underway in Poland and Hungary. We recognize that the political changes taking place in these countries will be difficult to sustain without economic progress. Each of us is prepared to support this process and to consider, as appropriate and in a coordinated fashion, economic assistance aimed at transforming and opening their economies in a durable manner. We believe that each of us should direct our assistance to these countries so as to sustain the momentum of reform through inward investment, joint ventures, transfer of managerial skills, professional training and other ventures which would help develop a more competitive economy.

Each of us is developing concrete initiatives designed to encourage economic reforms, to promote more competitive economies and to provide new opportunities for trade.

We agreed to work along with other interested countries and multilateral institutions to concert support for the process of reform underway in Hungary and Poland, in order to make our measures of support more effective and mutually reinforcing. We will encourage further creative efforts by interested governments and the public and private sectors in support of the reform process.

Concerning concerted support for reform in Poland and Hungary, we call for a meeting with all interested countries which will take place in the next few weeks. We underline, for Poland, the urgent need for food in present circumstances.

To these ends, we ask the Commission of the European Communities to take the necessary initiatives in agreement with the other Member States of the Community, and to associate, besides the Summit participants, all interested countries.

7. We are in favor of an early conclusion of the negotiations between the IMF [International Monetary Fund] and Poland. The strengthened debt strategy is applicable to Poland, provided it meets the conditions. We are ready to support in the Paris Club the rescheduling of Polish debt expeditiously and in a flexible and forthcoming manner.

8. We see good opportunities for the countries of West and East to work together to find just solutions to conflicts around the world, to fight against underdevelopment, to safeguard the resources and the environment and to build a freer and more open world.

SOURCE: Released by the Summit of the Arch, July 15, 1989.

DECLARATION ON HUMAN RIGHTS

July 15, 1989

In 1789, the rights of man and of the citizen were solemnly proclaimed. Just over forty years ago, the General Assembly of the United Nations adopted the Universal Declaration of Human Rights, which have been further developed and codified and are now embodied in the Covenants on Civil and Political Rights and on Economic, Social and Cultural Rights.

We reaffirm our commitment to freedom, democratic principles and human rights. We reaffirm our belief in the rule of law which respects and protects without fear or favor the rights and liberties of every citizen, and provides the setting in which the human spirit can develop in freedom and diversity.

Human rights are a matter of legitimate international concern. We commit ourselves again to encouraging and promoting universal respect for human rights and fundamental freedoms.

Looking towards the future, we see opportunities as well as threats; this impels us to pledge our firm commitment to uphold international standards of human rights and to confirm our willingness to reaffirm them and to develop them further.

We stress the protection of freedom of thought, conscience and religion, and of freedom of opinion and expression; for without these freedoms, other rights cannot be fully realized

We stress also respect for the rule of law and the plurality of opinion, for without them there can be neither representative government nor democracy.

We believe equally in freedom of association in a pluralist society.

We hold that the right of each individual to physical integrity and dignity must be guaranteed. We abhor and condemn torture in all its forms.

We believe that all human beings must act towards each other in a spirit of fraternity.

We believe that everyone has a right to equality of opportunity as well as to own property, alone or in association with others.

Extreme poverty and exclusion from society violate the dignity of everyone enduring them. Those who suffer or are in need should be supported.

We stress that the rights of the child, the disabled and the elderly require special protection.

We consider that developments in the human sciences, for instance the progress achieved in genetics and organ transplantation, must be applied in accordance with all human rights if the dignity of human beings is to be preserved.

We, the present generation, have an obligation to ensure that future generations will inherit a healthy environment.

We reaffirm our belief that these rights and freedoms cannot be properly safeguarded without the rule of law, impartial justice and genuine democratic institutions.

SOURCE: Released by the Summit of the Arch, July 15, 1989.

DECLARATION ON TERRORISM

July 15, 1989

1. We remain resolutely opposed to terrorism in all its forms. We confirm the commitment each of us has undertaken to the principle of making no concessions to terrorists or their sponsors and to cooperating, bilaterally and in all relevant international fora, in combatting terrorism. We reiterate our commitment to the policies agreed at previous summits; in particular we condemn state-sponsored terrorism. We are determined not to let terrorists remain unpunished, and to have them brought to justice within the framework of international law and in conformity with the rule of law. We call upon those states which have supported or encouraged terrorist acts to demonstrate by their actions that they have renounced such policies. We reaffirm in particular our absolute condemnation of the taking of hostages. We call on those holding hostages to release them immediately and unconditionally and on those with influence over hostage-takers to use it to this end.

2. Deeply concerned for the safety of all travelers and outraged by the murderous attacks perpetrated against international civil aviation and the frequent threat to air transport safety from terrorist groups, we reaffirm our commitment to the fight against all forms of terrorism affecting civil aviation. We reiterate our determination to contribute to reinforcing internationally agreed measures for protection against aircraft hijackings and sabotage.

3. We particularly condemn the recent attack on an aircraft over Scotland, which killed 270 people. We have agreed to give priority to preventing such attacks by further strengthening security measures. We attach importance to the implementation of the work plan recently adopted by the ICAO [International Civil Aviation Organization] Council for this purpose.

4. We have also agreed on the need for improved methods of detecting explosives. We endorse efforts currently underway in ICAO to develop, as a matter of high priority, an appropriate international regime for the marking of plastic and sheet explosives for detection.

SOURCE: Released by the Summit of the Arch, July 15, 1989.

COMMUNIQUE DE LA PRESIDENCE: CONFLIT ISRAELO–ARABE

15 juillet 1989

Les participants au Sommet restent profondément préoccupés par la situation au Proche Orient.

Certaines récentes déclarations partisanes en Israël, la violence persistante dans les territoires occupés, ainsi que la détérioration des conditions de vie en Cisjordanie et à Gaza montrent plus clairement que jamais qu'une solution respectant les droits politiques légitimes du peuple palestinien ainsi que le droit à la sécurité de tous les Etats de la Région, y compris Israël, revêt une nécessité urgente.

Plus que jamais, le temps est venu pour l'ouverture d'un dialogue entre les parties concernées en vue d'une négociation.

Les Sept pays considèrent que les élections en projet pour les territoires occupés pourraient marquer un pas en avant vers une reconnaissance mutuelle pour autant qu'elles aient lieu dans une atmosphère de libre expression et qu'elles fassent partie d'un réglement global sur la base des territoires contre la paix.

En outre, les Sept pays pensent que la réunion, le moment venu, d'une conférence internationale structurée de manière appropriée constituerait un cadre adapté pour promouvoir un dialogue direct entre toutes les parties et pour traiter tous les problèmes liés dont la solution commande un réglement pacifique au Proche Orient.

SOURCE: Released by the Summit of the Arch, July 15, 1989.

[UNOFFICIAL TRANSLATION]
STATEMENT ON THE ARAB–ISRAELI CONFLICT

July 15, 1989

The participants in the Summit remain profoundly concerned about the situation in the Near East.

Certain recent partisan declarations in Israel, the persistent violence in the occupied territories, as well as the deterioration of living conditions in West Bank and in Gaza show more clearly than ever that a solution concerning the legitimate political rights of the Palestinian people, as well as the right to security of all of the states in the region, including Israel, is once again an urgent necessity.

More than ever, the time has come to open a dialogue between the concerned parties, with a view toward negotiation.

The seven nations consider that the elections proposed for the occupied territories could mark a positive step toward mutual recognition, to the extent that they take place in an atmosphere of free expression and that they form part of a global settlement of territorial disputes that present obstacles to peace.

Furthermore, the seven nations believe that the holding, at the appropriate time, of an international conference structured in an appropriate manner would constitute a framework adapted to promoting direct dialogue among all the parties and to dealing with all of the related problems whose solution governs a peaceful settlement in the Near East.

COMMUNIQUE DE LA PRESIDENCE: AFRIQUE AUSTRALE

15 juillet 1989

Les participants au Sommet expriment leur condamnation de l'apartheid et leur détermination à travailler pour une Afrique du Sud démocratique, sans discrimination raciale. A cet égard ils demandent instamment au Gouvernement Sud africain de prendre des mesures concrètes pour commencer des négociations avec la majorité noire.

Ils insistent pour que le Gouvernement libère Nelson Mandela, et les autres prisonniers politiques, pour qu'il soit mis fin à l'état d'urgence, à l'interdiction de l'ANC [African National Congress], de l'UDF [United Democratic Front] et des autres organisations, et pour l'abrogation de la législation discriminatoire.

Les participants au Sommet se félicitent des progrès réalisés pour la mise en oeuvre de la résolution 435 du Conseil de Sécurité pour l'indépendance de la Namibie et demande à toutes les parties concernées de veiller à ce que rien n'entrave le processus. Ils espèrent que la récente rencontre au Sommet des dix-huit Chefs d'Etat africains à Gbadolite conduira à un réglement pacifique de la guerre civile en Angola et que des progrès seront faits pour la recherche d'une solution au conflit du Mozambique.

SOURCE: Released by the Summit of the Arch, July 15, 1989.

418

[UNOFFICIAL TRANSLATION]
STATEMENT ON SOUTHERN AFRICA

July 15, 1989

The participants in the Summit express their condemnation of apartheid and their determination to work for a democratic South Africa without racial discrimination. In this respect they urgently demand that the South African Government take concrete steps to begin negotiations with the black majority.

They insist that the Government free Nelson Mandela, and the other political prisoners, that an end be put to the state of emergency and to the interdiction of the ANC [African National Congress], of the UDF [United Democratic Front] and of the other organizations, and that the discriminatory legislation be repealed.

The participants in the Summit are pleased with the progress achieved toward the implementation of Resolution 435 of the Security Council for the independence of Namibia and ask all parties concerned to see that nothing hinders the process. They hope that the recent Summit meeting of eighteen African Heads of State in Gbadolite will lead to the peaceful settlement of the civil war in Angola and that progress will be made in the search for a solution to the conflict in Mozambique.

COMMUNIQUE DE LA PRESIDENCE: AMERIQUE CENTRALE

15 juillet 1989

Les participants au Sommet soutiennent les accords d'Esquipulas et de la Baie de Tesoro. Ils demandent aux pays de la région de remplir leurs engagements pour l'organisation d'elections libres et régulières, sous le contrôle d'une administration neutre et impartiale.

Ils appellent au respect des droits de l'homme et des règles de droit dans tous les pays de l'Amérique Centrale.

SOURCE: Released by the the Summit of the Arch, July 15, 1989.

[UNOFFICIAL TRANSLATION]
STATEMENT ON CENTRAL AMERICA

July 15, 1989

The Summit participants support the Esquipulas and Tesoro Bay agreements. They ask the countries of the region to fulfill their undertakings to organize free and orderly elections under neutral and impartial control.

They call for respect for human rights and the rule of law in all countries of Central America.

COMMUNIQUE DE LA PRESIDENCE: PANAMA

15 juillet 1989

Les participants ont examiné la situation à Panama, marquée par l'annulation des résultats des élections du 7 mai dernier et des mesures de répression contre l'opposition. Ils désapprouvent fermement ces pratiques.

Ils lancent un appel à l'Organisation des Etats Américains afin qu'elle continue ses efforts pour faire en sorte que soient pleinement respectés les règles démocratiques et le libre choix du peuple panaméen.

SOURCE: Released by the the Summit of the Arch, July 15, 1989.

[UNOFFICIAL TRANSLATION]
STATEMENT ON PANAMA

July 15, 1989

The participants examined the situation in Panama, marked by the invalidation of the results of the elections of May 7 last and by repressive measures against the opposition. They firmly disapprove of these practices.

They are sending an appeal to the Organization of American States to continue its efforts to see to it that democratic rules and the free choice of the Panamanian people are fully respected.

COMMUNIQUE DE LA PRESIDENCE: CAMBODGE

15 juillet 1989

Les participants au Sommet ont évoqué le problème du Cambodge.

Ils se félicitent de l'initiative prise par la France de convoquer une conférence internationale à Paris et lui apportent leur plein appui. Ils souhaitent que cette conférence conduise à un règlement politique global prévoyant, entre autre, le retrait vérifié des troupes vietnamiennes et l'autodétermination du peuple cambodgien. Ils insistent sur la nécessité d'un mécanisme international de contrôle efficace, comme composante essentielle de ce règlement.

Rendant hommage dans ce contexte aux efforts entrepris depuis plusieurs mois par les pays de l'ASEAN [Association of South East Asian Nations] pour la recherche d'une issue au conflit, ils estiment que l'occasion doit être saisie aujourd'hui de définir une solution réelle, complète et durable au problème cambodgien.

Les discussions ont montré une disponibilité générale à contribuer, le moment venu, aux efforts de reconstruction du Cambodge.

Source: Released by the the Summit of the Arch, July 15, 1989.

424

[UNOFFICIAL TRANSLATION]
STATEMENT ON CAMBODIA

July 15, 1989

The Summit participants recalled the problem of Cambodia.

They are pleased by, and fully support, the initiative of France to convene an international conference in Paris. They hope that this conference will lead to a global political settlement, providing, *inter alia*, for the verified withdrawal of Vietnamese troops and self-determination for the Cambodian people. They stress the need for an effective international control mechanism as an essential component of that settlement.

In this context, they pay homage to the efforts undertaken for several months by ASEAN [Association of South East Asian Nations] countries to seek an end to the conflict. They consider that the opportunity must be seized today to find a real, complete and lasting solution of the Cambodian problem.

The discussions showed a general receptivity to contribute, when the time comes, to the reconstruction of Cambodia.

COMMUNIQUE DE LA PRESIDENCE: LIBAN

15 juillet 1989

Les participants au Sommet ont consacré une attention particulière à la situation au Liban et ont été d'accord pour considérer que la communauté des nations ne pouvait ni ne devait rester indifférente devant les dangers qui menacent l'existence même de ce pays.

Ils expriment leur plein appui au Comité des trois Chefs d'Etat arabes chargés, en liaison avec la mission que le Conseil de Sécurite a confié au Secrétaire Général des Nations Unies, de trouver une solution à la crise libanaise. Ils appellent toutes les parties concernées à coopérer pleinement avec lui à l'établissement d'un cessez-le-feu effectif et complet et à la mise en oeuvre d'un réglement politique comportant la restauration des institutions de l'Etat et l'adoption des nécessaires réformes politiques.

Ils affirment leur attachement à la souveraineté, à l'indépendance, à l'unité et à l'intégrité territoriale du Liban, ce qui suppose le retrait de toutes les forces non-libanaises.

SOURCE: Released by the Summit of the Arch, July 15, 1989.

[UNOFFICIAL TRANSLATION]
STATEMENT ON LEBANON

July 15, 1989

The participants in the Summit have devoted particular attention to the situation in Lebanon and have agreed that the community of nations cannot and should not remain indifferent to the dangers that threaten the very existence of that country.

They express their full support for the Committee of the three Arab Heads of State who are charged with finding a solution to the Lebanese crisis, in conjunction with the mission which the Security Council has entrusted to the Secretary General of the United Nations. They call on all concerned parties to cooperate fully with the Committee in establishing an effective and complete cease-fire and in implementing a political settlement that permits the restoration of State institutions and the adoption of the necessary political reforms.

They affirm their support of the sovereignty, independence, unity, and territorial integrity of Lebanon, which presupposes the withdrawal of all non-Lebanese forces.

PRESS RELEASE FROM PRESIDENTS ABDOU DIOUF, MOHAMED HOSNI MUBARAK, CARLOS ANDRES PEREZ, AND PRIME MINISTER RAJIV GANDHI

July 13, 1989

In the light of the consultations we have had with the Heads of State or Government of both developed and developing countries assembled in Paris, we have come to the conclusion that it is now a propitious moment to initiate a process of regular consultations between developed and developing countries, at the Summit level.

We believe that steps should be taken to organize as soon as possible an appropriate meeting, at the Summit level, to deliberate on global economic and environmental issues of mutual interest. This should mark the beginning of the process of continuing consultations on such issues between the leaders of the North and the South.

This initiative will be pursued in full association with the Secretary-General of the United Nations and in cooperation with the relevant economic and financial international institutions.

The Group of 77 and the Movement of the Non-Aligned Countries will be kept informed.

To this end we invite President Mitterand to take the necessary measures for the concretization of this idea.

SOURCE: Released by the Summit of the Arch, July 13, 1989. *Note*: Although not an official Summit document, this important communication from four prominent Third World leaders on the eve of the Summit received the attention of the Seven.

[TEXTE DE LA LETTRE ADRESSEE PAR M. MIKHAIL GORBATCHEV AU PRESIDENT DE LA REPUBLIQUE FRANÇAISE]

14 juillet 1989

Monsieur le Président,

En m'adressant à vous en votre qualité de président de la XVe conférence économique annuelle des dirigeants des sept pays qui se tiendra à Paris les 15 et 16 juillet, et à travers vous aux autres participants à cette réunion, je tiens à vous faire part de quelques idées sur les problèmes-clés de l'économie mondiale qui exercent leur influence sur tous les pays sans exception.

L'interdépendance, tout en aidant à surmonter la division du monde, augmente considérablement le risque du heurt des intérêts, de l'explosion des contradictions.

Traditionnellement, pour résoudre les contradictions économiques entre Etats il était suffisant de trouver un équilibre sur la base des intérêts strictement nationaux. Toutefois, aujourd'hui un tel équilibre serait précaire si on essayait de l'asseoir sur autre chose que les intérêts universels de l'humanité.

Atteindre un véritable équilibre, assurer à l'interdépendance un caractère stable ne peut être que le fruit d'actions complémentaires. Un processus objectif de la formation de l'économie mondiale cohérente implique que le partenariat multilatéral économique soit placé à un niveau qualitativement nouveau.

Nous observons avec intérêt les efforts déployés par les sept Etats les plus développés du monde occidental en vue de mettre au point la coordination de la politique macroéconomique. Nous estimons qu'il est possible, grâce à la coordination, de rendre les processus de l'économie mondiale plus prévisibles. Or, ceci est une prémisse importante afin de garantir la sécurité économique internationale.

S'agissant de la sécurité économique, nous avons à l'esprit avant toute chose la formation de bases pour la cocréation stable, déidéologisée et mutuellement avantageuse et pour le codéveloppement.

Tout comme d'autres pays, l'Union Soviétique cherche à résoudre les tâches consistant à adapter son économie nationale à une nouvelle structure de la division internationale du travaile en gestation. Notre perestroïka est inséparable de la politique tendant à la participation pleine et entière à l'économie mondiale. Cette orientation-là, s'inscrivant dans le droit fil de la nouvelle pensée politique, est déterminée également par notre intérêt économique direct. Mais à l'évidence le reste du monde ne pourra que gagner à l'ouverture en direction de l'économie mondiale du marché tel que celui de l'URSS. Bien entendu, l'avantage mutuel suppose la responsabilité mutuelle et le respect des droits de tous les participants aux relations économiques internationales.

Il subsiste dans le domaine de ces relations pas mal de contradictions. Il n'en reste pas moins que la zone des intérêts communs, convergents des Etats est suffisamment large et peut servir de base à l'interaction. La preuve en est fournie notamment par les changements positifs intervenus dans les liens économiques bilatéraux de l'Union Soviétique avec beaucoup de pays occidentaux, par les ententes acquises à Vienne en matière de la "deuxième corbeille" de la coopération en Europe, par l'établissement des rapports CAEM–CEE.

Cependant la coopération multilatérale Est–Ouest sur les problèmes économiques globaux se trouve manifestement en retrait par rapport au développement des liens bilatéraux et régionaux. Cet état de choses ne paraît pas justifié compte tenu de poids de nos Etats dans l'économie mondiale, de la responsabilité qui est la leur dans son fonctionnement rationnel et efficace pour le bien de chaque peuple et de la communauté mondiale en général.

L'Union Soviétique se prononce pour une interaction constructive et libre de préjugés visant à résoudre ces tâches par les efforts communs. Nous voyons les points de convergence et la complémentarité dans les approches qu'ont les parties des problèmes globaux, en particulier du règlement de l'endettement de tiers monde. Peu importe de savoir à qui reviendra le mérite de la meilleure initiative. L'essentiel consiste à ce qu'il existe une possibilité réelle de contribuer ensemble à l'efficacité des mesures pratiques dans la sphère du règlement de la dette.

Nous sommes en faveur d'une assistance collective au développement, en faveur de la coordination des actions de créanciers et de débiteurs, de donneurs et de ceux qui recouvrent, en faveur de l'extension des formes d'aide multilatérales. Ceci peut devenir une des garanties matérielles considérables pour la participation égale en droits et responsable des pays en voie de développement à l'économie mondiale.

Des prémisses sont en train d'être réunies également pour le consensus sur les voies d'assurer un développement stable de tous les Etats, ce qui suppose la formation des stabilisateurs écologiques sûrs de l'édifice d'économie mondiale unie que l'on construit aujourd'hui.

Un autre problème qui nous est commun est lié aux tendances à l'intégration, qui prennent de plus en plus de vigueur dans diverses régions du monde. Nous voulons que leur développement aille dans le sens d'un partenariat universel. Aujourd'hui la vie elle-même détruit—progressivement et à grand-peine mais quand même détruit—les vieux obstacles dressés de façon artificielle entre différents systèmes économiques. Bien que chaque système conserve ses traits caractéristiques, ils ont emprunté beaucoup l'un à l'autre, utilisent les outils de gestion similaires.

Il devient urgent à nous entendre sur la méthodologie de mesure et d'harmonisation des processus économiques, méthodologie acceptable pour tous les pays et à usage universel. En perspective il pourra s'agir aussi des recherches de procédés pour faire arrimer, à l'échelle globale, les différents mécanismes de coordination macroéconomique.

Nous sommes prêts à engager un dialogue constructif sur ces questions. Pour le démarrer on pourrait établir les contacts professionnels dans divers domaines, par exemple sous forme de rencontres des experts gouvernementaux. Il importe ici de trouver dès le début un langage économique commun, procéder à un échange réciproque d'information, y compris sur les questions d'indicateurs de base du développement économique, de la régulation des liens de crédit et d'aide au tiers monde afin d'assurer la compatibilité méthodologique des données statistiques en tant que point de départ de la collaboration.

J'espère que ces réflexions seront utiles pour les participants de la rencontre au sommet de Paris et que les résultats de celle-ci iront dans le sens de recherches de l'équilibre des intérêts économiques nationaux, régionaux et universels.

Avec mes respects,

M. Gorbatchev

SOURCE: Released by the Summit of the Arch, July 14, 1989. *Note*: Although not an official Summit document, the Gorbachev letter was a major event during the Summit.—ED.

[UNOFFICIAL TRANSLATION: TEXT OF THE LETTER SENT BY MR. MIKHAIL GORBACHEV TO THE PRESIDENT OF THE FRENCH REPUBLIC]

July 14, 1989

Mr. President:

I address myself to you in your capacity as president of the 15th annual economic conference of the leaders of the seven countries, which will take place in Paris on July 15 and 16, and through you to the other participants in that meeting. I would like to share with you some ideas about the key problems of the world economy which exert their influence on all countries without exception.

Interdependence, while helping to overcome the division of the world, greatly increases the risk of conflicts of interests and of the explosion of contradictions.

Traditionally, to resolve economic contradictions between States it has been sufficient to find an equilibrium on the basis of strictly national interests. However, today such an equilibrium would be precarious if one tried to base it on anything other than the universal interests of humankind.

A true equilibrium, a stable interdependence, can result only from complementary actions. An objective process in the formation of a cohesive world economy implies that the multilateral economic partnership be placed on a qualitatively new level.

We observe with interest the efforts made by the seven most highly developed States of the Western world to enhance the coordination of macroeconomic policy. Thanks to this coordination, we consider it possible to make world economic processes more predictable. This is an important premise for guaranteeing international economic security.

On the topic of economic security, we have in mind above all else the formation of bases for stable, de-ideologized, and mutually advantageous co-creation and for joint development.

Like other countries, the Soviet Union seeks to complete the task of adapting its national economy to a new structure of the international division of labor which is developing. Our *perestroika* is inseparable from the policy that aims at full and complete participation in the world economy. That orientation, which is in keeping with current political thought, is equally determined by our direct economic interest. But it is clear that the rest of the world can only gain from the opening up to the global economy of a market like that of the USSR. Of course, mutual advantage implies mutual responsibility and respect for the rights of all the participants in international economic relations.

There exist many contradictions in these relations. At a minimum, it is necessary that the area of common, convergent interests of the States be sufficiently large and appropriate as a basis for interaction. The proof of this is furnished notably by the positive changes in bilateral economic ties between the Soviet Union and many Western nations, by the agreements reached in Vienna on the "second basket" of cooperation in Europe, by the establishment of relationships between the Council for Mutual Economic Co-operation and the European Economic Community.

Nevertheless, multilateral East–West cooperation on global economic problems finds itself manifestly behind in comparison to the development of bilateral and regional ties. This state of affairs does not seem justified considering the impact of our States on the world economy, and the responsibility which they have for its rational and efficient functioning, for the good of each country's citizens and of the world community in general.

The Soviet Union declares itself in favor of constructive, prejudice-free interaction aimed at completing these tasks through common efforts. We see the points of convergence and complementarity in the approaches taken by the States to global problems, in particular the settlement of Third World indebtedness. It matters little who receives the credit for the best initiative. What is essential is that there exists a real possibility of contributing to effective, practical measures regarding debt settlement.

We are in favor of collective assistance to development, in favor of coordinating the actions of creditors and debtors, of donors and debt-collectors, and in favor of extending multilateral forms of aid. This could become one of the considerable material guarantees for the participation of developing countries—with equal rights and responsibilities—in the world economy.

Some propositions are being assembled for a consensus on the means of assuring stable development for all States; this implies the formation of secure ecological guidelines for the structure of the unified world economy being built today.

Another problem that is common to us concerns the tendencies toward integration, which are growing more and more vigorous in various regions of the world. We want such development to go in the direction of a universal partnership. Today's way of life is destroying—albeit progressively and with much difficulty—the old artificial barriers between different economic systems. Although each system keeps its characteristic traits, they have borrowed a great deal from one another, utilizing similar tools of management.

It is becoming urgent that we understand each other concerning the methodology for measuring and harmonizing economic processes, a methodology acceptable to all countries and for universal use. Looking ahead, the question could be also one of research on the procedures for putting in place, on a global scale, the various mechanisms of macroeconomic coordination.

We are ready to engage in a constructive dialogue on these questions. To start this, one could establish professional contacts in various areas, for example, in the form of meetings of government experts. It is important to determine a common economic language at the start, to proceed to a reciprocal exchange of information, including questions on basic indicators of economic development, on regulation of lines of credit, and on aid to the Third World, so as to assure the methodological compatibility of statistical data as a point of departure for collaboration.

I hope that these reflections will be useful for the participants in the Paris Summit meeting and that its results will lead to a search for balance among national, regional, and universal economic interests.

Respectfully,

M. Gorbachev

Note: Although not an official Summit document, the Gorbachev letter was a major event during the Summit.

CONFERENCE DE PRESSE DE MONSIEUR FRANÇOIS MITTERRAND, PRESIDENT DE LA REPUBLIQUE, A L'ISSUE DU XVe SOMMET DES PAYS INDUSTRIALISES

16 juillet 1989

Le Président: Mesdames, Messieurs, bonjour. Maintenant, ce sont les journalistes qui vont s'exprimer. Je crois avoir assez parlé, plus que je ne l'aurais souhaité, mais je suis obligé de vous rendre compte d'un document fort important et copieux.

Vous l'avez entendue, je pense, cette lecture . . . non pas cette lecture, mais ce résumé.[2]

Vous avez dû noter, au passage, les points qui vous intéressent.

Donc, je ne vais pas inventer un nouveau préambule et dès maintenant, je vais vous demander de bien vouloir poser les questions de votre choix.

Question: Monsieur le Président, je voudrais commencer par l'article 1er où vous dites que le Sommet de l'Arche marque le début d'un nouveau cycle de sommets. Est-ce que vous pourriez nous préciser, nous commenter cette affirmation, assez étonnante à première vue puisque d'avance, on ne sait jamais si on commence un premier cycle.

Le Président: Je vous exprime une décision et une remarque, fruit des travaux des Sept. C'est écrit en toutes lettres là et je ne suis pas l'auteur de ce document. J'y ai simplement souscrit en tant que participant.

Il a été considéré, de façon générale, que nous étions arrivés par rapport aux travaux de quinze ans, à un certain terme. Le cycle débutant en 1982 correspondait à l'une des plus longues périodes de croissance depuis la seconde guerre mondiale.

---

[2]Just before the press conference, Mr. Mitterand, as host of the Paris Summit, had read the Economic Declaration, in accordance with established Summit procedure.—ED.

Le premier était celui de Rambouillet, en 1975. Donc 1975, 1982, 1989. Difficile de prévoir, vous avez raison, mais il me semble que l'on soit maintenant parvenu à une période différente. On pourrait dire que grosso modo les Sommets sont parvenus aux résultats qu'ils désiraient et ils observent à la fois les acquis dans la lutte contre l'inflation, dans la lutte pour une reprise de la croissance, dans l'organisation d'un minimum, je ne dirais pas de système, mais de politiques mondiales monétaires. Et on aperçoit aujourd'hui à la fois des progrès et un certain nombre de menaces, par exemple sur l'inflation. L'inflation était jugulée, et puis, elle ne l'était pas. Il semble donc bien que ce soit une période d'acquis et de reprise de responsabilité là où certains fléchissements apparaissent, avec un élargissement du domaine de nos réflexions et de nos décisions au domaine de l'environnement, de la lutte contre la drogue. Tout cela, indépendamment des résolutions politiques qui sont déjà connues de vous. Et je crois que la dimension environnement et que la dimension développement prennent aujourd'hui une nouvelle valeur et s'élargissent assez pour que l'on considère que les Sommets prennent une autre tournure.

Le temps consacré à la dette et au développement—la dette n'étant qu'un aspect particulier du développement—et le problème de l'environnement proprement dit n'ont jamais été l'objet d'autant de conversations et d'un aussi grand nombre de décisions ou d'intentions affirmées que cette fois-ci.

Voilà comment j'interprète cette notion de troisième période.

Question: Monsieur le Président, comment voyez-vous les rapports Est–Ouest, notamment avec l'Union Soviétique, après le Sommet? Comment pourraient-ils évoluer? Deuxième question: quelles ont été les réactions du Sommet à la lettre adressée par le Président Gorbatchev?

Le Président: Le Sommet n'a pas changé en profondeur la nature des relations entre l'Union Soviétique et les participants du Sommet. Ça n'était d'ailleurs pas l'objet de ce Sommet.

D'autre part, la lettre qui m'était adressée, que j'ai aussitôt communiquée aux membres du Sommet et qui a d'ailleurs été communiquée très rapidement à la presse, cette lettre n'appelle pas de réponse collective. Notre ordre du jour était déjà extrêmement rempli et il n'y a donc pas de réponse au Sommet de l'Arche à M. Gorbatchev. Cependant, je lui répondrai, nourri et inspiré par les considérations que j'ai entendues car nous en avons quand même parlé, surtout hors séance.

Nous avons voulu nous en tenir à notre ordre du jour. Je répondrai donc prochainement au Président Gorbatchev. Quant à la nature des relations, elle n'a pas fondamentalement changé et diverses résolutions sur les relations Est–Ouest vous ont été communiquées hier. Nous souhaitons la réussite de l'entreprise de démocratisation en Union Soviétique. Nous saluons le courage de cette entreprise. Nous ne sommes pas chargés d'en assurer la réussite mais, dans la mesure où nous pourrions le faire, nous y contribuerions. Mais les aspects de cette gestion sont de tous ordres: économique, politique, militaire et d'autres avancées sérieuses doivent être accomplies surtout sur le plan du désarmement avant que l'on puisse tirer des conclusions de caractère général. En tout cas, les dispositions des puissances réunies au cours de ce Sommet sont tout à fait ouvertes pour développer les relations, faciliter les échanges, permettre les évolutions qui seront significatives d'une plus grande liberté.

Question: M. le Président de la République, nous vous avons entendu tout à l'heure, pendant une cinquantaine de minutes, détailler les différents points du communiqué. Il y a eu également comme vous le signaliez, les déclarations politiques qui ont été prises hier. Alors, je voudrais vous demander si vous le voulez bien, de pratiquer l'exercice résolument inverse. S'il devait y avoir à votre avis un élément qui reste de ce Sommet, lequel serait-il?

Le Président: D'abord, ce travail c'est le vôtre . . . mais je veux bien répondre à votre question, habitué que je suis à nos dialogues que vous rendez habituellement constructifs.

Moi, mon impression personnelle, c'est une plus grande résolution de protéger les acquis de la politique, comme je le répondais à M. Fabra tout-à-l'heure. La politique économique suit, depuis l'origine, l'expression de cette vigilance dont j'ai fait état également, et donc l'appel à une plus grande coordination sur le plan économique. Mais il me semble que la note apportée à l'examen des problèmes de relations entre le Nord et le Sud et, particulièrement, de l'endettement, ressort de la masse des travaux. Il va y avoir maintenant d'une part de l'argent frais, la Banque Mondiale et le Fonds Monétaire International qui vont contribuer de façon importante à la réduction de l'encours et du service de la dette, d'autre part une multitude d'approches concrètes, souvent au cas par cas, on cite les Philippines, on cite le Bangladesh. Mais on pourrait citer beaucoup d'autres pays. Il y a donc une attention et une prise de conscience des problèmes du développement et de l'urgence des décisions. Hier, il s'agissait même d'une aide alimentaire urgente à un pays comme la Pologne. Je crois que, décidément, le problème des relations entre les pays riches et les pays pauvres est enfin entré dans la conscience des pays industriels les plus avancés. Et cela les conduira à adopter des politiques communes autant qu'il sera possible, à encourager les efforts particuliers, par exemple: les renoncements aux créances, les rééchelonnements et les moratoires de toutes sortes, avec la nécessité d'envisager non seulement le sort des pays les plus pauvres mais également celui des pays dits intermédiaires dont les problèmes ne se résolvent pas simplement, ne se réduisent pas à des questions d'argent, et qui ont besoin aussi de garanties de toutes sortes, d'accompagnement des échanges.

La troisième observation, c'est l'intrusion soudaine et considérable des problèmes de l'environnement sur lesquels un luxe de réponses a été apporté.

Donc ce sera trois idées.

Les pays industriels avancés veulent consolider les acquis, s'inquiètent des fluctuations qui ne vont pas toujours dans le bon sens, se coordonnent.

Les problèmes de l'endettement et des relations Nord–Sud entrent de plein fouet dans nos délibérations et l'environnement est désormais considéré comme une donnée humaine, économique et politique primordiale.

Je ne voudrais pas oublier les éléments que vous avez dû remarquer vous-même mais je ne veux pas alléger trop ma réponse. De la même manière ont été abordés les problèmes de la drogue.

Question: M. le Président, vous avez dit récemment que la France était l'avocat des pauvres. Il y avait des représentants des pays pauvres aussi à Paris cette semaine.

Est-ce que vous croyez que vous avez réussi à commencer au moins un dialogue Nord–Sud, même si l'idée un Sommet aura été refusée?

Le Président: La France ne se pose pas en unique avocat et défenseur des pays pauvres, mais elle entend prendre sa place dans la défense des justes intérêts de ces populations. Par rapport à toute une série de questions, je pourrais en citer certaines.

Une augmentation des quote-parts du Fonds Monétaire International et même une nouvelle amélioration des droits de tirage spéciaux, sur lesquels des polémiques s'étaient élevées lors de mes propositions devant les Nations Unies, restent en cours d'examen au conseil d'administration du Fonds Monétaire International. Et en réponse à la question que j'ai posée, je l'ai dit tout à l'heure, la Banque Mondiale et le Fonds Monétaire International fournissent des apports nouveaux.

Je pourrais continuer la liste, elle est longue, de toutes les réponses favorables qui ont été faites aux questions que nous posions. J'en ai là une liste, mais pour ne pas alourdir cette conversation elle vous sera fournie, c'est un document qui vous sera remis.

Maintenant, la demande m'a été faite par quatre pays de convaincre mes collègues de parvenir à une confrontation des points de vue au sein d'une conférence dont les contours n'ont pas encore été précisés. Ils en avaient d'abord parlé à nos partenaires, ce n'est pas sorti comme cela tout d'un coup. M. Gandhi avait longuement vu Mme Thatcher, d'autres s'étaient longuement entretenus, M. Moubarak ou M. Pérez, M. Gandhi avec le Président Bush . . . ce n'est pas sorti comme cela par miracle et par suprise.

Mais au fond, sachant les obstacles et les arguments réservés à l'égard d'une sorte de conférence Nord–Sud, et même d'une conférence limitée à un certain nombre de participants du type Cancún, j'ai bien l'intention de poursuivre cette démarche et de convaincre celles et ceux d'entre nous qui pourraient avoir des réticences, bien que je sois moi-même tout à fait raisonnable car je considère que ce qui a été finalement l'échec de Cancún, qui avait été convoquée avant mon accession à la Présidence de la République—cela a été la première grande réunion internationale à laquelle j'ai participé après mon élection en 1981—c'est-à-dire son absence de suite, a été dommageable à la cause qu'elle entendait servir.

Il faut donc se méfier de toute réunion diplomatique improvisée ou prématurée. Il n'empêche que j'entends poursuivre cette démarche dont j'ai entretenu mes collègues.

Question: A ce sujet, Monsieur le Président, "vous en avez parlé à vos collègues," est-ce que vous avez pu constater que certains marquaient un début de conviction? Est-ce que leurs réticences ont été ébranlées?

Le Président: D'une façon générale, on souhaite apporter une réponse au problème du développement. C'est un pas qui a été franchi et les dispositions pratiques qui vous seront communiquées sont nombreuses et importantes.

De là à franchir le pas qui va vers une conférence qui se déroulerait dans le cadre des institutions existantes, les grandes institutions internationales, il ne s'agit pas d'inventer une institution nouvelle, il s'agit d'une rencontre. . . . J'ai dit tout à l'heure que cette démarche serait poursuivie, en tous cas par moi-même. Elle fait des progrès, elle n'est pas acquise.

Tout à l'heure, j'ai entendu M. Bromberger parler de mes 50 ou 55 minutes. Croyez-moi, je suis l'interprète fidèle des travaux d'un Sommet, et encore j'ai résumé. Je ne sais pas si vous vous êtes rendu compte de mon effort? Non? Il ne semble pas. Eh bien si, pourtant oui, j'ai réduit, résumé et j'ai peut-être même aussi omis quelques det, qui vous auraient été utiles. Vous me le pardonnerez. Vous pouvez me pardonner sur ce point, sans quoi cela aurait été plus long.

Question: Monsieur le Président, maintenant que le Sommet est terminé, quel jugement portez-vous sur ceux qui en France ont critiqué la proximité des fêtes du Bicentenaire et du Sommet?

Le Président: Eh bien j'ai dit déjà dans une émission nationale télévisée, il y a 48 heures, que je pensais qu'il y avait une mauvaise information. Quand il y a mauvaise information, il faut s'en prendre à qui? A ceux qui devraient informer mieux ou à ceux qui n'ont pas voulu entendre les explications? Je n'en sais rien, je ne suis pas là pour démêler les responsabilités. Ce qui est vrai, c'est que, quand a été invité le Sommet des pays industrialisés à Paris, en même temps sont parties les invitations pour le Bicentenaire à un certain nombre de pays, mais pas en aussi grand nombre que ceux qui étaient là. Nous n'avions pas vu si grand. Mais très rapidement nous nous sommes aperçu que nous devions contenir le souhait très flatteur exprimé par beaucoup de pays d'être présents auprès de la France pour célébrer ce grand événement.

Il y a eu 35 invitations acceptées ou sollicitées et 34 présences. On a dit 33 parce que M. Hillery, Président de l'Irlande, n'est arrivé qu'en cours de cérémonie . . . donc 34, et l'un des 35 était empêché par des problèmes intérieurs, il s'agissait de l'Argentine, qui avait accepté.

Il y a eu en France un certain nombre de protestations, de manifestations. La presse y a largement collaboré. . . . Eh bien moi, j'ai pris cela comme cela venait. . . . Je suis un peu habitué. Il est vraiment rare qu'une initiative soit saluée par un concert de vivats ou de bravos. C'est très rare. . . . C'est encore une chance quand aprés coup les lazzi se transforment . . . en bravos. Mais on a constaté qu'un certain nombre de choses peuvent être réussies et utiles.

Alors je n'en pense rien, je prends les choses comme elles sont. Ce qui compte pour moi, c'est le résultat.

21 pays pauvres ou intermédiaires étaient présents à Paris. Quelques pays d'Europe, type Irlande, Portugal ou Grèce, non membres du Sommet se sont joints à nous, ainsi que les 7 pays industriels, disons les 6 autres. Il y avait aussi la Communauté Européenne, pendant deux jours et demi, cela a été le Bicente-

naire où tous avaient droit aux mêmes égards et ont participé aux mêmes manifestations. A partir du 14 après-midi, le Sommet a commencé. Il y a donc eu quelques heures pendant lesquelles tout se trouvait imbriqué dans le mouvement général et à partir du 15 au matin, il ne restait plus que le Sommet des Sept.

Je crois que cette conjonction a été ressentie, en tout cas par les participants, les uns et les autres, comme utile, comme une bonne chose.

Quant à l'opinion sur le fait d'avoir réuni des riches au moment d'un 14 juillet qui a été la victoire du Tiers Etat, c'est une observation qui mérite examen. Mais je ne peux pas non plus en vouloir aux pays démocratiques qui doiventpeut-être une partie de leur prospérité à leur démocratie.

Je ne vois pas pourquoi je sanctionnerais la Grande-Bretagne et les Etats-Unis d'Amérique qui, avant même la France, avaient déclenché le mouvement en faveur des Droits de l'Homme ou l'Etat du Massachusetts qui avait dessiné dans sa constitution quelques-unes des grandes lignes de ce qui fut la nôtre, ou plutôt la Déclaration des Droits de l'Homme. Au nom de quoi les écarter?

D'une part les grands pays industriels sont des grandes démocraties, ils avaient leur place. D'autre part tous les pays du Tiers Monde ne sont pas d'angéliques démocraties, mais ils ont pour eux d'être pauvres et de vouloir aspirer à la prospérité. C'est donc un phénomène très révolutionnaire constaté chaque fois qu'il s'est produit des grands tournants dans l'histoire de l'humanité. . . . Non, moi je me suis senti à l'aise avec tous et j'ai été heureux qu'ils fussent là les uns et les autres.

Question: Monsieur le Président, je voudrais revenir sur la déclaration politique concernant la Chine. Une dépêche officielle de l'Agence de presse Chine Nouvelle a annoncé le 11 juillet que la France avait versé 83 millions de francs à l'état chinois.

Qu'en est-il de ce versement? Pensez-vous qu'il soit en cohérence avec la déclaration politique d'hier concernant la Chine?

Le Président: Je n'étais pas du tout au courant. Ce n'est pas la

France qui a versé cet argent, il a été versé vraisemblablement par une institution particulière et certainement en application d'accords antérieurs. Nous n'avons pas décidé le non-respect des contrats. Donc je ne peux pas vous répondre autrement parce que je n'en sais rien. Je l'ai simplement entendu ce matin à la radio, avec un petit peu de surprise, et je dois dire un certain mécontentement. Je réserve mes observations à qui de droit après.

Dans les conditions où je viens de vous le dire, ce n'est pas scandaleux. Mais les décisions qui ont été prises, que la France avait déjà prises, tendent naturellement à observer dans ce domaine une retenue qui n'aurait pas été illustrée par le versement en question, mais je ne peux pas me prononcer sur un sujet que je ne connais pas assez.

Question: Monsieur le Président, ma question porte également sur la Chine.

Dans la déclaration politique, les Sept ont dit qu'ils voulaient qu'il y ait un délai pour les prêts de la Banque Mondiale à la Chine.

Dans quelles conditions les Sept seraient-ils favorables à ce que la Banque Mondiale reprenne les prêts?

Le Président: Cela n'a pas été dit. Je pense que cela dépendra de l'évolution intérieure de la Chine.

Nous avons fixé une politique restrictive pour marquer notre désaveu de ce qui s'est passé là-bas mais nous n'avons pas déjà prévu le moment où l'on pourrait changer d'attitude en raison de l'évolution intérieure de la Chine.

Je pense que si les faits qui ont commandé ce retrait demeurent semblables à eux-mêmes, cela ne permettra pas un retour.

Cela se discutera avec la Banque Mondiale dans les semaines qui viendront.

Question: Les 54 articles contenus dans cette déclaration concernent beaucoup de monde, beaucoup de pays dans le monde, surtout des pays en voie de développement. Pour les mettre en application, pensez-vous que les organismes internationaux peuvent jouer pleinement leur rôle, ou faut-il que la France, qui assure la Présidence, maintienne le contact avec tous ces pays pour mettre en applications ces articles-là?

Deuxièmement, est-ce que vous pensez qu'on va faire des consultations régulières entre pays en voie de développement et pays riches, avant chaque sommet des Sept?

Le Président: Les pays réunis au Sommet de l'Arche disposent d'une certaine influence sur les grandes institutions internationales, car ils y contribuent puissamment. Ils pourront donc faire connâitre directement, comme ils l'ont déjà fait à la Banque Mondiale et au Fonds Monétaire International, les orientations qui sont les leurs.

J'ai déjà indiqué tout à l'heure, dans ce long document que j'ai résumé, et non pas commenté, que sur 7 ou 8 points extrêmement concrets ces grandes institutions accompliront un certain nombre d'actes positifs, notamment dans la manière de traiter la dette, de la réduire, de l'échelonner, ou de préparer les temps nouveaux, c'est-à-dire d'alimenter la reprise économique de ces pays par de l'argent frais.

Il conviendra de suivre, de persévérer, de continuer dans cette voie.

Les décisions politiques qui sont prises par les Etats ou par l'Assemblée Générale des Etats et les institutions particulières, aussi importantes qu'elles soient, doivent s'inscrire dans cette volonté politique.

Il faut donc veiller à ce que la volonté politique soit maintenue et renforcée.

C'est pourquoi j'ai, en tant que Président Français, l'intention de poursuivre mon action:

1°) pour qu'il n'y ait pas de relâchement

2°) pour qu'on aille plus loin.

Question: Au cours du Sommet, vous avez exprimé très clairement vos préoccupations sur le problème de la dette et vous avez même déclaré l'autre jour que le Mexique était au bord d'une explosion et qu'un aboutissement satisfaisant des négociations de New-York était une de vos principales priorités ici.

Mais la déclaration finale ne mentionne pas les négociations et il n'y a pas de support direct aux négociations de New-York.

Je voudrais savoir pourquoi, Monsieur le Président, ne craignez-vous pas de créer, de générer un phénomène de déception généralisée au Mexique et en Amérique Latine?

Le Président: Pour l'instant, ce sont les banques privées qui négocient leurs créances et il importe de connâitre la position finale des banques privées avant d'ajouter autre chose. On ne peut pas séparer artificiellement banques privées et aides publiques, dans la mesure où l'on sait bien que, s'il y avait un krach mexicain plus prononcé, les banques en seraient elles-mêmes victimes et auraient tendance, même dans les pays les plus libéraux—mais cela, c'est une grande remarque purement personnelle—à se retourner du côté de la puissance publique. Donc, tout se tient.

Mais nous sommes dans une phase délicate et sensible, où il faut être extrêmement attentif. La discussion dure depuis quelques jours, avec des hauts et des bas. Rien ne doit venir la troubler. Je crois encore à ses chances de succès, sans pouvoir l'affirmer. Je considère ce règlement comme nécessaire, mais en raison de la concomitance de réunions sur la dette mexicaine et de la réunion du Sommet, toute intervention présente sur ce cas particulier (fort important, mais cas particulier) eut été imprudente.

C'est donc dans l'intérêt du Mexique qu'il n'a pas été jugé nécessaire d'adopter un texte, d'autant plus que d'heure en heure, ce texte aurait pu se révéler dépassé. Voilà la raison, ce n'est pas une raison de fond.

Question: Nous avons pris acte de la ferme volonté des participants à ce XVème Sommet de développer un autre type de coopération avec les pays en développement mais nous constatons que plus vous développez ces pays, plus ils sont sous-développés.

Est-ce que vous ne faites pas qu'appliquer cette parole de l'Evangile, prêchée, il y a quelque deux cents ans environ par vos missionnaires . . .

Le Président: Ce n'était pas les miens!

Question: . . . *"à celui qui n'a rien, il faut rendre même ce qu'il n'a pas?"*[3]

Le Président: C'est un très beau précepte, mais c'est un précepte moral et la morale ne s'est pas encore totalement substituée à la politique.

Cependant, tous les responsables du monde qui représentent de vraies civilisations savent bien que cette obligation morale doit, d'un jour à l'autre, se confondre avec les obligations politiques.

Donc, c'est un très beau précepte, pas commode à mettre en ouevre. . . . Vous voyez la tournure paradoxale prise précisément non pas par les missionnaires, mais par leur Maître, leur inspirateur, le Christ, à savoir: il faut donner même ce que l'on n'a pas! C'est une forme paradoxale qui dit bien ce qu'elle veut dire et que vous avez parfaitement comprise. C'est même un très beau précepte. Cela veut dire qu'il ne faut pas mesurer son effort lorsqu'il y a des gens en perdition. C'est ce que je pense.

Il reste bien entendu à créer un courant international, conforme aux voeux que vous exprimez.

Question: M. le Président, c'était le premier Sommet du Président Bush. Est-ce qu'au changement d'homme a correspondu, à votre avis, un changement politique?

Le Président: Vous savez, je ne vais pas me livrer à des comparaisons extrêmement délicates et je ne veux pas embarasser ceux dont nous parlons.

Un changement d'homme, c'est forcément un changement d'approche. Pas forcément un changement de politique. A quoi

---

[3]Paraphrased from Matthew 25:29.—Ed.

cela servirait de changer les hommes d'ailleurs? . . . si les démocraties ont prévu un terme à tous les mandats, au contraire des monarchies, c'est bien parce qu'il est bon de changer!

Donc je ne me situerai pas par comparaison avec M. Reagan que j'ai rencontré huit fois, c'est-à-dire pendant huit ans (il s'agissait pour moi de mon IVème Sommet).

Je dirai que M. Bush montre beaucoup d'ouverture d'esprit, beaucoup d'affabilité dans ses relations personnelles, un désir de réussir une bonne entente entre les pays ici réunis, et cette ouverture d'esprit de M. Bush qui connaît bien les problèmes de l'Europe et les problèmes du monde en raison de ses états de service antérieurs, me paraît de très bonne augure.

Question: M. le Président, est-ce que vous considérez maintenant que le cadre des Sommets, tel qu'il est, est totalement satisfaisant? Convient-il de l'élargir? et si oui, dans quel sens?

Le Président: On peut toujours améliorer. Même si cela ne vous est pas apparu—à cause d'une part, du Bicentenaire, et, d'autre part, à cause des lieux dans lesquels s'est déroulé le Sommet, c'est à dire la Pyramide du Louvre et l'Arche qui sont des monuments nouveaux et qui donc attirent la curiosité. A l'intérieur de ces grands bâtiments, les conditions d'intimité, de tranquilité et de sérénité ont été réunies. On a bien travaillé entre nous, sans jamais être dérangés. Cela n'a pas toujours été le cas dans le passé.

Donc, de ce point de vue, je suis très satisfait de la tournure prise par les Sommets, dont l'initiative qui est celle de M. Giscard d'Estaing, en 1975, a été précisément décidée afin que les responsables du monde qui se réunissent, se connaissent, se connaissent mieux.

Et puis, peu à peu, la présence de la presse, de plus en plus massive—cette fois-ci plus de 6 000 journalistes—l'effet médiatique, l'intérêt, les discussions passionnées, ont fait qu'il était difficile de préserver cette intimité de la relation directe entre les personnes. Mais je crois que le tir a été corrigé, depuis déjà quelques années suffisamment pour que l'on puisse juger de façon parfaitement acceptable la manière dont cela se déroule.

Il y a quelquefois une tentation de se mêler de tout ou de décider pour tous. Mais nous avons réussi à la surmonter et vous remarquerez que chaque fois qu'il s'agit d'initiatives nouvelles, il est écrit: "les pays réunis au Sommet, et tous autres pays intéressés, sont appelés à . . ." c'est à dire qu'il y a une ouverture des membres du Sommet sur les pays absents que l'on espère présents, sinon dans les Sommets, du moins dans la mise en oeuvre de politiques nouvelles, sur lesquelles ils auraient le même droit d'évocation et d'initiative que nous. C'est vrai de l'environnement en particulier.

Question: La lettre que vous a adressé M. Gorbatchev montre assez qu'il souhaiterait être associé au règlement des grandes affaires du monde. Est-ce qu'il vous paraît concevable qu'il puisse participer un jour à un Sommet tel que celui qui vient de s'achever ici à l'Arche?

Le Président: L'Union Soviétique est un très grand pays qui joue un rôle considérable dans le monde. Il est l'une des deux plus grandes puissances militaires de la planète, donc son rôle est éminent.

Les pays qui se rassemblent au sein du sommet des Sept sont des pays dont la définition de base est la démocratie, assortie d'institutions adéquates, d'institutions démocratiques.

L'un de ces pays deviendrait par malheur—c'est tout à fait imprévu—un pays qui s'éloignerait de la démocratie, il n'aurait plus sa place dans ces Sommets.

Les pays qui évoluent vers la démocratie, qui n'ont pas encore défini des règles d'existence démocratiques chez eux au même point ou nous y sommes parvenus au travers d'institutions et de pratiques car il n'y a pas que les institutions, il n'y a pas que ce qu'on écrit, il y a ce qu'on fait. Quel que soit l'intérêt remarquable que j'attache à l'évolution de l'Union Soviétique, sur le plan de l'éthique politique, nous n'en sommes pas au même point, nous n'en sommes pas là.

Quant à la valeur des Sommets économiques, puisque c'est leur nom, il semble également qu'un certain nombre d'événements doivent se produire pour que le dialogue soit fructueux au sein de ces Sommets. Je ne parle pas du dialogue à longueur d'année qui est tout à fait nécessaire.

Quant à me poser une question de caractère général: "pensez-vous qu'un jour cela soit possible?" . . . Bien entendu. Et je ne parle pas spécialement de M. Gorbatchev; je parle de son pays, comme d'autres pays qui devraient connaître une évolution, un progrès économique, et un progrès démocratique suffisants pour que cela soit possible.

Une observation de pure pratique: ces pays étaient cinq, ils sont maintenant sept. Un trop grand nombre rendrait plus difficiles les échanges de vues, mais en soi il n'y a pas d'obstacles à la perspective que vous venez de préciser.

SOURCE: Released by the Summit of the Arch, July 16, 1989.

[UNOFFICIAL TRANSLATION: PRESS CONFERENCE OF MR. FRANÇOIS MITTERAND, PRESIDENT OF THE FRENCH REPUBLIC, ON THE CONCLUSION OF THE FIFTEENTH SUMMIT OF INDUSTRIALIZED COUNTRIES]

July 16, 1989

The President: Ladies and gentlemen, good day. Now, it is the journalists who are going to express themselves. I believe I have spoken enough—more than I would have wished—but I am obligated to give you an account of a highly important and copious document.

You have heard, I think, this reading . . . not this reading but this summary.[4]

You must have noted, as it went along, the points which interest you.

Therefore, I am not going to invent a new preamble, and, from this point on, I am going to ask you if you would be so kind as to ask the questions of your choice.

Question: Mr. President, I would like to begin with Article 1, in which you say that the Summit of the Arch marks the beginning of a new round of Summits. Would you please elaborate on that statement, comment on it for us? It is rather astonishing at first glance, since one never knows in advance whether one is beginning a new cycle.

The President: I will tell you about one decision and make one remark, a result of the work of the Seven. It is spelled out there in full, and I did not write that document. I simply signed it as a participant.

It was generally thought that we saw the work of the last

---

[4]Just before the press conference, Mr. Mitterand, as host of the Paris Summit, had read the Economic Declaration, in accordance with established Summit procedure.—ED.

fifteen years as falling into certain time periods. The round that began in 1982 corresponds with one of the longest periods of growth since World War II.

The first round began with Rambouillet, in 1975. So 1975, 1982, 1989. But it seems to me that we have now entered a different period—you are correct in saying that this is difficult to foresee. One could say that, on the whole, the Summits are attaining the results they desired; note the concurrent achievements in the fight against inflation, in the fight for renewed growth, and in the organization of a minimum of—I would not say a full system of, but a minimum of—world monetary policies. Today, some progress and some threats may be noted at the same time, for example, on the topic of inflation. Inflation was at first suppressed, and then it was not suppressed. Therefore, it seems that this is a period of achievements and of renewed responsibility. Certain shifts are appearing, with more of our attention and decisions being related to the environment, to the war against drugs. All of that is independent of the political resolutions which you already know about. And I believe that today the environmental and development dimensions are gaining a new meaning and growing enough so that one could consider that the Summits are taking a new direction.

The time devoted to debt and to development—debt being nothing more than a specific aspect of development—and the problem of the environment have never been the subject of as many conversations and so many decisions or declared intentions as they have been this time.

That is how I interpret the notion of the third period.

Question: Mr. President, how do you see East–West relations, particularly with the Soviet Union, after the Summit? How might they develop? Second question: what have the reactions of the Summit been to the letter sent by President Gorbachev?

The President: The Summit has not profoundly changed the nature of relations between the Soviet Union and the participants in the Summit. That wasn't the objective of the Summit.

Moreover, the letter that was sent to me, which I immediately communicated to the members of the Summit and which was also communicated very rapidly to the press, this letter does not call for a collective response. Our agenda was already extremely full, so there was therefore no response by the Summit of the Arch to Mr. Gorbachev. Nevertheless, I shall respond to him, nourished and inspired by the thoughts which I have heard, for we have talked about it nonetheless, especially when we were not in session.

We wanted to keep to our agenda. I will respond to President Gorbachev shortly, to be sure. As for the nature of the relations, it has not changed fundamentally, and various resolutions on East–West relations were communicated to you yesterday. We hope that the attempt at democratization in the Soviet Union succeeds. We salute the courage of that attempt. We are not charged with assuring success but, to the extent that we can, we shall contribute to it. But there are many aspects to the situation: economic, political, military and other serious advances must be made, especially in disarmament, before any general conclusions can be drawn. In any case, the mood of the powers gathered together during this Summit is entirely open to developing relations, to facilitating exchanges, to permitting an evolution that signifies greater freedom.

Question: Mr. President of the Republic, for the past fifty minutes or so we have heard the different points of the communiqué detailed. There were also, as you indicate, the political declarations which were released yesterday. Now I would like to ask you, if you would, to engage in a directly inverse exercise. If there were an element of this Summit which endures, what would it be, in your opinion?

The President: First of all, that is your job . . . but I am quite willing to respond to your question, since I know that our discussions usually lead to something constructive.

My personal impression is that what is noteworthy is a greater determination to safeguard the political achievements, as I just said to Mr. Fabra. From the start, economic policy has been of primary importance in these Summits—and I value this just as highly—therefore we have the call for greater coordination in the economic area. But it seems to me that the importance given to examining the problems of North–South relations and, particularly, of debt, stands out from the bulk of the proceedings. On the one hand, there is going to be some new money, for the World Bank and the International Monetary Fund are going to contribute significantly to the reduction of indebtedness and debt servicing; on the other hand, there are a multitude of concrete approaches, varying from case to case, such as for the Philippines or for Bangladesh. One could cite many other countries. Hence there is attention to and awareness of the problems of development and of the urgent need for decisions. Yesterday, it was even a matter of urgent food aid for a country like Poland. I definitely believe that the most advanced industrial nations have finally become aware of the problem of relations between the rich nations and the poor nations. And that will lead them to adopt common policies, whenever possible, to encourage specific efforts; for example, debt forgiveness, and readjustments and moratoria of all sorts, with the need for seeing not only the condition of the poorest nations but equally that of the so-called intermediate nations, whose problems are not resolved easily or cannot be reduced to financial questions, and who also need guarantees of all sorts to accompany exchanges.

The third observation is the sudden and considerable intrusion of environmental problems, to which a profusion of responses has been provided.

So there are three ideas.

The advanced industrialized countries want to consolidate the achievements; they are anxious about the fluctuations which do not always go in the right direction; they coordinate.

The problems of indebtedness and of North–South relations were directly addressed during our deliberations, and the environment is henceforth considered as a paramount human, economic, and political fact.

I would not want to forget the elements which you yourself noted, but I do not want to dilute my answer. In the same manner, the problems of drugs have been taken up.

Question: Mr. President, you recently stated that France was the champion of the poor. Some representatives of poor nations have also been in Paris this week.

Do you believe that you have succeeded in at least beginning a North–South dialogue, even if the idea of a Summit were to be refused?

The President: France does not claim to be the only champion and defender of the poor countries, but she means to take her place in defending the just interests of those people. Numerous issues arose relating to this, and I can tell you about some of them.

An increase in the shares of the International Monetary Fund and even a new amelioration of the special drawing rights— proposals of mine that caused some controversy when I brought them up before the United Nations—are still being examined by the administrative council of the International Monetary Fund. And in response to the question I posed, as I have just said, the World Bank and the International Monetary Fund will be providing new funds.

I could continue the list—it is long—of all of the favorable responses which have been made to the questions which we asked. I have a list here, but in order not to weigh this conversation down, it will be furnished to you; it is a document which you will be sent.

At present, four countries have asked me to convince my colleagues to discuss their differing points of view in the forum of a conference, the outlines of which are not yet well defined. They had to be discussed first by our partners; it did not just happen all at once. Mr. Gandhi saw Mrs. Thatcher for a long time; others had lengthy discussions with us, Mr. Mubarak or Mr. Pérez, Mr. Gandhi with President Bush . . . it did not come about like a miracle and by surprise.

Basically, I realize the obstacles and the arguments with regard to a kind of North–South conference, even a conference limited to a certain number of participants, of the Cancún type. But I still fully intend to follow this course and to convince those among us who might be reluctant. I myself know that such reluctance is altogether reasonable, when I consider that the ultimate failure of Cancún, which had been called before my accession to the Presidency of the Republic—that was the first large international meeting I participated in after my election in 1981—the failure was its lack of follow-through, which damaged the cause it was meant to serve.

So it is necessary to be suspicious of any improvized or premature diplomatic meeting. And yet I mean to follow that course, about which I have talked to my colleagues.

Question: On that subject, Mr. President, "you have spoken to your colleagues about it," have you been able to ascertain whether some of them are beginning to believe in it? Are they any less reluctant?

The President: In a general way, one wishes to bring about a solution to the problem of development. It is a step which has been taken, and the practical arrangements, which you will hear about, are numerous and significant.

From there, the path leads to a conference which would take place within the framework of existing institutions, the great international institutions; it is not a question of inventing a new institution, it is a question of a meeting. . . . I have said just now that this course would be followed, by myself in any case. Progress is being made, but it has not yet been attained.

Just now, I heard Mr. Bromberger speak of my 50 or 55 minutes. Believe me, I am the faithful interpreter of the Summit's labors, and still I have only summarized. I do not know if you are aware of my effort. No? It doesn't seem so. Well, anyway, yes, I have reduced, summarized, and perhaps even omitted some details which you might have found useful. You will excuse me. You can excuse me on this point, without which it would have been longer.

Question: Mr. President, now that the Summit is over, what do you think of those in France who have criticized the proximity of the Bicentennial and Summit festivities?

The President: Well, I already said, on a nationally televised broadcast 48 hours ago, that I thought that was bad news reporting. When there is poor reporting, who is to blame? Those who should have given better information or those who did not want to hear the explanations? I do not know; I am not there to determine responsibility. What is true is that when the Summit of the industrialized nations was invited to Paris, invitations to the Bicentennial were sent out at the same time to a certain number of countries, but not as large a number as those who were here. We did not envision it so large. But very rapidly we saw that we would have to restrain the very flattering desire expressed by many countries to be present in France to celebrate this great event.

Thirty-five invitations were accepted or asked for and 34 were present. One should say 33 because Mr. Hillery, President of Ireland, only arrived during the ceremony . . . so 34, and one of the 35 who accepted was prevented from coming by domestic problems—that was Argentina.

There have been a number of protests in France, and demonstrations. The press has largely collaborated with them. . . . As for myself, I took that as it came . . . I am somewhat used to it. It is truly rare that an initiative is greeted by a chorus of hurrahs or bravos. It is very rare. . . . It is just chance when too late the jeers turn into . . . bravos. But one notes that a certain number of things can be successful and useful.

Now, I do not think anything of it, I take things as they are. What counts for me is the result.

Twenty-one poor or middle-income countries were present in Paris. Some countries from Europe, like Ireland, Portugal, or Greece, not members of the Summit, joined us, as did the 7 industrial nations—or, let us say, the 6 others. There was also the European Community. For two and a half days it was the Bicentennial, where all the countries were equally respected and all participated in the same ceremonies. After the afternoon of the 14th, the Summit began. There were thus several hours during which everything overlapped in the general hubbub, and after the morning of the 15th, there only remained the Summit of the Seven.

I believe that this conjunction was felt, by all the participants at least, to be useful, to be a good thing.

As for the opinion about having brought together some of the rich nations at the time of July 14th, which was the victory of the Third Estate, it is an observation that merits examination. But I cannot hold a grudge against the democratic countries who perhaps owe a part of their prosperity to their democracy.

I do not see why I should find fault with Great Britain and the United States of America who, even before France, started the movement in support of the Rights of Man, or Massachusetts, which traces in its state constitution some of the same great lines that are in ours, or rather, in the Declaration of the Rights of Man. In the name of what should they be discarded?

On one hand, the great industrial nations are great democracies; they have their place. On the other hand, all the nations of the Third World are not angelic democracies; they are poor and they want to aspire to prosperity. Therefore it is an extremely revolutionary phenomenon whenever these major turning-points occur in the history of humankind. . . . No, I am at ease with all and I was happy that they were all there.

Question: Mr. President, I would like to come back again to the political declaration concerning China. An official dispatch of the New China News Agency announced on July 11 that France had poured 83 million francs into the Chinese state.

What about that payment? Do you think it was in line with yesterday's political declaration concerning China?

The President: I was not informed of everything. It is not France who gave that money; it was given probably by a particular institution and certainly in implementation of earlier agreements. We have not decided to disregard contracts. So I cannot respond to you in any other way because I do not know any more about it. I simply heard it this morning on the radio, with a bit of surprise, and I should say a certain dissatisfaction. I reserve my comments for those involved in the matter.

Under the conditions I just mentioned to you, this is not scandalous. But the decisions that have been made in this area, that France has already taken, tend naturally to show some caution—which will not have been illustrated by the payment in question. But I cannot talk on a matter about which I do not know enough.

Question: Mr. President, my question also has to do with China.

In the political declaration, the Seven said that they would want to see a delay in the World Bank loans to China.

Under what conditions would the Seven favor the Bank's extending those loans again?

The President: It wasn't specified. I think it would depend on the domestic changes within China.

We established a restrictive policy to show our disapproval of what happened there, but we have not yet decided on the moment at which that attitude could be changed by virtue of the domestic evolution of China.

I think that if the conditions that led to the delay in loans stay the same, that would not permit a return.

This will be discussed with the World Bank in the coming weeks.

Question: The 54 articles contained in the declaration concern much of the world, many countries of the world, especially the developing countries. To implement them, do you think that the international organizations can play their role fully, or must France, which now holds the Presidency of the Summit, maintain contact with all of those countries to apply those articles?

Secondly, do you think there will be regular consultations between developing countries and rich countries, before every Summit of the Seven?

The President: The nations that met at the Summit of the Arch have a certain influence on the large international institutions, since they contribute heavily to them. They could therefore let their positions be known directly, as they already have with the World Bank and the International Monetary Fund.

I have just indicated, in the long document which I summa-

460

rized, and not commented on, that on 7 or 8 extremely concrete points these great institutions will accomplish a certain number of positive acts, notably in the ways in which debt is treated, is reduced, is arranged, or in which new terms are prepared, that is to say to feed economic recovery of those nations with fresh funds.

It will be advisable to follow, to persevere, to continue along that route.

The political decisions which are made by the States or by the General Assembly and the specialized Agencies, important though they may be, should be in keeping with this political will.

It will thus be necessary to see that this political will is maintained and reinforced.

That is why I, as President of France, intend to follow my course of action:

1) so that there is no slackening

2) so that one may go further.

Question: During the Summit, you expressed very clearly your concerns about the problem of debt. You even declared the other day that Mexico was on the verge of a breakthrough and that a satisfactory outcome of the negotiations in New York would be one of your principal priorities here.

But the final declaration does not mention the negotiations, and there is no direct support for the New York negotiations.

I would like to know why, Mr. President, you are not afraid of creating, of generating, a phenomenon of general disappointment in Mexico and in Latin America?

The President: For now, it is the private banks who are negotiating their loans, and it is important to know the final position of the private banks before adding anything else. One cannot artificially separate the private banks and public assistance, in the sense that we know full well that if there is a more pronounced Mexican financial crash, the banks themselves will be victims and there will be a tendency, even in the most liberal countries—but that is a sweeping and purely personal statement—to return to the side of public power. So everything is on hold.

But we are in a delicate and sensitive phase, in which it is necessary to be extremely attentive. The discussion has been going on for several days, with highs and lows. Nothing should disrupt it. I still believe in its chances for success, without being able to prove it. I consider a settlement necessary, but by reason of the concomitance of meetings on the Mexican debt and the Summit meeting, any present intervention in this particular case (most important, but a particular case) would have been imprudent.

It is thus in the interest of Mexico that it was not judged necessary to adopt a text, in addition to the fact that from hour to hour that text would have become outdated. That is the reason; it is not a profound reason.

Question: We note the firm resolve of the participants in this 15th Summit to develop another type of cooperation with the developing nations, but we have seen that the more you develop those countries the more they remain underdeveloped.

Are you only applying this Gospel, preached some two hundred years ago by your missionaries, of . . .

The President: They were not mine!

Question: . . . "to him who has nothing, one must give even that which he has not?"[5]

The President: That is a very fine precept, but it is a moral precept and the moral has not yet been totally substituted for the political.

However, all the responsible people in the world who represent true civilizations know full well that moral obligations must, from one day to the next, merge with political obligations.

---

[5]Paraphrased from Matthew 25:29.—ED.

Thus, it is a very fine precept, but not suited to being implemented. . . . You see the paradoxical turn taken precisely not by the missionaries but by their Master, their inspiration, Christ; namely, it is necessary to give even that which one does not have. It is a paradoxical form which says well what it means and which you have understood perfectly. It is indeed a very fine precept. That means that it is not necessary to measure the effort until there are people in distress. That is what I think.

It remains, of course, to create an international sentiment, conforming to the wishes you express.

Question: Mr. President, it was Mr. Bush's first Summit. Has the change of the man corresponded to a change of policy, in your opinion?

The President: You know, I am not going to indulge in extremely delicate comparisons and I do not wish to embarrass those of whom we speak.

A change of man necessarily means a change of approach. But not necessarily a change of policy. Otherwise, what else would it serve if the people were changed? . . . if democracies, unlike monarchies, envisioned a term of office for all authorities it is because it is good to change!

Thus I would not put myself in the position of comparisons with Mr. Reagan, whom I met eight times, that is, over eight years (it was my fourth Summit).

I would say that Mr. Bush shows a great deal of open-mindedness, a great deal of affability in personal relationships, a desire to achieve a good understanding among the countries gathered here; and this open-mindedness of Mr. Bush, who knows well the problems of Europe and the problems of the world by reason of his prior service, seems to me to be a very good sign.

Question: Mr. President, do you now consider that the membership in the Summits is totally satisfactory as is? Would it be advisable to enlarge it? If so, in what way?

The President: One can always improve. Even if you do not see how—by virtue, on the one hand, of the Bicentennial and, on the other hand, of the places in which in which the Summit took place, that is to say the Pyramid of the Louvre and the Arch, which are new monuments and which therefore attract curiosity. Inside these grand structures, the conditions of intimacy, of tranquility and of serenity were met. We worked well together, without ever becoming upset. That has not always been the case in the past.

Therefore, from that point of view, I am very satisfied with the turn taken by the Summits; in 1975, under the initiative of Mr. Giscard d'Estaing, it was precisely decided so that the world leaders who got together would know each other, and would know each other better.

And then, little by little, the presence of the press, ever more numerous—more than 6,000 journalists this time—the media effect, the interest, the passionate discussions, made it difficult to preserve the intimacy of direct relationships between the people. But I think that the aim has been corrected, for some years satisfactorily enough that one may judge in a perfectly acceptable way the manner in which it unfolds.

There is sometimes a temptation to become entangled in everything or to make decisions for everyone. But we have succeeded in overcoming it, and you will notice that each time there is a question of new initiatives, it is written: "the countries gathered at the Summit, and all other interested countries, are called to . . ."; that is to say, there is an overture by the members of the Summit to the absent countries that one wishes were present, if not in the Summits, then at least in the implementation of new policies, in which they would have the same right of proposals and initiative as we have. That is especially true for the environment.

Question: The letter which Mr. Gorbachev sent you shows well enough that he would like to be associated with the resolution of the grand affairs of the world. Does it seem conceivable to you that he might participate someday in a Summit such as the one that was just completed here at the Arch?

The President: The Soviet Union is a very large country which plays a considerable role in the world. It is one of the two greatest military powers on the planet, so its role is pre-eminent.

The countries that gather in the bosom of the Summit of the Seven are countries whose basic definition is democracy, furnished with adequate institutions, with democratic institutions.

If one of these countries should unhappily become—and this does not seem likely—a country which distances itself from democracy, it would no longer have its place in these Summits.

The countries which are evolving toward democracy have not yet defined the rules for a democratic existence to the same degree that we have defined ours through institutions and practice—since it is not what is written, it is what is done. Whatever the remarkable interest on the plane of political ethics which I have in the evolution of the Soviet Union, we are not all at the same point; we are not.

As for the value of the Economic Summits, since that is their name, it seems that a certain number of events should also take place so that the dialogue will be fruitful in these Summits. I am not speaking of dialogue throughout the year, which is quite necessary.

As for asking me a general question: "do you think that one day it might be possible . . .?" Of course. And I am not talking especially about Mr. Gorbachev; I am talking about his country, like other countries which must experience sufficient evolution, economic progress, and democratic progress for it to be possible.

A purely practical observation: the countries at the Summit used to be five; now they are seven. Too many countries would make it more difficult to exchange viewpoints, but this aspect is not in itself an obstacle to the possibility you have just raised.

Bibliography

BIBLIOGRAPHY

Armstrong, Robert. *Economic Summits: A British Perspective.* Bissell Paper no. 4. Toronto: Centre for International Studies, University of Toronto, 1988.

Artis, Michael J., and Sylvia Ostry. *International Economic Policy Coordination.* Chatham House Papers, vol. 30. London and New York: Routledge & Kegan Paul, 1986.

Brittan, Samuel. "How To Make Sense of the Tokyo Summit Indicators." In *Interdependence and Co-operation in Tomorrow's World: A Symposium Marking the Twenty-fifth Anniversary of the OECD.* : Organisation for Economic Co-operation and Development, 1987, pp. 95–101.

Cook, David. "The Selling of the Summit, 1983." *Johns Hopkins Magazine* 34, no. 4 (August 1983): 33–37.

De Menil, Georges. "De Rambouillet à Versailles: un bilan des sommets économiques" (From Rambouillet to Versailles: An Assessment of the Economic Summits). *Politique étrangère* 2 (June 1982): 403–17.

De Menil, Georges. "Si le sommet de Versailles n'avait pas eu lieu" (If the Versailles Summit Had Not Taken Place). *Commentaire* no. 20 (Winter 1982/1983): 571–79.

469

De Menil, Georges. *Les Sommets économiques: les politiques nationales à l'heure de l'interdépendance* (Economic Summits: National Policies at the Time of Interdependence). Paris: Economica, 1983.

De Menil, Georges, and Anthony M. Solomon. *Economic Summitry*. New York: Council on Foreign Relations, 1983.

Dimock, Blair. *The Benefits of Teamplay: Italy and the Seven Power Summits*. Country Study no. 5. Toronto: Centre for International Studies, University of Toronto, 1989.

Dornbusch, Rüdiger. *World Economic Problems for the Summit: Co-ordination, Debt and the Exchange Rate System*. Bissell Paper no. 6. Toronto: Centre for International Studies, University of Toronto, 1988.

Fowler, Henry H., and W. Randolph Burgess. *Harmonizing Economic Policy: Summit Meetings and Collective Leadership; Report of the Atlantic Council's Working Group on Economic Policy*. Atlantic Council of the United States Policy Papers. Boulder, Colo.: Westview Press, 1977.

Funabashi, Yoichi. *Managing the Dollar: From the Plaza to the Louvre*. Washington, D.C.: Institute for International Economics, 1988.

Funabashi, Yoichi. *Samitto no shiso* (Philosophy of the Summits). Tokyo: Asahi Shinbunsha, 1980.

Gotlieb, Allan. *Canada and the Economic Summits: Power and Responsibility*. Bissell Paper no. 1. Toronto: Centre for International Studies, University of Toronto, 1987.

Gotlieb, Allan. "The Western Economic Summit." Canada. Department of External Affairs. *Statements and Speeches* no. 81/13. Ottawa, 1981.

Heeney, Timothy. *Canadian Foreign Policy and the Seven Power Summits.* Country Study no. 1. Toronto: Centre for International Studies, University of Toronto, 1988.

Hein, John. *From Summit to Summit: Policymaking in an Interdependent World.* Conference Board Report no. 774. New York: The Conference Board, 1980.

Hellmann, Rainer. *Weltwirtschaftsgipfel Wozu?* (Whither Economic Summits?) Baden-Baden: Nomos Verlagsgesellschaft, 1982.

Henning, C. Randall. *Macroeconomic Diplomacy in the 1980s: Domestic Politics and International Conflict Among the United States, Japan, and Europe.* Atlantic Papers, no. 65. London; New York: Croom Helm for the Atlantic Institute for International Affairs, 1987.

Hiss, Dieter. "Weltwirtschaftsgipfel: Betrachtungen eines Insiders" (World Economic Summits: Observations of an Insider). In *Empirische Wirtschaftsforschung: Konzeptionen, Verfahren und Ergebnisse; Festschrift für Rolf Krengel aus Anlass seines 60. Geburtstages.* Ed. Joachim Frohn and Reiner Staeglin. Berlin: Duncker & Humblot, 1980, pp. 279–89.

Holmes, John W., and John J. Kirton, eds. *Canada and the New Internationalism.* Toronto: Canadian Institute of International Affairs and Centre for International Studies, University of Toronto, 1988.

Horne, Jocelyn P., and Paul R. Masson. "Scope and Limits of International Economic Cooperation and Policy Coordination." International Monetary Fund. *Staff Papers* 35, no. 2 (June 1988): 259–96.

Hornung, Robert. *Sharing Economic Responsibility: The United States and the Seven Power Summits.* Country Study no. 4.

Toronto: Centre for International Studies, University of Toronto, 1989.

Hunt, John, and Henry Owen. "Taking Stock of the Seven-Power Summits: Two Views." Review of *Hanging Together: The Seven-Power Summits*, by Robert D. Putnam and Nicholas Bayne. *International Affairs* 60, no. 4 (Autumn 1984): 657–61.

Ikenberry, G. John. "Market Solutions for State Problems: The International and Domestic Politics of American Oil Decontrol." *International Organization* 42, no. 1 (Winter 1988): 151–77.

International Monetary Fund. *Economic Policy Coordination; Proceedings of an International Seminar Held in Hamburg* [May 5–7, 1988]. Wilfried Goth, moderator. Washington, D.C.: International Monetary Fund; Hamburg: Institut für Wirtschaftsforschung, 1988.

Istituto Affari Internazionali. *Economic Summits, 1975–1986: Declarations.* Isola San Giorgio, Italy: Fondazione Cini, 1987.

Jervis, Robert. "From Balance To Concert: A Study of International Security Cooperation." In *Co-operation Under Anarchy.* Ed. Kenneth A. Oye. Princeton, N.J.: Princeton University Press, 1985, pp. 58–79.

Kaiser, Karl, Winston Lord, Thierry De Montbrial, and David Watt. *Western Security: What Has Changed? What Should Be Done?* [New York:] Council on Foreign Relations; [London:] Royal Institute of International Affairs, 1981.

Kenen, Peter, ed. *From Rambouillet to Versailles: A Symposium.* Essays in International Finance, no. 149. Princeton, N.J.: Dept. of Economics, International Finance Section, Princeton University, 1982.

Kirton, John J. "Managing Global Conflict: Canada and International Summitry." In *Canada Among Nations 1987: A World of*

Conflict. Ed. Maureen A. Molot and Brian W. Tomlin. Toronto: James Lorimer, 1988, pp. 22–40.

Kobayashi, Tomohiko. *The Japanese Perspective on the Toronto Economic Summit and the Uruguay Round.* Bissell Paper no. 8. Toronto: Centre for International Studies, University of Toronto, 1988.

Lamy, Pascal. *The Economic Summit and the European Community.* Bissell Paper no. 4. Toronto: Centre for International Studies, University of Toronto, 1988.

McMillan, Charles. *Comparing Canadian and Japanese Approaches to the Seven Power Summit.* Bissell Paper no. 2. Toronto: Centre for International Studies, University of Toronto, 1988.

Merlini, Cesare, ed. *Economic Summits and Western Decision-Making.* London: Croom Helm; New York: St. Martin's Press in association with the European Institute of Public Administration, 1984.

Merlini, Cesare, ed. *I Vertici: Cooperazione e Competizione tra Paesi Occidentali* (The Summits: Cooperation and Competition Among the Western Countries). Rome: ADN Kronos, 1985.

Ortona, Egidio. *The Problem of International Consultations: Report of the Trilateral Task Force on Consultative Procedures to the Trilateral Commission.* Egidio Ortona, J. Robert Schaetzel, and Nobuhiko Ushiba, rapporteurs. The Triangle Papers, vol. 12. New York: Trilateral Commission, 1976.

Ostry, Sylvia. *Summitry: The Medium and the Message.* Bissell Paper no. 3. Toronto: Centre for International Studies, University of Toronto, 1988.

Owen, Henry. "Summitry Revisited." *The Atlantic Monthly* 231, no. 3 (March 1973): 6–10.

Pons, Michael. *West German Foreign Policy and the Seven Power Summits.* Country Study no. 2. Toronto: Centre for International Studies, University of Toronto, 1988.

Putnam, Robert D. "Diplomacy and Domestic Politics: The Logic of Two-Level Games." *International Organization* 42, no. 3 (Summer 1988): 427–60.

Putnam, Robert D., and Nicholas Bayne. *Hanging Together: Cooperation and Conflict in the Seven-Power Summits.* Rev. ed. Cambridge, Mass.: Harvard University Press, 1987.

Putnam, Robert D., and Nicholas Bayne. *Hanging Together: The Seven-Power Summits.* Cambridge, Mass.: Harvard University Press, 1984.

Putnam, Robert D., and Nicholas Bayne. *Weltwirtschaftsgipfel im Wandel* (World Economic Summits Amid Change). Bonn: Europa Union Verlag, 1985.

Roberge, François. *French Foreign Policy and the Seven Power Summits.* Country Study no. 3. Toronto: Centre for International Studies, University of Toronto, 1988.

Sakurada, Daizo. *Managing the International Political Economy: Japan's Seven Power Summit Diplomacy.* Country Study no 6. Toronto: Centre for International Studies, University of Toronto and University of Toronto/York University Joint Centre on Asia-Pacific Studies, 1989.

Schaetzel, J. Robert, and H. B. Malmgren. "Talking Heads." *Foreign Policy* 39 (Summer 1980): 130–42.

Schmidt, Helmut. "The Inevitable Need for American Leadership." *The Economist* (February 26–March 4, 1983): 19–30.

The Seven-Power Summits. Tokyo: TBS-Britannica, 1986.

Shultz, George P., and Kenneth W. Dam. *Economic Policy Beyond the Headlines.* New York: W. W. Norton, 1977.

Smouts, Marie-Claude. "Les Sommets des pays industrialisés" (The Summits of Industrialized Countries). *Revue de droit international* (1980): 668–85.

Solomon, Hyman. "Summit Reflections." *International Perspectives* 17, no. 4 (July–August 1988): 8–10.

Sovrani Ma Interdipendenti: I Vertici dei Paesi Più Industrializzati (Sovereign but Interdependent: The Summits of the Most Industrialized Countries). Bologna: Il Mulino, 1987.

Summit Meetings and Collective Leadership in the 1980's. Charles Robinson and William C. Turner, co-chairmen; Harald B. Malmgren, rapporteur. Atlantic Council of the United States Policy Papers. Washington, D.C.: Working Group on Political Affairs, Atlantic Council of the United States, 1980.

Summitwatch: Prospects for the 1988 Toronto Summit. 3d ed. Toronto: The Research Group, Centre for International Studies, University of Toronto, 1988.

Thiel, Elke. "Atlantischer Wirtschaftskonflikt vor und nach Versailles" (Atlantic Economic Conflict Before and After Versailles). *Aussenpolitik* 33, no. 4 (1982): 371–84.

Thiel, Elke. "Wirtschaftsgipfel von Rambouillet bis Venedig" (Economic Summits from Rambouillet to Venice). *Aussenpolitik* 32, no. 1 (1981): 3–14.

Watt, David. *Next Steps for Summitry: Report of the Twentieth Century Fund International Conference on Economic Summitry; Background Paper.* New York: Priority Press, 1984.

Waverman, Leonard, and Tom Wilson, eds. "Macroeconomic

Policy Co-ordination and the Summit." *Canadian Public Policy* 15 (February 1989), Special Issue.

Whitehead, John C. *Towards a Stronger International Economy.* Bissell Paper no. 7. Toronto: Centre for International Studies, University of Toronto, 1988.

World Economic Summits: The Role of Representative Groups in the Governance of the World Economy. WIDER Study Group Series, no. 4. Helsinki: World Institute for Development Economics Research/United Nations University, 1989.

Index

INDEX

International Coal Industry Advisory
Board, 83
International Conference on Drug Abuse
and Illicit Trafficking (Vienna,
1987), 356, 406
International Conference on Kampuchea
(New York, 1981), 113
International Convention Against the
Taking of Hostages (New York,
1979), 91, 115
International Council of Scientific Un-
ions (ICSU), 342
International Covenant on Civil and Po-
litical Rights, 412
International Covenant on Economic, So-
cial and Cultural Rights, 412
International Development Association
(IDA), 40, 55, 86–87, 129, 187,
199, 209, 220, 236, 314–15, 340,
397
International Development Strategy, 85
International Energy Agency (IEA), 65,
82
International Energy Technology Group,
67, 84
International Fund for Agricultural Development (IFAD), 41, 86
International Labour Organisation (ILO),
150, 171
International Maritime Organization
(IMO), 318, 349, 404
International Monetary Fund (IMF), 7–
8, 16, 19, 24, 33–34, 37–40, 42, 56,
69, 88, 105, 129–31, 188, 192, 195,
197, 200–201, 210, 209, 213, 216–
18, 221–22, 235–36, 238, 247,
259, 261–62, 277, 291, 312, 314,
335–37, 340, 370, 393, 398–99,
411, 440–41, 446, 454, 456, 460.
See also Special Drawing Rights;
Surveillance
Executive Board, 393
Interim Committee, 8, 16, 28, 37, 262,
293
Structural Adjustment Facility, 315,
342, 371, 397
International monetary system. *See* Monetary issues
International Nuclear Fuel Cycle Evaluation Group, 84
International Organization for Standardization (ISO), 342
International trade. *See* General Agreement on Tariffs and Trade; Multilateral Trade Negotiations; United

Nations Conference on Trade and
Development; Trade
International Tropical Timber Organization, 403
Investment, 16, 18, 22, 34, 41, 48–49, 51,
54–55, 66, 68–69, 81–82, 97, 104–
105, 107, 126, 129, 134, 140, 142–
43, 146–49, 155, 161, 163–64,
167–70, 234, 239, 261–62, 272,
274, 288–91, 311–12, 314–15, 334,
337, 340–41, 365–66, 368–70, 390–
91, 394, 396, 398, 410. *See also*
Multilateral Investment Guarantee Agency (MIGA)
Iran, 92
Iran–Iraq war, 202, 223, 271, 275–76,
351, 381. *See also* Freedom of
navigation; Gulf situation
Ireland, 443, 458
Islamic Conference, 93–94
Israel, 178, 183, 190–91, 203, 211–12,
224, 251, 416–17. *See also* Arab–
Israeli dispute; Palestinian rights
Occupied territories, 353, 381, 416–17
Italy, 3, 5, 14–15, 23, 25, 32, 46–47, 49,
62, 64–65, 74, 78, 102, 108, 124,
194, 200, 215, 221, 232, 256, 264,
284, 289–90, 296, 308, 312–13,
317, 330, 344, 360, 373–75, 388,
391, 404

Jamaica agreement (IMF Interim Committee), 16, 28
Jamieson, Donald, 31, 45
Japan, 4–5, 14–15, 27, 32, 46–47, 49, 54,
62, 64–65, 72, 74, 78, 93, 102, 124,
127, 186, 194, 196, 208, 215, 217,
232, 256, 265, 284, 289, 294–97,
299, 302, 308, 323, 330, 337, 340,
343–44, 360, 364, 373, 375, 388,
392, 405
Jeanneney, Jean-Marcel, 101
Jenkins, Roy, 32, 46, 63, 79
Jobert, Michel, 200, 221
Johnstone, Robert, 45, 61

Kajiyama, Seiroku, 388
Kampuchea. *See* Cambodia
Kaneko, Ippeo, 62
Karmal, Babrak, 115
Kikuchi, Kiyoaki, 78, 102
Kissinger, Henry, 4, 14, 23–28
Kitamura, Hiroshi, 330, 360